Studien und Texte zu Antike und Christentum
Studies and Texts in Antiquity and Christianity

130

From Protology to Eschatology

Competing Views on the Origin and the End of the Cosmos in Platonism and Christian Thought

Edited by

Joseph Verheyden, Geert Roskam, and Gerd Van Riel

Mohr Siebeck

Joseph Verheyden is Professor of New Testament Studies in the Faculty of Theology and Religious Studies at the KU Leuven.

Geert Roskam is Professor of Ancient Greek Literature in the Arts Faculty at the KU Leuven.

Gerd Van Riel is Professor of Ancient Philosophy and Dean of the Institute of Philosophy at the KU Leuven.

ISBN 978-3-16-161009-7 / eISBN 978-3-16-161041-7
DOI 10.1628/978-3-16-161041-7

ISSN 1436-3003 / eISSN 2568-7433 (Studien und Texte zu Antike und Christentum)

The Deutsche Nationalbibliothek lists this publication in the Deutsche Nationalbibliographie; detailed bibliographic data are available at *http://dnb.dnb.de*.

The book was typeset, printed on non-aging paper and bound by Gulde Druck in Tübingen.

Printed in Germany.

Acknowledgements

The editors wish to thank the colleagues and PhD candidates who were involved in our overall research project which was funded by the KU Leuven Research Foundation, as was the conference from which this volume resulted.

This volume is dedicated to the memory of John D. Turner (July 15, 1938 – October 26, 2019), Cotner Professor of Religious Studies and Mach University Professor of Classics and History at the University of Nebraska-Lincoln, where he had been teaching religious studies since 1976 after earning his MA Theol. at Union Theological Seminary in Richmond VA and his PhD in religion at Duke University (1970) and having spent some years at Claremont working on the Nag Hammadi corpus with James Robinson. With John Turner, the scholarly world loses not only a world expert on the interconnections between Gnosticism and ancient philosophy, but also a fine person who some of us have come to know on a personal basis far too late.

Joseph Verheyden
Geert Roskam
Gerd Van Riel

Table of Contents

Acknowledgements V

JOSEPH VERHEYDEN / GEERT ROSKAM / GERD VAN RIEL
Introduction 1

ANDREA FALCON
Eternalism in Aristotle and After 7

ALAIN LERNOULD
L'interprétation proclienne de la création des âmes humaines dans le *Timée* de Platon 23

MARIJE MARTIJN
The (Meta)physics of Eating One's Children: Proclus' Interpretation of the Myth of Er 45

MARC-ANTOINE GAVRAY
Éternité ou génération? La controverse entre Simplicius et Jean Philopon sur l'origine du monde 69

JÖRG FREY
From Eternal Life to the Word That Was in the Beginning: The Logic of Johannine Theology 99

EINAR THOMASSEN
Protology and Eschatology in Gnostic Thought 119

JOHN D. TURNER†
"Where the Beginning Is, There Shall Be the End": Protology and Personal Eschatology in the Platonizing Sethian Apocalypses *Zostrianos* and *Allogenes* 133

Benjamin Gleede
"Above the Starry Canopy": Spatial and Non-Spatial Patristic Perspectives on the Christian Hope for Afterlife 153

George van Kooten
"Mind the Ontological Gap!": The Collateral Loss of the Pauline-Stoic Creation "From God" in the Joint Attack of the Arian-Nicene Creation "From Nothing" on the Platonic Creation "From Disorderly Matter" . 167

List of Contributors 239
Index of Ancient Authors and Texts 241
Index of Modern Authors 259

Introduction

Joseph Verheyden / Geert Roskam / Gerd Van Riel

This volume contains the proceedings of an international conference held in Leuven from 7 to 9 June 2017 and organised in the framework of a research project entitled “From Chaos to Order: The Creation of the World. New Views on the Reception of Platonic Cosmogony in Later Greek Thought, Pagan and Christian.” The conference was meant as a follow-up on an earlier one also held in Leuven, 4–6 February 2015, that focused on a number of works and authors from Greek (Platonic), Jewish-Hellenistic and Christian traditions who addressed aspects of this topic. The 2015 conference was meant to further dialogue in the respective fields by taking a comparative approach and to illustrate the rich variety of opinions that were developed in the respective traditions. Special attention was given to the dominant position of Platonic cosmogony which was the central reference point in Greek philosophical tradition, but also an important factor in Jewish and Christian reflection on the biblical creation account. The proceedings of this earlier conference were published in 2017 as *Light on Creation: Ancient Commentators in Dialogue and Debate on the Origin of the World*, ed. G. Roskam and J. Verheyden (STAC, 104).

The 2017 conference marked the conclusion of the project and was meant to widen the perspective and to further contextualise the debate on the origin of the world, with special attention to how it has been linked with reflections on the end of the world, hence the title “From Protology to Eschatology.”

The pagan Platonic and the Christian tradition share a number of important basic assumptions. Adherents to either of them accept there exists an ontological gap between the intelligible and the sensible, and they have developed (partly) similar ways of explaining how the intelligible order, in which all causative principles are situated, can still be linked to the material world. Moreover, the two traditions share a strong awareness that the order of the material world is not perfect. This common ontological framework conditions philosophical and theological reflections on the origin of the world (cosmology), on the status of human beings (anthropology), and on the potentials and limits of a moral life (ethics).

The 2017 conference intended to focus on the question of how, in Greek, mainly Platonic, philosophy and in Christian thought, views on the origin of the cosmos influence, and in part perhaps even determine, philosophical and theological reflection on the end or the aim towards which the cosmos is developing. The Judeo-Christian concept of a creation with temporal development and the philosophical notion of the eternity of the world evidently represent two very different views. Yet, despite these different starting points, there are also some clear traces of convergence and of influence from the latter on the former. There is a common interest in (Greek) philosophical and Christian tradition in reflecting not only on the principles that govern cosmology and on how the cosmos is reverting on its principles, but also on the answers provided in the own tradition in this regard. Plato and the Bible may be said or thought to contain the solution, but it is also felt that they need in turn to be interpreted.

Initially, the organisers had approached a number of colleagues with a sort of questionnaire on how beginning and end have been conceptualised, inviting them to reflect on what the works and authors they were asked to study tell us about such issues as whether/how the universe finally reverts upon its origin, what is the role of teleology or perfectibility, what it means that an original order is restored, both in its overall ontological structure and in the particular case of human beings, how the immortality of the soul is to be conceived in this perspective, and what are the ethical implications that have been linked to it. Many and quite variegated issues indeed, not all of which could be picked up by all speakers, but that was not the intention. The questionnaire was rather meant to help get some grip on the topic and somehow to illustrate its multiple facets. Several of the speakers told us that they had struggled with the task, in part because these are difficult questions and in part because the answers provided by the sources are all but clear. It created a fine sense of empathy amongst participants when one saw a colleague coping with a text to wring out from it some kind of answer.

After a quite severe selection nine papers were withheld for publication. For the sake of convenience they have been divided into two parts – a Christian and a non-Christian one. The editors have long pondered on whether and how to arrange the material. They finally have settled for this rather obvious and (too) simple division, all while realising that in several instances the lines are blurred; but after all, it definitely is a better option than trying to decide between philosophical and theological sources and approaches, as a fair share of "non-Christian" material and ways of reasoning or arguing shows up also in texts of Christian origin (hardly ever the other way around).

The "non-Christian" part contains four essays. *Andrea Falcon* studies the reception of Aristotle's view on the eternal character of the cosmos in the late and post-Hellenistic period. The development is gradual and diversified. If for (some) Peripatetics the doctrine seems to have been something like a litmus test for deciding whether one was a true member of the school (so apparently Critolaus of Phaselis), the notion also received some support from outsiders. The Stoic Panaetius of Rhodes seems to have sympathised with it as a kind of alternative for the conflagration theory. Ocellus Lucanus combined it with elements of Pythagorean tradition. This is all the more remarkable if one then also takes into consideration that some within the school itself, like Xenarchus of Seleucia, favoured only a weakened version of it. It leads Falcon to the conclusion that, generally, Aristotle is gradually being "domesticated," as he calls it, and explained in such a way that his outspoken position is softened and rendered less controversial, and therefore perhaps also made less interesting. *Alain Lernould* offers a close-reading analysis of Proclus' commentary on Plato's doctrine of the creation of the human soul as developed in the *Timaeus* (41d4–42d5). Lernould focuses above all on how Proclus in his typical way of creating triads develops a theory about the creation of the soul that allows him to locate the human soul in a raster existing of the original Platonic triad of "the intermediary essence," "the intermediary self," and "the intermediary other" of which each component is itself subdivided into three "ranks," the human souls each time taking the lower, third rank, after the divine and the demonic souls. He concludes by arguing that Proclus' interpretation is inspired by the central myth of the *Phaedrus* and should be seen as one more example of the overall attempt to explain Plato's view as part of a coherent and intended system, while at the same time also going beyond the source when dealing with the generation of the human soul. *Marije Martijn* also deals with Proclus' reading of Plato, more specifically the latter's version of the so-called "Myth of Er" as found in his *Republic*, but that also shows up in other writings of Plato. The "Myth" is a notoriously strange passage addressing the question of individual eschatology or the transition to a new life upon death. The major problem with it is that it creates a tension by giving such a prominent place to Fate and cosmic order at the expense of the concept of justice linked to free will and responsibility one naturally expects to play a role in issues of coming to terms with one's life and which indeed receive quite some attention in other parts of the *Republic*. Proclus surmounts the problem by adopting a view on justice that combines and in fact creates some sort of harmony between cosmic and individual justice. Martijn's investigation of Proclus' comment leads her to single out three quite remarkable elements in the latter's analysis: his open attitude to cannibalism in times of great famine, his interest in cosmic justice, and his views on justified retribution for the individual. The last essay in this part opens up a window to the Christian side, all while staying within the orbit of Neo-Platonism. *Marc-Antoine Gavray* focuses on the controversy between Simplicius and John Philoponus on the origin of the world centring around the latter's refutation of the opinions of Aristotle and Proclus about its eternity and looking in particular to the argumentative strategies both sides are using. With regard to content, Simplicius takes issue with four elements of Philoponus' criticism, that involve either an attack on the notion of God as Creator or on a core aspect of Neo-Platonic argumentation. He reproaches him of diminishing the status of the world by making it a creature, of devaluating the status of the divine Creator as one who can only produce a perishable creation, of ignoring heaven a divine status, and of destroying or rather invalidating the principle that the inferior can only be explained from its superior. As for style, not infrequently, controversy mixes up with irony and insult, which is all the more acute if one realises how profoundly both parties, not just Simplicius, are tributary to the Platonic-Aristotelian tradition. They share several axioms and arguments, but they are using them for opposite purposes. The latter raises the question of the validity of any such argumentation, but it shows above all the limits of such philosophical debates on questions of protology and eschatology, something both participants in the discussion are not completely unaware of.

Jörg Frey opens the second part with an essay on "the logic of Johannine theology" in addressing issues of cosmology and protology. The author of a classic three-volume work on Johannine eschatology, Frey nicely shows how the latter is intrinsically interconnected with the evangelist's views on the pre-existence of Christ as presented in the opening lines of the Prologue, in particular through the soteriological task Christ is said to have come to fulfil. The doctrine of Christ's pre-existence is not only a way to express divine origin or authority, but to root human salvation, beyond the historical level, in God's eternal plan with the world and humanity. Frey continues by analysing how this take on Christ's existence affects the choice of one's reading strategy of the Gospel, briefly evoking, but then also relativising, the famous battle between Käsemann and Bultmann on whether verse 14b or 14a is the key to reading the Prologue and then also the Gospel as a whole and arguing for a reading from the perspective of Jesus' death and resurrection that forms the climax of the Gospel. He combines with it a proposal for a (hypothetical) reconstruction of John's Christology from an early (Jewish) Messianic perspective to the high Christology that characterises the Fourth Gospel. Two essays deal with Gnostic material. Picking up on his previous research on the topic *Einar Thomassen* begins his essay with presenting the way redemption is conceived of in the *Gospel of Truth* and goes on with a more general reflection on the relation between protology and eschatology as this can be found or extracted from various sources of Valentinian origin, focusing in particular on the "parallelism" there is in using these two concepts, but also on the ritual dimension that is brought out in speaking about the Saviour's redemptive task, before broadening his survey to include also sources of non-Valentinian origin. The second essay on Gnostic texts is by the regretted *John D. Turner* who studied the relation between protology and personal eschatology in the tractates *Zostrianos* and *Allogenes*, both of them, as he sees it, Platonising apocalypses of Sethian origin. Starting from the notion of realised eschatology, for which Turner finds some evidence in John's gospel, but also in Paul, he then concentrates above all on issues of ritual in Sethian tradition and on the metaphysics that guided the authors of the two treatises, in particular Plotinus' noetic triad "Being-Life-Mind" in evoking scenarios for transforming earthly into heavenly liturgy and reaching from earthly baptism to forms of mystical union or internal assimilation with the divine as culmination points of a trajectory that leads the individual to his/her final destination. The last two essays open up much broader perspectives. *Benjamin Gleede* surveys how Christian authors from the second to the fifth century have handled the question of where human beings will reside after death. Linked to it are not just issues of judgement, reward and retribution, but also the question of whether or not to use spatial categories, and which ones. It is not enough to speak of heaven and hell in this context, for such concepts are linked to specific views on cosmology. In particular, Gleede looks into counter-positions to the (almost) generally accepted views, as these can be found in the rather idiosyncratic writings of the mysterious Cosmas Indicopleustes with regard to cosmography and in Gregory of Nyssa's teaching on the resurrection of the body that makes superfluous any such discussion because the human body is completely transformed and does no longer need any form of spatiality. *George van Kooten* casts an even wider net stretching his interests from Plato to the Council of Nicaea and beyond in retracing the trajectory from Plato's views of creation as a transformation from disorder to order to the "Stoic-Pauline" notion of a creation "from God" to the concept of a creation "ex nihilo" that received some ambiguous support at the Council in the margin of the dispute with Arius. As van Kooten sees it, the second of these was a collateral victim of attacks on the first and of the outcome of the Arian dispute. This challenging thesis is developed in two steps: first, a detailed analysis of Paul's view as presented in, above all, Romans and 1 Corinthians, and carried further in the Deutero-Pauline letter to the Ephesians and the one to the Colossians; second, a critical survey of the origin and development of the rivalling view of the creation "from nothing" which was made a crucial element of his reflection on the relation between God and Christ the Son by Arius, only to meet a rather more ambivalent fate at Nicaea which firmly countered Arian Christology in asserting that the Son is created from the Father all while assuming, though not stating, that the world is created from nothing.

Two general comments by way of conclusion. First, (post-)modern readers may be puzzled (or shocked) by the apparently limitless confidence ancient philosophers and theologians display in their willingness to scrutinise issues we all know are utterly unsolvable for the human mind. There is little place for doubt, let alone for recognising one's lack of knowledge of such borderline topics. Second, and partly as a consequence of the former, difference of opinion reigns, so it seems, and this not only between the theological and the philosophical approach or between the Christian and the non-Christian tradition, but also within the respective traditions themselves. However, it is only by juxtaposing and confronting the different insights that the peculiarities, the nuances, and maybe also some elements of agreement can be detected and perhaps reasonably validated. That was the ultimate purpose of the meeting and the editors very much hope that something of this overarching aim can be discovered in the essays included in this volume.

Eternalism in Aristotle and After

Andrea Falcon

I. Introduction

By "eternalism" I mean the doctrine that the world has always existed, and will always exist, in its present structure. In other words, according to this doctrine, the world-order (*kosmos*), as we know it, is not subject to generation or destruction but is eternal.

In this essay, I am interested in the original formulation of the doctrine by Aristotle and how it was received in the late Hellenistic and early post-Hellenistic times.[1] I will focus on the following figures: Critolaus of Phaselis, Panaetius of Rhodes, Ocellus of Lucania, and Xenarchus of Seleucia. In the case of Ocellus, we have a text, so his stance on the debate on the eternity of the world can be easily established and assessed. In the other three cases, the positions defended can be reconstructed only through the information transmitted by our ancient sources. As is often the case with Hellenistic and post-Hellenistic authors, the surviving information is not only fragmentary but also of uneven quality. Our ancient sources do not always have direct access to what was written by earlier authors but know their views or ideas only via one (or more than one) intermediate witness(es). This is certainly true for Xenarchus of Seleucia, for whom the ultimate source of information is Alexander of Aphrodisias and his lost commentary on the *De caelo*, and there is no reason to think that we are in a much better situation with respect to Critolaus of Phaselis and Panaetius of Rhodes. Still, I am persuaded that a careful study of the extant information – even when it is second- or even third-hand – is valuable because it can be used to establish that eternalism was not a homogeneous front; rather, it was a constellation of different, and often competing, positions.

[1] This essays combines, and indeed reworks, some of the findings already published in Falcon 2016a and Falcon 2017. What motivates those essays, as well as this one, is the belief that a study of the appropriation of Aristotle's views on the eternity of the world, and their adaptation to a new and different context, can serve to throw Aristotle's original formulation of his position into a sharper relief.

In this essay, I will show that different, and at times alternative, theoretical commitments may underpin the claim that the world is eternal. I will also show that none of the post-Aristotelian positions discussed in this essay really capture what is unique about the original formulation by Aristotle. I believe that establishing these results is important for at least two reasons. First, at the most general level, we learn that Aristotle and the Aristotelian tradition (broadly understood so as to include positions that are inspired by Aristotle but do not belong to the Peripatetic tradition) are not one and the same thing, and that a study of the latter does not necessarily translate into a study of the former. The gap that separates Aristotle and the Aristotelian tradition must not be overlooked or minimized. Quite the opposite: it must be carefully evaluated in order to assess what is specific, if not even unique, about the original position defended by Aristotle. This leads to my second reason for engaging in a close study of the early reception of Aristotle's views on the topic of the eternity of the world: we can better appreciate Aristotle's theoretical commitments by studying how they were received and selectively used in the subsequent philosophical tradition. In this sense, the study of the Aristotelian tradition can teach us something about Aristotle, although it can do so only indirectly.

II. Aristotle's Theoretical Commitments

Getting to the bottom of Aristotle's commitment to the eternity of the world is not an easy task. Aristotle argues for the eternity of motion in *Physics* 8, and for the eternity of the world in *De caelo* 1,10–12. For Aristotle, the eternity of motion entails the eternity of the world.[2] It is therefore possible, at least in principle, to derive the eternity of the world from the eternity of motion – but this is not, interestingly enough, how Aristotle proceeds in the *De caelo*. Moreover, Aristotle seems to have concerned himself with the eternity of the word also in the now lost *De philosophia*. In this section, I would like to elaborate briefly on the exegetical problems that any interpreter has to face when he or she would like to reconstruct Aristotle's position on the topic of the eternity of the world.

In *Physics* 8, Aristotle shows that the eternity of motion entails the existence of a principle that moves the first heavens by being itself outside the chain of motion – in short, he establishes the existence of a first mover that is absolutely unmoved. Establishing the existence of such a principle can be seen as the culmination of the argument offered in *Physics* 8, or as an indispensable step in the

[2] This inference cannot be generalized. It is not true, for instance, for ancient atomism. Both Leucippus and Democritus were committed to the eternity of motion, but they were not committed to the eternity of our world (*kosmos*). On the one hand, they believed that atoms always moved in a void. On the other hand, they believed that the random motion of the atom gave rise to an infinite number of worlds (*kosmoi*), all subject to generation and corruption.

course of an argument that is primarily meant to establish the existence of a single continuous (that is, uninterrupted) motion – namely, the circular motion of the heavens.[3] Either way, the doctrine of the first unmoved mover is certainly the most obvious result that one should take away from *Physics* 8.

It is, however, far from clear that this doctrine is absolutely necessary for the project attempted in *De caelo*.[4] Moreover, Aristotle's opening move in the *De caelo* is at least as controversial as his claim that there exists a first unmoved mover outside the chain of motion. He argues that the heavens are made of a special simple body different from earth, water, air, and fire, and argues that this body naturally moves in a circle (*De caelo* 1,2). He goes on to explain that, precisely because it is naturally moves in a circle, this body is not subject to generation and destruction (*De caelo* 1,3).

We may think that either one of these two commitments – the commitment to the existence of a first unmoved mover that moves the heavens by being itself outside the chain of motion, and the commitment to the existence of a special celestial simple body that naturally moves in a circle – is on its own enough to establish that the world has always existed and will always exist. If, on the one hand, Aristotle is successful in establishing the existence of a first unmoved mover that moves the heavens by being itself outside the chain of motion, why does he need to posit that they are made of a special simple body that move naturally in a circle? If, on the other hand, he is successful in establishing that the heavens are made of such a celestial simple body, why does he have to commit himself to the existence of a first unmoved mover that moves the heavens by being itself outside the chain of motion?

There is no evidence that the thesis that there exists a mover that is absolutely unmoved (defended in *Physics* 8) and the thesis that the heavens are made of a simple celestial body (defended in the *De caelo*) serve the same function, so Aristotle is not forced to choose one thesis over the other. Rather, his commitment to the eternity of the world is the result of a commitment to both theses. The outcome is an especially strong version of the eternalist position, which makes Aristotle stand out as a true anomaly in the ancient cosmological tradition.

A further complication we face in getting to the bottom of Aristotle's commitment to the eternity of the world is that Aristotle seems to have also argued for the eternity of the world in the *De philosophia*. Scholars have tried to reconstruct the contents of the *De philosophia*. Werner Jaeger has famously argued that in the *De philosophia* Aristotle defended his two most important innovations in the field of ancient physics, namely the thesis that the world is eternal,

---

3 I argued for the second reading in Falcon 2015.

4 We find references to the doctrine of the first unmoved mover in the *De caelo*. But those references do not establish that an unmoved mover is needed for the project attempted in the *De caelo*.

and the claim that the heavens are made of a special simple body, unique to them.[5] Moreover, David Furley has suggested that the doctrine of the eternity of the world and the doctrine of the fifth substance were connected in the lost *De philosophia*, and that Aristotle might have defended the formed by using the latter.[6] Unfortunately, this suggestion cannot be substantiated. For one thing, the presence of the doctrine of the fifth substance in our work is far from a sure thing.[7] For another, we have no information about the context in which the doctrine of the eternity of the world was introduced or the strategy that was adopted to defend this doctrine. Philo of Alexandria (first century AD) is our only source of information for the arguments that Aristotle *may* have employed to defend the eternity of the world.

[Arg. 1] the world cannot be destroyed by anything outside it or by anything inside it; hence, the world is not subject to destruction (Philo, *De aeternitate mundi* 20–24 = fr. 19a Ross 1958).
[Arg. 2] Destruction entails return of parts to their natural places, but the parts of the world are already in their nature places; hence, the world is not subject to destruction (Philo, *De aeternitate mundi* 28–34 = fr. 19b Ross).
[Arg. 3] God has no motive to destroy the world, whether permanently or in order to replace it with another (sc. better) world; hence, the world is not subject to destruction (Philo, *De aeternitate mundi* 39–44 = fr. 19c Ross).[8]

We cannot be certain that these arguments go back to the *De philosophia* because there is no explicit reference to the *De philosophia* in Philo of Alexandria. In the best-case scenario, the arguments preserved by Philo go back to the lost *De philosophia* via an unknown (Peripatetic) source. Hence, they are at most *vestiges* of Aristotle's original arguments. What is clear, however, is that the arguments transmitted by Philo have very little in common with those we can read in *Physics* 8 and *De caelo* 1,10–12. As a result, we are left with three independent attempts to argue for the eternity of the world, and we are also left with the problem of how to reconcile them. More directly, any interpreter who is interested on Aristotle's original formulation of the eternalist position will have to reconcile not only what Aristotle says in *Physics* 8 with what he says *De caelo* 1,10–12, but also what Aristotle says in these two works with the surviving information about the argumentative strategy (or strategies) adopted in the lost *De philosophia*.

---

[5] Jaeger [2]1948: "it was this work, now lost but much read in antiquity, that contained the two philosophical views then considered most characteristic of Aristotle: the adoption of the ether as the element of the heavens, and the assertion that the cosmos is indestructible and uncreated. The doxographers commonly mention the two together as his distinctive additions to Plato's cosmology, and this is correct" (140).

[6] Furley 1989, 209–11.

[7] I refer the reader to Hahm 1982.

[8] My presentation of the three arguments is an adaptation of Sharples 2008, 61.

Trying to reconcile what Aristotle says on the topic of the eternity of the world is not a task that I will pursue in this essay. Here I am content to make two quick observations. My first observation concerns the historical significance of the lost *De philosophia* and its role in the early reception of Aristotle's ideas on the topic of the eternity of the world. The *De philosophia* circulated in the late Hellenistic times and played a significant role in the formation of what we can describe as "Aristotelian eternalism." It remains to be seen whether this position, or rather the various positions that can be subsumed under this general description, and the significance of which goes emphatically beyond the Peripatetic tradition, are the same as Aristotle's original position – at least as the latter is known from *Physics* 8 and the *De caelo*.

My second observation concerns the question of how we should approach *Physics* 8 and the *De caelo*. It is not enough to say that Aristotle is engaged in different projects in these two writings. Rather, he is engaged in different *kinds* of projects. In *Physics* 8, Aristotle deals with the question of the eternity of motion at the most general level possible. As a result, he refrains from making assumptions about the particular bodies that populate the sublunary and celestial worlds. He establishes that there has to be a single continuous (that is, uninterrupted) motion by employing the resources that he has made available for himself in the course of the whole *Physics*. But, again, those resources are very general and teach us very little (in fact, nothing) about the bodies that populate the heavens or the sublunary world. We can think of the whole *Physics*, including *Physics* 8, as a prolegomenon to a detailed study of the physical world – and of the *De caelo* as the first instalment of such a detailed study. It is telling that the opening lines of the *De caelo* serves as a programmatic passage, the significance of which goes well beyond the narrow boundaries of the *De caelo*. At the outset of the *De caelo*, Aristotle announces that "the science of nature is manifestly concerned for the most part with bodies and magnitudes and their properties and motions."[9] It is only after this general description of the subject matter of physics that Aristotle is ready to turn to the study of the physical world. He does so by way of a study of the different bodies that populate it. Moreover, his first and most controversial step in this project is the introduction of a celestial simple body that naturally moves in a circle and is not reducible to earth, water, air, and fire.

[9] Aristotle, *De caelo* 1,1,268a1–3. I offer a full discussion of the opening lines of the *De caelo* in Falcon 2016b.

III. Aristotle's Original Position

The ancient doxographical tradition introduces eternalism with the help the following tripartition:

(a) the world is subject to generation and destruction;
(b) the world is subject to generation but is not subject to destruction;
(c) the world is subject neither to generation nor to destruction.[10]

Aristotle's position would fall under (c). But it is far from clear that the thesis advanced in (c) captures what is specific about his position. In his extant writings, Aristotle is committed to a stronger thesis: that the world is *of necessity* ungenerated and indestructible. This thesis is the result of the combination of his two other commitments – namely, the view that the heavens are made of a special simple body, unique to them, and the claim that a full explanation of celestial motion requires the existence of a first principle that moves by remaining absolutely unmoved, the first unmoved mover.

I will try to illustrate what I take to be Aristotle's position with the help of a discussion offered in the *De motu animalum* (hereafter *De motu*). In *De motu* 3 and 4, Aristotle is concerned with two distinct, though related, *aporiai*. The first *aporia* is as following: every motion requires a point of rest, and celestial motion is no exception to the rule. Where is that point? Can it be inside the world? The idea is illustrated with the help of an image: a giant, Atlas, who could set the heavens in motion by supporting himself against the earth. This model would be physically impossible because the earth is too small to serve as a point of support. The earth would be displaced from its natural place as soon as Atlas tried to set the heavens in motion. The discussion of the first *aporia* goes some way toward explaining why Aristotle thinks that we need to posit the existence of a body that is naturally endowed with circular motion. However, it does not explain why we need an unmoved mover in addition to such a body.

Let us turn to the second *aporia*. We begin with the idea that the earth could be displaced from the center of the world if we had a sufficient force. Had we a sufficient force, we could also stop the heavens from rotating around the earth. However, Aristotle is not content with the claim that the earth occupies the center of the world because there is no force available that can displace it. Nor is he content with the claim that the heavens rotates around the earth because there is no force that could stop them. By his lights, this particular arrangement is rather a necessary truth. This position generates the second *aporia*, which goes something like this: How is it possible to establish the desired conclusion, namely that *necessarily* the earth is at the center of the cosmos, and that the

[10] Philo, *De aeternitate mundi* 10–11 (= fr. 18 Ross). A full discussion of this doxographical tradition is found in Runia 2005.

heavens *necessarily* rotate forever around it? The existence of a mover that is absolutely unmoved is the solution to the *aporia*. This mover is the controlling principle that in virtue of being absolutely unmoved is responsible for the fact that the arrangement of the world is not only an eternal but also a necessary truth.

I have elaborated on this discussion for two reasons. The first is that it is still common to think that there is a redundancy in Aristotle's physical theory. Many have argued that it is not clear why we need to posit the existence of an absolutely unmoved mover in addition to a body that eternally moves in a circle. This perceived redundancy disappears as soon as we realize that we need both a mover that is absolutely unmoved and a body that naturally moves in a circle in order to secure the especially strong version of eternalism that Aristotle seems to endorse in his writings on natural philosophy. The second reason can be introduced with the help of the following question: Can Aristotle's actual position be reconstructed without access to the school treatises (not only *Physics* 8 and the *De caelo* but also the *De motu*)? My answer to this question is an emphatic "no." If we had only the doxographical information about the ancient debate on the eternity of the world at our disposal, we could not reconstruct Aristotle's actual position.

The extant evidence from the *De philosophia* is not very helpful with respect to the two commitments that contribute to establishing his distinctive version of the eternalist position. There is some evidence that Aristotle offered an argument for the view that god is unchangeable. Admittedly, it is open to us to find in this argument a commitment to the existence of a first mover that is absolutely unmoved.[11] But the presence in the *De philosophia* of the doctrine of the fifth substance is far from established. On the contrary, we have already seen that there are good reasons to doubt its presence. But without a firm commitment to the existence of a special matter, unique to the celestial bodies, the strong version of the eternalist position that can be extracted from Aristotle's writings on natural philosophy can neither be secured also for the *De philosophia*.

IV. Eternalism after Aristotle

In the Hellenistic period, the thesis that the world is eternal did not enjoy great success beyond the Peripatos. Epicureans and Stoics defended different, and mutually incompatible, styles of physics, but they agreed on the following point: the world-order, as we know it, is not eternal. Things changed toward the end of the Hellenistic period. In the second century BC, a few philosophers

---

[11] Simplicius, *In De caelo* 288,28–289,15 (= fr. 16 Ross).

working in different philosophical traditions, and responding to different theoretical pressures, adopted the view that the world is eternal.

Critolaus of Phaselis was the champion of the Peripatetic tradition in the late Hellenistic period. As head of the Peripatos, he took part in the diplomatic mission of philosophers to Rome in 155 BC. In physics, Critolaus endorsed the Aristotelian thesis that the world is eternal. The remaining evidence is scarce, but it suggests that the activity of defending this thesis (as well as others) was very important, if not even essential, to his identity as Peripatetic philosopher.[12]

That a member of the school founded by Aristotle in Athens argued for the eternity of the world is unsurprising. After all, we know that not only Aristotle but also Theophrastus defended this thesis.[13] What is surprising is that, beginning in the second century BC, this thesis can be found *outside the* Peripatos. For example, a notable defender of the eternity of the world was Panaetius of Rhodes.[14] Panaetius was the most important *Stoic* philosopher of the second century BC. When we come to Panaetius, we can safely say that the doctrine of universal conflagration (*ekpurôsis*) was no longer regarded as a non-negotiable Stoic doctrine. Rather, it seems to have become an expendable thesis. Before Panaetius, Boethus of Sidon and his teacher Diogenes of Babylon had already rejected this thesis.[15] Before them, Zeno of Tarsus too seems to have doubted it.[16] We can only speculate on the reasons that may have motivated Panaetius, Boethus, Diogenes, and maybe Zeno, to modify the Stoic physics on this point. It is possible that this modification is a direct response to theoretical pressures coming from outside the Stoic school. The doctrine of universal conflagration was an increasingly difficult thesis to defend.[17] As a result, some Stoic philosophers may have felt that it was possible to drop it without major consequences for the Stoic physical theory as a whole. This explanation need not be in competition with one that invokes the fact that Panaetius was also an admirer of Aristotle (a *philaristotelês)* and an admirer of Plato (a *philoplatôn*). On the contrary, one may argue that it is because the doctrine of universal conflagration was an in-

---

[12] Philo, *De aeternitate mundi* 55–64. On Critolaus, see Hahm 2007. For a discussion of Critolaus' arguments on the eternity of the world as preserved by Philo, I refer the reader to Sharples 2008.

[13] See Philo, *De aeternitate mundi* 117–49. For a discussion of Theophrastus' arguments and their fortune in antiquity, see Sedley 1998.

[14] Philo, *De aeternitate mundi* 76–77.

[15] Our source of information is Philo, *De aeternitate mundi* 76–77 (= *SVF* III, *Diogenes Babylonius* 27 and *Boethus Sidonius* 7) The *Stoic* Boethus is not to be confused with the *Peripatetic* Boethus who was also a native of Sidon. Since the Stoic Boethus was a student of Diogenes of Babylon, his activity is to be dated to the second half of the second century BC. As for Diogenes of Babylon, he took part in the diplomatic mission to Rome in his capacity as head of the Stoa in 156–57.

[16] Arius Didymus (*apud* Diels 1879: fr. 36; = *SVF* III, *Zeno Tarsensis* 5).

[17] For a first impression of the sort of objections moved to the doctrine of universal conflagration see Philo, *De aeternitate mundi* 45–51.

creasingly difficult thesis to defend for a Stoic philosopher that Panaetius, who was *also* an admirer of Aristotle and Plato, returned to their writings and found in these writings the resources to modify the original Stoic position.[18] We have to stop here because the information in our possession is not sufficient to establish whether the Stoics were influenced by Peripatetic philosophers such as Critolaus, or whether their commitment to eternalism was the result of a direct engagement with Aristotle's writings. If they were reading his works, a further question is whether they were reading the *De philosophia* or the writings that are still extant. We really do not know, and we should refrain from speculating on this point in the complete absence of any information.

What we can take away from this brief review of the extant evidence for eternalism in the second century BC is that this view enjoyed some success outside the Peripatetic tradition, most notably in the Stoic tradition. With this in mind, we can now turn to the Pythagorean tradition. The work that interests us is the short essays *On the Nature of the Universe* attributed to Ocellus Lucanus. Both the title of the work and its attribution to Ocellus are based on what we read in the opening sentence of the work: "Ocellus of Lucania has written the following things on the nature of the Universe."[19] We cannot date this work with precision, but both Harder, its modern editor, and Theiler, who reviewed his critical edition for *Gnomon*, dated it to the second half of the second century BC.[20] This work is the earliest extant evidence of the reception of Critolaus' arguments for the eternity of the world. More directly, this work contains indisputable evidence that its author appropriated not only Aristotle but also the Peripatetic tradition, and in particular Critolaus, for the Pythagorean tradition. At least the following argument goes back to Critolaus:

> Fire, which imparts the heat to another thing, is self-hot, honey which is sweet to the taste is self-sweet. The principles of demonstrations, which conclude to things unapparent, are self-evident. Therefore, the cause of the perfection of other things is itself perfect. What preserves and renders permanent other things must itself be preserved and permanent. What harmonizes must itself be self-harmonic. Now, as the world is the cause of the existence, preservation, and perfection of other things, the world must itself be perpetual and perfect; and because its duration is everlasting, it becomes the cause of the permanence of all other things (trans. by Guthrie 1987).[21]

---

[18] At the same time, we should not assume that all the Stoic philosophers who dropped the doctrine of universal conflagration did it for the same reason. For example, we cannot rule out that the reasons that motivated Diogenes and Boethus to reject *ekpurôsis* were different from those that motivated Panaetius.

[19] When I say "Ocellus" in the rest of this essay, I mean the unknown author who says that he is Ocellus. *On the Nature of the Universe* is already taken to be the title of his work by Philo of Alexandria in the first century AD (see below).

[20] Harder 1926; ²1966. See, in particular, the concluding remarks (especially 149–50). Cf. Theiler 1926.

[21] Ocellus Lucanus 13,5–17 = § 9. We know that this argument goes back to Critolaus because Philo (*De aeternitate mundi* 70 = Wehrli 1969, fr. 12 = Sharples 2010, 20B) credits Cri-

In addition to the appropriation of arguments for the eternity of the world that go back to the Peripatetic tradition (which may have been inspired, or even shaped, by the arguments offered in the *De philosophia*),[22] the author speaking for Ocellus makes use of a physical theory that can be traced back to the second book of Aristotle's *De generatione et corruptione*. He does not acknowledge the original source of his theory, nor does he invoke the authority of Aristotle. Instead, he presents the original material as ideas and arguments put forward by Ocellus. And yet, this use of Aristotle is a fact whose significance can hardly be overestimated. The use of ideas and doctrines that can be traced back to Aristotle's writings are extremely rare in the Hellenistic period to the point that some scholars have concluded that these writings were not known and did not circulate in this period.[23]

But what happened to the Aristotelian doctrines that the author speaking for Ocellus appropriated for the Pythagorean tradition? To answer this question, we need to look at the contents of his work. We can divide this work into four more or less self-sufficient pieces.[24] This does not mean, I hasten to say, that our text is just a compilation of materials of various provenance. Clearly, there is a single argument running through the first three pieces. We can safely say that the main thesis that the author defends is in place only at the end of the third

tolaus with a version of it: "Continuing his contention, Critolaus also used an argument like the following: 'what is the cause of its own health does not suffer disease. What is the cause of its own wakefulness too does not sleep. But if this is so, what is the cause of its own existence is eternal. But the world is the cause of its own existence, if it is the cause of the existence of all other things. So the world is eternal'" (trans. Sharples 2010, 175–76).

22 The following argument may be derived (directly or indirectly) from Aristotle's *De philosophia* (cf. Philo, *De aeternitate mundi* 20–24 = *De philosophia* 19a Ross and 19a Walzer): "if somebody should think that it [*sc.* the world, cosmos] can be corrupted, it must be corrupted either from something external to or contained in the universe; but it cannot be corrupted by anything external to it, for nothing such exists, since all other things are comprehended in the universe; but it cannot be corrupted by anything external to it, for nothing such exists, since all other things are comprehended in the universe, and the world is the whole and the all. Nor can it be corrupted by the things it contains, which would imply their greater power. This, however, is impossible, for all things are led and governed by the universe, and thereby are preserved and adjusted, possessing life and soul. But if the universe can neither be corrupted by anything external to it, nor by anything contained within it, the world must therefore be incorruptible and indestructible, for we consider the world identical with the universe" (Ocellus Lucanus 13,24–14,5 = § 11, trans. by Guthrie 1987).

23 The most notable defender of this view was F.H. Sandbach, who felt compelled to discuss our text precisely because it posed an obvious challenge to his thesis – especially so since he accepted the early date for Ocellus suggested by Harder and Theiler (second century BC). See, in particular, Sandbach 1985, 63–64. Sandbach denied that this work is evidence that Aristotle's works in general, and *On Generation and Corruption* in particular, may have circulated before the time of Andronicus. He argues that "the quotations [in Ocellus] may have been part of the material inherited from the early days of the school when knowledge of that work is easier to credit" (64).

24 Piece 1: §§ 2–17; Piece 2: §§ 18–37; Piece 3: §§ 38–43; Piece 4: §§ 44–57.

piece. It is telling that the third piece ends with a recapitulation of the main results reached up to that point:

> So much about the whole and the universe, the generation and corruption of natures generated in it, of how they subsist, and forever, one part of the universe consisting of a nature which is perpetually moved, and another part being passive and of how the former rules and how the latter is ever ruled (Ocellus Lucanus 21,15–18 = § 43, trans. by Guthrie 1987, with modifications).

Clearly, the universe is envisioned as a causal arrangement in which one part – the region above the moon – *always* acts on the other. Moreover, this other part – the region below the moon – is *always* acted upon such that generation and corruption go on forever without interruption. The following aspect of the explanatory strategy adopted in this work is especially interesting: no cause that comes from outside the world is invoked to explain the existence of this specific causal arrangement. It really looks as though our author, presenting himself as Ocellus, regards the world as a causal system that has within itself the resources to maintain itself forever. In other words, the world is conceived as *a self-maintaining system*. Needless to say, this is not Aristotle's position. Aristotle never intended to give the impression that a full explanation of why the world is eternal can be given by remaining within the boundaries of the physical world. On the contrary, in *Physics* 8, Aristotle invokes the existence of an unmoved mover as a causal factor in the explanation of the existence of an unbroken continuous chain of motion. This unmoved mover is needed to secure the continuity of a celestial motion, which in turn is required to explain the fact that the sublunary world can be conceived as an unbroken chain of things that come into existence and go out of existence.

There are two possible ways of understanding how the unknown author speaking as Ocellus uses Aristotle in his work. A first possibility is that he uses Aristotle *selectively*. In this scenario, the main textual basis for the picture of the physical world as a self-maintaining causal system is Aristotle's *De generatione et corruptione* (hereafter *GC*). In addition to relying on (a selection from) *GC* II 2–3, the author appropriates for Ocellus the thesis that the sun is the *proximate* efficient cause invoked to explain the continuity of generation and corruption.[25] This is a thesis that Aristotle defends in *GC* II 9–10. In this first scenario, the author speaking for Ocellus knows and uses *GC* II. However, we cannot rule out a second possibility. This author does not use Aristotle but rather ideas and arguments that go back to Critolaus. For one thing, Critolaus appears to have adopted the view that the physical world is a result of the causal action of the imperishable celestial world (a world made of an intelligent, and indeed rational, element, which he may have called *aithêr*) upon the sublunary world. He seems to have invoked this element to explain not only the imperish-

25 Ocellus Lucanus 20,1–7 = § 37 *partim*.

ability of the heavens but also the Aristotelian view that world is a causal system in which the heavens act upon the sublunary world, but cannot be acted upon by it. If this element is imperishable and intelligent, it is also divine. It may be not just *a* god but rather *the* god listed as one of the two principles (the other being matter) in the doxographical tradition preserved by Epiphanius. All of this would have made the unmoved mover expendable from Critolaus' physical theory. As a result, the gap between Stoic and Aristotelian physics would be reduced considerably.[26]

It is worth stressing a further possible point of contact with what we know about Critolaus. Critolaus seems to have adopted the view that the heavens are made of *aithêr.* The unknown author who presents himself as Ocellus has very little to say on the region above the moon. It really looks like his interest in this part of the world is limited to its causal role in the explanation of the continuous and unbroken chain of generation and corruption taking place in the sublunary world. Toward the end of the second piece, however, he sums up his position as follows:

> Thus, what generates in something else is in the region above the moon while what generates in itself is in the region below the moon; what consists of both of them, *the ever-running divine part* and the ever-mutable generated part, is the cosmos (Ocellus Lucanus 20,7–11 = § 37 *partim*).[27]

It is tempting to read in the description of the celestial part of the cosmos a reference to the etymology of *aithêr* as ever-running (*aithêr = aei thein*).[28] This is certainly how Sextus Empiricus (or rather his doxographical source) seems to have understood our text:

> Ocellus of Lucania and Aristotle [hold that all things have come to be] from five: for along with the four elements they also adopted the fifth body that moves in a circle, and from which they say that the heavenly objects are derived (Sextus, *Adv. math.* 10,316, trans. R. G. Bury).

But even if we adopt the second scenario, and argue that the conception of the world attributed to Ocellus derives from Critolaus (rather than Aristotle), we

[26] For this reconstruction of Critolaus' physical theory, I am relying on Sharples 2002, especially 14 and Hahm 2007, 82–87. The two key texts for this reconstruction are found in doxographical tradition. They are Epiphanius (*apud* Diels 1879: 592.9-20) and Aëtius (*Placita* 1,7,21).

[27] Guthrie 1987 translates as follows: "Different, therefore, is the generator, which is superlunary, while that which is generated is sublunary; and that which consists of both of these, namely, an ever-running body, and an every-mutable generated nature, is the world itself." This conception of the world occurs also in Ps-Philolaus, *De anima*. In addition to the eternity of the world, both texts are committed to the claim that the world is a self-maintaining system due to its division into a superlunary and a sublunary part.

[28] For this etymology, see Plato, *Cratylus* 410b6–7. Cf. Aristotle, *De caelo* 1,3,270b20–23. This etymology is accepted by the author of the *De mundo* 392a5–9. For more on this etymology, as well as its theoretical implications, see Falcon 2005, 113–21.

still have to say that the doctrine of inter-transformation – offered as the explanation for how generation and corruption is possible in the sublunary world – derives, ultimately, from Aristotle. In sum, in either one of the two scenarios I have outlined, our text is a hybrid of arguments that go back, on the one hand, to the Peripatetic tradition of Late Hellenistic time and, on the other hand, to Aristotle. As such, our work gives us a unique insight into the transition from late Hellenistic philosophy to post-Hellenistic philosophy.

It is time to try to evaluate the position attributed to Ocellus. This position can be usefully contrasted with another eternalist position. The latter can be reconstructed on the basis of the extant evidence we have for Xenarchus, a Peripatetic philosopher who lived in the second half of the first century BC.[29] Xenarchus famously rejected the doctrine that the heavens are made of a special celestial body. He also developed a theory of natural motion that allowed him to claim that the heavens are made of an ever-running fire. Briefly, fire moves upward until it reaches its natural place, but then it does not stop moving. Why? The answer is: Because that would be in conflict with its non-stationary nature. Once fire has reached its natural place, it begins moving in a circle. Moreover, because of its non-stationary nature, fire keeps moving in a circle *forever*, since there is nothing that can prevent it from moving in a circle. On my reconstruction of the extant evidence, Xenarchus too was committed to the view that the world is eternal. He was committed to this view by being committed to the eternity of the heavenly region. But he was *not* able to give us a sufficiently robust version of the eternalist position. Very briefly: the fire that has reached its natural place may be removed from the cycle of generation and corruption that takes place in the sublunary world, but it still keeps its natural capacity to change into the other simple bodies. This means that, *at least in principle*, the heavens could be destroyed, even though they are never destroyed.

Let us stop to expand on this last point by reflecting on the meaning of the Greek *phtharton*. This term can be used to refer to something that will be eventually destroyed. But it can also be used to refer to something that is merely *capable of being destroyed*, whether or not it will eventually undergo destruction. One may exploit this ambiguity of the Greek *phtharton* to argue that the world is capable of being destroyed but it will never undergo destruction. If Xenarchus adopted the view that the world is a self-maintaining system, he also adopted a rather weak version of this thesis. For Aristotle, the world is eternal in a much stronger sense: the world cannot, *even in principle*, undergo (generation and) destruction. In fact, one of the reasons that may have motivated Aristotle to adopt the controversial thesis that the heavens are made of a special celestial body unique to them may have been his desire to secure a sufficiently strong version of the view that the world is eternal.

---

[29] See my reconstruction of Xenarchus' position in Falcon 2011, 25–42.

There is another view that should be on the table as we reflect on the precise nature of the commitment to the eternity of the world attributed to Ocellus. That the world could be destroyed, even if it will never be destroyed, is an idea that we find also in Plato's *Timaeus*. Consider, for instance, the following passage in which the divine demiurge addresses the lesser gods involved in the creation of the world:

O Gods, works divine whose maker and father I am, whatever has come to be by my hands cannot be undone but by consent. Now, *while it is true that anything that is bound is liable to being undone, still, only one who is evil would consent to the undoing of what has been well fitted together and is in fine condition* (Plato, *Tim.* 41a–b, trans. by D.J. Zeyl, italics are mine).

The main idea conveyed in this passage is that all that has been bound is at least *in principle* dissolvable. More to the point: *it would dissolve* if it were not for the benevolence of its creator. This is how this idea was received in the doxographical tradition that goes back to Aëtius:

Plato claims that the world is perishable to the extent that it is so by nature; but it will never be destroyed because of the divine providence which maintains it in existence (Aëtius, *Placita* 2,4,2).

After having recalled the view that Xenarchus put forward, and with this particular reading of the *Timaeus* in place, we can return to the text attributed to Ocellus in order to evaluate the eternalist position adopted in that text. If the author speaking for Ocellus is adopting the position that Critolaus seems to have defended – namely, the view that the heavens are made of a non-stationary body, different from and not reducible to earth, water, air, and fire, called *aithêr* – his position is not vulnerable to the objection that we have discussed in connection with Xenarchus. Nor is it equivalent to the position that the doxographical tradition ascribes to Plato. Our work commits Ocellus to a third, distinct position. But is this position sufficiently robust, at least by Aristotle's lights?

We are back to the question that opened my essay: How much of Aristotle's original position is left not only in Ocellus but also in Panaetius, Critolaus, and Xenarchus? My answer is: Not much. Recall what I said about Aristotle's commitments: at least for Aristotle, it is not sufficient to claim that the world, in its present structure, is ungenerated and incorruptible. Rather, his view is that the world, as we know it is *of necessity* ungenerated and incorruptible. We do not find this position in the subsequent traditions. Instead, we find distinct attempts to promote a weaker version of his eternalist position. They are best regarded as independent attempts to adopt Aristotle's original formulation and update it to a new context. It should not be lost, however, that the result is a "domesticated Aristotle" to the extent that his original position is not only much stronger but also more controversial, and as such more interesting, than any of the subsequent positions I have reviewed in these pages.

Bibliography

Diels, H. (1879), *Doxographi graeci*, Berlin: Reimer.
Dillon, J. (1977), *The Middle Platonists: A Study of Platonism 80 B.C. to A.D. 200*. London: Duckworth.
Effe, B. (1970), *Studien zur Kosmologie und Theologie der Aristotelischen Schrift "Über die Philosophie"* (Zetemata 50), München: Beck.
Falcon, A. (2005), *Aristotle and the Science of Nature: Unity without Uniformity*, Cambridge: Cambridge University Press.
– (2011), *Aristotelianism in the First Century BCE: Xenarchus of Seleucia*, Cambridge: Cambridge University Press.
– (2015), 'The Argument of *Physics* 8', in: *Aristotle's Physics: A Critical Guide*, ed. M. Leunissen, Cambridge: Cambridge University Press, 265–83.
– (2016a), 'The Reception of Aristotle's *Physics* in Antiquity: Ps-Ocellus and the Doctrine of the Eternity of the World in Late Hellenistic and Early Post-Hellenistic World (2nd and 1st Century BC)', *Philosophia* 46: 154–69.
– (2016b), 'The Subject Matter of Aristotle's Physics', in: *ΣΩΜΑ: Körperkonzepte und körperliche Existenz in der antiken Philosophie und Literatur*, ed. Th. Buchheim, D. Meißner, and N. Wachsmann, Hamburg: Felix Meiner Verlag, 422–36.
– (2017), 'La dottrina dell'eternità del mondo in Aristotele e nell'aristotelismo degli inizi', in: *Immanenza e trascendenza in Aristotele*, ed. L. Grecchi, Pistoia: Petite Plaisance, 201–15.
Furley, D. (1989), 'Aristotelian Material in Cicero's', in: *Cicero's Knowledge of the Peripatos*, ed. W.W. Fortenbaugh, New Brunswick, NJ: Transaction Publishers, 201–19.
Guthrie, K.S. (1987), *The Pythagorean Sourcebook and Library: An Anthology of Ancient Writings Which Relate to Pythagoras and Phytagorean Philosophy*, compiled and translated by –. Introduced and edited by D.R. Fideler, Grand Rapids, MI: Phanes Press.
Hahm, D. (1982), 'The Fifth Element in Aristotle's *De Philosophia*: A Critical Re-examination', *The Journal of Hellenic Studies* 102: 60–74.
– (2007), 'Critolaus and Late Hellenistic Peripatetic Philosophy', in: *Pyrrhonists, Patricians, Platonizers: Hellenistic Philosophy in the Period 155–86 BC*, ed. A.M. Ioppolo and D.N. Sedley, Naples: Bibliopolis, 47–101.
Harder, R. (²1966), *Ocellus Lucanus: Text und Kommentar*, Berlin: Weidmann, 1926.
Jaeger, W. (²1948), *Aristotle: Fundamentals of the History of His Development*, Oxford: Clarendon.
Mansfeld, J. and Runia, D.T. (1997), *Aëtiana: The Method and Intellectual Context of a Doxographer*. Vol. I: *The Sources* (Philosophia antiqua 73), Leiden – Boston, MA: Brill.
Ross, W.D. (1958), *Aristotelis Fragmenta selecta* (Scriptorum classicorum bibliotheca Oxoniensis), Oxford: Clarendon.
Runia, D.T. (2005), 'A Difficult Chapter in Aëtius Book II on Cosmology', in: *Philosophy and Doxography in the Imperial Age* (Studi – Accademia toscana di scienze e lettere La Colombaria 228), Firenze: Olschki, 1–25.
– (2008), 'Philo and Hellenistic Doxography', in: *Philo of Alexandria and Post-Aristotelian Philosophy*, ed. F. Alesse, Leiden – Boston, MA: Brill, 13–54.
Sandbach, F.H. (1985), *Aristotle and the Stoics* (Cambridge Philological Society. Supplementary Vol. X), Cambridge: Cambridge Philological Society.

Sedley, D. N. (1998), 'Theophrastus and Epicurean Physics', in: *Theophrastus: Reappraising the Sources*, ed. J. van Opuishjen and M. van Raalte, New Brunswick, NJ: Transaction Publishers, 131–42.
Sharples, R. W. (2002), 'Aristotelian Theology after Aristotle', in: *Traditions of Theology: Studies in Hellenistic Theology: Its Background and Aftermath*, ed. D. Frede and A. Laks (Philosophia antiqua 89), Leiden – Boston, MA: Brill, 1–40.
– (2008), 'Philo and Post-Aristotelian Peripatetics', in: *Philo of Alexandria and Post-Aristotelian Philosophy*, ed. F. Alesse, Leiden – Boston, MA: Brill, 55–73.
– (2010), *Peripatetic Philosophy 200 BC to AD 200: An Introduction and Collection of Sources in Translation*, Cambridge: Cambridge University Press.
Theiler, W. (1926), '"Ocellus Lucanus": Text und Kommentar von Richard Harder', *Gnomon* 2: 585–97.
Wehrli, F. (1969), *Hieronymos von Rhodos, Kritolaos und seine Schüler. Rückblick: Der Peripatos in vorchristlicher Zeit* (Die Schule des Aristoteles 10), Basel – Stuttgart: Schwabe & Co. Verlag.

L'interprétation proclienne de la création des âmes humaines dans le *Timée* de Platon

Alain Lernould

Le récit imagé en *Timée* 41d4–42d5 de la création de la partie immortelle de l'âme humaine est dense et suscite nombre de problèmes. F.M. Cornford, dans son commentaire cursif du *Timée*, note, quand il en arrive à la création de l'âme humaine:

In all this section of the dialogue the veil of myth grows thicker again, and it is useless to discuss problems that would arise only if the statements were meant literally[1].

Le commentaire de Proclus sur cette section du *Timée* (41d4–42d5) couvre 67 pages dans l'édition allemande de Diehl (*In Tim.* 3,242,9–310,2)[2], 80 pages dans la traduction française de Festugière[3]. Assurément, au regard du jugement de Cornford, Proclus a perdu un peu de son temps. Et que dire de celui qui consacre à son tour du temps et quelques efforts pour analyser le commentaire de Proclus et en tirer quelques éléments en vue d'une synthèse doctrinale! Une synthèse doctrinale demanderait par ailleurs de compléter l'analyse du commentaire sur le *Timée* par celles d'autres textes de Proclus, en premier lieu la *Théologie platonicienne* (Livres 5 et 6)[4], le commentaire sur la *République*[5] (toute la section sur le mythe d'Er), toute la section finale des *Éléments de théologie*[6] consacrée aux âmes (Propositions 184–211), sans compter le commentaire sur le *Phèdre* rédigé par Hermias[7], l'élève, au côté de Proclus, de Syrianus. Mais ce serait là l'objet d'une importante monographie. Dans le cadre du présent article je me limite au commentaire sur le *Timée* (avec parfois des références à des passages parallèles

[1] Cornford 1937, 143.

[2] Les références au texte grec du commentaire de Proclus sur le *Timée* sont à l'édition de Diehl 1903–06. Les traductions en français de l'*In Timaeum* sont tirées de Festugière 1966–68, parfois modifiées.

[3] Festugière 1966–68, V, 109–89.

[4] Saffrey et Westerink 1968–97.

[5] Kroll 1899–1901. Trad. fr.: Festugière 1970.

[6] Cf. Dodds 1933; [2]1963. Trad. fr.: Trouillard 1965.

[7] Lucarini et Moreschini 2012. Voir aussi Couvreur 1901.

tirés d'autres textes de Proclus) et me propose de dégager de ce commentaire quelques lignes directrices de l'interprétation proclienne de *Timée* 41d8–e4[8].

Commençons par le texte de Platon lui-même. Le Démiurge a créé le Monde comme totalité, comme Vivant divin, d'abord le Corps du Monde (*Tim.* 31b–34b), puis l'Âme du Monde (34b–37c), puis le Temps qui implique la création des vivants divins partiels que sont les planètes (37c–39e) et les astres fixes (39e–40e). Reste à créer le vivant mortel, c'est-à-dire l'homme. Avant de céder la place aux «jeunes dieux»[9] pour la fabrication de ce vivant mortel, le Démiurge s'adresse à eux et leur dit que c'est lui seul qui peut créer la partie immortelle dans le vivant mortel qu'est l'homme, à savoir l'âme immortelle humaine. Après son discours (41a7–d3) le Démiurge revient au cratère dans lequel il avait opéré pour la création de l'Âme du Monde un premier mélange, avec pour éléments: l'Essence indivisible et l'Essence divisible, le Même indivisible et le Même divisible, l'Autre indivisible et l'Autre divisible[10]. Un second mélange, presque le même que le premier, est alors fait en vue de la création des âmes humaines. Ce qui différencie le second mélange du premier, c'est le fait que dans le second mélange les éléments mêlés sont «moins purs»:

---

[8] On trouvera dans Finamore et Kutash 2017 une bonne synthèse de la philosophie proclienne de l'Âme (Âme du Monde et âmes individuelles). La section consacrée aux âmes individuelles est basée sur les *Éléments de théologie*. Le commentaire sur le *Timée* est utilisé seulement pour la doctrine du véhicule de l'âme.

[9] C'est-à-dire les dieux sublunaires (les dieux traditionnels), cf. *Tim.* 40d6–41a6. Sur ces «jeunes dieux» sur lesquels Proclus fait présider Dionysos, cf. Opsomer 2003.

[10] Je parle de «premier mélange» pour faire référence à celui opéré en vue de la constitution de l'Âme du Monde, par opposition au «second mélange», qui est fait en vue de la création des âmes (immortelles) partielles, i.e. humaines. Mais ce «premier mélange», à partir duquel est créée l'Âme du Monde, se dédouble lui-même en deux moments successifs. On a d'abord (1) Les mélanges, respectivement, de l'Essence indivisible et de l'Essence divisible, du Même indivisible et du Même divisible, de l'Autre indivisible et de l'Autre divisible, qui conduisent à la production de trois ingrédients intermédiaires: l'Essence intermédiaire, le Même intermédiaire, l'Autre intermédiaire; (2) ces trois ingrédients intermédiaires sont à leur tour mélangés pour produire cette «essence intermédiaire» entre l'Intelligible et le Sensible qu'est l'Âme du Monde; là-dessus cf. le schéma donné par Cornford 1937, 61 et repris par Brisson 1992, 283:

Premier mélange	*Second mélange*	*Résultat*
Essence indivisible } Essence divisible	Essence intermédiaire	
Même indivisible } Même divisible	Même intermédiaire	Âme du Monde
Autre indivisible } Autre divisible	Autre intermédiaire	

> Il dit ces mots; puis revenu au cratère dans lequel il avait auparavant composé par un mélange l'Âme de l'Univers, il s'employa à fondre le reste des ingrédients utilisés antérieurement, en réalisant presque le même mélange, un mélange dont les ingrédients n'étaient plus aussi purs qu'avant mais qui était de second et de troisième ordre. Puis, ayant combiné le tout, il le partagea en un nombre d'âmes égal à celui des astres – διεῖλεν ψυχὰς ἰσαρίθμους τοῖς ἄστροις (*Tim.* 41d4–e1; trad. Brisson 1992).

Taylor[11] a parfaitement raison de souligner que, dans διεῖλεν ψυχὰς (41d8), ψυχὰς est un «inner accusative», un accusatif résultatif; il ne s'agit pas comme l'a compris Chalcidius d'un découpage des âmes individuelles en deux cercles (celui du Même et celui de l'Autre) et en intervalles harmoniques, semblable au découpage opéré dans la création de l'Âme du Monde[12]. Certes les âmes partielles (humaines) elles aussi sont structurées par des rapports mathématiques, mais ce dont il est question ici c'est de la création des âmes partielles à partir d'un second mélange. On peut comparer cela à la fabrication de pains par un boulanger à partir d'une pâte, mais en précisant que les «pains» sont ici des âmes individuelles humaines, destinées à devenir des «personnes», qui vont constituer la première génération d'hommes. Il ne s'agit pas de simples portions d'une substance psychique primitive et indifférenciée[13]. Le Démiurge, poursuit Platon (*Tim.* 41d8–42d2), «distribue» (ἔνειμεν, *Tim.* 41e1) ensuite les âmes en attribuant chacune d'elles à un astre. Il installe les âmes dans leur astre comme dans un char. Il leur révèle les lois de leur destinée: une fois plongées dans le Devenir, celles qui parviennent à dominer les affections irrationnelles induites par leur implantation dans un corps et à vivre ainsi dans la justice, celles-là donc retourneront dans l'astre qui leur a été affecté et vivront une vie bienheureuse; celles qui au contraire ne pourront dominer par la raison les désordres violents provoqués par les passions, celles-là subiront un enchaînement de métamorphoses en vivants de plus en plus inférieurs, depuis la femme jusqu'aux bêtes, en fonction du degré de leur déchéance morale. Mais rien n'exclut un retour à la forme primitive, pourvu que l'âme parvienne à soumettre à la révolution du Même toute «cette masse tumultueuse et déraisonnable, faite de feu, d'eau, d'air et de terre» venue s'adjoindre à sa nature première.

---

[11] Taylor 1928, 256.

[12] Cf. Calcidius, *Commentaire au Timée de Platon* §§ 140–41, éd. Bakhouche 2011. Sur la division de l'Âme du Monde en intervalles harmoniques cf. *Tim.* 35b–36b où est exposée la constitution de l'Âme du Monde à la façon d'une sphère armillaire. Là-dessus, cf. Cornford 1937, 76–77; Brisson 1992, 284–91. Le Démiurge, tel un forgeron, fait du mélange primitif, qui sert de matériau pour fabriquer l'Âme du Monde, quelque chose comme une plaque, en laquelle il introduit des divisions de manière à obtenir une série d'intervalles ordonnés selon une double progression géométrique: 1, 2, 3, 4, 8, 9, 27, intervalles qu'il remplit de médiétés arithmétiques et harmoniques. Puis il découpe cette plaque en deux bandes, qu'il recourbe l'une sur l'autre en les faisant coïncider par leurs milieux, «comme un chi».

[13] Cf. Taylor 1928, 256–57.

La dernière tâche qui revient au Démiurge, avant qu'il ne passe en quelque sorte le relais aux «jeunes dieux», est celle de «semer» les âmes dans les instruments du Temps, c'est-à-dire les planètes:

Après avoir fait connaître tous ces décrets pour ne pas être responsable du mal que par la suite pourrait commettre l'une ou l'autre, il sema ces âmes, les unes sur la terre, les autres sur la lune, et celles qui restaient sur tous les autres instruments du Temps (*Tim.* 42d2–5; trad. Brisson 1992, légèrement modifiée).

Depuis Taylor il est admis que la «distribution» des âmes se fait dans les astres fixes, par opposition à l'ensemencement des âmes qui se fait sur la Terre et sur les planètes. Et aussi qu'il est attribué une âme par astre fixe, tandis qu'il est semé plusieurs âmes sur chacune des planètes[14]. Les astres fixes (les étoiles) constituent l'espèce céleste des dieux, la première espèce des vivants (partiels) compris dans le Monde. Leur structure est de feu pour qu'elle soit brillante (et donc belle) et ils ont la forme d'une sphère, à l'imitation du Tout. Il y a un nombre fini d'âmes, égal au nombre fini d'astres fixes, ce qui permet l'attribution à chaque âme d'un astre fixe qui lui est propre. Les astres fixes ne présentent pas de différence de nature entre eux. On peut donc raisonnablement penser qu'au moment de leur distribution et de leur montée sur leur astre, toutes les âmes sont encore, à ce stade, sans destin. Leurs destinées individuelles apparaissent seulement après l'implantation des âmes en des corps. Dans le cadre des «lois fatales» auxquelles les âmes sont assujetties par le Démiurge, selon que les âmes dominent ou non les affections engendrées nécessairement par cette implantation, une juste récompense ou punition sanctionne la vie juste ou injuste dont les âmes seules sont entièrement responsables.

J'en viens maintenant au commentaire de Proclus, en procédant étape par étape.

I. Le second mélange et la création des âmes partielles, i. e. humaines[15] (*In Tim.* 3,242,9–260,4)

Chez Proclus la création des âmes humaines vient après celle des âmes (encosmiques) divines, i. e. après celle de l'Âme du Monde, des astres fixes et des planètes, et après celle des âmes supérieures[16]. Dans le *Timée* la création de l'Âme

---

[14] Cf. Taylor 1928, 255–56: «The procedure is quite clear if we understand that the ἄστρα meant are *stars*, not *planets*, and that this procedure is separate from and preliminary to the 'sowing' of the souls in the planets»; Cornford 1937, 143: «The souls are equal in number to the stars, among which they are distributed, one to each star. (The 'sowing' into the planets comes later)».

[15] Par «âmes partielles» sont désignées souvent les âmes humaines, non pas parce qu'elles sont les seules âmes partielles, mais parce qu'elles sont les plus partielles des âmes partielles.

[16] On trouvera en annexe ci-dessous un tableau de la hiérarchie des degrés du divin chez Proclus.

du Monde est opérée à partir d'un premier mélange des genres intermédiaires, le Même intermédiaire, l'Autre intermédiaire, l'Essence intermédiaire[17]. Par «second mélange» il faut donc entendre chez Platon celui qui prépare la création des âmes humaines. Pour distinguer maintenant la création d'une part de l'Âme du Monde et des autres âme divines encosmiques, de celle, d'autre part, des âmes humaines (plus exactement, de la partie immortelle des âmes humaines), Proclus va complexifier le schéma hérité de Platon. Les trois éléments intermédiaires que sont l'Essence intermédiaire, le Même intermédiaire et l'Autre intermédiaire, font maintenant l'objet d'une différenciation triadique interne. De manière typiquement proclienne on a ainsi une structuration triadique de chacun des termes d'une triade car parmi ces genres intermédiaires, «certains sont suprêmes et intellectifs, d'autres médians, d'autres du dernier rang» (*In Tim.* 3,257,10–11). Soit le schéma suivant:

L'Essence intermédiaire
- de 1^{ier} rang = E. int.1
- de $2^{\text{ième}}$ rang = E. int.2
- de $3^{\text{ième}}$ rang = E. int.3

Le Même intermédiaire
- de 1^{ier} rang = M. int.1
- de $2^{\text{ième}}$ rang = M. int.2
- de $3^{\text{ième}}$ rang = M. int.3

L'Autre intermédiaire
- de 1^{ier} rang = A. int.1
- de $2^{\text{ième}}$ rang = A. int.2
- de $3^{\text{ième}}$ rang = A. int.3

Les âmes encosmiques divines (dont fait partie l'Âme du Monde) sont créées à partir du mélange de l'Essence intermédiaire de premier rang avec le Même intermédiaire de premier rang, et avec l'Autre intermédiaire de premier rang: E. int. (1) + M. int. (1) + A int. (1). Les «ingrédients» intermédiaires de second et troisième rang sont utilisés quant à eux pour entrer dans deux autres mélanges à partir desquels sont créées respectivement les âmes supérieures, et les âmes humaines (celles qui sont les plus partielles)[18]. Soit les trois mélanges suivants:

---

[17] Cf. *supra*, note 9 et Proclus, *In Tim.* 2,148,21–150,5: l'Âme (i.e. l'essence de l'Âme) du Monde est fabriquée à partir d'un mélange de l'Essence intermédiaire, du Même intermédiaire, de l'Autre intermédiaire. Le Repos et le Mouvement intermédiaires entrent en compte seulement pour les activités de l'Âme. À noter que par «Essence divisible dans les corps» et par «Essence indivisible» Proclus entend la Nature et l'Intellect cosmique (i.e. le Démiurge). Pour Proclus l'Âme est intermédiaire non pas simplement entre l'Intelligible et le Sensible, mais entre l'Intellect divin et la Nature, cf. *In Tim.* 2,140,11–142,14 (voir aussi *In Tim.* 2,148,31–149,16). Sur l'identification de la Nature avec l'Essence divisible dans les corps et comme «essence incorporelle non séparée des corps» (*In Tim.* 1,12,26–27), cf. Lernould 2012.

[18] *In Tim.* 3,257,18–20: «Par le moyen des premiers (*sc.* les genres intermédiaires de premier

E. int.1 + M. int.1 + A. int.1 ⟶ âmes divines
E. int.2 + M. int.2 + A. int.2 ⟶ âmes supérieures (anges, démons, héros)
E. int.3 + M. int.3 + A. int.3 ⟶ âmes humaines

Quand il est dit que le Démiurge a pris «le reste des ingrédients utilisés précédemment» (*Tim.* 41d5–6), il ne faut donc pas comprendre, ajoute Proclus, que le Démiurge a pris ce qui restait du premier mélange car toute cette première mixture – i. e. le mélange des genres intermédiaires de premier rang, «a été entièrement dépensée dans la production, la division, l'harmonie de l'Âme du Monde»[19]. Il faut comprendre que Démiurge prend maintenant pour la création des âmes *humaines* les genres intermédiaires *de dernier rang*, qu'il fond dans ce mélange. Parce que Proclus suit le *Timée*, qui n'expose que la création de l'Âme du Monde puis celle des âmes partielles, i. e. humaines, Proclus passe ici en quelque sorte par-dessus la production des âmes supérieures, qui se fait à partir du mélange des genres intermédiaires médians. C'est pourquoi il peut dire, comme il est dit dans le *Timée*, que «la classe des âmes partielles (sc. humaines) a été produite au jour par un second arrangement», et ajouter qu'«elle a été complètement séparée des âmes divines» (*In Tim.* 3,244,22–24)[20]. À côté de la «séparation» complète d'avec les âmes divines, Proclus ajoute une autre propriété importante des âmes qui viennent après les âmes divines, à savoir qu'elles sont «compagnes» des âmes divines, ainsi en *In Tim.* 3,260,17–18: le Démiurge «après avoir créé les âmes divines produit, comme leurs compagnes (ὀπαδούς)[21], les âmes partielles». «Compagnes» des dieux veut donc dire, chez Proclus, «non divines». Un peu plus haut dans son commentaire (*In Tim.* 3,259,11–27) Proclus est plus précis. Les âmes «compagnes des dieux» constitue une classe d'âmes qui fait l'objet d'une subdivision selon que ces âmes sont ou non capables de demeurer toujours dans la compagnie des dieux (i. e. des âmes divines). Proclus livre ainsi une hiérarchie des âmes encosmiques plus complète, sous forme de la quadripartition

---

rang) Platon a créé les âmes divines, par le moyen des médians les âmes démoniques, par le moyen des derniers les âmes partielles». Cf. aussi *In Tim.* 3,245,14–19, où il est dit que «l'altérité est plus grande dans le cas des âmes partielles (sc. humaines)».

[19] Cf. *In Tim.* 3,257,5–9, où Proclus se réfère à *Tim.* 36b6. Taylor (1928, 254) a bien vu ce point: «The ὑπόλοιπα τῶν πρόσθεν are not 'remains' of the former mixture; that all went into the ψυχή of the οὐρανός» (avec un envoi à *Tim.* 36b6). Cornford (1937, 142) au contraire commet ici une erreur: «They (sc. the individual souls which are to be incarnated first in human form) are composed of what was left of the original ingredients used to compound the World-Soul».

[20] La séparation complète d'avec les âmes divines a pour conséquence que l'âme humaine n'est pas consubstantielle aux âmes divines, cf. *In Tim.* 3,245,19–246,28. Sur le fait que cette séparation des âmes divines (en particulier de l'Âme du Monde) d'avec les âmes humaines n'a pas toujours été respectée dans la tradition platonicienne, cf. Baltes 2002, B. 159,3, 68–70 et 267–68.

[21] Le terme ὀπαδοί vient de *Phèdre* 252c4 (cf. aussi 248a2) et *Tim.* 41c6–8.

suivante[22]: (i) âmes divines; (ii) âmes qui sont toujours compagnes des dieux, (iii) âmes qui ne sont pas toujours compagnes des dieux et descendent dans la *genesis*, mais sans souillure, (iv) âmes qui descendent jusqu'au Tartare, i.e. la «race aux mille errances»[23]. À la lumière des commentaires de Proclus sur le *Phèdre*, le *Cratyle* et la *République* on peut se faire une idée plus précise de la hiérarchie complexe des âmes établie par le Lycien[24]. Appartiennent à la première classe l'Âme du Monde, les âmes des astres (fixes et planètes); à la seconde, les âmes supérieures (anges, démons, héros); à la troisième, les âmes humaines *héroïques* (*In Tim.* 2,230,7–9) et *démoniques*[25] envoyées sur la Terre pour sauver l'humanité; à la quatrième, les âmes humaines communes. Ces deux dernières classes d'âmes constituent, on le voit, une subdivision de la classe d'âmes issue du mélange des ingrédients intermédiaires de troisième rang. Cette classe d'âmes est celle des âmes humaines, qui ne sont pas toujours compagnes des dieux. Certaines ne le sont d'ailleurs jamais.

Il est important de souligner que toutes ces classifications ne sont pas, bien sûr, élaborées en quelque sorte hors-sol, puisqu'elles sont le fruit d'une exégèse de dialogues platoniciens. Je ne retiendrai ici, en me référant au commentaire sur le *Timée*, qu'un exemple. La tripartition (i) âmes divines – (ii) âmes supérieures – (iii) âmes humaines correspond à une première grande distinction, tirée du *Timée*, entre un premier mélange préparatoire à la création de l'âme divine qu'est l'Âme du Monde, et le seconde mélange préparatoire à la création des âmes humaines. Est inséré ici entre ces deux mélanges celui préparatoire à la création des âmes supérieures. La création des âmes partielles, i.e. non divines, est donc ainsi dédoublée, puisque les âmes partielles, par opposition aux âmes divines, comprennent les âmes supérieures et les âmes humaines. Ce dédoublement et la triade complète des mélanges et des classes d'âmes leur correspondant, Proclus les trouve inscrits en *Timée* 41d6–7: dans le second mélange qui préside à la création des âmes humaines les ingrédients «ne sont plus aussi purs» (ἀκήρατα δὲ οὐκέτι) que dans le premier, «mais de second et de troisième degré de pureté» (ἀλλὰ δεύτερα καὶ τρίτα). À ma connaissance, personne parmi les Modernes ne s'est jamais véritablement arrêté sur ce qu'il faut entendre par ces mots quelque peu énigmatiques: «de deuxième et troisième valeur», ou «de second et troisième

[22] Cf. aussi *In Tim.* 3,264,19–265,1 et *El. Theol.* 185 où l'on a une tripartition «Toutes les âmes divines sont des dieux au niveau psychique; toutes celles qui participent de l'intelligence intellective sont continuellement compagnes des dieux; toutes celles qui sont susceptibles de changements sont parfois compagnes des dieux»; voir aussi *El. Theol.* 184; 202–03.

[23] Cf. aussi, *In Tim.* 1,111,14–19; *In Remp.* 2,331,10–332,3.

[24] Pour la hiérarchie des âmes encosmiques, voir Dodds 1933, 294–96 (= commentaire aux Propositions 181–83 et 184 des *Éléments de théologie* de Proclus); O'Meara 1989, 150–52. Voir aussi Brisson (à paraître) «Les anges chez Proclus».

[25] Le passage de «démon» et «héros» à «démonique» et «héroïque» indique une dégradation d'ordre ontologique.

degré de pureté» pour en proposer une interprétation argumentée[26]. Il faut reconnaître que l'explication proclienne, fondée sur une lecture très précise du *Timée*, ne manque pas de cohérence et qu'elle est plutôt convaincante.

Le caractère proprement systématique de cette explication est accentué par le fait que l'exégèse du *Timée* est ici nourrie par le *Phèdre* de Platon. L'expression «compagnes» des dieux[27] vient, comme on l'a noté plus haut, de *Phèdre* 252c4. Et c'est à partir du mythe central du *Phèdre*, auquel il se réfère de nombreuses fois[28], que Proclus explique *Timée* 41d6–7 et enrichit la triade des classes d'âmes encosmiques pour établir la quadripartition mentionnée plus haut[29].

II. La distribution (διανομή) hypercosmique[30]

Le mot *διανομή* est formé sur le verbe νέμω (cf. *Timée* 41e1 ἔνειμεν) qui signifie «distribuer», «découper (en parts)», et plus particulièrement: attribuer à un troupeau une partie d'un pré, et de là, attribuer un troupeau à son berger. On peut ainsi comprendre pourquoi Proclus appelle les dieux auxquels est attribué tel ou tel groupe d'âmes, «Chefs de troupeaux» – ἀγελάρχαι, en référence au *Politique* de Platon [31]. Ici chaque âme est affectée à un astre, c'est-à-dire à l'âme divine de chaque astre. La distribution ne se fait pas en effet dans les astres en tant que corps,

---

26 Taylor 1928, 255, parle bien de «second and third vintage», mais sans plus d'explication. Cornford avance de manière rapide une hypothèse peu satisfaisante, cf. Cornford 1937, 143: «'Second or third degree in purity', if it does not mean 'second or even worse', may refer to the superiority of man's soul over woman's (42a)». Mais Cornford n'évoque ici que deux termes (homme et femme), deux «générations» (celle des âmes masculines et celle des âmes féminines), alors que l'on a explicitement dans le *Timée* trois degrés dans la dégradation de l'âme humaine (homme, femme, bête). Pour Proclus, il ne s'agit pas ici de la dégradation impliquée dans la destinée des âmes humaines, mais de la dégradation qui confuit des âmes divines aux âmes humaines en passant par les âmes supérieures. Finamore et Kutash font remarquer, sans plus, que Platon n'éclaire ici en rien son lecteur, cf. Finamore et Kutash 2017, 138, n. 37: «Plato never explained how the ingredients could be less pure since they are already of an intermediate nature between Intelligible and material Being».

27 Cf. *In Tim.* 3,260,18; 3,262,7; voir aussi 3,259,15; 3,262,1; 3,262,30.

28 Cf. e.g. *In Tim.* 3,258,10 et 20.

29 On notera que lorsqu'il évoque la classe des âmes démoniques comme ayant en propre le caractère d'être intermédiaire entre les âmes divines et les âmes humaines (cf. e.g. *In Tim.* 3,165,5; 3,290,30–291,6) Proclus ne se réfère pas au *Banquet* de Platon, en particulier au passage bien connu (cf. 202e9) où Érôs est dit être un grand démon, intermédiaire entre les dieux et les hommes. En fait le *Banquet* est peu présent dans le commentaire sur le *Timée* (cf. Festugière 1966–68, V, 260, s.v. *Symposium*). Sur l'expression «compagnons des dieux» pour caractériser les démons chez Proclus, cf. e.g. *In Remp.* 2, 3,9. Sur les différentes classes d'âmes, cf. aussi *El. Theol.* 184, 202–03.

30 Cf. *In Tim.* 3,263,22–265,12.

31 Cf. 271d6–8 où hommes et animaux sont dits avoir été «gardés», tels des troupeaux, par des génies divins. On retrouve le terme ἀγελάρχαι par exemple en *In Tim.* 3,265,8; 3,308,26.

car «les astres» (*Tim.* 41e1) signifie les âmes des corps astraux (*In Tim.* 3,263,25–26).

De cette distribution des âmes partielles Proclus dit qu'elle est «hypercosmique»[32]. Pourtant les dieux «Chefs de troupeaux» sont bien ici encosmiques. Mais on peut comprendre que la distribution soit dite «hypercosmique». Avant leur «montée» sur leur astre, comme en un char, les âmes ne sont pas encore dans le monde, elles ne sont pas encore encosmiques. Elles sont par essence «au-dessus du Monde» (ὑπερκόσμιοι). Proclus insiste sur ce point, et j'y reviendrai. Par ailleurs la distribution des âmes partielles humaines peut être dite «hypercosmique» en ce sens qu'elle doit être rattachée à une distribution antérieure, celle des âmes partielles relativement aux Douze Dieux du *Phèdre*:

In Tim. 3,263,22–265,12, sp. 263,22–264,11: Il se fait ici une première distribution des âmes partielles relativement aux divines, avant même qu'elles (sc. les âmes partielles) ne soient entrées dans le Monde – πρὶν καὶ ἐγκόσμιοι γένωνται. En effet dans l'ordonnance hypercosmique comme dans l'encosmique[33], les parties s'entretissent aux touts… Car les âmes divines elles-mêmes se distribuent en relation avec les puissances de l'Âme Totale: elles ont procédé en effet selon les puissances multiformes immanentes en l'Âme Totale et elles ont été établies les unes dans le Cercle du Même (*sc.* les fixes) de l'Âme Totale, les autres dans les cercles de l'Autre (*sc.* les planètes). Les âmes partielles à leur tour se distribuent en relation avec les âmes divines … De même donc que ces âmes divines encosmiques s'élèvent au lieu supracéleste par l'entremise des Douze Dieux, de même aussi les âmes partielles par l'entremise des divines: car elles sont unies à ces âmes (*sc.* les âmes hypercosmiques que sont les Dieux-Chefs) en vertu de l'ordonnance hypercosmique, que Platon a appelée *dianomê* vu qu'elle se fait selon le *Nomos* divin, qui est établi auprès de Zeus. … Il existe donc et une même ressemblance entre toutes les âmes partielles et une division de ces âmes selon les hégémonies des dieux.

Les âmes humaines sont distribuées relativement aux âmes divines qui elles-mêmes sont distribuées relativement aux puissances de l'Âme du Monde (*sc.* le cercle du Même et celui de l'Autre). Et Proclus d'ajouter que ces âmes divines s'élèvent jusqu'au lieu supracéleste «par l'entremise des Douze Dieux» (τῶν δώδεκα θεῶν), ainsi que le font les âmes partielles par l'entremise des âmes divines. Dans la théologie proclienne, le «lieu supracéleste» correspond à la première triade des dieux intelligibles-intellectifs; mais ici il est semble-t-il assimilé aussi au rang des dieux hypercosmiques. Les Douze Dieux, ou dieux «séparés» (sc. du Monde) correspondent aux âmes hypercosmiques-encosmiques. Il est donc ici signifié que les âmes encosmiques (divines et humaines) passent *par*

[32] *In Tim.* 3,291,7–17: «Platon a fait naître les âmes à partir de la Cause démiurgique et de la Cause zoogonique (*sc.* le Cratère), et, après leur naissance, il les a subordonnées l'une à telle âme divine, l'autre à telle autre, faisant ainsi de leur procession et de leur distribution choses hypercosmiques». Sur le Cratère, «déité vivifiante», cf. *In Tim.* 3,247,26–250,28.

[33] Par «ordonnance hypercosmique» (ὑπερκόσμιος σύνταξις) je comprends la distribution des âmes et par «ordonnance encosmique» (ἐγκόσμιος σύνταξις) la montée des âmes sur leurs véhicules, plutôt que l'ensemencement des âmes (voir plus bas, le développement sur la montée sur les véhicules).

l'intermédiaire (διὰ) des Douze Dieux hypercosmiques-encosmiques pour remonter jusqu'aux dieux hypercosmiques – voire même jusqu'à la première triade des dieux intelligibles-intellectifs; dans sa *Théologie platonicienne* 6,15 Proclus nous dit qu'un des caractères appartenant à la classe des dieux hypercosmiques-encosmiques est d'«être élévatrice en tant qu'elle fait tendre les dieux encosmiques vers les hauteurs intelligibles-intellectives»[34]. La distribution des âmes humaines (comme celle, antérieure, des âmes divines) est donc bien «hypercosmique» en ce sens qu'elle se fait «selon le *Nomos* divin, établi auprès de Zeus», le dieu qui vient en tête du cortège des Douze Dieux du *Phèdre*, par l'intermédiaire desquels elles se rattachent aux dieux hypercosmiques[35].

On n'aura pas manqué de remarquer que toute cette explication de la «distribution» des âmes humaines est développée sur fond d'une lecture, encore une fois, du mythe central du *Phèdre*, auquel Proclus fait implicitement référence quand il parle (cf. *In Tim.* 3,264,4) des «Douze Dieux» dont il est question en *Phèdre* 247a1–2.

III. L'installation dans les véhicules[36]

La montée sur leurs véhicules fait que les âmes partielles, par essence (i. e. en tant qu'âmes) au-dessus du Monde, deviennent encosmiques:

> *In Tim.* 3,275,26–30: Par essence, les âmes sont au-dessus de la Nature, au-dessus du Monde (ὑπερκόσμιοι), au-delà de l'Heimarménê, parce qu'elles ont leur premier mode d'existence séparé de ce Monde-ci. Mais, par leurs véhicules et les lots qu'elles ont eu pour sort d'administrer, elles sont devenues choses du Monde (ἐγκόσμιοι)[37].

Selon Proclus, lorsque Platon dit que le Démiurge installe les âmes dans leurs véhicules, il montre par là qu'il fait du Démiurge le créateur des véhicules[38]. Et

---

[34] Cf. *Théol. plat.* 6,15,74,27–75,1. Voir aussi *Théol. plat.* 6,18,85,3–5: Platon dit que «l'armée triadique des dieux encosmiques, élevée par la classe des dieux séparés du monde vers les dieux intellectifs et vers les dieux intelligibles, est rattachée aux causes toutes premières».

[35] Voir *infra*, «Annexe. Les degrés du divin chez Proclus».

[36] Cf. *In Tim.* 3,265,15–268,21. Sur le véhicule de l'âme, voir pour commencer Dodds 1933, ²1963, 313–21, «The Astral Body in Neoplatonism»; voir aussi Finamore et Kutash 2017, 133–34.

[37] Cf. *In Tim.* 3,235,28–30: «Comment serait-il possible que l'âme fût chose du monde (ἐγκόσμιον) à moins d'avoir un véhicule dans l'Univers. Tout être encosmique a en effet siège fixe et place dans le cosmos et en remplit une portion»; 3,266,5–7 «dès là qu'elles montent sur le véhicule, les âmes deviennent co-citoyennes de l'Univers (πολίτιδας), entrent dans le cosmos et se subordonnent au cosmos entier»; 3,298,27–28: «Ainsi donc le véhicule congénital à l'âme rend l'âme encosmique (ἐγκόσμιον)»; Voir aussi *In Tim.* 1,5,3–5; *In Tim.* 3,238,5; 3,276,23.

[38] Cf. *In Tim.* 3,267,5–10: «Mais ils (sc. les véhicules) ont aussi pour créateur le Démiurge même du Tout, et il est leur premier créateur. C'est pourquoi maintenant aussi, il fait monter les âmes sur les véhicules, évidemment après avoir produit le véhicule. Car même si, dans le récit précédent, on n'a pas parlé. De sa formation, néanmoins le Démiurge l'a créé lui aussi avec

tandis que Platon fait de l'astre le véhicule de l'âme, Proclus distingue très nettement les âmes divines (les astres) auxquelles sont attribuées les âmes humaines et les véhicules:

In Tim. 3,266,1–5: Si donc il faut se conformer à la réalité des choses et à l'enseignement de Platon, on doit dire qu'autre chose est la Nature du Tout que le Démiurge révèle, autre chose l'astre, cet astre incorporel sous lequel est rangée l'âme, autre chose le véhicule-ci, qui est au service des âmes.

Le «véhicule» dont il est ici question, fabriqué par le Démiurge, est le «premier véhicule» (ou «premier corps») de l'âme partielle, véhicule immatériel, impassible et non sujet à la corruption. Ce véhicule est aussi «congénital» à l'âme; en d'autres termes, l'âme ne s'en sépare jamais. Ce véhicule est éthérien, comme le sont les véhicules (les corps) des âmes divines, «puisque le nôtre aussi (sc. véhicule) est astréiforme» (*In Tim.* 3,308,17). Mais il y a une différence entre les âmes divines et les âmes partielles (humaines):

In Tim. 3,268,10–20: Dans le cas des divines, le Démiurge avait placé les corps dans les âmes comme enveloppés de tout côté par elles, et ces âmes ne se tournaient pas vers ce qu'elles administrent, mais jouissaient d'une intellection une et inébranlable. Dans le cas des âmes partielles, il fait monter les âmes sur les véhicules: car ces âmes sont destinées par nature à être souvent dominées par les corps et à se tourner vers ce qu'elles administrent, quand elles deviennent elles aussi parties du Tout, comme leurs véhicules, qu'elles sont les esclaves des Lois Fatales et ne vivent plus tout du long en pureté sous la lumière divine de la Providence.

L'installation *dans* leur véhicule est propre aux âmes humaines. Elle marque leur *dégradation* par rapport aux âmes divines. Celles-ci enveloppent leur corps et leur véhicule. C'est ainsi que dans le *Timée* l'Âme du Monde est dite «envelopper le Ciel» (*Tim.* 36e3). Les véhicules des âmes humaines leur sont certes «congénitaux», mais dans le fait que ces véhicules leur sont donnés par le Démiurge, qu'elles y montent pour s'y installer, se trouve impliquée, me semble-t-il, une forme d'extériorité, d'acquisition.

---

tout le reste, et c'est seulement ensuite qu'il fait monter sur lui les âmes et qu'il leur donne le commandement sur leurs instruments». Le Démiurge est dit ici être le «premier créateur» des véhicules, «car les véhicules ont sans doute pour créateur le Fabricant de toute la substance corporelle, qui prépare d'avance aux dieux leurs lieux de séjour dans le Monde» (3,267,1–3). Festugière (1966–68, V, 141, n. 5) se demande qui est désigné par l'expression «le Fabricant de toute la substance corporelle». Je crois qu'il s'agit d'Héphaestos, qui est le dieu qui «produit la substance du monde corporel» (*In Tim.* 2,70,27), et qui «appartient à la 'chaîne' fabricatrice» (*In Tim.* 1,142,20–21); voir aussi 1, 144,12–15 «Les âmes Athénaïques (sc. appartenant à la série d'Athéna) reçoivent principalement d'Héphaestos, en vertu de son activité [fabricatrice], leurs véhicules, et viennent se loger en des corps issus des principes créatifs d'Héphaestos et de la Terre». Sur le Démiurge Universel, (premier) créateur des véhicules, voir aussi *In Tim.* 3,235,25–29: «C'est à partir du Démiurge que Platon fait exister le véhicule: car c'est le Démiurge lui-même qui 'place l'âme sur un véhicule' (41e1–2) à la ressemblance des âmes divines».

À côté de ce premier véhicule, qui fait de l'âme une réalité encosmique, Proclus en distingue deux autres: le véhicule irrationnel, i.e. le corps pneumatique immatériel, qui fait de l'âme une «citoyenne de la *genesis*», et le «véhicule ostréeux», ou corps terrestre, qui marque le terme de la chute de l'âme vers le partiel, et qui fait que celle-ci, quand elle s'attache à ce dernier, «projette la vie de tel homme particulier»[39].

Je passe ici, provisoirement, par-dessus la révélation par le Démiurge des lois de la destinée des âmes, révélation que Proclus associe étroitement avec la montée sur les véhicules. Je reviendrai sur cette révélation dans le développement que je consacre à l'*apocatastasis* des âmes. J'en arrive donc à l'opération que constitue l'ensemencement des âmes, ce qui me conduira à revenir aussi sur la distribution des âmes et à préciser quels sont les dieux que Proclus englobe dans le mot «astres».

IV. La montée sur les véhicules et l'ensemencement

L'ensemencement de l'âme avec son (premier) véhicule n'a pas pour seule conséquence le fait que l'âme devienne encosmique. Le fait de devenir encosmique est déjà la conséquence de la montée sur les véhicules. L'ensemencement a pour résultat que l'âme se range sous la conduite de tel ou tel Dieu-Chef et acquiert par là une «forme» déterminée:

In Tim. 3,276,22–30: Le premier ensemencement des véhicules[40] ne fait pas seulement de l'âme une «chose du Monde» (ἐγκόσμιον), il en met aussi toute la substance sous l'influence d'un Chef particulier. Autre chose en effet est d'être encosmique, autre chose d'être Séléniaque ou Hermaïque. Car c'est là un type de vie plus particulier, et de même que, une fois montée sur un véhicule, l'âme devient concitoyenne de l'Âme du Monde, de même, quand elle a été semée avec son véhicule, elle devient citoyenne du cercle de la Lune ou du cercle du Soleil ou de quelque autre.

En prenant les exemples du Soleil et d'Hermès (Mercure) Proclus laisse entendre semble-t-il que l'ensemencent a lieu comme dans le *Timée* seulement dans les planètes. En fait telle n'est pas la doctrine de Proclus.

[39] Cf. *In Tim.* 3,298,2–299,9. Voir aussi *In Tim.* 3,236,31–238,26.
[40] Et non pas «dans les véhicules» comme le traduit Festugière 1966–68, V, 153.

V. Ensemencement, distribution et ce que sont les astres ou âmes divines[41]

Platon distingue nettement distribution et ensemencement, astres fixes et planètes. La distribution se fait relativement aux astres fixes, l'ensemencement, dans les planètes. Proclus est soucieux bien sûr de montrer qu'il respecte ces différences. «La distribution est autre que l'ensemencement» (ἄλλη δὲ ἡ νομὴ τῆς σπορᾶς, *In Tim.* 3,307,26). Et il consacre un long développement sur ce sujet[42]. Il y affirme qu'«il n'y a distribution que des âmes seules, mais ensemencement des âmes avec leurs véhicules». Ce qui est semé ce sont des hommes[43]. Un peu plus haut, dans le cadre d'une explication générale de ce qu'est la dissémination, il nous dit qu'en tant qu'âmes (n'ayant pas encore un corps) les âmes partielles sont *distribuées* par rapport aux astres, c'est-à-dire distribuées par rapport à leurs Dieux-Chefs, comme par lots; et il ajoute: en tant que le Démiurge leur a donné un véhicule, autrement dit en tant qu'elles sont devenues encosmiques et qu'elles ont à leur tour reçu en lot des vivants, elles sont *disséminées*, c'est-à-dire subordonnées à certaines des révolutions divines:

In Tim. 3,304,30–305,4: Avant toute l'autre démiurgie qui reste, celle des dieux récents, prend place la dissémination (ἡ σπορά) des âmes avec leurs véhicules en ces dieux[44]. Il faut en effet que non seulement les âmes comme âmes aient des Chefs, mais aussi que, comme encosmiques et comme ayant reçu en lot des vivants, elles soient subordonnées à certaines des révolutions divines – ὑποτάττεσθαί τισι τῶν θείων περιφορῶν.

Les âmes humaines sont ici reconduites à deux classes d'âmes divines hiérarchisées, les Dieux-Chefs, c'est-à-dire les dieux hypercosmiques (auxquelles les âmes partielles sont rattachées par l'entremise des douze dieux du *Phèdre*), et les «jeunes dieux» que sont les âmes encosmiques des astres fixes, celles des planètes et celles des neuf dieux sublunaires. Quand Proclus dit ici que la dissémination, ou ensemencement, des âmes avec leur véhicule se fait dans les dieux récents faut-il comprendre que cette dissémination se fait aussi dans les âmes des astres fixes, auquel cas le partage bien établi chez Platon entre «distribution» dans les fixes et «ensemencement» dans les planètes devient chez Proclus moins clair? En même temps on n'aura pas manqué de noter l'introduction dans le texte du déterminant τισι deux lignes plus bas: les âmes humaines sont subor-

[41] Sur la distribution relativement aux astres, cf. *In Tim.* 3,261,12–263,22. Sur l'ensemencement, 3,305,11–307,12.

[42] Sur la différence entre l'ensemencement et la distribution, *In Tim.* 3,307,26–309,20.

[43] Sur ce point Proclus a bien vu le passage du féminin σπαρείσας αὐτὰς (41e5) au masculin ἔσπειρεν τοὺς μὲν … τοὺς δὲ (42d4). Cf. aussi *In Tim.* 3,131,18–20: «Si en outre il a été semé dans les Sept des âmes humaines (μερικαὶ ψυχαί), certaines dans le soleil, d'autres dans la lune, d'autres dans chacune des autres planètes».

[44] Et non pas: «en tel ou tel de ces dieux» comme le traduit Festugière, certainement par superposition avec «certaines des révolutions divines».

données à «*certaines* des révolutions divines»[45]. Par «certaines des révolutions divines» faut-il entendre les planètes? En fait la réponse est: non. Lorsque Proclus dit que la dissémination «prend place en ces dieux (sc. encosmiques)», il faut comprendre que la dissémination ne se fait pas exclusivement dans les planètes.

Revenons à ce développement que Proclus consacre à la différence en distribution et ensemencement:

In Tim. 3,307,32–308,7: Puis donc que ces deux opérations sont différentes, et que l'une a été dite avoir eu lieu dans les astres, l'autre dans les instruments du temps, il semblerait (δόξειεν) qu'elles eussent lieu en des endroits différents. Car ni la Terre n'est un astre, en sorte qu'il ne saurait y avoir distribution en elle, ni les astres fixes (τὰ ἀπλανῆ) n'ont été dits «instruments du Temps», en sorte qu'il ne saurait y avoir ensemencement en eux: seules les planètes (πλανώμενα) sont à la fois des astres et des instruments du Temps, en sorte que les deux opérations les concernent, et la distribution et l'ensemencement.

Commençons par une remarque terminologique touchant le mot «astre». Dans l'affirmation: «seules les planètes sont à fois astres et instruments du temps» (*In Tim.* 3,308,5–6), le mot «astres» ne peut vouloir dire «astres fixes», c'est-à-dire «étoiles» par opposition à «planètes»; les planètes ne peuvent être en même temps étoiles (au sens d'«astres fixes») et planètes. «Astres» signifie ici, au sens large, «corps célestes» (qui englobent les «étoiles» ou astres fixes, et les «planètes» ou astres errants). C'est d'ailleurs un sens bien attesté[46], par exemple, entre autres passages, en *Timée* 38c5: «le Soleil, la Lune et les cinq autres astres, ceux qu'on appelle errants»[47]. N'oublions pas enfin que pour Proclus le mot «astres» ne désigne pas seulement les astres en tant que corps. Il désigne aussi, et surtout, comme l'a vu, les astres en tant qu'âmes divines.

Ce texte appelle par ailleurs une autre remarque, touchant un point de doctrine. On aura noté l'expression «il semblerait» qui marque de la part de Proclus une prise de distance par rapport à l'idée que distribution et ensemencement puissent être des opérations admises ou exclues selon la nature du corps céleste (plus exactement du vivant divin) destinataire de ces opérations. Si l'on suit Platon à la lettre, suggère Proclus, il n'y a pas de distribution dans le cas de la Terre, qui n'est pas un astre, i.e. un corps céleste. Et il n'y a pas de dissémination dans le cas des astres fixes, qui ne sont pas les «instruments du temps». Or ce que

[45] Harrold Tarrant ne traduit pas τισι, cf. Tarrant 2017, 195: «it was necessary that they (*sc.* the souls) should be enlisted under divine orbits».

[46] Cf *LSJ*, s.v. ἄστρον, p. 263.

[47] En français on dit parfois encore «étoiles errantes» pour planètes. Ce sens figure dans les dictionnaires avec la mention «vieilli», ou «désuet». Mais on dit encore couramment «l'étoile du berger» pour désigner la planète Vénus. De même en anglais on a le couple «wandering stars» *versus* «fixed stars» (cf. e.g. Taylor [1928], 191). Dans la traduction de Tarrant 2017, 198: «only the planets are both stars and instruments of time», «stars» ne peut signifier «étoiles» qu'au sens large de «corps célestes». Pour un emploi de ἄστρον = «étoile» au sens d'«étoile fixe» par opposition à «planète», cf. Aristote, *De caelo* 290a20.

Proclus n'admet pas c'est que les deux opérations ne concernent pas également et les fixes et la Terre:

In Tim. 3,308,7–9: Qu'il soit étrange (ἄτοπον) néanmoins que les deux n'aient pas concerné la Terre et les astres fixes, c'est évident. Car si le Démiurge est l'auteur et de ce qu'il distribue et de ce qu'il sème, ces deux appartiennent aux âmes par essence.

On n'aura pas manqué de noter l'expression ὅτι δὲ ἄτοπον «qu'il soit étrange», qu'on pourrait aussi traduire par «qu'il soit absurde». Aux yeux de Proclus, le texte de Platon, pris à la lettre, conduit à une absurdité. La vraie doctrine (la vraie «pensée implicite», qu'il faut bien sûr attribuer, au-delà de la lettre du texte, à Platon) est que distribution et ensemencement, pris ensemble, concernent et la Terre, et les planètes, et les astres fixes. Il y a distribution et ensemencement dans le cas la Terre, distribution et ensemencement dans le cas des planètes, distribution et ensemencement dans le cas des fixes. Il peut y avoir distribution dans le cas de la Terre car la Terre est aussi un astre en vertu de son véhicule éthérien. Et il peut inversement y avoir dissémination dans les astres fixes en tant que ceux-ci sont aussi des instruments du Temps:

In Tim. 3,308,14–18: Si donc cette doctrine est vraie, il faut dire que la Terre est un astre, non selon la masse apparente, mais selon son véhicule éthérien qui est astréiforme – puisque le nôtre aussi est astréiforme –, et que les astres fixes «contribuent à réaliser le Temps»[48].

C'est à partir de cette doctrine que l'on peut comprendre un des passages les plus déroutants du commentaire sur le *Timée*, celui où Proclus commettrait l'erreur grossière de confondre astres fixes et planètes. On se souvient que dans le *Timée* le Démiurge après le partage du second mélange en un nombre d'âmes égal à celui des astres, distribue ces âmes dans les astres, chacune à chacun: διεῖλεν ψυχὰς ἰσαρίθμους τοῖς ἄστροις, ἔνειμέν θ' ἑκάστην πρὸς ἕκαστον – *il partagea (le mélange) en un nombre d'âmes égal à celui des astres et il distribua ces âmes dans les astres, chacune à chacun* (41d8–e1). Proclus pose alors la question de savoir comment comprendre ἰσαρίθμους τοῖς ἄστροις[49] et ἑκάστην πρὸς ἕκαστον:

In Tim. 3,261,12–19: Maintenant, «en nombre égal à», comment l'entendre? Dira-t-on que c'est en ce sens qu'une seule âme partielle a été rangée sous une seule des âmes astrales, et qu'il y a quantitativement autant d'âmes partielles qu'il y a de dieux astraux? C'est ce que semble en tout cas suggérer Platon, puisqu'il a été ajouté «chacune à chacun». Mais comment dire que telle est l'opinion de Platon, puisqu'il dit un peu plus loin: «il

---

48 Pour l'idée qu'il y a ensemencement dans les astres fixes, cf. *In Tim.*3,306,13–307,12, sp. 305,30–306,2: «Car tous les astres contribuent à la naissance du Temps, les uns par eux-mêmes (*sc.* les planètes), les autres en union avec le Tout, comme les astres fixes, et ils sont tous 'instruments du Temps'».

49 On pourrait donner au datif le sens suivant: les âmes sont données *aux astres* en nombre égal, ce qui impliquerait que plusieurs âmes sont attribuées à chaque astre (cf. Tarrant 2017, 147, n. 402). Mais cette lecture est difficilement compatible avec le grec ἑκάστην πρὸς ἕκαστον.

dissémina les uns sur la terre», d'autres dans le soleil, «d'autres dans la lune». D'après ce texte, c'est un grand nombre d'âmes que Platon réserve à chaque astre.

Selon Taylor[50] Proclus confond ici astres fixes et planètes. Ce serait le cas si, comme Taylor, on pense que le mot «astre» n'a que le sens étroit d'astre fixe. Mais chez Proclus, comme chez Platon, «astre» veut dire «corps céleste». On peut donc légitimement comprendre, comme Proclus le fait, (i) que la distribution ne concerne pas exclusivement les astres fixes – ce qui va, je le rappelle, à l'encontre de l'*opinio communis* parmi les Modernes, (ii) que l'ensemencement ne concerne pas uniquement les planètes, (iii) que pour chacune de ces deux opérations, c'est «un grand nombre d'âmes que Platon réserve (καταλείπει) *à chaque astre*»; il faut comprendre: à chaque astre, fixe et planète (en ajoutant: et aussi à la Terre).

Deux problèmes se posent alors. Le premier, que Proclus pose, est de concilier cette lecture qui contredit la lettre du texte. De manière ingénieuse Proclus donne deux réponses pour résoudre la contradiction. Première réponse (*In Tim.* 3,261,20–262,6): par «en nombre égal» il ne faut pas entendre unité par unité (une âme humaine par astre), mais de manière analogique, comme 10 et 50 (qui sont des dizaines) sont analogues à 1 et 5 (des unités). Deuxième réponse, clairement plus satisfaisante (262,6–263,5): les âmes partielles (humaines) ont une forme, i. e. un nombre, qui «provient de la forme des Dieux-Chefs» (Kronos, Zeus, Hélios, etc.). Il ne s'agit donc pas d'une égalité numérique et d'une correspondance terme à terme (à tel astre, telle âme), mais d'un rapport entre le nombre des Dieux-Chefs et le nombre de formes de vie, lesquelles procèdent des Dieux-Chefs et «pénètrent» jusqu'aux âmes partielles qui font cortège les unes à tel Dieu-Chef, les autres à tel autre.

Mais si l'on peut concéder à Proclus qu'il ne confond pas grossièrement fixes et planètes, n'est-il pas ici pris en flagrant délit de commettre une autre confusion tout aussi grossière, celle entre distribution et ensemencement? Je reviendrai sur ce point un peu plus bas. Car pour répondre à la question il faut apporter un élément de doctrine complémentaire, à savoir que la distribution concerne aussi tous les dieux sublunaires:

In Tim. 3,265,6–12: Et de fait il serait étrange que les âmes partielles eussent été distribuées (διανενέμηνται) en relation avec seulement les astres proprement dits et que ne fussent pas *chefs de troupeaux* (ἀγελάρχαι) les autres dieux qui, dans chaque élément, correspondent aux astres, dieux de l'air, de l'eau, de la terre, au sujet desquels Platon a dit (41a4) qu'«ils se montrent dans la mesure où il leur plaît».

Les dieux sublunaires sont eux aussi des «astres», par analogie (ἀνὰ λόγον: 265,9) avec les astres (les corps célestes) au sens propre du terme. De même que distribution et ensemencement concernent et les astres fixes, et les planètes, de même

50 Taylor 1928, 256.

il y a eu et distribution et ensemencement d'âmes dans les sphères sublunaires selon chaque élément:

In Tim. 3,305,26–28: Il apparaît en second lieu qu'il y a eu ensemencement et dans le monde sublunaire selon chaque élément (cf. 230,15; 280,22) et dans les sphères célestes et dans les astres.

Et Proclus d'ajouter un peu plus loin:

*In Tim.*3,308,24–309,2: Toutes les régions du Monde ont reçu un *ensemencement* d'âmes partielles, et tout dieu encosmique est «chef de troupeau» (ἀγελάρχης) d'âmes partielles qui lui ont été *attribuées* (νεμηθεισῶν) et qui ont été semées en lui selon l'intention du Démiurge (souligné par moi).

Le glissement ici de l'opération de l'ensemencement à celle de l'attribution est significatif. Ce n'est pas le seul exemple. Proclus, dans son explication de ce qu'est l'ensemencement ou dissémination des âmes, commence par affirmer que cette dissémination est le fait *et* du Démiurge, *et* de l'âme partielle (humaine), qui choisit librement l'astre en lequel elle est semée:

In Tim. 3,304,3–11: Cette *dissémination* (σποράν)des âmes, il ne faut penser ni qu'elle se fasse au hasard – car où l'indéfini peut-il se glisser dans ce qui est toujours identiquement le même – ni qu'elle soit simplement une *distribution* (διανομήν) accomplie par le Créateur – car ce qui est disséminé n'est ni mû par un autre ni dénué de libre choix – mais on doit estimer que d'une part elle s'accomplit d'en haut selon l'Intellect Démiurgique et que d'autre part la volonté aussi des âmes mêmes y contribue: car chaque âme connaît et choisit son propre rang, et vient se fixer, elle-même ainsi que son véhicule, dans les portons appropriées du Tout (souligné par moi)[51].

Nous sommes ainsi ramenés à la question de savoir si Proclus confond véritablement ces deux opérations. La réponse est: non.

VI. L'apocatastasis

Chez Proclus la distinction entre «distribution» et «ensemencement» tend, dans une certaine mesure, à s'effacer. D'abord parce que les deux opérations concernent également et les fixes et les planètes (les dieux célestes), et les dieux dans le monde sublunaire, en un mot tous les dieux encosmiques. Ensuite, Proclus utilise les deux mots comme s'ils étaient interchangeables. À tout le moins, il peut donner à un mot un sens strict et un sens large[52]. L'ensemencement est

---

[51] Pour un autre passage parallèle qui confirme que Proclus emploie «distribution» et «ensemencement» quasiment comme des synonymes, cf. *In Tim.* 3,309,2–10, cité *infra*.

[52] C'est ainsi que Proclus peut parler de la montée sur les véhicules comme étant le premier ensemencement, cf. *In Tim.* 3,276,22: «Le premier ensemencement dans les véhicules ne fait pas seulement de l'âme une 'chose du Monde' (ἐγκόσμιον), il en met aussi toute la substance sous l'influence d'un Chef particulier» (cité *supra*).

ainsi «une sorte de seconde distribution»[53]. Mais on ne peut pas dire que Proclus confond «ensemencement» et «attribution». Comme on l'a vu Proclus souligne lui-même cette distinction. Il veut mieux dire que Proclus *conjoint* ou *superpose* «ensemencement» et «distribution». La raison de cette «conjonction» est d'ordre doctrinal et touche à la question du retour de l'âme à son astre. La distribution et l'ensemencement d'une âme partielle se fait dans le même astre. Car si l'on pose une distribution dans tel astre et un ensemencement en tel autre, il faudrait alors poser deux retours, l'un dans l'astre auquel l'âme a été attribuée, l'autre dans l'astre dans lequel elle a été semée, ce qui, pour Proclus, ne peut se produire:

In Tim. 3,308,10–24: Et s'il en est ainsi il faut bien que les deux (*sc.* distribution et ensemencement) concernent le même astre, pour que le retour au point de départ se fasse, pour toute âme, à un astre unique, et que l'âme ne soit pas forcée, après être retournée à l'astre confraternel (τὸ σύννομον ἄστρον)[54] à cause de la distribution, de retourner à un autre astre à cause de l'ensemencement en cet astre: car ce qui est semé est toujours approprié à ce dans quoi il a été semé par essence.

Distribution et ensemencement n'impliquent pas des régions différentes, pour éviter un retour dans tel astre, suivi d'un retour dans tel autre. Si c'était le cas le retour ainsi dédoublé ne serait jamais accompli, mais en quelque sorte toujours «contrarié». Proclus ajoute une autre raison qui exclut un double retour. C'est le Démiurge qui «distribue» et qui «sème», si bien que «ces deux opérations appartiennent aux âmes par essence»[55]. Le raisonnement est ici un peu elliptique. Je comprends que l'unicité de la Cause qui à la fois distribue et sème implique le retour à un seul et même astre à partir du moment où distribution et ensemencement se font dans le même astre et à partir du moment où «distribution» et «ensemencement» peuvent être assimilés à des attributs essentiels de l'âme. Si donc une âme a été attribuée à un astre fixe, elle a été aussi ensemencée avec son véhicule dans cet astre fixe. Et si elle a été ensemencée dans un astre fixe c'est à cet astre fixe qu'elle remonte:

In Tim. 3,306,29–307,5: Cependant il vaut mieux dire que l'ensemencement des véhicules se fait aussi dans les astres fixes, et que c'est aussi jusqu'à cette sphère-là que remontent les véhicules entièrement purifiés, devenus astréiformes et bien dégagés de la matière, dont la vie exclut toute composition et dont le mouvement est tout centré sur l'intellect et la sagesse, puisqu'ils suivent la révolution du Même. Il serait ridicule en effet, ou que, alors que l'âme a été attribuée (νεμηθείσης) aux astres fixes, l'ensemencement (τὴν σπορὰν) du véhicule eût lieu ailleurs – car de même que telle âme [partielle est attribuée] à telle

[53] *In Tim.* 3,276,8–9.

[54] «Lawful partner star», Tarrant 2017, 198.

[55] *In Tim.* 3,308,9: εἰ γὰρ ὁ δημιουργὸς καὶ ὃ νέμει καὶ ὃ σπείρει, κατ 'οὐσίαν ἄμφω ταῖς ψυχαῖς ὑπάρχει. La traduction de Festugière (1966–68), V, 186 est inexacte: «Car si le Démiurge est l'auteur et *de ce* qu'il distribue et *de ce* qu'il sème, ces deux appartiennent aux âmes par essence» (souligné par moi).

âme [divine][56] de même son véhicule se combine avec tel véhicule divin – ou que l'âme qui avait été semée dans un astre fixe ne remontât pas aussi jusqu'à cet astre fixe.

Et puisque la Terre est aussi, comme on l'a vu, un astre et qu'il y distribution des âmes sur la Terre, il peut donc y avoir un retour des âmes aussi sur la Terre:

In Tim. 3,309,2–10: Dès lors donc, étant admis qu'il y a distribution (νομή) de l'âme sur la Terre, c'est néanmoins dans la mesure où la Terre a quelque chose d'astréiforme et d'incorporel ... il faut donc admettre qu'il peut y avoir aussi apocatastase sur la Terre de ce qui a été semé (σπαρέντων) sur elle, et qu'il peut y avoir des destinées posthumes (λήξεις) qui s'accomplissent sur la Terre[57].

****

À partir de ce que F.M. Cornford jugeait être un mythe obscur, inintelligible, Proclus a élaboré une doctrine complexe certes, mais très cohérente, fondée sur une lecture très minutieuse du texte. L'acribie proclienne se révèle dans l'interprétation des détails du texte, auxquels il confère parfois une grande portée doctrinale. C'est le cas notamment avec l'explication de «deuxième et de troisième valeur», en *Tim.* 41d6–7, qui conduit à éclairer de manière très heureuse ce qui caractérise la teneur spécifique de chacun des deux mélanges distincts opérés en vue de la création d'abord de l'Âme du Monde et de la création ensuite, à partir d'un mélange «moins pur», des âmes humaines. Cette explication est aussi pour nous l'occasion de redresser une «erreur» ou «négligence» de la part de cette immense autorité qu'est Cornford, qui n'a pas bien vu ce qu'il faut comprendre par «le reste des ingrédients» quand il est dit (*Tim.* 41d5) que le Démiurge, pour la création des âmes humaines, «s'est employé à fondre le reste des ingrédients utilisés antérieurement». En même temps cette lecture très soucieuse du détail du texte n'empêche pas Proclus de s'écarter, très consciemment, du sens littéral, comme on l'a vu dans les pages qu'il consacre à la «distribution» et l'«ensemencement» des âmes humaines. Ces deux opérations ne peuvent à ses yeux impliquer des lieux différents. Elles procèdent en effet d'une Cause unique, et elles appartiennent aux âmes «par essence». L'interprétation proclienne, forte, va à l'encontre de l'*opinio communis* chez les Modernes, et par là nous invite à un réexamen de celle-ci. On voit aussi enfin comment l'interprétation du *Timée* par Proclus s'élabore dans la perspective d'une compréhension (au sens figuré et au sens propre du terme) des textes de Platon comme faisant «système». Ici, c'est

---

[56] *In Tim.* 3,307,3: ἡ ψυχὴ πρὸς τὴν ψυχήν, cf. *Tim.* 41e1: ἑκάστην πρὸς ἕκαστον.

[57] Cf. aussi *In Tim.* 3,290,18–23: «L'*astre confraternel* (*Tim.* 42b5) est celui dans lequel ont lieu l'ensemencement et la distribution (ἡ σπορὰ καὶ ἡ διανομή) tant des âmes que des véhicules. En sorte que, si certaines âmes ont eu pour lot, dès le principe, la Terre, ces âmes-là, si elles ont obéi à la justice et aux dieux, vont aussi, après la première naissance, abandonnant le corps terreux, se retirer dans le véhicule éthérien de la Terre totale».

très nettement le mythe central du *Phèdre* qui est à l'arrière-plan de toute l'exégèse proclienne de *Timée* 41d–42d.

****

Annexe
Les degrés du divin chez Proclus

Proclus adopte la tripartition «pythagoricienne» du réel: l'Intelligible, le Psychique, le Sensible. L'intelligible est lui-même structuré triadiquement en: Intelligible, Intelligible-Intellectif, Intellectif. Les deux premières classes forment elles-mêmes une triade, tandis que l'Intellectif forme un hebdomade. Le plan du Psychique présente à son tour une triade, avec trois degrés: l'Hypercosmique, l'Hypercosmique-Encosmique, l'Encosmique. Je donne ici un tableau simplifié[58] des différents degrés de la hiérarchie des dieux chez Proclus, en mettant en évidence les divinités dont il est plus particulièrement question dans le commentaire sur le *Timée* en général, et plus spécifiquement dans le commentaire à *Tim.* 41d8–e4.

L'Intelligible

Les dieux intelligibles
1ière triade: l'Un-étant = l'Être intelligible
2ième triade: l'Éternité = la Vie intelligible
3ième triade: le Vivant-en-Soi = Intellect intelligible = le **Modèle** (dans le *Timée*)

Les dieux intelligibles-intellectifs
1ière triade = le **«Lieu supracéleste»**
2ième triade = le «Ciel»
3ième triade = la «Voûte subcéleste»

Les dieux intellectifs
1ière triade = les «Parents» Kronos, Hécate, **Zeus** (le **Démiurge** dans le *Timée*)
2ième triade = les «Dieux immaculés»
Septième divinité

Le Psychique

Les dieux hypercosmiques = Dieux-Chefs
Les dieux hypercosmiques-encosmiques = **les 12 Dieux du *Phèdre***
Les dieux encosmiques = les **«jeunes dieux» du *Timée*** = Dionysos + fixes et planètes + les 9 dieux sublunaires.
Âmes divines célestes (Âme du Monde, âmes des fixes et les planètes)
Les âmes supérieures (anges, démons, héros).
Les âmes humaines (leur partie immortelle).

---

[58] On trouvera dans le très beau livre *All from One: A Guide to Proclus* (éd. D'Hoine et Martijn 2017, Appendix I) un tableau très complet et très clair de tous les degrés d'êtres chez Proclus.

L'expression «dieux recteurs», ou «dieux-chefs», vient du *Phèdre* (246e4). Elle désigne, chez Proclus, d'abord les dieux hypercosmiques, auxquels seuls convient le caractère de commandant et de chef, et, en second lieu, les dieux hypercosmiques-encosmiques, ou dieux «séparés», qui sont à la fois «chefs» et «rangés en bon ordre» – tandis que les dieux encosmiques sont seulement «rangés en bon ordre» (cf. *Théol. plat.* 6,21,96,10–29). Les «dieux-chefs» séparés sont les douze dieux du *Phèdre* (246e–47a), c'est-à-dire Zeus et les dieux qui le suivent, chefs des onze sections de dieux et démons (cf. *Théol. plat.* 6,18–22); ces douze dieux-chefs du *Phèdre* guident tous les dieux encosmiques et toutes les troupes de démons dans leur ascension vers la nature intelligible (cf. *Théol. plat.* 4,4,18,1–2; 4,5,19,17–21). Les âmes divines sont à leur tour «chefs» des âmes partielles (humaines), «chefs de troupeaux» (ἀγελάρχαι).

Ces dieux-chefs, que sont les âmes divines (ou «astres») par rapport aux âmes partielles (i. e. humaines), sont portés par les huit sphères célestes (pour les fixes et les planètes) et par les quatre sphères sublunaires correspondant aux quatre éléments (pour les dieux sublunaires) soit un total de douze sphères. Proclus peut ainsi rapporter aux douze dieux du *Phèdre* la multitude des dieux-chefs (ou «astres») dont dépendent les âmes humaines.

Les neuf dieux sublunaires (cf. *Tim.* 40d6–41a2), ou «dieux générateurs» (i. e. liés à la *genesis*) sont Ouranos, Gê, Okéanos, Tethys, Kronos, Rhéa, Phorkys, Zeus et Héra. Sur la question de savoir pourquoi ils sont neuf, cf. Proclus, *In Tim.* 3,193,18–194,15.

Bibliographie

Bakhouche, B., éd. (2011), *Calcidius, Commentaire au Timée de Platon*. Édition critique et traduction française, Paris: Vrin.

Baltes, M. (2002), *Der Platonismus in der Antike*, VI 2, Stuttgart, Frommann-Holzboog.

Brisson, L. (1992), *Platon, Timée. Critias*. Traduction inédite, introduction et notes par —, Paris: Flammarion.

— (à paraître), 'Les anges chez Proclus', dans *Inventer les anges de l'Antiquité à Byzance: conception, représentation, perception* (Travaux et Mémoires du Centre d'Histoire et Civilisation de Byzance).

Cornford, F. M. (1937, [6]1971), *Plato's Cosmology: The* Timaeus *of Plato*, London: Hackett Publishing Company.

Couvreur, P., éd. (1901), *Hermiae Alexandrini In Platonis Phaedrum Scholia* (Bibliothèque de l'École des Hautes Études 133), Paris: ad fidem Codicis (réimpression, Hildesheim: Olms, 1971, avec un index par C. Zintzen).

D'Hoine, P. et Martijn, M. eds (2017), *All from One: A Guide to Proclus*, Oxford: Oxford University Press.

Diehl, E. (1903–06), *Procli Diadochi In Platonis Timaeum commentaria*, 3 tomes (5 livres), Leipzig: Teubner (réimpression, Amsterdam: Hakkert, 1965).

Dodds, E.R. (1933; [2]1963), *Proclus, The Elements of Theology*. A Revised Text with Translation, Introduction, and Commentary by —, Oxford: Clarendon.

Festugière, A.-J. (1966–68), *Proclus, Commentaire sur le Timée*. Traduction et notes par —, 5 livres, Paris: Vrin.

— (1970), *Proclus, Commentaire sur la République*. Traduction et notes par —, 3 tomes, Paris: Vrin.

Finamore, J.F. et Kutash, E. (2017), 'Proclus on the Psychè: World Soul and the Individual Soul', dans: *All from One: A Guide to Proclus*, éd. P. D'Hoine et M. Martijn, Oxford: Oxford University Press, 122–38.

Kroll, W. (1899–1901), *Procli Diadochi in Platonis Rem publicam commentarii*, Leipzig: Teubner (réimpression, Amsterdam: Hakkert, 1965).

Lernould, A. (2012), 'Nature in Proclus: from irrational immanent principle to goddess', dans: *Neoplatonism and the Philosophy of Nature*, éd. J. Wilberding et Chr. Horn, Oxford, Oxford University Press, 68–102.

Lucarini, C.M. et Moreschini, C., éds (2012), *Hermias Alexandrinus, In Platonis Phaedrum Scholia* (Bibliotheca scriptorum Graecorum et Romanorum Teubneriana), Berlin: De Gruyter.

O'Meara, D. J. (1989), *Pythagoras Revived: Mathematics and Philosophy in Late Antiquity*, Oxford: Clarendon.

Opsomer, J. (2003), 'La démiurgie des jeunes dieux selon Proclus', *Les Études classiques* 71: 5–49.

Saffrey, H.D. et Westerink, L.G. (1968–97), *Proclus, Théologie platonicienne*, 6 tomes (Collection des Universités de France), Paris: Les Belles Lettres.

Tarrant, H. (2017), *Proclus, Commentary on Plato's* Timaeus, vol. VI, Cambridge: Cambridge University Press.

Taylor, A.E. (1928), *A Commentary on Plato's* Timaeus, Oxford: Clarendon.

Trouillard, J. (1965), *Proclos, Éléments de Théologie*. Traduction inédite, introduction et notes par —, Paris: Aubier.

The (Meta)physics of Eating One's Children

Proclus' Interpretation of the Myth of Er

Marije Martijn

I. Introduction

In Proclus' philosophy, there is no eschatology describing the end of time or of the world. The world, in his view, is eternally being created in time.[1] Instead, the eschatology we find is about the end of an earthly life, and the afterlife as the transition to the next life. Undoubtedly the most famous Platonic eschatological myth – and one which Proclus addresses extensively in his commentary – is the Myth of Er.[2] This myth remains a problematic feature for many interpreters. The most extreme verdict, besides that of those who simply do not discuss it at all,[3] is probably that of Julia Annas, who thinks that the myth "is a painful shock; its vulgarity seems to pull us right down to the level of Cephalus, where you take justice seriously when you start thinking about hell-fire."[4] She finds it of a "jarring childishness," and suggests that, in its consequentialist view of justice, it undermines Plato's serious effort at a non-consequentialist theory of justice. For her, as for many contemporary readers, the myth is in that sense a blemish on what is tentatively considered a systematic treatise of justice. For those readers who take a more literary approach to the *Republic*, instead, it is one of the highlights of the dialogue.[5]

* Work on this article was made possible by the C.J. de Vogel Foundation. I thank the members of the Research Group History of Philosophy VU, and especially Marina Uzunova and Ype de Boer, for their helpful comments on an earlier version.

[1] For Proclus on the cosmos as a created, composite entity that is eternally being generated, see *In Tim.* 1,277,32–286,19; 1,366,20–368,11.

[2] See also *Phaedo* 107c–15a; *Gorgias* 523a–27e; *Phaedrus* 246a–49d; *Tim.* 42bd, 90e–92c; *Laws* 903b–05d.

[3] As Santas 2010, or Averroes, who calls it "stories of no account," because it is "remote imitation" (third treatise, Lerner 1974, 105). Cf. the criticism of the Epicurean Colotes mentioned by Proclus, *In Remp.* 2,105,24–106,14.

[4] Annas 1981, 349.

[5] Cf. the much more appreciative tone in Halliwell 2007, 445; Destrée 2014; and Morgan 2000, 207. The latter criticizes Annas' view and posits instead that the myth "carries the concerns of the dialogue to their logical conclusion." Delcomminette 2014, gives a convincing,

In this article, I will discuss Proclus' perspective on the myth. For a Neoplatonist reader of the *Republic*, the starting point is always that Platonic dialogues offer a systematic treatment of a central notion.[6] Moreover, a second starting point maintains that there is no such thing as a blemish on that treatment – that is, if part of a dialogue does not seem to fit in, the fault is ours. These starting points also underlie Proclus' exegesis of Platonic eschatology, as phrased in the Myth of Er. He summarizes the myth and analyzes some key images in essay 15 of the *Commentary on the Republic* (*In Remp.* 2,92,20–95,24) and discusses it in quite some detail in essay 16.[7]

The summary of the myth, in essay 15, consists in a division into four parts (*In Remp.* 2,92–93).[8] Of the four parts Proclus distinguishes, the first treats the types of souls in Hades, the place of the tribunal, the judges, and the journey underneath the earth. The second presents the order of the cosmos, the heavens, and the monads with their powers. The third concerns the types of existence and the choice of the soul, and especially the transition from rational to irrational, or vice versa, from rational to rational and from irrational to irrational. The fourth part concerns the descent into the body.

As is clear from the beginning of essay 16, Proclus interprets the myth both literally and metaphorically – literally as presenting the rewards of justice, and metaphorically – or one could also say analogically, which in turn comes down to metaphysically – as representing the cosmos as the paradigm of the Socratic state (*In Remp.* 2,99,12–101,12).[9] The two come together in the ultimate aim of the myth, teaching us about cosmic order or justice (*In Remp.* 2,100,24–101,10). Proclus ends his first summary of the myth by pointing out that "all these things are required for showing that justice grants great goods, both in the allotment [i.e. of next lives, MM], and in the second descent into genesis." In other words, Proclus takes the myth to function within the *skopos* of the dialogue as a whole, which he considers a treatise on personal and political justice

non-literary, reading of the myth as emphasizing the inadequacy of consequentialist notions of justice by pointing out that consequentialism cannot guarantee the correctness of our choices – which philosophical justice can.

[6] For this exegetical principle of εἷς σκοπός, the formulation of which is ascribed to Iamblichus, cf. *In Remp.* 1,6,1–4. See also Baltzly 2017, for a recent interpretation of the working of the principle in Proclus' academic practice.

[7] Note that of the two titles/summaries of essay 16, as given by Kroll 1899, one is probably wrong: at *In Remp.* 1,4,29 we read Πῶς ἡ τῶν παίδων βρῶσις γίνεται ἐκ τοῦ παντός, καὶ πῶς *τοῦτο φιλεῖται ψυχῇ* ἐκ τοῦ οὐρανοῦ κατιούσῃ. At *In Remp.* 2,292,23, however, we find Πῶς ἡ τῶν παίδων βρῶσις γίνεται ἐκ τοῦ παντός, καὶ πῶς *τοῦτο ὀφείλεται ψυχῇ* ἐκ τοῦ οὐρανοῦ κατιούσῃ. Considering the content of the discussion, the second is more likely to be correct.

[8] "Lexis" being the word by word or phrase by phrase "reading" of Platonic passages. See Festugière 1963.

[9] For Proclus' defence of Plato's eschatological myths in general as to be taken literally, see *In Remp.* 1,121,23–27 and Sheppard 1980. For emphasis on the allegorical side of Proclus' commentary, see Dillon 2015.

(*In Remp.* 1,11,5–14,14) – in the myth, specifically, he thinks this aim is displayed in its full and cosmic scope, by showing justice as having advantages not just during the just life, and not even only for the afterlife, but also for what comes after the afterlife: the rebirth into the next life.[10] The vision of the cosmos at *Resp.* 616bc puts the rest of the dialogue in its proper perspective.

A highly interesting passage in Proclus' exegesis of the Myth shows how this pans out in what is for many one of the most frustrating parts of the myth: the fate of the poor first chooser, the tyrant-to-be. He is a person whose living a good life did get him to go to heaven, but who then ends up choosing the wrong next life, which will involve him eating his children.[11] It is his case we will focus on here, as a good example of the tension between cosmic and individual justice. As we will see, Proclus takes great pains in justifying this story – such great pains, in fact, that one wonders whether he was bothered by its contents himself. Two interesting further aspects of his interpretation are that he implicitly disagrees with Porphyry in a number of respects, despite speaking highly of his commentary on the Myth of Er (*In Remp.* 2,96,10–15). And second, that he relies on the physics of the *Timaeus* for the main part of his justification.

II. The Tyrant to Be, Choice, and Fate

At *Resp.* 619b7–d1, Plato presents the beginning of a tyrannical life in "the first choice," i. e. the choice of the soul that gets to pick the next life before anyone else does:

> …the one who drew the first lot came up and immediately chose the greatest tyranny. In his foolishness and greed, you see, he chose it without adequately examining everything, and did not notice that it involved being fated to eat his own children, among other evils. When he examined the life at leisure, however, he beat his breast and bemoaned his choice, ignoring the warning of the spokesman. For he did not blame himself for these evils, but chance, *daimones*, and everything except himself. He was one of those who had come down from heaven, having lived his previous life in an orderly constitution, sharing in virtue through habit but without philosophy.[12]

---

[10] *In Remp.* 2,93,11–13: Ταῦτα δὴ ἀναγκαῖα πάντα πρὸς τὸ δεῖξαι τὴν δικαιοσύνην μεγάλα προξενοῦσαν ἀγαθὰ καὶ ἐν ταῖς λήξεσιν καὶ ἐν ταῖς δευτέραις καθόδοις εἰς τὴν γένεσιν.

[11] For the association of tyrants with violence and bloodshed as a trope in Greek literature, see Arruzza 2018, 23–24. For cannibalism, and the Greek preference for child victims, see Henrichs 1980, 224–32. For a discussion of Cronus' child eating, see Versnel 1990, 94 and n. 12.

[12] Plato, *Resp.* 619b7–d1 (trans. C. D E. Reeve) Εἰπόντος δὲ ταῦτα τὸν πρῶτον λαχόντα ἔφη εὐθὺς ἐπιόντα τὴν μεγίστην τυραννίδα ἑλέσθαι, καὶ ὑπὸ ἀφροσύνης τε καὶ λαιμαργίας οὐ πάντα ἱκανῶς ἀνασκεψάμενον ἑλέσθαι, ἀλλ' αὐτὸν λαθεῖν ἐνοῦσαν εἱμαρμένην παίδων αὑτοῦ βρώσεις καὶ ἄλλα κακά· ἐπειδὴ δὲ κατὰ σχολὴν σκέψασθαι, κόπτεσθαί τε καὶ ὀδύρεσθαι τὴν αἵρεσιν, οὐκ ἐμμένοντα τοῖς προρρηθεῖσιν ὑπὸ τοῦ προφήτου· οὐ γὰρ ἑαυτὸν αἰτιᾶσθαι τῶν κακῶν, ἀλλὰ τύχην τε καὶ δαίμονας καὶ πάντα μᾶλλον ἀνθ' ἑαυτοῦ. εἶναι δὲ αὐτὸν τῶν ἐκ τοῦ οὐρανοῦ ἡκόντων, ἐν

This beautiful Platonic version of a tragic *peripeteia*,[13] describes how the first person to choose, because his virtue in his previous life was not founded in reflection, opts, again, without proper reflection, for becoming the greatest tyrant. In Proclus' understanding, four elements or phases are to be distinguished in this event: (1) choice, (2) consequences, (3) blame, and (4) cause vs. responsibility. After (1) the unreflected choice, the first soul to choose comes to (2) the realization of the consequences, or of the true nature of the life chosen: namely that the life chosen will necessarily be lived. Proclus takes the breast-beating and other "tragic" behavior of the chooser as indicating awareness of this inevitability, *In Remp.* 2,291,5–11, and as involving all kinds of evils, including that of devouring his own offspring – note that the realization of the inevitability of the consequences of the choice is not in Plato's text, and that in Plato instead it is the choice as such that is bemoaned; next comes (3) the chooser blaming chance, demons, and everything except himself, for the evils to come; and finally (4) the matter of causation and responsibility is (rather implicitly) introduced: he is himself responsible, due to his previous, unphilosophical life. As we will see, however, for Proclus that does not and cannot mean that he is the sole cause of the outcome.

One of the main difficulties of the Myth of Er for contemporary readers, is the tension caused by the emphatic introduction of Fate and cosmic order, as opposed to the notion of justice as argued for in the remainder of the *Republic*, i.e. as internal harmony resulting from personal choices and training – and hence also as relating to free will and responsibility.[14] The most common interpretation of the Myth of Er in this context is that it emphasizes the eternity of the soul, and the cosmic embedding of justice. But the idea that "justice is guaranteed by the cosmic order; the universe is such that overall justice is rewarded and evil punished,"[15] does not fit this overall picture. This view is hence considered unsatisfactory – "depressing," not inspiring[16] – in that it, again, undermines Plato's project as locating justice within the individual. The alternative Annas tentatively proposes, is to demythologize the myth, in which case its message becomes that the just life is worth living because it helps us make the right choices.[17]

τεταγμένῃ πολιτείᾳ ἐν τῷ προτέρῳ βίῳ βεβιωκότα, ἔθει ἄνευ φιλοσοφίας ἀρετῆς μετειληφότα. For the trope of tyrants involved in cannibalism, see Hook 2005 and Versnel 1990, 94 n. 12. The tyrant Plato is often taken to have in mind is Thyestes, who was fed his own children by Atreus (Aeschylus, *Agamemnon* 1223–26). For Cronus, probably the most famous case of child-eating, see section VI.

[13] Cf. Halliwell 2007, 451: "The myth, in other words, echoes the psychological tones of tragedy in order to negate them with the force of a kind of cosmic irony."

[14] Esp. *Resp.* 4.

[15] Annas 1981, 350.

[16] Cf. Annas 1982.

[17] Annas 1981, 352–53. For a reading that considers the tension a conscious choice of Pla-

For Proclus, there is no need to demythologize the myth, as he has a view of justice and human morality more broadly speaking that allows for, even requires, a combination of cosmic and individual justice. In order to see how this combination pans out in this specific context, let us first turn to Proclus' interpretation of the "lots" (κλῆροι, *Resp.* 617d5), i.e. the numbers determining the order in which the souls get to pick their next life.

The second part of essay 15 consists in a *lexis*-type allegorical interpretation of some key elements from the myth (*In Remp.* 2,93–95), such as the meadow, the 1000-year journey – and the lots. The aim of this exercise is to show that, to the trained reader, the dialogue is full of metaphysical truths.[18] The metaphysical truth underlying the mention of the lots, for Proclus, is the cosmic order which determines the type of life fitting each soul – as opposed to the types of life themselves, representing the types of living beings, and the choices made, standing for the *connections* of the souls to the cosmic order.[19] Or as Proclus later formulates it, the distribution of the lots is determined by cosmic intellect, on the basis of the merits of the souls (cf. *In Remp.* 2,256,27). Importantly, however, the lot is not just a number, and does not just determine the order of picking. Instead, also the range of possibilities, or the sum of all the types of life we get to choose from is included (*In Remp.* 2,263,17–18: κλῆρος μὲν γάρ ἐστιν σύμπας ὁ ἀριθμὸς τῶν βίων, ὧν ἑκάστῃ προτείνει τὸ πᾶν διὰ τῶν ἑαυτοῦ περιοορῶν).[20] In a fascinating move which will come in handy in Proclus' determination of responsibility, he distinguishes, besides this first lot, a second one, namely everything that comes with that life (ὅσα ἄλλα προσήρτηται τοῖς βίοις, ὁ δὲ ὁλότης τῶν ἑκάστῳ βίῳ παρακολουθούντων 264,4–16), such as your parents, and good and bad fortune (τύχας).[21] This second lot is not explicitly mentioned in Plato's *Republic*, and Proclus does not adduce any textual evidence for it, but if we re-

to's, see Destrée 2014. Destrée explicitly opposes Proclus' view, but unfortunately starts from what we will see is too limited a reading of Proclus, as merely interested in the individual's responsibility. Instead, Proclus is very interested in the combination of individual responsibility and metaphysical determinism.

[18] *In Remp.* 2,95,21–24: Τοσαῦτα καὶ περὶ τῶν ἐν τῷ μύθῳ σπέρματα νοημάτων ἀναγεγράφθω προκείμενα τοῖς ἐξεργάζεσθαι βουλομένοις τε καὶ δυναμένοις ἀνελίττειν.

[19] *In Remp.* 2,94,26–95,7: οἱ δὲ αὖ κλῆροι σημαίνουσι τὴν κοσμικὴν τάξιν τὴν ἀφορίζουσαν ταῖς ψυχαῖς τοὺς ὀφειλομένους ἑκάστῃ κατὰ τὴν ἀξίαν βίους, ἧς ἡ τὸν ὅλον οὐρανὸν διατάττουσα Λάχεσίς ἐστιν ἡγεμών· οἱ δὲ βίοι τὰ εἴδη τῶν γενεσιουργῶν ζωῶν τῶν ἐκ τοῦ παντὸς ἀπονεμομένων ταῖς κατιούσαις ψυχαῖς, πλειόνων ἢ ἐλασσόνων· αἱ δὲ αἱρέσεις προβολὰς λόγων κατὰ τὴν αὐτενέργητον τῶν ψυχῶν δύναμιν ἐναρμοζομένων τῇ τάξει τοῦ παντός· αἱ δὲ εἰς διάφορα ζῷα μετατάξεις ἀμείνω καὶ χείρω τῆς ζωῆς ποικίλας διεξόδους κατὰ τὰς διαφόρους δυνάμεις λογικὰς ἢ ἀλόγους, τῶν ὁμοίων ἀεὶ πρὸς τὰ ὅμοια φερομένων κατὰ τὴν ἐν τῷ κόσμῳ δίκην

[20] On this passage, see also Dillon 2015, 141–43.

[21] *In Remp.* 2,264,5–16: ὅσα δὲ πάλιν ἑλομέναις προστίθησιν τὸ πᾶν, κλῆροι δεύτεροι μετὰ τὴν αἵρεσιν, οἷον πατέρων τωνδὶ γενέσθαι καὶ τύχας τοιάσδε ἔχειν καὶ ὅσα ἄλλα προσήρτηται τοῖς βίοις. διττὸς οὖν ὁ κλῆρος, ὁ μὲν πρὸ τῆς αἱρέσεως, ὁ δὲ μετὰ τὴν αἵρεσιν· ὁ μὲν ὁλότης ὢν τῶν βίων, οὗ μέρος ἕκαστος βίος, ὁ δὲ ὁλότης τῶν ἑκάστῳ βίῳ παρακολουθούντων, ὃν ὁ κόσμος ἀπονέμει· καὶ ἑκάτερος ἀπὸ τοῦ παντός, ἐν μέσῳ δὲ αὐτῶν ἡ αἵρεσις τῆς ψυχῆς καὶ οὕτω δὴ μένει

turn to the contents of Plato's Myth and Proclus' exegesis of it in essay 16 we will find a possible source. It is probably in the above quoted passage from the *Republic* that we are to locate the textual evidence for the second lot, namely in what we might call "the small print" of the lots – the details or consequences which our chooser is not aware of until he scrutinizes the life he has already picked (291,16–17, μετὰ δὲ τὴν ἐπίσκεψιν τοῦ βίου τὰ ἑπόμενα τίνα ἐστίν).[22]

By splitting the lots into these two phases, Proclus can clearly show how the two elements of freedom and cosmic order are combined, albeit with a different motivation from contemporary readers. His aim is not so much to ensure the possibility of free will, but to ensure that the Cosmos remains sovereign despite the existence of free will: it both pre-determines our range of possibilities, before our free choice, and determines the consequences of our choice.[23] Free will comes in explicitly only in the very brief but crucial intermediate stage: the choice of the next life.[24]

It looks like Proclus may be building on, but also criticizing, the distinction Porphyry made in his essay on the Myth of Er (*On What Is Up to Us*), between the two lives we choose. First, there is a completely free pre-birth choice of a type of life (or biological life) – limited only by the order in which we get to pick. Then, there is another after-birth "life" consisting of additional characteristics, which in part consist of necessary consequences due to the time and place we are born, and in part are a matter of choice – of embracing or rejecting the life one is born in (268F, ed. A. Smith).[25] Proclus, we have seen, proposes a more limited range of freedom than that offered by Porphyry, by limiting the choice offered in the first place, and by adding the necessary consequences even before birth.

μὲν ἡ αὐτεξούσιος φορά, σώζονται δὲ τῆς δίκης ὅροι, τὴν ἀξίαν διανέμοντες ταῖς ψυχαῖς, οὐχ ὧν εἵλοντο μόνον, ἀλλὰ καὶ ὧν αἱρήσονται· προκατάρχει δὲ τὸ πᾶν καὶ ἐπακολουθεῖ ταῖς αἱρέσεσιν.

22 Another way to read the nature of the necessity of eating children is offered in McPherran 2010, 140 n. 24: "One solution to this dismal picture might perhaps be this: the necessity that Plato speaks of at 617e3, 618b3, and 619c1 may also be a contingent one. That is, the fateful requirement that the first soul who chooses a tyrant's life eat his own children might be a necessity that comes into play only after that particular soul picks that particular life." In the note, McPherran thanks Julia Annas for the suggestion.

23 *In Remp.* 2,264,15–16: προκατάρχει δὲ τὸ πᾶν καὶ ἐπακολουθεῖ ταῖς αἱρέσεσιν. For the extensive discussion on the relation between cosmic order and free will, see *In Remp.* 2,257,24–266,26. In modern terms, this combination is nicely put by Halliwell as the myth "[echoing] the psychological tones of tragedy in order to negate them with the force of a kind of cosmic irony." Halliwell 2007, 451.

24 That is, this is where freedom is located in the discussion of the myth of Er (pace Dillon 2015, 143). More generally, however, there is freedom within the life chosen, as well, in moral choices made along the way.

25 See Greenbaum 2018, 103ff., esp. 109 and Wilberding 2013 for a thorough discussion, Wilberding 2011, 123–31 for some similarities between Proclus and Porphyry, and Adamson (2014), for the relation between free choice and necessary consequences in late antiquity more generally.

Proclus embraces the narrow window Porphyry was trying to widen, and thereby escapes the difficulties the case of the tyrant posed for the latter.[26]

III. Intermezzo: Fate (*In Tim.* 3,274–75)

At this point, it may be worth our while to take a first detour to the *Timaeus* commentary, specifically the section on the so-called "first birth" of the soul, and its relation to fate:

> [The demiurge] described to [the souls] the fated laws. They would all be assigned the same initial birth (*Tim.* 41e2–3; *In Tim.* 3,274–75).

In analyzing what it means that the Demiurge showed the souls the "fated laws" before their "initial birth," Proclus explains their working in terms of the Aristotelian theory of the natural motions of the elements.[27] The laws "written into the souls" by the Demiurge (*In Tim.* 3,274,23–24) are the encosmic counterparts of hypercosmic Fate, and make souls conduct themselves in a certain manner, fitting the lives they have chosen (25): the "errant" soul "moving to" what is dark and impious, the pious soul going up to the heavens (26–28). The motions up and down in this context are not those of the afterlife described in the Myth of Er,[28] but regard the focus a soul has during its embodied life: to the heavens if it is rational, to the material world if it is irrational. Proclus explains this using an analogy with the elements, comparing the working of the laws of fate in souls to the working of the powers of nature in matter and bodies: earth is given a natural downward motion through the power of heaviness, fire a natural upward motion through the power of lightness.[29] Likewise, he suggests, some souls move up, and some move down, through the fate within them – fate being a thing's nature, an internal power necessitating certain behavior.[30] There are obvious differences between the elements and souls, of course, first of all that for the latter there is a value judgement involved: their motion upwards or downwards is associated with doing right or wrong. Second, these moral quali-

---

26 Cf. Wilberding 2013, 102.

27 Aristotle on natural motion: *De caelo* 1,2,269a8–9. On Fate as Nature and in relation to intellectual and intramundane Necessity in Proclus, see Linguiti 2009.

28 In that case, Proclus would have had in mind the fate of the souls in the afterlife, as going to heaven or Hades (which is called "dark and unlit" at 352,26 – a passage that is problematic for our tyrant, because Proclus there points out that after a life without education we go to the underworld to be purified), but this seems less likely, as the context is that of internal powers moving souls that have just incarnated.

29 *In Tim.* 3,275,1–5. The source of inspiration, besides Aristotle, of course, is clearly *Laws* 904.

30 For fate as the nature of the human body, maintaining it, see *Prov.* 11–12 with Russi 2009.

ties are the result of the souls' *prohairesis*, which the elements do not have.[31] *Prohairesis* here should not be understood as a (first or prior) choice,[32] but as character or ethical stance, as is clear from Proclus' reference further down to two people who both chose a priestly life, where one lives it well and the other badly (*In Tim.* 3,279,20–22).[33] Likewise, in the *Republic* the tyrant's life could still have been a good life, as we will see – if, we can say on the basis of this passage, the one who chose it had not had the wrong *prohairesis* or ethical stance. In *Prov.* 56–60, *prohairesis* is defined as the rational faculty of moral choice, a "crossroads" within us that leads both to real and to apparent goods.[34] It does seem, however, that Proclus assumes, in *Prov.* as in the passage mentioned above, that this faculty has (or is) a certain habitus or tendency.[35]

And finally, as opposed to the elements, souls take up a certain rank on the basis of prior existence (πρόσφορον τοῖς προϋπηργμένοις ἑαυταῖς ... τάξιν, *In Tim.* 3,275,14–15). It is not entirely clear to me whether Proclus wants this prior existence to refer to the transcendent existence prior to incarnation, or to a prior incarnated life. He does not, however, take Plato to think of a literal first birth of the soul, as souls are immortal. The first birth of the soul is the very first descent from the intelligible realm, as opposed to further descents (3,277,3–5; cf. 278,25–32). Fate, which is already inscribed in each soul as its internal power (analogous to the internal power of the elements to move to their natural places), kicks into action afterwards, with the second birth or descent "into generation" (*In Tim.* 3,275,15–280,32). There are three stages to this descent into generation (which is how Proclus understands the *Moirai*): first, the cloaking of the soul in a bodily vehicle, which involves its becoming subject to Fate; a second element is the moment of choice, where the soul picks its next life, which implies that it will then necessarily live that life; and third, the universe carries the soul to its natural place,[36] i.e. it plays a part in the All in accordance with the life it has chosen (*In Tim.* 3,277,7–31).[37]

Returning briefly to the two lots in the Republic, we may then tentatively map the two commentaries onto one another, and state that the first lot corresponds to the options made available to it in the first stage of the second birth, whereas after the second stage, when the soul has picked the type of life it will

---

[31] *In Tim.* 3,275,12–13 διὰ μὲν τὴν προαίρεσιν ἁμαρτάνουσαι καὶ κατορθοῦσαι.

[32] Pace Tarrant 2017, ad loc., but cf. his translation of 279,21.

[33] *In Tim.* 3,279,21–24 κἂν γὰρ τελεστικὸν ἀμφότεραι βίον ἕλωνται, δυνατὸν τὴν μὲν ὀρθῶς περὶ αὐτὸν διαγενέσθαι, τὴν δὲ διαστρόφως· ἕκαστος γὰρ τῶν βίων ἐπιδέχεται τό τε εὖ καὶ τὸ κακῶς.

[34] See also Proclus' discussion at *In Remp.* 2,257–64.

[35] Cf. the description of virtuous people who always opt for the real good (*Prov.* 61). On *prohairesis* as rational faculty, see Riggs 2015.

[36] ἄγεται μὲν γὰρ ἕκαστον ὡς πέφυκε, 277,22–23 – cf. Aristotle on natural motion.

[37] For Proclus' views on the descent of the mortal soul, see Finamore and Kutash (2017, 131–35) and Opsomer 2006.

lead, comes the second lot, or the necessary consequences of the choice, i.e. the soul's natural place in the All.

Despite the differences between elements and souls, we may assume that the analogy from physics is chosen on purpose in the context of eschatology, and especially rebirth. Besides solving certain specific problems, Proclus thereby also emphasizes that human beings are entirely descended and incarnated souls (*El. Th.* 211), and that their lives in the encosmic realm are subject to certain far-reaching necessities, anchored at higher metaphysical levels. Perhaps Proclus would even go so far as to connect our moral stance to our physical constitution: those with a more "earthy" body are more prone to being pulled down to the irrational. This will remain a mere suggestion, however.

Let us return to our tyrant. Although for Proclus our prenatal choice of life is crucial, it is merely a fraction of a much larger structure: the lots, including the range of types of life on offer, as such pre-exist the choices made by individual souls, and hence the availability of certain types of life – especially the immoral ones – requires a justification at a level higher than that of the individual.[38]

This understanding of the lots is also quite different from the contemporary view, as described e.g. by Ilievski, that Plato is emphasizing the element of chance, which is supposed to free the gods from responsibility of evil – *theos anaitios* (*Resp.* 617e5).[39] McPherran does think that the description of the throwing of the lots by a prophet (617e6), suggests that who gets which lot is not a matter of chance, but a matter of divine providence – but contrary to Proclus, he considers this a providence "Plato is unwilling to expose and explain," and one that concerns the order of life-picking, more than the available selection.[40]

Instead, for Proclus this divine side is what the myth is all about. As has been shown, free will and choice, according to Proclus, can be located in a Stoically narrow range of moral choices and actions.[41] This is also, in his view, where evils are to be located.[42] As a consequence, the problems of the future tyrant's life, for Proclus, are not so much the cosmic limitations imposed on his personal choices: it is after all the soul itself which chooses from the wealth of possible lives, and it is the soul's gluttony (λαιμαργία, *Resp.* 619b9, cf. *In Remp.* 1,104,28; 2,291,12) and its thoughtlessness (ἀφροσύνη, *In Remp.* 2,291,12) that are "the causes of such a tragedy." What Proclus does struggle with, however, is the element of apparent evil at the level of cosmic necessity: the lives on offer come

[38] This also fits his overall interpretation of the Myth in essay 16, as both displaying the rewards of justice, and presenting the cosmic paradigm of the Socratic state (2,99,12–101,12).

[39] Ilievski 2016, in reply to McPherran 2010.

[40] McPherran 2010, 139 suggests that in a divinely manipulated lottery we would expect the philosopher to receive lot #1, but I would suggest that the broad selection available to the tyrant-to-be reflects Plato's warning that souls with the best natures, who receive bad education, do more harm than less talented souls (*Resp.* 491de).

[41] Steel 2014 and for the Myth of Er Dillon 2015.

[42] Steel 2017.

from the lap of Lachesis, daughter of Necessity (*Resp.* 617d). So although the responsibility of the choice is with the chooser (617e5), the mere *possibility* of eating your children is both necessary from a cosmic perspective and morally questionable. In that case, how can *theos anaitios* be maintained?

IV. Justifying the Tyrant's Life (*In Remp.* 2,292–98)

After summarizing how "the first choice" insofar as it is a choice emphasizes the truth of the prophet's words that the gods are not to blame (*In Remp.* 2,290,25–292,22), Proclus still feels the need to dedicate an in-depth analysis to the question how the eating of children (ἡ τῶν παίδων βρῶσις) "derives from the All," in order to solve this paradox of the cosmic facilitation of evil. A second question he addresses in that context is how eating your children can be due reward for a soul coming from heaven (as one would rather expect it to be punishment for those who did not live a good life):

> How the devouring of children originates from the all, and how that fits a soul which comes down from heaven.[43]

The problem is not the presence of tyranny in the cosmos. There is no surprise there, says Proclus, because tyrannical power could be used for the good.[44] The assumptions underlying this justification are, of course, first of all the more neutral meaning of "τύραννος" as "all-powerful ruler," and second, that whatever stems from the All is, indeed, in principle good. This emphasis on the possibility of good tyranny, in fact, could count in favor of assuming that Proclus would agree with Annas about the contingent necessity of eating your children: if a philosopher had chosen the life of the tyrant, this ghastly deed would probably not have been included among the consequences. This is supported, perhaps, by the splitting of the lots, if we interpret it as the first lot referring to the selection offered on the basis of the quality of the previous life, and the second lot, i.e. the evil fate, as determined by the combination of the life chosen with the character of the person choosing.[45]

But even then, the possibility of eating one's offspring is pre-ordained in the texture of the All. And since it is hardly obvious how that could be used for the good, it requires a further justification.

---

43 *In Remp.* 2,292,23–25: Πῶς ἡ τῶν παίδων βρῶσις γίνεται ἐκ τοῦ παντός, καὶ πῶς τοῦτο ὀφείλεται ψυχῇ ἐκ τοῦ οὐρανοῦ κατιούσῃ.

44 *In Remp.* 2,292,12–13, cf. Porphyry, *On What Is Up to Us* 79–81.

45 Comparable also, apparently, to what Porphyry had in mind. Cf. Wilberding 2013, 103.

Of course, since we are in the middle of a myth, Proclus could explain it as an image.[46] This is not what he does, however. Instead, he takes the tyrant's possible worst behavior quite literally, and elaborates the two *aporiai*:

(1) The first *aporia* concerns the causal role of the All: either the All merely indicates (σημαίνειν) to the future tyrant what he will do, or in a sense the All makes it happen and thereby is its cause or at least secondary cause (συναιτία) (292,12–16);
(2) The second *aporia* is in what sense such a life can be just, since the person who chooses it lived a life (βίος) that was good enough, and in a good enough city, for him to end up in heaven. So why, then, was such a life (βίος) offered to him, what kind of life (ζωῆ) did he have that would merit such a fate (292,17–21)?

The last question is partly answered right away: "For here we do not have some prior life (προβιοτή) to blame for such a penalty."[47]

Festugière, who translates "vie" for both βίος and ζωῆ, takes Proclus to mean simply that in the case of the tyrant to be, we already know that he did not live a bad life, and therefore the prior life is not the cause of the punishment. That is unsatisfactory, insofar as it leaves unanswered the question "What kind of life would merit such a fate?" – or even unanswerable in the sense that now the prior life seems excluded as element in the equation. If the prior life cannot be blamed for the punishment, then how does it make sense to ask what kind of life merits his fate? I see two possible interpretations that could solve this problem. First, perhaps this is one of the occasions in Greek thought where βίος and ζωῆ mean slightly different things. It is at the very least interesting that ζωῆ is used only once in this context, and precisely where we need something other than the life lived. Earlier in the *Commentary on the Republic*, ζωῆ and βίος refer to a general type of life and specific differences in the attributes of a type respectively (e.g. short tyranny or lasting tyranny), following Porphyry's distinction.[48] This distinction seems to map onto that of the two lots – where ζωῆ would be the first lot, and βίος the second – but that would only help us here if the *type of life* chosen, i.e. a tyranny, would at the same time be that which earns the poor soul

[46] For the interpretation of evil ascribed to the gods as referring to their excellences instead, see Sheppard 2017, 279 and n. 7.

[47] *In Remp.* 2,292,21–22: οὐ γὰρ ἔχομεν ἐνταῦθα προβιοτὴν αἰτιᾶσθαί τινα τῆς τοιαύτης ποινῆς.

[48] *In Remp.* 2,282,13–16. Cf. also the sequel, until 2,283,1. For Porphyry, see above. Also relevant may be the distinction between the type of life (τὸ εἶδος τῆς ζωῆς) and the misfortune attached to it by the All (τὸ ἐκ τοῦ παντὸς αὐτῷ συνηρτημένον ἀτύχημα), at 2,292,5–10. Proclus uses the word ἀτύχημα only twice, here and in *In Alc.* 17, of Alcibiades who "unwittingly falls into misfortune" due to lack of self-knowledge. The latter seems to suggest that Proclus uses the word to indicate mishaps which you could have prevented through reflection – or better, philosophy. It may also be that Proclus has in mind the Aristotelian explanation of ἀτύχημα as unexpected misadventure the origin of which lies outside oneself (Aristotle, *EN* 5,8 1135b16–19, cf. *Rhet.* 2,13,1374b6), as it is the All which joins the misfortune to the type of life. Combined, we get the picture of bad luck as the second lot, necessarily joined to a type of life by the All on the basis of a lack of reflection.

his dramatic fate. To some extent, that is true, as the tyranny is the necessary condition, but it is not also sufficient: tyrannical power could be used for the good, we need the character of the soul picking it as well.

A common misconception regarding the difference between βίος and ζωῆ as they are used by Aristotle is that one means "moral life" and the other "bare life."[49] We can say, however, that in Stoa and late antiquity we sometimes find a distinction between animal life (ζωῆ) and rational life (βίος), or between being alive and living a (rational) life. In that case, a second possible interpretation is that it is the specific behavior or character our soul displays *in heaven* – an "animal life," which in itself *is* due to the prior life, which is to blame: the voracity in picking a life without studying it, which is in its turn the result of the absence of philosophy in the prior life. This would mean all but reducing ζωῆ to irrational life. We will not decide here but return to this below.

After the brief preliminaries on the second *aporia*, Proclus goes on to elaborate both *aporiai* in more detail. In the following, we will focus mainly on the former, and, of the four sections in the argument distinguished by Festugière, mainly on the first: eating children is a natural transformation.[50]

V. Eating Offspring as a Natural Transformation (292,26–294,3)

Proclus first addresses his first question, whether the All only indicates that the tyrant will eat his children, or also causes it to happen in some sense. To explain what he means by "indicating" (σημαίνειν) (as opposed to causing), Proclus adds "as birds do" (292,27). This is a reference to auspices, for whom birds in the sky indicate certain events. These birds, Proclus implies, do not also cause the events by flying by (that would be upward causation). More complex is the astrological case mentioned by Porphyry and referred to by Festugière, of the planets either merely indicating a certain way of life, or also causing it. Porphyry follows what he considers the Platonic view, that the planets merely indicate a certain way of life.[51] Not surprisingly, however, for Proclus the answer is that the All is the productive cause of events in our lives. First, it fits Proclus' (Ptolemaic) metaphysics in which, as opposed to the birds flying by, heavenly processes such as stellar configurations and motions have effects in the sublunary realm and for

[49] Often ascribed to Aristotle following a suggestion of H. Arendt's. It has been shown, that that ascription is hardly justified. See e.g. Backman 2017, discussing G. Agamben's use of her distinction.

[50] The other sections are: Such transformations are in accordance with Justice; Role of demon punishers; Conclusion.

[51] In the fragments *On Free Will* he takes Platonic astrology as the planets merely indicating a certain way of life, but not also necessitating it (271F, 87–95 Smith). See also Wilberding 2013, 98–99 and Greenbaum 2018, 108.

human lives: "every cosmic movement is efficient" (δραστήριος, 293,1).[52] Second, it fits the argument, as in order to subsequently justify the eating as a punishment, it has to first be established as part and parcel of cosmic developments: only then can it be served by higher powers judging the soul.

Although the conclusion that the All is the productive cause of the tragic events resolves the first *aporia*, Proclus now faces the problem of theodicy: how can the All in all its goodness be the cause of something that is apparently despicable? Fortunately, he has an ingenious solution to offer: eating children is not despicable, to the extent that it is simply an example of the dissolution of composite bodies into their simple components. As we read in Proclus' conclusion:

The devouring of children occurs by Fate (εἱμαρμένη), as the leader of all dissolution of bodies into bodies.[53]

The more common role of Fate in Proclus is that of composing and maintaining, not of dissolving bodies.[54] That we here find it as the leader of dissolution, may be due to the role Fate has in Plato's *Statesman* (272e5–6), when the steersman lets go and Fate is in charge of the ensuing entropy.

More important for our purposes, however, is that he core of the solution to the *aporia* lies in taking up a physical point of view. The first steps of the argument supporting the conclusion presented above consist in elaborating the more proximate causes of destruction: (1) cosmic motions are efficient, i.e. they produce either generation or destruction; (2) beings are destroyed either by themselves, or by others, and in the case of others, either by co-ordinate entities, or by causes, or by effects (τὰ μὲν ὑφ' ἑαυτῶν, τὰ δὲ δι' ἄλλων, καὶ ἤτοι τῶν συστοίχων ἢ τῶν αἰτίων ἢ τῶν αἰτιατῶν).[55]

This, as Festugière remarks, very elliptic passage requires further analysis. It refers to the "three natural laws of transformation of bodies," underlying which is the one general principle that all bodies must be generated from other bodies, and subsequently dissolve back into the bodies they were generated from (293,4–6). The three laws are that (a) that which is produced dissolves into its producer ("destroyed by causes"), (b) co-ordinate bodies contribute to mutual generation, and (c) that which produces feeds that which is produced ("destroyed by products") (293,26–29). "Co-ordinate" here means that there is no ontological relation of prior to posterior and vice versa between the entities involved.

---

52 See also *In Remp.* 2,261,3–264,30 and Dillon 2015, 139–40.

53 *In Remp.* 2,297,15–17: ἡ τῶν παίδων βρῶσις γίνεται μὲν καθ' εἱμαρμένην ὡς πάσης ἀναλύσεως σωμάτων εἰς σώματα προστάτιν. Proclus refers to the *Statesman* passage on a number of occasions, among which *In Tim.* 3,273,25–274,13, for which see below. On the passage in Proclus, and Fate as part of the chain of Necessity, see also Van Riel 2009, 235–37.

54 See *Prov.* 10–11, and Linguiti 2009.

55 *In Remp.* 2,293,1–294,3.

The laws hold for (i) simple bodies – e.g. air coming from fire and returning to fire, for (ii) complex bodies generated from simple ones, and hence, Proclus says, "it only makes sense that the remaining option is also the case," for (iii) complex bodies produced from complex bodies (293,7–21). The encosmic demiurges create the composites, Proclus says, quoting the *Timaeus* (42e), "borrowing parts" from the cosmos which are "to be returned some day." We will return to this reference below.

The next step in the argument is to apply this general structure to eating living beings (ζῴων βρώσεις) as an example of decomposition. Proclus distinguishes three options: one animal species eating another, or eating fruits (iii-b, the composite counterpart of the simple fire "eating" air), and the parents and children within one species eating one another – where the parents are complex bodies generating complex bodies at a lower ontological level, namely children (iii-a and b). In the first example – and this may help us understand the justification of child eating – there does not seem to be a bidirectional relation between eater and food: when we eat fish, that is not a resolution of something generated by us back into us. (There is no reason to limit this example to food we have grown ourselves, because in that case it would not apply to non-human animals eating other species or vegetation.) Instead, as we will see, there is a cosmic relation underlying the process, that is bidirectional.

Note that the horizontal option of complex bodies dissolving complex bodies is not elaborated until we reach the conclusion of the entire argument (where Proclus mentions one animal species eating another, or animals eating fruits, 297,21), here instead he goes straight to the vertical case of animals bringing forth other, inferior, animals of the same kind and eating them. This eating, Proclus emphasizes, happens in accordance with a certain natural order and a corporeal transformation of the product into the producer.[56]

To make this notion more palatable, it seems, Proclus then moves straight to the inverse case, where children "are fed by" (τρέφηται) their parents. Since the argument requires that this feeding is actually a production of the child from the parent themselves, this may simply refer to the corporeal components involved in procreation, sperm and blood, but in light of the verb used, it could also be that Proclus is thinking of nursing, in which a child literally eats its parent and thereby grows.[57]

We may render the different options as follows:

[56] *In Remp.* 2,293,19–22: ὥστε καὶ ζῴων βρώσεις ὑπὸ τῶν γεννησαμένων αὐτὰ γιγνόμεναι κατά τινα τάξιν ἀποτελοῦνται φυσικὴν καὶ σωματικὴν εἰς ἐκεῖνα μεταβολὴν ἐξ ὧν γέγονεν.

[57] For a reference to a child's first feeding on milk (as relating to the Milky Way), see *In Remp.* 2,130,1–2.

Table 1: Corporeal transformations

Direction	Simple to simple: generation (g) + dissolution (d)	Simple to complex: generation	Complex to simple: dissolution	Complex to complex: generation + dissolution
Horizontal				Different species:
Examples	Fire to air and vv (g+d)	–	–	Eating fruit or meat (d) (+ cosmic processes?) (g)
Vertical				Same species
Examples	–	Earth and water to mud (g)	Mud to earth and water (d)	Gestation/breastfeeding (g) + **eating children** (d)

Proclus emphasizes the corporeal side of eating children, by making it part of a scholastic analysis of options of corporeal transformation, as the counterpart of gestation or breastfeeding, and by introducing the more general composition of complex bodies from the simple elements which together constitute the All. To emphasize the role of the All in the context of the dissolution of such complex bodies into their components, Proclus makes good use of the physics of the *Timaeus*, specifically the obligations of the younger gods or encosmic demiurges mentioned above. These children of the Demiurge are made responsible for the temporary formation of bodies out of the primary elements:

His children ... borrowed parts of fire, earth, water and air from the world, intending to pay them back again, and bonded together into a unity the parts they had taken.[58]

The most manifest reason for Proclus' reference to this passage is the fact that the younger gods have the intention of *giving back* what they borrow: they form bodies by combining borrowed portions of the different elements, "to be returned someday" (ἀποδοθησόμενα πάλιν) – not just dissolved, but returned to "the Father," i.e. the Demiurge, in accordance with his wishes (βούλεται ... ἐκεῖνος). Creating bodies isolates parts of the four wholes of elemental matter as created by the Demiurge, and in order to ensure ongoing generation, ongoing destruction has to be ensured as well, preventing that the gods run out of matter.[59] The destruction of bodies is a cosmic necessity.

58 ...οἱ παῖδες ... λαβόντες ἀθάνατον ἀρχὴν θνητοῦ ζῴου, μιμούμενοι τὸν σφέτερον δημιουργόν, πυρὸς καὶ γῆς ὕδατός τε καὶ ἀέρος ἀπὸ τοῦ κόσμου δανειζόμενοι μόρια ὡς ἀποδοθησόμενα πάλιν, εἰς ταὐτὸν τὰ λαμβανόμενα συνεκόλλων (*Tim.* 42e). Diehl 1906 refers to 42c, see below. The metaphysical parallel in *In Remp.* is tricky in several respects, as not all children are eaten by their parents – but then perhaps Proclus thinks not all bodies are dissolved, and the All, not the younger gods, is considered mediately responsible for the dissolution of the children into their parents.

59 *In Tim.* 3,318,27–31. On the identity and work of the younger gods in Proclus, see Opsomer 2003.

Moreover, at first sight, this passage also seems chosen by Proclus because it discusses the *bilateral* aspect of the material exchange and hence puts what is actually a horizontal transformation of simple elements into complex bodies (comparable to the horizontal transformation of complex bodies into one another, e.g. animals eating fruit) in a *parental*, i.e. vertical, context, which brings it closer to the eating of children: the children are "returned" to their father the tyrant. In this reading, however, it is not clear what, in the story of the tyrant, would be a parallel for the younger gods.

If we take a closer look, Proclus' reference to the *Timaeus* adds further, suggestive layers of depth to the argument, going beyond the corporeal give and take between generations. First of all, it includes a reference to demiurgic causality, as presiding over elemental composition and dissolution: thus we now have the picture of the immediate cause, the younger gods (if they instead are the analogue for the tyrant parent), as well as a higher demiurgic cause (analogous to the All or Cosmos, in charge of the cyclic process of composition and dissolution). So although it is the tyrant who will eat his children, and he is himself responsible for this action, it is preordained at a higher level. He "returns" what he "borrowed" to the Cosmos[60] – in accordance with its "wishes" (cf. βούλεται … ἐκεῖνος, *In Tim.* 3,318,30).

Let us also briefly consider another very interesting aspect of the reference to the *Timaeus*, namely the context of the passage alluded to. First, it is immediately preceded by the *Timaeus*' eschatology:[61] the Demiurge had just explained to the souls, before sowing them, that they would themselves be responsible for the lives to be led – there may be a higher demiurgic cause, but he is *anaitios* – god is without blame. Although this prior passage is not referred to explicitly in the *Commentary on the Republic*, Proclus' readers are bound to think of it themselves, especially in light of the parallel with *theos anaitios* here: although the tyrant's fate is caused at a cosmic level, only the tyrant is to blame. And second, the *Timaeus* passage is especially apposite, because it is not just about composition of complex bodies, it is about the composition of *human* bodies.

We could, therefore, read Proclus' interpretation of the Myth of Er as reducing the cannibalism to the death and dissolution of the body, which in turn is no more than its return to that to which it belongs primarily: the universe (rather than us). In the *Timaeus* commentary, Proclus explicitly says that we should not grieve at death: "…why do humans grieve at their destruction? Why is this dissolution a terrible thing?" (*In Tim.* 3,319,29–320,2) Translated again to our tyrant: when a father eats his children, this is neither sad nor evil, but instead both necessary and innocent, insofar as it is "merely" the eating, i.e. dissolution, of

[60] As we will see, the evil side of his behavior consists in the method of returning. See below, section VI.

[61] This is probably why Diehl 1906 refers to 42c, rather than 42e.

the body. The latter, perhaps not surprisingly, remains rather implicit in Proclus' discussion of the Myth of Er.

There may be two reasons for this corporeal understanding of the tyrant's fate remaining somewhat implicit. First, the analogy does not really fit, as it seems to counter what is called the one-seed theory of procreation: the idea that children receive their form uniquely from their father, and their matter from their mother.[62] This would mean that for the argument of transformation to work it requires a female tyrant taking back the matter she provided – it is unlikely that this is what Proclus wanted to imply.[63] Second, and more importantly, we are now confronted with a new problem, namely that the defense of the tyrant's fate works too well: it almost becomes an injustice not to eat your children. At the same time, however, we can safely assume that Proclus grew up with a tradition vehemently criticizing cannibalism – the most obvious examples being Greek myths (such as that of Thyestes) and Porphyry's condemnation of cannibalism in the strongest of terms in his invective against the Christians.[64] But this would not be the only reason for Proclus not to advertise eating children: he is interpreting Plato, and so he still has to be able to show the fate of the tyrant to be a form of punishment.[65]

VI. The Transformations Are Unnatural but in Accordance with Justice

After elaborating the resemblance between eating your children and elementary decomposition, Proclus tackles the second *aporia*: how this type of existence can be justified, what sort of life is deserving of it, and how come that someone who ends up in heaven, receives this punishment? His treatment of these questions will provide us with solutions to two issues discussed above: the paradox of the good prior life, and the paradox of justified yet evil child-eating.

That the All is the productive cause of the fate of the tyrant, does not imply that it is to blame for the evil in the future life. Cosmic justice hands out numbers based on the prior life one led. But how does that work in this case? It is a well-known paradox of the Myth of Er that ending up in heaven is no guarantee for a good next life. In this case, the previous life was virtuous, but its virtue was not the result of reflection. So when Proclus points out that the "dissolution" (of the kids) is punishment (*In Remp.* 2,294,5–10, 20–21), a closer look reveals that the punished is served his punishment not so much in light of the unphilosoph-

[62] On this theory, see Wilberding 2017.
[63] For Proclus' views on women, see Baltzly 2013, and Schultz (forthcoming).
[64] *Against the Christians* (fragm. 69 A. von Harnack). See also Henrichs 1980, 227.
[65] It is interesting, for example, that Proclus does not refer to well-known and respectable examples of child-eating, most notably Cronus. But see below.

ical life, as because of the gluttony and lack of reflection involved in picking the next life (294,25–26)[66] – although these characteristics are of course in turn the result of the unphilosophical life (294,18–20). The afterlife has, it seems, become a life of its own, which is characterized by an intermediate status, i.e. both as a temporal transition between the prior life and the next life, and, more importantly, between the relative goodness of the prior life and the shocking evil in the next life. The changing circumstances between the first life and the afterlife (parallel to the ring of Gyges in *Republic* 2: what would you do if anything was possible?) lead to the revelation of the true disposition of our future tyrant: immoderate and irrational in picking the next life (*In Remp.* 2,295,3–6). His "voracity" then turns against the voracious person himself, says Proclus, when the life chosen involves satisfying his appetite with unnatural food: eating his own children (*In Remp.* 2,295,3; 295,10–12).

Perhaps Proclus has, again, the *Timaeus*' eschatology in the back of his head, when he emphasizes that it is this disposition as revealed in the afterlife that is to blame (cf. 295,21–24) – the resulting mitigation of the transition from the good life to the bad life fits the prescription in the *Timaeus* that opposite lives cannot follow one another immediately (cf. *In Tim.* 3,295,20).

Alternatively, we may now tentatively answer the question why Proclus says the prior life cannot be blamed and still wonders what kind of life merits eating your children. In the passages here discussed, Proclus hardly uses "βίος," but a lot of "ζωῆ."[67] Since the immoderate disposition is the result of an unreflected and in that sense irrational life, which reduces our future tyrant to a beast, we may now conclude that the question what kind of life merits eating your children, is answered by assuming the Stoic distinction between animal life (ζωῆ) and rational life (βίος): it is not the deeds of the previous life that are punished, but the underlying irrational, animal-like character or disposition which comes to the fore in his behavior in heaven.

The question why Proclus can still maintain that eating your children is punishment, and an unnatural and impious deed, despite arguing earlier that there is something completely natural about this process, lies, again, in a subtle but crucial change in terminology: whereas earlier it was the corporeal *transformation* or dissolution that was justified, of children into their parents, here Proclus emphasizes that the *food* (τροφή) is unholy and unnatural.[68] He elaborates this

[66] Adduced in *In Tim.* 3,235,11–21 as evidence for Plato's opinion with respect to an afterlife of the irrational part of the soul. Note that picking the life of a tyrant in itself is not necessarily a bad thing according to Proclus: at *In Alc.* 137,13–19 he considers those who opt for a tyrannical life superior to more modest choices, because of a desire to excel over others, albeit in the wrong domain (becoming, rather than Being). See the discussion in Van den Berg 2017, esp. 154.

[67] Exception is *In Remp.* 2,295,17–18, where the two seem equivalent.

[68] *In Remp.* 2,294,26–27. It is tempting to assume that Proclus has in mind a Stoic view of cannibalism as defended in Hook 2005, esp. 36, 39: under certain circumstances (e.g. famine),

in a discussion of the demon punishers, who can be found at the lowest end of any metaphysical chain of divinities, and are the wrong "gods" to follow: at the bottom of the chain of Ares, god of ambition, opposition, war, and division in the material and passionate realm,[69] are "Areic" demons, who take perverse pleasure in the cutting up of bodies (*In Remp.* 2,296,1–15). It is here that Proclus finally introduces the impressive intellective prime-cannibal and ancestor of Ares himself (who belongs at the hypercosmic-encosmic level) as well as these Areic demons: high up the metaphysical chain, we find the paradigmatic – intellective – variety of a parent eating his children: he is not mentioned explicitly, but Festugière must be right in suggesting that Proclus has in mind Cronus.

Of all Greek child-devourers, Cronus is probably the most famous. He moreover plays a pivotal role in Neoplatonic metaphysics as the Intelligible Intellect,[70] and the cause of all reversion (*In Remp.* 2,75,8–10). Cronus' "outrageous" (ὑβριστικῶς)[71] reign, and especially his devouring his children[72] is in fact the image of reversion: "he who turns even those that have emerged from him back upon himself and envelops them and establishes them firmly within himself."[73]

For a human soul, following Cronus means producing thoughts, i.e. intellective offspring, and keeping them unified inside (*In Remp.* 2,296,18–21). Consorting with the bottom of the chain, however, i.e. with the ultimate declension of Areic demons, inspires the human soul to dissolving its own offspring by dividing it, irrationally and bestially (ζῳωδῶς) (16–18, 22–27).

To put it in terms of the problem formulated in section IV, and the analogy of the elements: that the matter of the childrens' bodies is returned to its cause is justified from a cosmic perspective, because strictly speaking, bodies – whether those of fish, apples, or humans – are offspring of nature or fate (*Prov.* 11; *In Tim.* 1,429,6–7), and need to be returned at some point. But the soul attempting to revert through its material products, rather than its thoughts, commits a crime and is punished for it at the same time.[74]

only the wise will be justified in eating human flesh, because they understand it to be in agreement with Nature. However, since he wants to maintain the link between being subject to strong desire and cannibalism (see also below), we should not give in to this temptation.

[69] For Proclus' ideas on the leader-gods, inspired by the *Phaedrus* myth, see also *El. Th.* 204, and Finamore and Kutash 2017, 132–33. For Ares, see e.g. *In Tim.* 1,34,21–23; 79,6–9; 167,30–32; 3,279,11–30; 3,162,1–166,29.

[70] For his position in Proclus' metaphysical system, see D'Hoine and Martijn 2017, Appendix I.

[71] *In Crat.* 105; *Theologia platonica* 5,5,24.

[72] Hesiod, *Theogony* 453–62.

[73] *In Crat.* 107,11–13 ὅς γε καὶ τοὺς ἀπ' αὐτοῦ προκύψαντας εἰς ἑαυτὸν αὖθις ἐπέστρεψεν καὶ ἐνεκολπίσατο καὶ ἐν ἑαυτῷ σταθερῶς ἵδρυσεν. For references to Cronus as διαιρετικός, see Festugière 2012, 254 n. 6.

[74] Thanks to Marina Uzunova for pointing me in this direction.

Interestingly enough, Proclus shortly after returns to Cronus in a less circumspect way. The text is rather corrupted there,[75] but it is clear that this passage functions as a sort of argument from authority or pedigree of the combination of tyranny and child-eating, but also explains why introducing Cronus is problematic. A first problem, on an allegorical/ metaphysical understanding of Cronus' child-eating, is probably that referring to Cronus would suggest that the human tyrant's future deed would at least resemble a metaphysical and intellectual one, parallel to the working of the intelligible Intellect,[76] rather than a physical and irrational one, of devouring bodies. So it would neither fit the fact that the tyrant-to-be caused his fate by lacking in reflection and philosophy, nor the justification of the devouring from a cosmic perspective as a physical affair. To counter this, however, Cronus is brought in in an indirect manner (presumably only for those who are already in the know), and after the metaphysical chain and its lowest, physical declension have been emphatically introduced.

And second, on a more literal reading, an obvious reason for not introducing this high-up parallel to the tyrant-to-be, is explicit in Proclus' own words: "Maybe the eating of children, if I have to take courage and say it, appeared for the first time together with the greatest tyranny."[77] Saying more or less out loud that Cronus' deeds are like the evil deeds of the tyrant-to-be, borders on blasphemy. On the other hand, however, it does provide a metaphysical origin of the evil in the life of the tyrant-to-be, which is what Proclus set out to give us in the first place.

In elaborating the theologians' myth of Cronus, Proclus adds further depth to his justification. Eating his children is Cronus' punishment for him castrating his father (*In Remp.* 2,297,10–15). So here we have another possible answer to the paradox of lives: the life that merits the punishment may be the very life during which it is served. Likewise, our tyrant may be punished both for and by acting like a tyrant.

VII. Conclusion

By way of conclusion, let me first point to two interesting new elements from Proclus' own conclusion. First of all, a fascinating tidbit in Proclus' conclusion

[75] Considering what remains, however (for which see Kroll 1899 and Festugière 2012, ad loc.), it seems clear that the text is especially close to *In Crat.* 149 and refers to Cronus as separating the Titanic order from the connective gods, symbolized by him castrating his father. In our context, the relevance of that myth is, as we see in the sequel, the usurpation of power – analogous to the tyrant-to-be. (Festugière mentions other parallels, but they concern mainly Cronus as image of division. See above n. 73).

[76] Cf. *Theologia platonica* 5,28,20–25.

[77] *In Remp.* 2,297,5–7: τάχα καὶ τῆς τῶν παίδων βρώσεως, εἰ χρὴ τολμήσαντα εἰπεῖν, ὁμοῦ τῇ μεγίστῃ τυραννίδι πρῶτον ἐκφανείσης.

is his reference to historical context – something Proclus hardly ever gives us. When stating that among humans, eating offspring occurs due to excessive passion of spirit or desire, he mentions famine as a frequent cause (πολλοί). By way of illustration, he refers to an invasion of Thessaly – which must have been the "ravaging" invasion of the Ostrogoths under Theodoric in 482, three years before Proclus' death.[78] Apparently, that invasion resulted in a famine that kindled the desires to the extent that they overruled law and decency – which Proclus does not condemn in any way.[79]

Also interesting, although somewhat gruesome, is that all the way at the end of his conclusion, Proclus even lays some blame for being eaten with the poor children: cosmic justice demands the dissolution of bodies, but when this takes the form of being eating by your father, that means that you must have violated the piety owed to parents, and hence deserved that specific form of punishment (*In Remp.* 2,298,3–5) – again, Cronus' case serves as the example: the gods are punished for rising up against their father.

Thus the conclusion adds two new elements to the discussion: a parallel from recent history, of extreme circumstances evoking extreme desire; and justification of the suffering involved as a form of punishment for the one who suffers.

The overall picture arising from Proclus' comments on the fate of the first soul to pick, is that of a (Stoicizing) narrow view of free will and cosmic justice, a strong emphasis on the importance of the character or disposition underlying our choices and on the completely descended, corporeal life of human beings, a strong relation between the eschatology of the *Timaeus* and the *Republic*, and implicit criticism of both Porphyry's broader notion of freedom and his stronger position regarding cannibalism. If you end up eating your children, or being eaten by your parents, you probably had it coming.

Bibliography

Adamson, P. (2014), 'Freedom, Providence and Fate', in: *The Routledge Handbook of Neoplatonism*, ed. P. Remes and S. Slaveva-Griffin, Abingdon, TN: Routledge, 437–52.

Annas, J. (1981), *An Introduction to Plato's Republic*, Oxford: Oxford University Press.

– (1982), 'Plato's Myths of Judgement', *Phronesis* 27: 119–43.

Arruzza, C. (2018), *A Wolf in the City: Tyranny and the Tyrant in Plato's Republic*, Oxford: Oxford University Press.

[78] *In Remp.* 2,297,26–28: πολλοὶ γοῦν καὶ διὰ λιμὸν ἥψαντο τῶν τέκνων, ὥσπερ ἐν Θετταλίᾳ μετὰ τὴν τῶν βαρβάρων ἔφοδον ἔναγχος. For the dating see Festugière 2012 ad loc. See also Marcellinus' *Chronicles*, sub a. (ed. B. Croke). Marcellinus does not mention a subsequent famine.

[79] Cf. again the position of Porphyry, *De abstinentia* 2,8.

Backman, J. (2017), 'Aristotle', in: *Agamben's Philosophical Lineage*, ed. A. Kotsko and C. Salzani, Edinburgh: Edinburgh University Press, 15–26.
Baltzly, D. (2013), 'Proclus and Theodore of Asine on Female Philosopher-Rulers', *Ancient Philosophy* 33: 403–24.
– (2017), 'The Skopos Assumption: Its Justification and Function in the Neoplatonic Commentaries on Plato', *International Journal of the Platonic Tradition* 11: 173–95.
Delcomminette, S. (2014), 'Liberté et caractère dans le mythe d'Er', in: *Fate, Providence and Moral Responsibility in Ancient, Medieval and Early Modern Thought: Studies in Honour of Carlos Steel*, ed. P. D'Hoine and G. Van Riel, Leuven: Leuven University Press, 39–57.
Destrée, P. (2014), 'Comment être responsable de son destin? Platon et le mythe d'Er', in: *Fate, Providence and Moral Responsibility in Ancient, Medieval and Early Modern Thought: Studies in Honour of Carlos Steel*, ed. P. D'Hoine and G. Van Riel, Leuven: Leuven University Press, 23–38.
D'Hoine, P. and Martijn, M., eds. (2017), *All from One: A Guide to Proclus*, Oxford: Oxford University Press.
Diehl, E., ed. (1906), *Procli Diadochi In Platonis Timaeum commentaria*, vol. III, Leipzig: Teubner.
Dillon, J. (2015), 'Proclus on the Myth of Er', *Dionysius* 33: 132–44.
Festugière, A.-J. (1963), 'Modes de composition des commentaires de Proclus', *Museum Helveticum* 20: 77–100.
– (2012), *Proclus, Commentaire sur la République*. Vol. III: *Dissertations XV–XVII (*République *X)* (Textes philosophiques), Paris: Vrin.
Finamore, J.F. and Kutash, E. (2017), 'Proclus on the Psychē: World Soul and the Individual Soul', in: *All from One: A Guide to Proclus*, ed. P. D'Hoine and M. Martijn, Oxford: Oxford University Press, 122–38.
Greenbaum, D.G. (2018), 'Porphyry of Tyre on the Daimon, Birth and the Stars', in: *Neoplatonic Demons and Angels*, ed. L. Brisson, S. O'Neill, and A. Timotin, Leiden – Boston, MA: Brill, 102–39.
Halliwell, F.S. (2007), 'The Life-and-Death Journey of the Soul: Interpreting the Myth of Er', in: *The Cambridge Companion to Plato's Republic*, ed. G.R.F. Ferrari, Cambridge: Cambridge University Press, 445–73.
Henrichs, A. (1980), 'Human Sacrifice in Greek Religion', in: *Le sacrifice dans l'Antiquité*, ed. J. Rudhardt and O. Reverdin (Entretiens Fondation Hardt 27), Vandoeuvres – Geneva: Fondation Hardt, 195–235.
Hook, B.S. (2005), 'Oedipus and Thyestes among the Philosophers: Incest and Cannibalism in Plato, Diogenes, and Zeno', *Classical Philology* 100: 17–40.
Ilievski, V. (2016), 'Lot-Casting, Divine Interference and Chance in the Myth of Er', *Apeiron* 50: 67–79.
Kroll, W. (1899–1901), *Procli Diadochi in Platonis Rem publicam commentarii*, Leipzig: Teubner.
Lerner, R. (1974), *Averroes on Plato's Republic*, translated with an introduction and notes by –, Ithaca, NY – London: Cornell University Press.
Linguiti, A. (2009), 'Physis as Heimarmene: On Some Fundamental Principles of the Neoplatonic Philosophy of Nature', in: *Physics and Philosophy of Nature in Greek Neoplatonism*, ed. R. Chiaradonna and F. Trabattoni (Philosophia antiqua 115), Leiden: Brill, 173–88.

McPherran, M.L. (2010), 'Virtue, Luck, and Choice at the End of the Republic', in: *Plato's 'Republic': A Critical Guide*, ed. M.L. McPherran, Cambridge: Cambridge University Press, 132–46.
Morgan, K. (2000), *Myth and Philosophy from the Presocratics to Plato*, Cambridge: Cambridge University Press.
Opsomer, J. (2003), 'La démiurgie des jeunes dieux selon Proclus', *Les études classiques* 71: 5–49.
– (2006), 'Was sind irrationale Seelen?', in: *Proklos: Methode, Seelenlehre, Metaphysik: Akten der Konferenz in Jena vom 18.–20. September 2003*, ed. M. Perkams and R.-M. Piccione (Philosophia antiqua 98), Leiden: Brill, 136–66.
Riggs, T. (2015), 'Authentic Selfhood in the Philosophy of Proclus: Rational Soul and Its Significance for the Individual', *International Journal of the Platonic Tradition* 9: 177–204.
Russi, C. (2009), 'Causality and Sensible Objects: A Comparison between Plotinus and Proclus', in: *Physics and Philosophy of Nature in Greek Neoplatonism*, ed. R. Chiaradonna and F. Trabattoni (Philosophia antiqua 115), Leiden: Brill, 145–71.
Santas, G. (2010), *Understanding Plato's Republic*, Oxford: Wiley-Blackwell.
Schultz, J. (forthcoming), *Women and the Female in Neoplatonism*, Leiden: Brill.
Sheppard, A. (1980), *Studies on the 5th and 6th Essays of Proclus' Commentary on the Republic*, Göttingen: Vandenhoeck & Ruprecht.
– (2017), 'Literary Theory and Aesthetics', in: *All From One: A Guide to Proclus*, ed. P. D'Hoine and M. Martijn, Oxford: Oxford University Press, 276–89.
Steel, C. (2014), 'Human or Divine Freedom: Proclus on What Is Up to Us', in: *What Is Up to Us? Studies on Agency and Responsibility in Ancient Philosophy*, ed. P. Destrée, R. Salles, and M. Zingano, Sankt Augustin: Academia Verlag, 311–28.
– (2017), 'Providence and Evil', in: *All From One: A Guide to Proclus*, ed. P. D'Hoine and M. Martijn, Oxford: Oxford University Press, 240–57.
Tarrant, H. (2017), *Proclus, Commentary on Plato's* Timaeus, vol. VI, Cambridge: Cambridge University Press, 2017.
Van den Berg, R.M. (2017), 'Proclus and Damascius on φιλοτιμία: The Neoplatonic Psychology of a Political Emotion', *Philosophie antique* 17: 149–65.
Van Riel, G. (2009), 'Proclus on Matter and Physical Necessity', in: *Physics and Philosophy of Nature in Greek Neoplatonism*, ed. R. Chiaradonna and F. Trabattoni (Philosophia antiqua 115), Leiden: Brill, 231–57.
Versnel, H.S. (1990), *Inconsistencies in Greek and Roman Religion*. Vol. II: *Transition and Reversal in Myth and Ritual* (Studies in Greek and Roman Religion 6/2), Leiden: Brill.
Wilberding, J. (2011), *Porphyry: To Gaurus on How Embryos Are Ensouled and on What Is in Our Power*, translated by – (Ancient Commentators on Aristotle), London: Bristol Classical Press.
– (2013), 'The Myth of Er and the Problem of Constitutive Luck', in: *Ancient Approaches to Plato's 'Republic'*, ed. A. Sheppard (Bulletin of the Institute of Classical Studies Supplements 117), London: Institute of Classical Studies, 87–105.
– (2017), *Forms, Souls, and Embryos*, London: Routledge.

Éternité ou génération?

La controverse entre Simplicius et Jean Philopon sur l'origine du monde

Marc-Antoine Gavray

I. Simplicius *versus* Philopon

La controverse qui opposa Simplicius à Jean Philopon fut certainement l'une des plus vives de l'Antiquité tardive[1]. Prenant pour fond la cosmologie aristotélicienne, elle s'inscrit dans le cadre plus large de l'affrontement entre le christianisme et sa doctrine créationniste d'un côté, l'hellénisme et son système émanatiste de l'autre. Sa caractéristique majeure tient sans doute à son déséquilibre, puisqu'elle opère à sens unique et consiste en la réponse de Simplicius aux traités polémiques de Philopon, l'un contre Proclus, l'autre contre Aristote – ce dernier ne subsistant plus que par fragments dont la plupart proviennent de Simplicius[2]. Philopon de son côté ne paraît pas avoir eu connaissance des objections de son adversaire et, bien que les deux hommes aient été disciples d'Ammonius à Alexandrie[3], ils ne s'y seraient jamais rencontrés.

Or, aussi partielle qu'elle soit, la controverse ne s'en trouve pas moins au cœur de l'œuvre de Simplicius[4], qui entame son dialogue avec le *Contre Aristote* de Philopon dès le début de son commentaire au *De Cælo*, le prolonge dans son

[1] La vie et l'œuvre de ces deux auteurs actifs dans le deuxième quart du VIe siècle PCN ont fait – et font encore – l'objet de discussions. Pour un aperçu des positions en présence, je renvoie, pour Philopon, à Évrard 1953; Verrycken 1990; Golitsis 2008; Sorabji 2016; et, pour Simplicius, à Hadot 2014.

[2] Ces fragments ont été rassemblés dans Wildberg 1987a (abrégé en W). Ce dernier estime que Simplicius se juge tellement supérieur à son adversaire qu'il donne de ses thèses un compte rendu fidèle (1987a, 30). Mais les arguments de Philopon peuvent être nuancés grâce aux parallèles conservés *in extenso* dans le *Contra Proclum*.

[3] Philopon éditera plusieurs cours d'Ammonius sous la forme de commentaires lemmatiques sur Aristote («avec des annotations personnelles», comme le notent les manuscrits; Golitsis 2019), tandis que Simplicius le désigne comme «notre maître», ὁ ἡμέτερος καθηγεμών (*In De c.* 271,19; 462,20; *in Ph.* 59,23; 183,18; 192,14). En *in Ph.* 1363,8–9, il signale, par la formule Ἀμμωνίῳ τῷ ἐμῷ καθηγεμόνι, que ce dernier avait écrit un traité prouvant que, pour Aristote, dieu était également la cause efficiente de l'univers: souligner qu'il s'agit de *son maître* à lui est peut-être une manière de refuser qu'il ait pu être en même temps celui de Philopon.

[4] Selon l'hypothèse formulée par Golitsis 2016.

commentaire à *Physique* 8 et le clôture en quelque sorte dans ses considérations préalables aux *Catégories* sur l'attitude du bon exégète d'Aristote[5]. Ce caractère central justifie assurément la virulence du propos. Simplicius adopte vis-à-vis de Philopon, tout comme ce dernier vis-à-vis de Proclus, un ton ironique, si ce n'est insultant[6]: il critique sa prolixité, sa recherche de réputation, ses propos destinés à séduire une foule imbécile qui aime tout ce qui est étranger – les Chrétiens. Sur le fond, il lui reproche de

- vouloir démontrer que le monde est périssable (et engendré)
- dévaluer le statut du dieu créateur et de le réduire au domaine du périssable
- dévaluer le ciel lui-même en lui refusant le statut divin
- renverser le schéma néoplatonicien de la procession en décrétant le supérieur (le ciel) en vue de l'inférieur (les hommes)

De façon générale, la polémique tourne autour du statut du ciel et de son créateur, la question étant de savoir si le monde est éternel ou engendré/corruptible. Je n'en suivrai pas ici tous les aspects, car certains ont déjà fait l'objet d'études approfondies, en particulier la discussion sur la nature du ciel qui occupe les cinq premiers livres du *Contre Aristote*[7]. Je me pencherai davantage sur le livre 6 – le livre 7 ayant totalement disparu et le livre 8 se réduisant désormais à un seul fragment qui en résume les deux premiers chapitres[8] –, ainsi que sur un autre court traité, dont Simplicius ne donne pas le titre mais qu'il discute vers la fin de son commentaire à *Physique* 8[9]: autant de passages relatifs à la production du monde et, dans une moindre mesure, à son éventuelle destruction. Et c'est à ce niveau cosmologique que la question protologique intervient dans le débat.

Les deux auteurs s'inscrivent dans un même horizon platonicien et partagent de nombreuses thèses. Ils estiment que tout ce qui a un début a nécessairement une fin et, par conséquent, que tout ce qui est généré est nécessairement destructible. Ils s'accordent pour reconnaître la dépendance *immédiate* du monde à l'égard d'une cause première, que tous deux identifient au démiurge du *Timée:* entre le dieu et sa création, il n'y a aucun intermédiaire, ce qui confère à cette dernière un statut particulier. Mais l'accord s'arrête là. Commandés par des raisons sans doute plus religieuses que philosophiques[10], leurs postulats initiaux les conduisent à s'opposer sur l'action du dieu créateur et, par voie de conséquence,

---

[5] *In Cat.* 7,23–32, où Simplicius dénonce les exégètes refusant d'examiner la portée réelle des propos d'Aristote.

[6] Pour une étude des aspects formels de la polémique, Hoffmann 1987. Pour un aperçu du ton, Philopon, *CA* Prologue W (= Simplicius, *In De c.* 25,22–6,7).

[7] Voir Hoffmann 1987, 210–21; Wildberg 1988. Cf. Évrard 1961 (2020).

[8] Sur l'état du texte, Wildberg 1987b.

[9] Les deux hypothèses sont formulées dans Wildberg 1991, 100.

[10] L'idée que leur opposition est religieuse avant d'être philosophique est soutenue par Golitsis 2016, 419–20.

à formuler des définitions distinctes des concepts mobilisés – génération (γενητός), capacité productive (δύναμις) et temporalité. Telles sont les portes d'entrée que j'emprunterai dans cette controverse sur l'origine et la fin du monde pour reconstituer les positions respectives de nos deux auteurs et mesurer la portée des objections qu'ils s'adressent. À bien des égards, toute leur opposition est contenue dans l'extrait suivant de Simplicius, dont on appréciera la subtilité du lexique et dont je tenterai un commentaire tout au long de cet article:

T1 Si seulement il avait su ce que cela signifie d'être créé immédiatement par le dieu démiurge (τὸ ἀμέσως ὑπὸ τοῦ δημιουργοῦ θεοῦ γίνεσθαι), à mon avis il ne serait pas tombé dans ces blasphèmes à propos du ciel. Nous aussi, en effet, nous soutenons que le démiurge n'a fourni le sujet (τὸ ὑποκείμενον τῷ δημιουργῷ παρασκευασθῆναι) ni au hasard ni par quelque autre cause. Mais nous affirmons que le dieu démiurge a produit directement (ἀμέσως παραγαγεῖν) le sujet du ciel, si on peut dire, en même temps que sa forme (ἅμα τῷ εἴδει). Et cela ne s'est pas produit au moyen de la génération ni au sens où ce qui n'est pas d'abord survient ensuite, mais à cause de la bonté du dieu (διὰ τὴν ἀγαθότητα τοῦ θεοῦ): il a été produit par celui-ci, du fait même qu'il est dieu, et non pas du fait qu'il décide et fait tantôt ceci tantôt cela (οὐ τῷ ἄλλοτε ἀλλοῖα προαιρεῖσθαι καὶ ἐνεργεῖν). Il dépend toujours de la bonté du dieu et de la permanence de son être éternel (τῆς ἀγαθότητος αὐτοῦ καὶ τῆς τοῦ εἶναι διαιωνίου διαμονῆς), comme ces gens ont l'habitude de le dire du Fils (τὸν Υἱόν)[11].

II. Production du monde et démiurgie

La raison que ces philosophes ont d'admettre la dépendance immédiate du monde vis-à-vis du démiurge est d'attribuer un mode particulier à cette production et, partant, de la distinguer des productions de la nature. Chacun investit cependant cette différence d'une façon propre.

Commençons par Philopon. À ses yeux, la différence entre production naturelle et production divine correspond à celle entre production immanente et production transcendante. Parce que la nature a sa réalité dans un sujet (ἐν ὑποκειμένῳ) et n'est rien d'autre que ce sujet, c'est dans ce dernier – en définitive en elle-même – qu'elle puise la matière nécessaire à sa production. Dans ces conditions, elle produit une forme qu'elle introduit dans la matière qui existe déjà et qui lui est en quelque sorte immanente. Toutefois, cette nécessité ne s'impose pas à dieu[12]. La transcendance divine signifie en effet que dieu ne dépend nullement d'un sujet extérieur pour créer, mais qu'il produit ce dernier en même temps que la forme. Dans le cas contraire, il ne différerait en rien de la nature. C'est donc la transcendance radicale de dieu qui rend possible la création *ex nihilo:* parce qu'il n'est dans aucun sujet et ne dépend donc d'aucun sujet pour agir ou exister, dieu a le pouvoir de créer ce dernier, à partir duquel il peut en-

[11] Simplicius, *In De c.* 137,19–28.

[12] Philopon, *CA* fr. 115 W (= Simplicius, *In Ph.* 1141,11–24); Simplicius, *In Ph.* 1145,7–11.

suite façonner le monde[13]. Sa supériorité résulte de ce qu'il crée la matière première à partir du non-être, ce qui contredit ouvertement l'axiome aristotélicien selon lequel «rien ne se produit absolument à partir du non-être»[14], c'est-à-dire du non-être en tant que non-être.

Philopon propose aussi un raisonnement *a fortiori* fondé sur une analogie entre l'art, la nature et dieu[15]. Quand un menuisier réunit des planches de bois pour former une porte, il assemble des substances existantes pour produire une figure (σχῆμα). Il ne crée rien qui n'existait déjà. Quand la nature cette fois engendre des individus, elle se sert des éléments pour produire des substances et des formes individuelles (des os, du sang, des facultés vitales). Elle utilise donc une matière existante pour produire une substance ou une forme individuelle qui n'existait pas encore[16]. Or, si dieu se trouve à l'égard de la nature dans un rapport de supériorité analogue à celui de la nature sur l'art, il ne se contente pas de produire les formes à partir d'une matière préexistante. Il produit surtout cette matière même, le sujet de ce qu'il crée et dont la nature se sert à son tour pour produire. La supériorité divine en fait de production résulte de la capacité de dieu à faire exister ce que la nature utilise comme sujet pour sa propre production.

Simplicius rejette la solution de Philopon, car elle revient selon lui à restreindre l'intervention de dieu à la création des éléments comme tels et à le dépouiller de toute responsabilité dans la genèse des corps périssables: dans ces termes, l'intervention divine s'arrête avec la matière, à la suite de quoi la nature prend le relais pour la transformation réciproque des éléments[17]. Pour sa part, il admet l'existence d'une différence entre production divine et production naturelle, qu'il situe au niveau de la temporalité, dans la différence entre éternité et génération[18]. Toute production naturelle implique une chronologie, l'antériorité et la préexistence d'une chose à l'égard d'une autre. Ce qu'il convient d'appeler la génération au sens propre est lié au temps, dès lors que non seulement le père précède le fils – tant sur le plan causal que temporel –, mais ce qui est produit existe nécessairement dans le temps[19]. À l'inverse, ce que dieu produit directement est nécessairement éternel et ne vient pas à proprement parler à l'être (γίνεται), comme il le rappelle dans son commentaire à *Physique* 8. Sans doute est-ce la raison pour laquelle, dans l'extrait précédent du commentaire au traité *Du Ciel* (**T1**), Simplicius évite avec soin le registre de la génération, sauf pour l'évacuer et, en ce sens, l'attribuer à son adversaire – parlant de *mise en place*

---

13 Je reviendrai plus loin sur les différences temporelles entre ces deux processus productifs.

14 Aristote, *Ph.* 1,8,91b13–14: γίγνεσθαι μηθὲν ἁπλῶς ἐκ μὴ ὄντος.

15 Philopon, *CP* 9,9,340,25–1,23.

16 Cf. Philopon, *CA* fr. 131 W (= Simplicius, *In Ph.* 1177,22–24).

17 Simplicius, *In Ph.* 1152,2–5.

18 Simplicius, *In Ph.* 1150,34–1151,6.

19 Cf. Simplicius, *In Ph.* 1144,10–12.

(παρασκευασθῆναι) et de *mise au jour* (παραγαγεῖν) pour maintenir à distance la production *ex nihilo*. La production divine n'est ni création ni génération d'une réalité nouvelle. Elle est l'arrangement ou la mise en mouvement continue d'un sujet toujours existant.

D'après Simplicius, la production divine concerne donc un domaine d'objets qui partagent par proximité avec leur producteur un fragment de son immutabilité et de son éternité. Ce faisant, il entend restaurer la responsabilité de dieu sur l'ensemble du monde. Celui-ci produit certes les corps célestes, qui possèdent l'éternité à titre individuel (κατ' ἀριθμόν), mais également les caractères communs des êtres sublunaires, qui possèdent une éternité spécifique (κατ' εἶδος)[20]. Il ne s'agit pas d'objecter que dieu, plutôt que de créer la matière comme le pense Philopon, crée les formes intelligibles. Simplicius parle du démiurge, d'un dieu inférieur à ce niveau de la production dans l'ordre de la procession. Il n'entend pas non plus lui attribuer la production des formes matérielles, individuelles, qui restent la prérogative de la nature. Pour Simplicius, le démiurge produit les caractères communs (κοινότητες), le fond intimement lié à la matière qui assure la participation des formes individuelles aux intelligibles et réalise ainsi la jonction formelle entre les individus. Par conséquent, quand Simplicius affirme que «le dieu démiurge a produit directement le sujet du ciel [...] en même temps que sa forme», c'est au sens où il a introduit un ordre formel dans le sujet du monde, qui s'avère lui être coextensif et coéternel.

En bref, Philopon associe la dépendance directe à l'égard de dieu à une question ontologique: dieu crée la matière, c'est-à-dire la condition sans laquelle la nature et ses produits ne peuvent exister. Il reçoit ainsi la responsabilité de l'ensemble de la création en ce qu'il se tient derrière la subsistance de chaque individu auquel la nature donne tour à tour naissance. Simplicius en revanche associe la fonction démiurgique à l'introduction de l'éternité dans le monde. De ce point de vue, dieu confère sa permanence au monde, en garantissant la subsistance formelle des espèces et des êtres éternels. Son action se situe sur ce point moins du côté de la cause matérielle que des causes formelle et motrice. L'opposition entre les deux adversaires va ainsi se creuser sur deux fronts: celui de l'origine de l'être et celui de la relation entre le moteur et le mobile, prolongeant cette divergence de vue entre différence radicale et proximité du dieu.

1. Du non-être à l'être...

D'après Philopon, la preuve aristotélicienne de l'éternité du mouvement repose sur l'axiome – repris par les néoplatoniciens[21] – selon lequel «rien ne naît de rien, mais tout naît de quelque chose d'antérieur»[22]. Sa stratégie pour réfuter la thèse

---

20 Simplicius, *In Ph.* 1152,5–10.

21 Comme le rappelle Philopon, *CP* 9,17,380,10–17.

22 Philopon, *CA* fr. 114 W (= Simplicius, *In Ph.* 1140,11–17); Simplicius, *In Ph.* 1143,20–22.

de l'éternité du monde consiste donc à établir la proposition inverse, notamment grâce à sa hiérarchisation des modes de production.

Philopon estime que toute production se fait à partir du non-être et toute destruction se résout en non-être. Il se concentre en effet sur ce qui, dans la génération du composé hylémorphique, correspond à une véritable génération, c'est-à-dire à l'apparition d'une nouveauté. Or dans ce cas, la matière ne vient pas à l'être, étant donné qu'elle supporte le changement. La génération de la substance composée se fait seulement du point de vue de la forme (κατὰ τὸ εἶδος) et est génération de la forme: seule celle-ci donne lieu à une génération au sens propre, à partir du non-être, vu que la forme individuelle n'existe pas auparavant – tout comme sa destruction est disparition dans le non-être[23]. La démonstration ressemble à une pétition de principe, du fait d'évacuer ce qui subsiste à travers le changement (le sujet, la matière) pour se concentrer sur la forme qui survient (et qui, en termes aristotéliciens, n'est qu'un non-être par accident). Elle déplace en réalité le regard porté sur la génération et la destruction, en insistant sur ce qui naît et disparaît – la forme individuelle, qui n'est pas là avant la génération et ne subsiste pas après la destruction. Sous cet angle, l'art et la nature eux-mêmes produisent à partir du non-être, dès lors qu'ils créent une figure ou une forme nouvelle[24]. Ce renversement suppose toutefois de ne pas prendre les productions techniques et naturelles pour modèles, caractérisées par une sortie hors de l'être, mais de partir de la forme suprême de production – la production divine.

Philopon applique le même raisonnement à la matière. Le principe d'inhérence lui interdit de résulter d'autre chose: en tant que sujet du changement *dans* lequel arrive la forme, elle n'est pas elle-même *dans* un sujet et n'a besoin d'aucun autre sujet pour exister[25]. Si elle doit être engendrée, ce ne sera pas à partir d'un être, autre sujet ou autre matière, mais d'un non-être[26]. Aussi est-ce la subsistance de la matière à travers la génération, en vertu de laquelle Aristote concluait que l'être naît de l'être, qui mène Philopon à renverser son axiome. Non seulement la forme individuelle est nouvelle et ne naît de rien, mais son sujet ne provient pas d'un autre. Il ne peut provenir que de rien, car rien d'autre ne peut le supporter. Ce constat valable pour la matière particulière recevant la forme particulière, constat qui évite la régression à l'infini, Philopon l'étend par analogie à la matière comme telle (ἁπλῶς), qui entretient un rapport semblable avec la forme comme telle (ἁπλῶς)[27]. Quand dieu crée la matière, il le fait à partir de

[23] Philopon, *CA* fr. 116 W (= Simplicius, *In Ph.* 1142,4–14); *CP* 9,17,378,25–379,25.

[24] Simplicius, *In Ph.* 1145,7–13.

[25] Philopon, *CP* 11,10,449,13–450,25. Philopon retient du *Timée* que le réceptacle conserve sa propre nature, la tridimensionnalité qui lui permet d'être le réceptacle de toutes les formes (*CP* 9,11,350,9–351,1; 11,10,448,3–14). Sur sa théorie de la matière, de Haas 1997, 251–95 et Mueller-Jourdan 2011, 71–163.

[26] Philopon, *CP* 11,12,458,19–26.

[27] Philopon, *CP* 11,10,455,15–25.

rien. C'est donc la rencontre entre un argument axiologique (la supériorité de dieu sur la nature) et une déduction logique (rien ne naît de quelque chose) qui, chez Philopon, sert à asseoir l'idée de la création divine du monde *ex nihilo*.

De tels arguments exaspèrent Simplicius, qui en dénonce la longueur et l'inconséquence[28]. Sa réaction traduit surtout une incompréhension si radicale qu'elle empêche toute discussion. Le premier problème, d'ordre conceptuel, résulte de la polysémie du terme génération. Philopon l'interprète clairement sur le plan ontologique de la création d'un être nouveau. Elle se révèle exclusive de l'éternité, puisqu'elle s'applique à des réalités qui ont nécessairement un début – et une fin en ce qui concerne la destruction. Simplicius estime au contraire que le mot renvoie aux réalités associées par essence au temps, au sens où elles s'étendent sur une partie de celui-ci[29]. Sous cet angle, la génération ne s'avère pas absolument incompatible avec l'éternité, car elle vaut également pour ce qui s'étend sur la totalité du temps, en tant qu'il reçoit son être dans le temps. Si nos auteurs s'accordent pour associer génération et temporalité, le premier insiste sur la dimension ontologique de la génération, le second sur sa nature temporelle.

Cette divergence mène au second problème. Dans les faits, la contradiction entre nos auteurs résulte d'une incapacité à se placer dans la perspective de l'adversaire et à adopter pour un temps son horizon conceptuel: aucune charité herméneutique chez ces philosophes davantage enclins au sarcasme. Ainsi, pour Philopon, il suffit de prouver que tout ne naît pas d'un être, au sens où il n'y a pas toujours déjà de sujet, pour invalider la démonstration aristotélicienne de l'éternité du monde – sans constater que cette dernière vise avant tout à établir l'éternité du mouvement et à en déduire l'éternité de ce qui est, comme le note Simplicius dans le prologue au livre 8[30]. Simplicius reproche pour sa part à Philopon de vouloir démontrer que ce qui est éternel provient du non-être, tant il juge absurde d'interroger l'origine temporelle de ce qui existe toujours[31]: dès lors que la génération suppose une privation de soi que résorbe la venue à l'être, il trouve aberrant d'appliquer ce concept à une réalité dont la propriété est justement de ne jamais faire défaut. La critique repose toutefois sur un détournement du projet initial de Philopon. Ce dernier admet en effet la nécessité qu'une matière préexiste à chaque production de la nature, assertion dont Simplicius déduit abusivement qu'il admet l'éternité de la matière, alors qu'il examine ensuite, en toute absurdité, son origine. Ce faisant, Simplicius néglige la suite de l'argument: si Philopon reconnaît la préexistence de la matière dans la produc-

[28] Simplicius, *In Ph.* 1142,28–1143,2. Le reproche, fréquent chez Simplicius, fait écho au passage cité plus haut.

[29] Simplicius, *In Ph.* 1144,10–12; 1145,22–24.

[30] Simplicius, *In Ph.* 1117,6–12.

[31] Simplicius, *In Ph.* 1144,16–21. Comme le note Michael Chase (Bodnár, Chase, et Share 2012, n. 93), quelques lignes plus loin (*In Ph.* 1144,30–31), Simplicius atteste de sa connaissance que Philopon développe une thèse monophysite loin de faire l'unanimité parmi les Chrétiens (je remercie Simon Fortier d'avoir attiré mon attention sur ce point).

tion naturelle, il montre que la matière trouve son origine, tout comme les formes, dans la création divine dotée de la capacité à produire à partir du non-être. Il n'y a donc pas là deux façons de concevoir l'éternité, mais d'un côté un refus d'associer éternité et génération, de l'autre une tentative pour les réconcilier sur le plan de la causalité – Simplicius ajoutant par précaution que, même si l'argument de Philopon était valide et si dieu créait les êtres éternels à partir du non-être, ce serait sur un mode différent des êtres naturels: il en serait la cause, tout en restant hors du temps[32].

2. …et retour?

La situation change quelque peu autour de la destruction, à propos de laquelle Simplicius croit déceler une contradiction chez son adversaire. La démonstration de Philopon concluait, par analogie avec la génération, au passage de l'être au non-être dans la destruction.

T2 Car, même si la nature, dit-il, ne produit pas la matière première, dieu le fait mais pas à partir de la matière, de sorte qu'il la détruit aussi quand il le veut en non-être, d'où elle est issue; de la même façon que la forme, dit-il, ne s'altère pas en une autre forme, mais retourne au non-être absolu d'où elle est également issue[33].

Simplicius s'étonne que Philopon soutienne ensuite que la destruction du monde ne se résolve pas dans le non-être:

T3 Après ces propos, il déclare montrer que la transformation du monde ne mène pas à sa non-existence totale (εἰς ἀνυπαρξίαν παντελῆ), mais à quelque chose de supérieur et plus divin. Il est étonnant que, d'un côté, il estime que la destruction soit un changement du monde en un être plus divin (τοῦ κόσμου μεταβολὴν εἰς ὄν τι καὶ θειότερον) et, de l'autre, qu'il nie que le monde ait une génération à partir de l'être. Il démontre que ce monde change en un monde plus divin – ce à quoi il s'emploie dans les livres suivants –, sans remarquer que ce n'est pas une destruction du monde, mais un achèvement (τελείωσις)[34].

La contradiction semble manifeste: Philopon affirme à la fois que le monde se transforme en un être supérieur et que la destruction est retour au non-être. Il paraît même difficile d'accuser Simplicius de lui prêter des propos étrangers, étant donné qu'une source extérieure corrobore son compte rendu – je cite la traduction de l'arabe que Chr. Wildberg donne pour les titres des deux premiers chapitres du livre 8 du *Contre Aristote*, malheureusement les seuls vestiges de la suite de son traité polémique, où Philopon développait ce point:

T4 Our argument affirms that that which is subject to resolution into not-being is not wicked on its own and by itself, and that that into which the world will be resolved is not not-being.

---

[32] Simplicius, *In Ph.* 1145,25–7. Je reviens sur cette question de la création atemporelle.
[33] Philopon, *CA* fr. 131 W (= Simplicius, *In Ph.* 1177,22–26): cf. *CA*, fr. 116 W.
[34] Philopon, *CA* fr. 132 W (= Simplicius, *In Ph.* 1177,38–1178,5).

However, the world will not be resolved into not-being, because the words of God are not resolved into not-being either, and we clearly speak of new heavens and a new earth[35].

La thèse de la parousie mènerait Philopon dans l'impasse. L'objection manque néanmoins sa cible, tant la contradiction s'avère superficielle: Philopon ne soutient pas des propos opposés en même temps et sous le même rapport. D'un côté, il développe une théorie physique selon laquelle la destruction signifie le passage dans le non-être, autrement dit la résorption de la matière et de la forme dans le néant. De l'autre, il adopte un discours théologique selon lequel la fin du monde culmine dans la création d'un ordre meilleur. Dans ce contexte, il n'est plus question de la matière créée par dieu, mais de la situation d'un être particulier, le monde dans lequel nous vivons, qui est amené à subir une transformation aussi radicale qu'exceptionnelle. Au lieu d'aboutir à un néant comparable à celui qui a précédé sa création, comme c'est le cas du reste des êtres générés et corruptibles, le monde serait sublimé à la suite de sa destruction, du fait de la bonté divine[36].

Or, à y regarder de plus près, la subtilité n'échappe pas à Simplicius. Dans un univers fini, la matière créée par dieu correspond au sujet du monde. La destruction de l'une implique donc celle de l'autre, et la contradiction plane sur le système de Philopon. En filigrane, s'esquisse la distinction entre deux conceptions des rapports entre physique et théologie. En définitive, ce que Simplicius dénonce chez son adversaire, c'est la rupture d'un principe physique pour un motif théologique. Cela revient selon lui à admettre que la logique des principes s'impose du bas vers le haut, de la matière et du monde vers dieu, puisque, pour préserver sa création, périssable par essence, dieu est contraint de contrevenir aux lois physiques qu'il a édictées: il doit briser leur régularité pour produire une exception, en raison d'un défaut de providence en quelque sorte. Simplicius ne peut s'accommoder de la rupture de l'ordre qu'impose le dogme chrétien assumé par Philopon. Au contraire, une physique théologique comme la fait Aristote doit dégager les principes divins, éternels et immuables, à l'œuvre derrière les mécanismes de la nature d'où ils tirent leur régularité.

La position de Philopon n'en reste pas moins cohérente dans l'économie de son œuvre. En un sens, la supériorité de dieu se manifeste à nouveau dans sa capacité à échapper au principe qui régit la nature: il peut sublimer le monde, plutôt que de l'abandonner aux lois naturelles qui le régissent et le condamnent à la destruction. Dans cette perspective, la fin du monde, comme du reste son début, est un lieu qui échappe à la physique pour ressortir à la théologie, en vertu d'une coupure radicale entre les règles qui gouvernent l'une et celles qui gouvernent l'autre. La supériorité de dieu sur la nature, et de la théologie sur la

---

[35] Philopon, *CA* fr. 134 W (= Brit. Mus. ms. add. 17 214, fol. 72vb,36–73ra,19).

[36] Cf. *CP* 6,4–6: en tant qu'il sait comment créer le monde, dieu sait aussi comment le détruire: délier le monde n'est pas un mal pour dieu, mais le résultat de sa bonté.

physique, rompt avec l'idée de réaliser une physique théologique, au profit d'une physique soumise à la théologie.

3. Moteur et mobile

La question de la génération et de la destruction s'inscrit dans le cadre plus large de la théorie du mouvement. L'examen de la démonstration aristotélicienne sur l'éternité du mouvement en *Physique* 8 conduit ainsi nos auteurs à s'interroger sur le statut du mobile, sur l'origine et sur la fin du mouvement. Partant tous deux de la définition d'Aristote, ils adoptent des angles très différents. Commençons par Philopon, dont Simplicius divise la démonstration en quatre temps:

1) Il relève une contradiction entre la possibilité du mouvement éternel et une conséquence qu'Aristote tire de la définition du mouvement – le mobile préexiste dans le temps au mouvement[37]. Il en déduit que soit la définition du mouvement ne s'applique pas au mouvement éternel, ce qui contrevient au principe d'universalité de la définition; soit le mouvement éternel ne l'est pas vraiment, si quelque chose lui préexiste dans le temps; soit, enfin, la définition du mouvement n'implique pas la préexistence du mobile. Au vu de l'absurdité des deux premières options, Philopon retient la dernière.

2) Il montre ensuite la simultanéité du mouvement et du mobile. Le mobile n'est pas ce qui a le mouvement en puissance et qui lui préexiste (le bois capable de brûler), mais ce qui est mû au moment où il l'est en tant qu'il peut se mouvoir (le feu qui se meut vers le haut). En ce sens, le mouvement vers le haut n'est pas l'actualisation du bois, mais celle du feu, qui est contemporaine du feu, puisqu'il n'appartient pas à la nature du bois de se mouvoir vers le haut[38].

3) Par extension, Philopon note qu'en vertu de la transformation réciproque des éléments, en cas de rejet de l'hypothèse précédente, tous les mouvements devraient leur appartenir par nature – ce qui est absurde, puisque cela inclut des mouvements contraires[39].

4) Pour cette raison, Philopon constate que le mouvement est l'actualisation des capacités immédiates: la croissance est l'actualisation de la chair et non de la nourriture, s'élever est le mouvement du feu et non du bois[40]. Par conséquent, s'agissant du mouvement non éternel, le mobile potentiel ne préexiste pas au mouvement – à moins d'être empêché dans l'actualisation de son mouvement.

Étant donné qu'elle ne garantit pas toujours la préexistence du mobile, Philopon conclut que la définition aristotélicienne du mouvement ne prouve en rien son éternité[41]. En filigrane de ce raisonnement, transparaît une théorie du mou-

[37] Philopon, *CA* fr. 108 W (= Simplicius, *In Ph.* 1129,28–1131,7).
[38] Philopon, *CA* fr. 109 W (= Simplicius, *In Ph.* 1133,16–1134,29).
[39] Philopon, *CA* fr. 110 W (= Simplicius, *In Ph.* 1134,29–33).
[40] Philopon, *CA* fr. 111 W (= Simplicius, *In Ph.* 1134,33–1135,15).
[41] Philopon, *CA* fr. 112–13 W (= Simplicius, *In Ph.* 1135,28–32 et 1140,4–8).

vement qui, sans rejeter la définition d'Aristote, en modifie la signification. Loin de rejeter catégoriquement l'antériorité du mobile, Philopon change plutôt la perspective et inverse en quelque sorte le paradigme. Comme en attestent ses exemples, et dans la suite de nos constats précédents, il ne prend pas pour modèle d'analyse le mouvement contraint ou non naturel, celui de la pierre ou du char qu'il faut pousser pour les faire avancer, voire du bois qu'il faut brûler pour qu'il s'élève. Il se concentre sur les premiers mouvements naturels, ceux des éléments qui sont mus dès leur apparition. Ce faisant, il établit la simultanéité naturelle entre mouvement et mobile, évacuant du même coup la nécessité de poser une autre forme d'antériorité que celle du moteur. Par ce changement de modèle, c'est-à-dire en partant des éléments naturels, Philopon évite le risque d'une régression à l'infini en posant clairement un début au mouvement. Ce faisant, il conforme la théorie aristotélicienne du mouvement à la possibilité d'une création *ex nihilo*.

S'il s'accorde avec lui sur deux points – la portée universelle de la définition et la coexistence nécessaire du mouvement et du potentiel –, Simplicius objecte à son adversaire un manque de clarté et de distinction conceptuelle. Il introduit donc deux nuances, qui révèlent les limites de leur accord apparent[42]. S'agissant de la coexistence du mouvement et du potentiel, Simplicius reconnaît qu'elle résulte de la définition du mouvement: celui-ci est une activité incomplète tout au long de laquelle le mobile conserve sa capacité à être mû. Dans ce cas, la coexistence renvoie moins à la contemporanéité qu'à la préservation de la mobilité du mobile à travers le processus d'actualisation. Elle ne s'avère dès lors en rien exclusive de la préexistence ni de la subsistance temporelle du mobile. Seconde nuance, Simplicius corrige Philopon sur la nature du mouvement éternel: le mouvement éternel ne désigne pas un processus unique et continu qui se poursuit de toute éternité, mais plutôt une succession ininterrompue de mouvements qui diffèrent selon le temps et s'enchaînent ἐπ' ἄπειρον[43]. En d'autres termes, il n'y a pas toujours *un* mouvement; il y a toujours *du* mouvement – ce qui préserve l'universalité de la définition et de sa conséquence, étant donné que la capacité à être mû préexiste toujours au mouvement.

D'après Simplicius, l'erreur de Philopon provient d'un manque de distinction sur l'expression τὸ δυνάμενον κινεῖσθαι, qu'il s'emploie à clarifier[44]. Dans un premier sens, elle désigne «ce qui possède la capacité parfaite projective de l'acte, que l'acte accompagne (τὸ τὴν τελείαν ἔχον δύναμιν τὴν προβλητικὴν τῆς ἐνεργείας, ᾗ σύνεστιν ἡ ἐνέργεια)», ce dont l'actualisation n'épuise jamais la puissance, car elle la suit et l'accompagne tout au long du mouvement. En exemple, Simplicius cite la capacité naturelle de l'eau au mouvement descendant et du feu au mouve-

[42] Simplicius, *In Ph.* 1131,9–19.
[43] Simplicius, *In Ph.* 1131,29–1132,3 et 1135,15–21. La question de l'infinité se posera plus loin à propos du temps.
[44] Simplicius, *In Ph.* 1136,3–10.

ment ascendant. C'est ce sens que Philopon associe manifestement à la définition du mouvement. Quant au second, il qualifie «le mobile en puissance, qui n'a pas encore la capacité parfaite porteuse de l'acte, mais qui y tend par nature (τὸ δυνάμει κινητόν, ὃ οὔπω μὲν τὴν τελείαν ἔχει δύναμιν τὴν οἰστικὴν τῆς ἐνεργείας, πέφυκε δὲ ἴσχειν)», ce qui pourra se mouvoir sans être encore en mesure de le faire. D'après Simplicius, c'est en ce sens qu'il faut entendre la préexistence du mobile par rapport au mouvement. Aussi reproche-t-il à Philopon de confondre entre puissance parfaite et puissance imparfaite, la première passant à l'acte au moment seulement où la seconde se transforme[45].

L'objection s'avère pertinente, du moins dans une perspective néoplatonicienne qui prend le mouvement non naturel comme paradigme. Entre les théories de Simplicius et de Philopon, la différence réside au fond dans la limite fixée à la capacité d'un corps à se mouvoir. Soit elle est restreinte au mouvement que le corps peut subir en tant qu'il est ce qu'il est (le feu, en tant que feu, qui s'élève) – ce que Philopon nomme la capacité immédiate. Le mouvement suivant n'est plus celui du corps comme tel, mais le mouvement qui survient après une transformation (ou génération) potentielle. Cette théorie repose sur une conception stricte de la potentialité à se mouvoir. Soit cette limite inclut le mouvement issu de la transformation suivante du corps (le bois susceptible de s'élever une fois qu'il brûlera), en considérant que la génération est un mouvement comme les autres[46]. Elle s'articule alors à une échelle de la perfection hiérarchisée en fonction de la possibilité de s'actualiser pour une puissance à se mouvoir[47]. En clôture de ce débat sur la génération, soulignons que l'enjeu de toute cette discussion autour de la théorie du mouvement tient à la possibilité (ou non) d'attribuer un terme au mouvement, selon que ce qui le précède et le suit appartient au mouvement d'un corps donné.

III. Puissance ou puissance?

Nous le voyons, le débat autour de l'antériorité du mobile par rapport au mouvement achoppe sur deux points en particulier: la temporalité et la signification de l'antériorité; la puissance et la capacité à agir/subir. Je creuserai tout d'abord la question de la δύναμις, en partant cette fois du versant qui concerne la nature de la capacité productive du monde.

---

[45] Simplicius, *In Ph.* 1138,29–1139,2.

[46] Simplicius répond ensuite aux autres arguments de Philopon. S'agissant de l'attribution au bois du mouvement vers le haut (2), il invoque la distinction entre acte et puissance, entre par soi et par accident (*In Ph.* 1137,27–1138,11). Il résout juste après la transformation réciproque des éléments (3) de la même façon (1138,12–16), puis celle de la nourriture (4) (1138,16–29). Ces réponses supposent évidemment d'admettre la différence sémantique que Philopon rejette et de considérer que la génération n'échappe pas à une forme de préexistence.

[47] Simplicius, *In Ph.* 1139,2–10.

1. *L'actualisation de la puissance seconde n'est pas un mouvement*

Comme il ressort de **T1**, Simplicius endosse sur ce point la thèse classique du néoplatonisme athénien, celle que Philopon affronte dans le *Contra Proclum*: «Si le démiurge est démiurge de quelque chose, soit il est toujours démiurge en acte, soit il l'est parfois en puissance mais n'est pas toujours démiurge»[48]. Dans ces termes, l'éternité du monde résulte de l'expression permanente de la puissance et de l'être de dieu. Le démiurge ne décide de rien et n'agit pas dans l'instant: il est producteur de façon essentielle[49]. Il ne peut donc en aucun cas être un dieu destructeur, parce que détruire le monde impliquerait la fin de son existence en tant que dieu producteur, empêché qu'il serait dans son activité essentielle. La question protologique se voit reconduite à une décomposition causale qui révèle la dépendance hiérarchique du monde vis-à-vis du principe immédiatement supérieur. Quant à la question eschatologique, elle se limite à admettre la possibilité que le monde soit détruit, en tant que réalité en devenir, et à écarter aussitôt que cela puisse arriver du fait de la nature même du démiurge.

Philopon conteste l'utilisation que Proclus fait de la δύναμις dans ce raisonnement – selon ce qui semble être un usage dans cette polémique[50]. Il lui reproche de ne pas tenir compte de la distinction opérée par Aristote (et «admise par tout un chacun») entre deux manières d'être en puissance et deux manières d'être en acte. Par souci de clarté, il reprend donc la typologie suivante[51]. La puissance première désigne la convenance naturelle – ἐπιτηδειότης – à devenir quelque chose, par exemple l'enfant qui est grammairien en puissance. La puissance seconde est celle qui résulte de l'actualisation de la précédente, mais en dehors de son exercice: le grammairien alors qu'il est en train de manger. Du côté de l'acte, le premier est équivalent à la puissance seconde, mais considérée du point de vue de sa réalisation, c'est-à-dire le grammairien en tant qu'il a acquis les règles de la grammaire. Enfin, l'acte second désigne l'exercice de la capacité, lorsque le grammairien enseigne ces théorèmes à un élève. L'enjeu de cette typologie est en définitive d'y situer les capacités essentielles. Proclus les range très clairement au niveau de l'acte second: de son point de vue, ce qui fait partie de l'essence doit s'exprimer en permanence. Philopon estime en revanche qu'elles relèvent de

[48] Philopon, *CP* 3,42,2–4: εἰ ὁ δημιουργὸς τινός ἐστιν δημιουργός, ἤτοι κατ' ἐνέργειαν ἔσται δημιουργὸς ἀεὶ ἢ δυνάμει ποτὲ μὴ ἀεὶ δημιουργῶν. Il s'agit du troisième argument de Proclus, qui couvre *CP* 3,42,1–43,24.

[49] Simplicius juge cette thèse ô combien plus belle et plus convenable à la nature de dieu, *In Ph.* 1330,37–1331,7.

[50] Philopon estime que Proclus bascule dans la sophistique et manque de la plus élémentaire rigueur dialectique: Philopon, *CP* 3,45,6–19.

[51] Philopon, *CP* 3,2,46,3–47,17. Il se base sur Aristote, *DA* 2,5,417a21–b2, qu'il cite *in extenso* plus loin, en 4,7,13–70,1. Le tableau que dresse Philopon rejoint celui que donne Porphyre dans l'*Ad Gaurum*, qui insère la notion d'ἐπιτηδειότης dans l'échelle aristotélicienne: e.g. 1,26; 12,20; 12,23; 13,62; 14,35–36 Dorandi 2012. Sur cette dernière notion chez Porphyre, Aubry 2008, 143–47.

l'acte premier. Il en va ainsi de la création: Dieu peut être par essence un producteur en acte tout en possédant la capacité de créer le monde: s'il ne crée pas le monde en permanence, son essence n'en est pour autant affectée en aucune façon, et il n'en reste pas moins parfait[52]. Admettre le contraire revient en effet à faire dépendre dieu de sa création et à subordonner le principe supérieur à ce qui en découle directement[53].

Il reste à répondre aux objections de Proclus. Le passage de l'acte premier à l'acte second ne suppose en dieu ni l'intervention d'une cause extérieure, ni un changement dans son être. D'une part, dieu agit comme le grammairien, qui n'a besoin d'aucune cause extérieure (un autre grammairien) pour exercer sa capacité (mais seulement pour l'acquérir): la décision de créer le monde, le passage de la puissance seconde ou de l'acte premier à l'acte second, procède uniquement de la volonté divine, qui n'a besoin de rien d'extérieur pour créer *ex nihilo*[54]. D'autre part, comme le dit Aristote[55], l'actualisation de la puissance seconde diffère d'un mouvement au sens propre, en tant qu'elle est le passage d'un acte (premier) à un acte (second), sans altération du sujet. Autrement dit, le passage à l'acte second n'implique aucun changement en dieu, au sens où l'actualisation de sa puissance créatrice s'apparente à un développement en soi-même qui n'entraîne aucun changement formel: elle est l'expression de sa disposition (τῆς ἕξεως φανέρωσις)[56], l'expression de son être et de son essence.

À l'appui de sa thèse, Philopon invoque la nature purement intellectuelle de dieu et recourt à un argument *a fortiori* fondé sur la distinction entre deux aspects du savoir (ἐπιστήμη)[57]: la disposition psychique, de l'ordre de la capacité (la θεωρία et la νόησις), et l'activité communicationnelle (verbale et pratique). Si les pensées pouvaient subsister dans leur nudité (γυμνάς), comme pures expressions de l'âme déliées de l'ancrage corporel, elles entreraient en contact direct. La différence entre l'activité communicationnelle et la réflexion en serait alors supprimée, puisque la communication d'une pensée produirait chez autrui un effet semblable à celui de la θεωρία ou de la νόησις chez leur auteur. De la même façon, si l'âme était capable de concrétiser ses pensées sans passer par le corps, il reviendrait au même de les penser ou de les mettre en œuvre[58]. Par analogie, étant donné que dieu agit seulement par la pensée, ne se produit en lui aucun changement physique justifiant que l'actualisation de sa puissance contrevienne à sa

52 De la même façon, qu'il y ait ou non quelque chose à chauffer, le feu n'en est pas moins chauffant et complet (Philopon, *CP* 4,11,83,15–84,7).

53 Philopon, *CP* 4,12,85,1–88,11, qui généralise des arguments de Zacharie de Gaza, cf. Sorabji 2015, 77–79.

54 Philopon, *CP* 3,4,48,14–49,8.

55 Aristote, *DA* 2,5,417b8–419.

56 Philopon, *CP* 4,7,73,20–74,1; cf. 3,63,2–16; 4,68,23–69,4; 7,74,7–19.

57 Philopon, *CP* 4,9,77,5–78,6.

58 Cette conception de la δύναμις de la pensée rappelle Platon, *Soph.* 248d. Je me permets de renvoyer à Gavray 2006, 42–45.

perfection. Par conséquent, dans la perspective de Philopon, à partir du moment où la capacité de créer le monde appartient en acte à l'essence de dieu, il n'y a aucun obstacle à ce que le geste créateur ne se produise pas de toute éternité, mais qu'il fasse venir le monde à l'existence à un moment déterminé par l'exercice d'une pensée en rien différente de sa capacité de penser les concepts de toutes les êtres. La création du monde, tout comme sa destruction, sont ainsi reconduites à des activités purement intellectuelles dont les effets physiques n'affectent en rien l'essence du dieu qui les met en œuvre.

2. L'actualisation de la puissance du monde

S'il accepte la typologie aristotélicienne, Simplicius ne peut concéder à Philopon sa vision de l'actualisation de la puissance seconde de dieu. Malheureusement, il ne donne pas de réponse directe à l'argument du *Contra Proclum*, mais conteste indirectement sa conclusion sur deux points: la nature de la puissance de la création et la raison (suffisante) pour dieu de passer de l'acte premier à l'acte second. Je développerai le second dans le chapitre suivant.

Dans une section du commentaire à *Physique* 8,10 que Hermann Diels a baptisée *Contra Philoponum*, Simplicius discute un bref traité de Philopon intitulé «Que chaque corps est fini et possède une puissance finie»[59], dont il résume l'objet de la façon suivante:

T5 Ce grammairien, que j'ai évoqué au début de mes leçons sur ce livre, fait grand cas de mener nombre de profanes à mépriser le ciel et le monde tout entier au motif qu'ils seraient aussi corruptibles qu'eux; et, évidemment, à mépriser le démiurge lui-même, s'il était démontré être le producteur d'un monde engendré et corruptible, lui qui, avant l'acte démiurgique et de toute éternité, n'eût été ni démiurge, ni dieu, ni père, ni soutien de tous les êtres, puisqu'il n'y avait alors aucun des êtres de maintenant[60].

Simplicius retourne l'argument de Philopon sur la puissance divine. Là où celui-ci jugeait que l'hypothèse d'une actualisation permanente de la puissance créatrice revenait à soumettre à sa création la réalisation de l'essence de dieu (pour être pleinement, dieu devrait créer le monde en permanence), Simplicius objecte que dénier à dieu la capacité de produire davantage qu'un monde fini implique de lui attribuer une puissance finie, soit un statut semblable à celui de sa création[61]. Le point de discorde se situe au niveau de la relation entre l'acte divin et la création – entre la puissance de créer et celle d'être créé. Si nos deux auteurs admettent une différence, ils se séparent sur sa nature.

---

59 Simplicius, *In Ph.* 1326,38–1336,34. Le titre est rétabli d'après une source arabe, cf. Wildberg 1991, 100 n. 7.

60 Simplicius, *In Ph.* 1326,38–1327,5.

61 Ce que les Chrétiens, selon lui, considèrent comme de la piété, θεοσέβεια, *In Ph.* 1327,19–20.

Dans ce traité, Philopon prouve que le monde possède nécessairement une puissance finie et qu'il est par conséquent périssable. Pour ce faire, il s'appuie sur la thèse aristotélicienne selon laquelle aucun corps fini n'a de capacité pour un temps infini[62], ce qu'il interprète comme la négation absolue pour un corps de posséder une puissance infinie. Cette thèse lui permet de dissocier radicalement la puissance divine de celle du monde, étant donné que la première se caractérise par son infinité, la seconde par sa finitude[63]. Dans ces conditions, nier la création et la fin du monde impliquerait, une fois encore, de contraindre dieu à œuvrer en permanence à la préservation du monde.

À l'inverse, Simplicius entend rétablir la relation entre la puissance divine et la puissance du monde, en retrouvant de part et d'autre une forme d'infinité. Il s'inscrit en effet dans la vision du néoplatonisme tardif selon laquelle les relations de dépendance causale obéissent à la loi de l'affinité du semblable avec le semblable, qui justifie une procession de proche en proche[64]. Poser, comme le fait Philopon, un passage de la puissance infinie à la puissance finie s'avère trop fort[65]. Au contraire, dieu et sa création doivent partager un type de puissance semblable: soit finie, soit infinie. Suivant cette seconde option – la première étant la raison pour laquelle Simplicius considère que les Chrétiens dévaluent le statut de dieu –, il formule une objection qui passe à nouveau par la distinction entre deux types de puissance, et plus particulièrement entre deux types de puissance infinie. Il montre ainsi que de la capacité finie à la périssabilité la conséquence

[62] Aristote, *Ph.* 8,9,266a23–266b6.

[63] Philopon utilise quatre arguments au service de sa thèse: (1) (1329,19–33) ce qui est composé de matière en a besoin pour exister et n'est donc pas autosuffisant. Pour cette raison, il ne peut être infini. Simplicius répond que le ciel est constitué d'une matière impérissable – thèse que précisément Philopon conteste dans les cinq premiers livres du *CA* (cf. Wildberg 1987a); (2) (1329,33–1331,7) si, par essence, la matière accueille toutes les formes mais ne peut en accueillir plusieurs simultanément, elle ne peut en accueillir aucune éternellement. La première réponse de Simplicius est, à nouveau, d'opposer la quintessence. La seconde est de noter qu'il n'est pas nécessaire pour le monde de périr dans son ensemble, mais successivement selon ses parties. (3) (1331,7–1335,16) en raison de leur composition, les corps sont et restent périssables malgré la capacité de dieu à empêcher leur destruction. Simplicius répond que, si dieu peut conserver le monde fini, c'est grâce à la capacité intrinsèque de ce dernier. (4) (1335,17–1336,34) le tout possède une puissance finie, dès lors que ses parties ont elles-mêmes une puissance finie. Simplicius répond que la puissance infinie réside dans la totalité, du fait que les parties tiennent leur être de l'enchaînement infini des générations.

[64] Cf. Proclus, *El. Th.* 7; 26; 28; 29; 77.

[65] Rappelons d'ailleurs l'argument *ad hominem* de Simplicius en **T1**. Selon la doctrine monophysite à laquelle souscrit Philopon, le Fils est issu du Père, ce qui le rend divin et, du même coup, éternel et infini. Philopon paraît admettre ce type de dépendance causale, en vertu de laquelle un acte infini produit un être tout aussi infini. Aux yeux de Simplicius, ce point souligne l'inconséquence de son adversaire: quoiqu'il parle dans les deux cas d'une production immédiate par dieu, il oublie ses effets en passant du registre théologique au registre cosmologique. L'argument était attendu: Philopon reprochait déjà à Proclus de s'être mis en quête de contester la vérité des Écritures et de tourner ses adversaires chrétiens au ridicule en les consignant au statut de novices dans les matières physiques (*CP* 4,8,75,4–21). Sur le rapport de Proclus aux Chrétiens, Hoffmann 2012.

n'est pas nécessaire[66]. D'un côté, il y a «ce qui est infini d'un seul et même coup» (τὸ ἅμα ὅλον ἄπειρον ὄν), l'infini ἀθρόον qui appartient au moteur éternel (à dieu). De l'autre, il y a «ce qui est à l'infini» (τὸ ἐπ' ἄπειρον), tel que ce qui est mû éternellement. On le voit, Simplicius mobilise la théorie qu'il a formulée dans le commentaire à *Physique* 3,6[67], qui distingue l'infini en acte du procès à l'infini, afin de distinguer entre la puissance active de mouvoir et la puissance passive d'être mû. Le moteur divin est une puissance infinie tout entière en acte (second), un infini au sens propre du point de vue de l'acte (κυρίως et κατ' ἐνέργειαν). Simplicius reproche dès lors à Philopon de ne pas comprendre la nature du procès à l'infini, pourtant essentielle à la définition du mouvement: le mouvement ne peut être infini en acte, étant donné qu'il est un processus d'actualisation. Imaginer le contraire impliquerait de le rendre parfaitement immobile[68]. Le mouvement ne peut donc jamais recevoir l'existence d'un coup, mais il se constitue à travers une chaîne de générations.

De cette façon, Simplicius ne rompt pas avec l'axiome d'Aristote, il le complète: aucun corps ne possède de puissance infinie *en acte*. Le monde est dans son ensemble une puissance d'être mû à l'infini; il n'est infini que sous un aspect, en tant qu'il est considéré du point de vue de la puissance[69]. Simplicius rétablit ainsi la continuité entre l'infinité du moteur et l'infinité du mobile, de dieu et du monde, sans pour autant nier que ce dernier, en tant que corps, soit fini: l'infinité en acte du premier moteur assure la continuité infinie du mouvement de ce corps fini, dans l'enchaînement de toutes ses parties. En définitive, la question n'est pas de savoir si le monde est fini – il l'est –, mais de démontrer que sa finitude n'implique pas nécessairement sa périssabilité. En tant que totalité qui se déploie à l'infini, le monde n'a ni début ni fin, car le dieu, en tant que principe démiurgique, le maintient éternellement à l'existence du fait que, tout en demeurant fini, il possède la capacité adéquate de devenir impérissable[70].

IV. Temps et génération

Passons à présent à la temporalité, second problème découlant de la relation entre moteur et mobile. Avec le monde arrivent le temps et le mouvement. Philopon et Simplicius s'accordent sur cet héritage du *Timée*, qui pose toutefois la question de la temporalité de la production: comment comprendre cette si-

---

66 Simplicius, *In Ph.* 1328,5–7.

67 En particulier le commentaire à *Ph.* 3,6,206a21–23 et 29–33, en *In Ph.* 492,12–495,17. Soulier 2014, 146–56 et 156–60 (pour la polémique avec Philopon).

68 Simplicius, *In Ph.* 1328,23–30.

69 Simplicius, *In Ph.* 1179,31–36.

70 Tout comme Philopon, Simplicius peut se réclamer du *Timée*, où le démiurge déclare que le monde ne sera pas détruit du fait de sa volonté (*Tim.* 41a7–d3), *In Ph.* 1331,7–25; 1334,34–39. Cf. Proclus, *In Tim.* 1,267,12–268,6.

multanéité inhérente à l'acte démiurgique, s'il survient alors que le temps n'existe pas encore? Nos deux auteurs reconnaissent que, contrairement à la nature, dieu n'a besoin d'aucun temps pour produire le monde: il agit nécessairement hors du temps, de façon préalable, immédiate et instantanée, étant donné qu'il ne peut y avoir de temps avant le temps[71]. Ils divergent pourtant dans la compréhension de cette instantanéité et de sa relation à la temporalité en général: l'origine (et la fin possible) du temps offre une nouvelle occasion à la polémique, avec en ligne de mire le temps sous-jacent à la démiurgie.

1. L'origine du temps selon Philopon

S'agissant du temps, la polémique s'articule autour du passage suivant du *Timée*:

T6 Le temps est né (γέγονεν) avec le ciel, afin que, nés en même temps, ils soient dissous en même temps (ἅμα γεννηθέντες ἅμα καὶ λυθῶσιν), si la dissolution de l'un d'eux devait jamais se produire; et sur le modèle de la nature éternelle, afin de lui être le plus semblable possible. Le modèle est en effet de toute éternité (πάντα αἰῶνά) au présent (ἐστιν ὄν), tandis que le ciel, de part en part (διὰ τέλους), sur toute l'étendue du temps (τὸν ἅπαντα χρόνον), est au passé, au présent et au futur (γεγονώς τε καὶ ὢν καὶ ἐσόμενος)[72].

Pour interpréter la génération simultanée du monde et du temps, Philopon analyse cet extrait à la lumière de la tradition dont Proclus se réclame. De Taurus à Porphyre, les platoniciens ont distingué quatre sens en vertu desquels le monde pouvait être dit γενητός: (1) ce qui appartient au genre de l'engendré; (2) ce qui est conceptuellement composé de matière et de forme; (3) ce qui est dans un perpétuel devenir; (4) ce dont l'être lui vient d'ailleurs, en l'occurrence de dieu[73]. Porphyre ajoutait à la liste de Taurus un cinquième sens, plus familier, pour l'exclure aussitôt du champ des possibles: ce qui a pour début un point du temps. Or c'est précisément le seul que retienne Philopon, au terme d'une réfutation focalisée sur deux points. Il voit tout d'abord dans les autres sens autant de détournements licencieux de l'usage ordinaire, sans le moindre fondement exégétique, qui du reste n'invalident en rien la nécessité d'un début dans le temps[74]. En effet, et c'est son second point, Platon n'écrit pas que le monde est *engendré* (γενητός), mais qu'*il est né* (γέγονεν): il ne s'enquiert pas de sa catégorie ontologique, qu'il aurait indiquée au moyen de l'adjectif, mais il montre son origine passée, tempo-

---

[71] Philopon, *CA* fr. 115–16 W; Simplicius, *In Ph.* 1122,3–11.

[72] Platon, *Tim.* 38b6–c3.

[73] Philopon, *CP* 6,8,144,16–149,26. Sur ce passage et sa réception arabe, Rashed 2016, 707–28. Cette liste peut être comparée à celle des sens de ἀγένητος que Philopon dresse en *CA* fr. 63 W (= Simplicius, *In De c.* 119,7–120,12), qui répond à Aristote, *De c.* 1,11,280b1–20.

[74] Philopon, *CP* 6,11,155,5–158,23. Les chapitres suivants (13–29) poursuivent une discussion exégétique destinée à confirmer l'interprétation de Philopon. Notons que, pas plus que Porphyre, Simplicius ne nie cette signification temporelle de γίνεσθαι. Toutefois, il en réserve l'usage à Aristote et aux physiciens, sans l'attribuer à Platon (*In Ph.* 1140,10–12).

relle, par le recours au parfait[75]. Au contraire, si Platon avait voulu souligner la nature processuelle de sa génération, il aurait opté pour le présent. Philopon s'inscrit en faux par rapport à la tradition platonicienne, tout en revendiquant la bonne exégèse de Platon[76]. Dans ces termes, ce passage souligne non seulement la coïncidence du monde et du temps, mais il pose du même coup l'existence d'un début temporel au monde, une origine associée au temps.

À côté de cet argument exégétique, Philopon montre que le temps ne préexiste pas au monde sur la base de sa définition (aristotélicienne) comme nombre du mouvement. Il en déduit que le temps occupe le troisième ou quatrième rang à partir des corps, vu qu'il suppose l'existence des corps, (de la capacité cinétique) et du mouvement[77]. Il en tire deux conséquences, partant dans les deux directions opposées. La première, évidente, concerne la priorité du monde sur le temps: la venue à l'être du monde ne peut se faire dans le temps, dans la mesure où le second vient logiquement après le premier, dès lors qu'il dépend logiquement de lui. La seconde, par extension, souligne que ce qui est ontologiquement au-delà du corps, au sens où il ne dépend pas du corps pour exister, ne dépend *a fortiori* pas du temps pour agir ou exister. Ainsi, dieu crée-t-il le monde indépendamment du temps qu'il fait exister. Par voie de conséquence, étant donné qu'il n'en dépend pas, il peut lui-même subsister après la fin du monde et du temps.

Les deux arguments paraissent contradictoires, dans la mesure où l'un pose la simultanéité du temps par rapport au monde, l'autre sa postériorité. En réalité, les relations qu'ils décrivent ne se placent pas sur un même plan. Le premier insiste sur la coïncidence temporelle, le second sur la dépendance logique. Mais ces deux raisonnements révèlent surtout l'attachement ferme de Philopon à une conception aristotélicienne du temps qui, confrontée au texte platonicien, aboutit à une conception finie du temps (et du monde). Si le monde est en effet fini, *a fortiori* le temps qui en dépend le sera également.

La solution soulève toutefois une objection majeure[78]: si le monde et le temps ont un début et une fin, pourquoi leur génération ou leur destruction surviendraient-elles à un moment plutôt qu'à un autre? Cette absence de raison suffisante pour distinguer un moment particulier sur le cours de l'éternité a conduit les philosophes grecs, depuis Parménide, à conclure à l'éternité du monde. Avec Philopon, le problème prend un tour particulier. Si dieu est parfait et toujours identique, pourquoi se mettrait-il subitement à créer le monde? Pour le formuler

[75] Philopon, *CP* 6,9,153,9–16.

[76] Il se garde néanmoins de se faire le sectateur de Platon et de chercher à le sauver à tous prix, cf. *CP* 8,4 et 9,1.

[77] Il lui attribue le troisième rang en *CP* 5,3,110,21–28 (il ne mentionne pas la capacité cinétique) et le quatrième en *CA* fr. 121 W (= Simplicius, *In Ph.* 1157,6–9) et Simplicius, *In Ph.* 1159,8–27.

[78] L'objection est adressée à Philopon par Simplicius, *In De c.* 138,3–6.

autrement, si le monde possède un début et une fin dans le temps, comment dieu pourrait-il en décider sans inévitablement sortir de sa perfection? La question implique de lever deux difficultés: d'une part trouver une raison suffisante à l'origine (et à la fin) du monde, d'autre part démontrer que la création (et la destruction) n'entraîne pas, à nouveau, une temporalisation de dieu.

Philopon lie la raison suffisante à la providence divine[79]. Contrairement à la nécessité aveugle de la nature qu'il transcende, dieu n'est pas contraint de faire exister dans l'immédiat toutes les choses futures qu'il connaît de toute éternité. Il les crée *sous l'effet de sa volonté* – et non par simple émanation de son être – et *au moment opportun* – dont la détermination dépend de ce qui est bon pour chaque chose et lui correspond par nature[80]. Or la thèse expose son auteur à une double objection: dans sa bonté, dieu devrait vouloir que tout soit éternel; et ses actes de volonté s'apparentent à autant d'altérations contraires à sa perfection. Philopon répond en invoquant la bonté divine: en tant que pure bonté, dieu ne veut rien d'autre que le bien (pour chaque chose) et, par conséquent, sa volonté s'avère une et simple. Il ne s'altère aucunement à créer le monde à tel moment, car seules changent les choses créées: par leur participation à sa bonté, celles-ci reçoivent un *bon* moment pour exister, sans que les variations de leur point de vue n'altèrent la bonté à laquelle toutes participent[81]. Il n'y a ainsi aucun obstacle à admettre qu'un début et une fin du monde se détachent sur la trame de l'éternité, dès lors que la raison suffisante s'en trouve inscrite dans chaque chose à créer. Il en résulte que les individus, dont dieu connaît les raisons (λόγοι), voient le temps de leur existence inscrit dans la connaissance divine, dès lors que cette providence sait à quel moment chacun doit naître et disparaître. Leur début et leur fin sont déjà en dieu.

En un sens, cette solution déplace le problème vers deux points aveugles à son auteur. Tout d'abord, elle asservit le créateur à sa création, étant donné que cette dernière impose à dieu le temps qui lui convient par nature pour exister. Ensuite, bien qu'elle définisse une chronologie relative, elle ne résout pas l'aporie de la relation entre l'éternité et le temps, dès lors qu'elle n'explique pas comment surviennent des différences qualitatives sur le cours, nécessairement invariable, identique de l'éternité. Dieu seul sait où passent ces distinctions.

[79] La démonstration repose sur les deux postulats déjà évoqués (n. 56): (1) dieu possède les concepts (νοήσεις) et raisons (λόγοι) de toutes choses de toute éternité; (2) en lui, puissance et activité se confondent, qu'il exerce ou non son activité créatrice. Cf. Philopon, *CP* 4,9,76,22–77,5.

[80] Philopon, *CP* 4,9,78,6–79,15. Cf. *CP* 4,14–16.

[81] Philopon, *CP* 4,10,79,16–81,28. Par ailleurs, dieu est une cause plus éminente que la cause immédiate et il atteint jusqu'au dernier individu (cf. *CP* 4,13).

2. La temporalité de la création selon Philopon

En admettant que dieu transcende le temps, dans quelles conditions se livre-t-il à la création et introduit-il une différence dans le *continuum* de l'éternité? Philopon répond en supprimant la temporalité du processus producteur et en écartant la possibilité de distinguer des moments du temps en dehors du temps. Il soutient la thèse d'une production instantanée, qui corrobore l'absence d'altération dans le passage de la puissance seconde à l'acte second. Au service de sa démonstration, il invoque plusieurs processus dont la temporalité pose question.

Pour créer ou détruire le monde, dieu n'a besoin d'aucun intervalle de temps (ἄνευ χρονικῆς παρατάσεως)[82]. Certes, dans la mesure où la création divine n'est pas un mouvement, il paraît exclu qu'elle prenne du temps. Mais ce n'est pas la seule raison:

T7 La mise en œuvre d'une activité à partir d'une disposition n'implique pas de temps (ἄχρονος γίνεται). En effet, le terme du fait de ne pas produire et le début de celui de produire surviennent au même moment (ἐν τῷ αὐτῷ). C'est selon un seul et même instant (καθ' ἓν καὶ τὸ αὐτὸ νῦν) que quelqu'un cesserait de ne pas écrire pour se mettre à écrire, et il en va de même dans tous les cas. Par conséquent, il n'y a aucun temps entre le fait de ne pas produire et celui de produire, ni de façon générale entre toute disposition et l'acte qui se produit à partir d'elle. Car s'il y avait du temps entre le fait de ne pas produire et celui de produire, et en général de tous les termes de la contradiction, dans celui-ci l'agent ne sera ni en train de ne pas produire (car il aura cessé de ne pas produire) ni en train de produire (car il n'aura pas encore commencé à produire). Par conséquent, dans le même temps, il ne sera ni en train de produire ni de ne pas produire, ce qui est impossible, parce que les deux termes de la contradiction seront vrais en même temps[83].

De la continuité du processus producteur, c'est-à-dire de l'absence d'intermédiaire entre non-production et production dans l'exercice d'une capacité seconde, résulte l'instantanéité de la production en général: le passage à l'acte se fait dans l'instant, qui est la limite intermédiaire et commune entre les deux moments du processus. Par conséquent, le passage à la production et à la destruction du monde n'entraîne aucun temps, dieu n'est soumis à aucun mouvement et, du même coup, ne subit aucune temporalité. Cela étant, il reste à expliquer pourquoi nous sommes enclins à introduire du temps dans ce processus, à penser qu'il y avait du temps avant le temps et qu'il y en aura après, raison pour laquelle nous concluons à l'éternité du temps. Philopon invoque deux cas où

[82] Philopon, *CA* fr. 116 W (= Simplicius, *In Ph.* 1142,21–28) et fr. 129 W (= Simplicius, *In Ph.* 1173,11–13).

[83] Philopon, *CP* 4,3,63,4–16. Philopon exclut du reste la possibilité, qui correspond à la thèse néoplatonicienne, que la production soit un mouvement et que dieu soit dans une production permanente: il serait alors pris dans un mouvement permanent et, par contamination de l'incomplétude qui caractérise ce dernier, il serait imparfait.

l'assomption temporelle est manifestement erronée: l'activité intellectuelle et les expressions de temps[84].

Le premier argument explique en quoi l'activité de dieu échappe au temps, en dépit de notre tendance à la temporaliser[85]. Il s'agit de montrer que dieu est lié à la succession et capable de la penser sans pourtant se temporaliser. Sur le premier point, Philopon part du fonctionnement général de l'intelligence, qui connaît les idées successivement. Dans la réflexion, les pensées arrivent en effet non pas simultanément, mais bien les unes après les autres. Cette succession échappe cependant au temps, car elle s'exerce séparément du corps et dès lors du mouvement qui lui est propre. *A fortiori*, puisque dieu est une pure intelligence qui transcende les autres formes d'intelligence, il échappe à la succession temporelle. Quant au second point, en tant que providence, dieu anticipe la succession des événements sans subir leur temporalité: sa connaissance de l'avant et de l'après échappe à une division temporelle en son sein. En conclusion, de l'usage de marqueurs temporels pour qualifier l'activité divine, nous ne pouvons conclure à une quelconque temporalité de dieu. Philopon généralise ensuite ce point à l'ensemble des expressions temporelles.

Le second argument vise l'usage du temps dans la langue ordinaire. Nous utilisons sans cesse des marqueurs temporels dont nous induisons une temporalité réelle, ce que Philopon dénonce comme une projection et un abus de langage. Ainsi, lorsque nous renvoyons à la création ou à la destruction du monde, nous supposons qu'elles sont précédées ou suivies d'un temps, parce que nous disons: «le temps n'existait pas *avant* d'être créé»[86]. Qu'y avait-il avant le temps, si le temps ne pouvait pas encore le mesurer? En réalité, cette expression signifie seulement que le temps n'a pas été précédé par du temps.

T8 Aussi n'est-ce pas dans tous les cas que les marqueurs temporels (τὰ χρονικὰ προσρήματα), là où ils sont employés, signifient directement un temps. Qu'est-ce qui empêche donc dans le cas présent, quand on dit «il y aura un moment où le temps n'existera pas» (ἔσται ποτέ, ὅτε οὐκ ἔσται χρόνος), qu'«un moment» (ποτέ) ne signifie pas un temps mais une limite du temps, en tant que le temps cessera d'exister? Et si on dit que le temps est venu à l'être à un moment donné (ποτέ) et qu'il n'existe pas éternellement, alors à l'inverse cela désigne le début du temps, c'est-à-dire le premier instant (τὸ πρῶτον σημεῖον) ou le maintenant (τὸ νῦν), en tant qu'il a commencé à exister[87]?

Philopon juge purement verbaux les arguments qui jouent sur les mots «quand», «avant» et «après». Or il suffit de remplacer l'expression «avant le temps, il y avait déjà du temps» par «le temps a un début et une fin» pour écarter l'implication temporelle de ce qui dépasse les limites du temps. De la même façon, objecte-t-il, si nous introduisions du temps à chaque fois que nous utilisons un

[84] Philopon discute ces arguments tant dans le *CA* (fr. 121–22 W) que dans le *CP* (5,2–4).
[85] Philopon, *CA* fr. 121 W (= Simplicius, *In Ph.* 1157,27–1158,29).
[86] Philopon, *CA* fr. 122 W (= Simplicius, *In Ph.* 1158,29–1159,7).
[87] Philopon, *CP* 5,3,108,5–13.

marqueur temporel, toute phrase complexe, contenant plusieurs verbes, contiendrait aussi plusieurs temps[88]. Ces expressions réfèrent soit à une existence, soit à une limite du temps qui, par définition, n'est pas elle-même encadrée par du temps[89]. L'emploi de marqueurs temporels ne renvoie donc pas nécessairement à un temps réel. Nous y recourons à cause de notre incapacité à penser et à exprimer les relations logiques (en particulier celles qui excèdent le temps) sans y glisser des liens de consécution, parce que, contrairement à dieu qui pense atemporellement (ἀχρόνως) ce qui est temporel, nous devons penser temporellement ce qui est atemporel. Ainsi en va-t-il de la création et de la destruction: elles sont des limites du temps au-delà desquelles le temps n'existe pas.

En conclusion, Philopon prolonge et harmonise les définitions du temps laissées par Platon et Aristote, tout en rejetant leur lecture éternaliste – notamment la conséquence tirée par Aristote lui-même d'une infinité du temps – qu'il range parmi les argumentations sophistiques. Il en résulte une conception du temps qui l'associe intimement au mouvement des corps, plus qu'à la succession (de la même façon que la succession des nombres n'implique pas entre eux de relation temporelle), et autorise à fixer des bornes au temps, à son début comme à son terme. Dès lors, pour penser correctement le début et la fin du monde, nous devons nous extraire de la conceptualité associée au temps dans lequel nous vivons et prendre le point de vue de dieu.

3. Éternité et temporalité selon Simplicius

Selon Simplicius, dans le livre 6 du *Contre Aristote*, Philopon prétend nier l'immutabilité de dieu et l'éternité du monde en rejetant l'infinité du mouvement[90]. Il ne concède évidemment aucun point à son adversaire, mais il réfute patiemment ses conclusions tant sur la temporalité de la production que sur le rapport du temps à l'éternité. Son argumentation se concentre sur la relation entre le temps et l'éternité.

S'inscrivant dans la lignée des interprétations platoniciennes du *Timée*[91], Simplicius justifie la génération du monde (et du temps) au moyen d'une production hors du temps, instantanée. Il se démarque toutefois de Philopon en raisonnant non plus à partir du producteur, mais bien du produit. Son objection porte sur la différence sémantique entre processus *en bloc* (ἀθρόα) et processus *atemporel* (ἄχρονος). L'adjectif ἀθρόον qu'emploie Aristote ne caractérise pas le processus

[88] Suivant la définition aristotélicienne du ῥῆμα comme ὄνομα auquel s'ajoute un temps, Aristote, *DI* 3,16b6–25.

[89] Philopon, *CP* 5,3,113,28–114,14.

[90] Simplicius, *In Ph.* 1182,28–39.

[91] Simplicius reproche à Philopon d'avoir manqué la différence entre les emplois de γενητός chez Platon et chez Aristote, pourtant établie par les exégètes, pour imposer le sens qui lui convient: Simplicius, *In Ph.* 1165,3–10. Sur l'interprétation de γενητός, voir *In Dec.* 140,9–12. Je me permets de renvoyer à Gavray (2018, 114–19).

dans son ensemble, mais il décrit uniquement son terme (κατὰ τὸ τέλος), le moment où le changement s'accomplit – où la génération, la destruction ou l'altération deviennent effectives. Par exemple, construire une maison n'est pas un événement atemporel, mais un processus qui s'achève subitement avec la pose de la dernière tuile: c'est à ce moment-là, et à ce moment-là seulement, que la maison est pleinement construite, parce qu'une matière reçoit la forme de la maison. À l'inverse sa destruction *débute* dès que la première tuile s'envole[92]. Il y a certes une contraction de l'intervalle temporel (συνῃρημένη ἡ παράτασις) qui achève le processus, mais celui-ci n'en reste pas moins un processus. Là où Philopon, qui raisonne sur la cause productrice en prenant en un sens le point de vue de dieu, isole l'instant où l'acte se manifeste, Simplicius, en changeant la perspective sur la génération et la destruction pour se concentrer sur le sujet du changement, souligne la dimension processuelle. L'objection porte plus particulièrement s'agissant de la fin du monde, dans la mesure où la destruction implique une dégradation progressive dont les effets devraient (déjà) être perceptibles – à tout le moins à suivre le calendrier chrétien, qui place nos auteurs plus proches de la fin que du début[93].

Toutefois, Simplicius envisage aussi l'argument de son adversaire du point de vue de la cause productrice et dénonce la combinaison qu'il réalise entre des choses pourtant inconciliables, à savoir ce qui est hors du temps (ἄχρονον) et ce qui implique une alternance temporelle (ποτὲ μὲν ποτὲ δὲ οὔ)[94]. Le récit de la *Genèse* paraît incompatible avec une production atemporelle, étant donné qu'il impose, d'une part, que dieu se mette subitement à créer *après* ne pas avoir créé et *avant* de s'arrêter et, d'autre part, que sa création mobilise une succession temporelle dont le programme se déroule sur six jours. Dans ces conditions, dieu est soumis au temps. La seule acception possible d'une production divine atemporelle, conclut Simplicius, consiste dès lors à admettre que, puisque dieu produit le monde directement, il le fait aussi éternellement et lui transmet son éternité, tout comme au temps[95]. Dans les sections précédentes, nous avons examiné la réponse de Philopon à cette objection sur l'usage inadapté de marqueurs temporels quand ils s'appliquent à dieu et à sa création – du moins dans sa formulation par Proclus. Ici, l'originalité de Simplicius tient à son diagnostic: Philopon attribue à dieu une production hors du temps de façon purement verbale (μέχρι ὀνόματος μόνον), alors que lui attribuer un mode d'action temporel revient à l'anthropomorphiser[96]. Par là, Simplicius retourne l'argument de son ad-

[92] Simplicius, *In Ph.* 1173,20–31 (réponse à *CA* fr. 129 W); 1198,18–20 (il reprend Alexandre).

[93] Simplicius, *In Ph.* 1334,40–1335,16: d'après les Chrétiens, le monde aurait 6000 ans et serait dans ses derniers jours, bien qu'aucun signe avant-coureur de ralentissement ou de dégradation ne soit perceptible.

[94] Simplicius, *In Ph.* 1174,6–33.

[95] Cf. Simplicius, *In Ph.* 1152,2–10.

[96] Simplicius, *In Ph.* 1175,5–10.

versaire pour lui reprocher son incapacité à sortir de schèmes humains de pensée qui, en outre, soumettent l'éternité au temps, si dieu dépend du monde pour fixer le moment de sa création.

Enfin, Simplicius examine la thèse de la succession non temporelle. L'argument de Philopon reposait sur une définition qui liait étroitement le temps au mouvement des corps et éloignait du même coup dieu et l'intelligence de la temporalité. Or, dans le cadre de son commentaire à la *Physique*, dans la continuité de son *Corollarium de tempore*[97], Simplicius revendique une définition alternative du temps, selon laquelle ce dernier mesure aussi l'extension de l'être (ἡ τοῦ εἶναι παράτασις) et l'extension selon les qualités (κατὰ τὰς ποιότητας)[98], car «le temps est mesure du flux de l'être, non pas seulement selon la substance, mais aussi selon l'acte»[99]. Cette définition du temps autorise dès lors une temporalisation et des mouvements de réalités qui transcendent les corps, ce qui permet à Simplicius de revenir à l'intelligence. Philopon admet que la discursivité, à laquelle est sujette l'intelligence inférieure à dieu, implique une succession, dont Simplicius entend prouver qu'elle marque nécessairement une temporalité. À cette fin, il avance deux arguments. Tout d'abord, que cette intelligence soit l'âme rationnelle (celle qui pratique les syllogismes), qui est liée au corps, ou une intelligence située entre cette dernière et la substance intellective, elle est immanquablement liée au temps, étant inférieure à dieu. Ensuite, invoquant Aristote, il note que la succession s'entend en trois sens seulement: par position (θέσει), par nature (φύσει) ou par substance (οὐσίᾳ), temporellement (χρόνῳ)[100]. Dans la mesure où il n'y a pas de position dans les intelligibles, si ce n'est métaphoriquement (et quand bien même, l'intellect peut concevoir la substance et le centre simultanément), et où il n'est pas question de relation entre genres et espèces, il reste à considérer que l'intelligence discursive est temporelle. En conclusion, estime Simplicius, Philopon mobilise des concepts dont les implications lui échappent complètement: il confond ainsi la capacité de l'intellect à penser sans transition (ἀμεταβάτως) la relation entre ce qui est premier et ce qui est second, parce que déjà distingués (διακεκριμένα), avec le fait de penser dans la succession[101]. Car pour penser la distinction entre les Formes, l'intellect n'a besoin ni de temps ni de succession.

Simplicius dénonce l'homonymie dont, à ses yeux, Philopon abuse dans ses objections. S'il est vrai que dieu, en tant que providence, connaît les événements futurs de façon atemporelle, sans que leur succession ne l'affecte d'une quel-

---

97 Simplicius, *In Ph.* 773,8–800,25.

98 Simplicius, *In Ph.* 1159,11–14.

99 Simplicius, *In Ph.* 774,35–37: ἔστιν οὖν ὁ χρόνος μέτρον τῆς τοῦ εἶναι ῥοῆς, εἶναι δὲ λέγω οὐ τοῦ κατὰ τὴν οὐσίαν μόνον, ἀλλὰ καὶ τοῦ κατὰ τὴν ἐνέργειαν. Simplicius paraphrase là le traité (perdu) de Damascius *Sur le nombre, le lieu et le temps*.

100 Simplicius, *In Ph.* 1160,20–40. Cf. Aristote, *Cat.* 12,14a26–b23.

101 Simplicius, *In Ph.* 1160,40–41,9 et 1161,29–1162,2.

conque façon, en lui, du strict point de vue de la connaissance, tous ces événements sont simultanés, bien qu'il sache lesquels sont antérieurs et lesquels postérieurs[102]. Il n'en reste pas moins que les marqueurs temporels qui caractérisent leurs positions respectives renvoient à une temporalité, qui certes n'est pas celle de dieu, mais des événements eux-mêmes. Aussi leur présence indique-t-elle nécessairement une succession temporelle, que dieu connaît dans la simultanéité, et pas simplement une relation d'antériorité et postériorité qu'il faudrait entendre *par position*, voire selon le rang causal ou naturel. Pour Simplicius, il paraît bien exclu que les marqueurs temporels échappent jamais au temps – ce que Philopon aurait constaté s'il avait jamais examiné les différents sens possibles[103]. Il faut en déduire qu'*avant* le temps, il y avait nécessairement du temps, tout comme *après* le temps, il y en aura encore.

Fondée sur une autre définition du temps, toute l'argumentation de Simplicius vise à asseoir la différence radicale et l'incompatibilité logique entre l'éternité et le temps, dieu et le monde. Il exclut qu'un processus décrive autre chose qu'une temporalité, de sorte qu'il est impossible pour dieu, éternel, de créer et détruire le monde de façon temporelle et limitée, parce que cela impliquerait inéluctablement de le temporaliser. La seule option reste l'infinité du temps et du monde, produit immédiat et permanent de l'éternité divine.

V. Conclusion

En dépit de désaccords profonds, nos deux auteurs partagent de nombreuses thèses héritées de la tradition platonico-aristotélicienne, notamment le fait que tout ce qui a un début a aussi une fin. Au-delà des traits communs cependant, leurs visions du monde s'affrontent sur un fond de querelle théologique, où ils rivalisent par leur capacité à expliquer sa génération, sa puissance et sa temporalité, les deux parties en présence atteignant dans l'ensemble un même degré de cohérence et de validité. Nos auteurs utilisent ainsi des postulats et des arguments semblables, mais à des fins contraires. Car, plus qu'une simple dispute rhétorique, la controverse implique un véritable choix dans le sens des concepts destinés à autoriser les thèses en présence. Ainsi, à côté des raisonnements dialectiques et des démonstrations ordinaires, Simplicius et Philopon recourent aux mêmes procédés afin de désarçonner leur adversaire. Par exemple, pour réduire des arguments à des bavardages infondés, il leur arrive d'en appeler à l'opinion commune ou à l'expérience sensible[104]. Ils se servent aussi de l'argument du

---

102 *In Ph.* 1163,3–24.

103 *In Ph.* 1163,25–1164,6.

104 Voir Philopon, *CA* fr. 77 W (= Simplicius, *In De c.* 139,23–27) ou fr. 79 W (= Al-Sijistānī, *Muntakhab Siwān al Hikmah*, 237), où Philopon objecte à Aristote que (1) il ne suffit pas dire que tous les hommes prient en croyant que le ciel est inengendré et impérissable pour

nombre, qui s'avère à double tranchant[105]. Ils dénoncent enfin un recours à l'usage ordinaire des mots, pourtant peu adapté à la discussion philosophique[106]. Or de tels arguments révèlent rapidement leur faiblesse.

S'agissant de protologie et d'eschatologie, du début et de la fin du monde, les démonstrations connaissent des limites dont Simplicius et Philopon semblent plus ou moins conscients, selon qu'il leur paraît possible d'ancrer définitivement leur thèse sur la génération ou l'éternité du monde dans l'expérience. Ils peuvent certes se disputer pour savoir si le monde a un début ou s'il est éternel, comme ils le montrent toutefois, ils doivent souvent se contenter de réfutations *ad hoc* ou verbales. L'impossibilité de faire l'expérience de l'origine, de la fin ou au contraire de l'éternité rend la question insoluble de façon définitive et positive. Elle présente cependant l'immense intérêt, face à un tel débat, de révéler les limites du néoplatonisme tardif et de sa version chrétienne.

Bibliographie

Aubry, G. (2008), 'Capacité et convenance: La notion d'*epitêdeiotês* dans la théorie porphyrienne de l'embryon', in: *L'Embryon: Formation et animation. Antiquité grecque et latine, traditions hébraïque, chrétienne et islamique*, éd. L. Brisson, M.-H. Congourdeau, et J.-L. Solère, Paris: Vrin, 139–55.

Bodnár, I., Chase, M., et Share, M. (2012), *Simplicius, On Aristotle's Physics 8.1–5* (Ancient Commentators on Aristotle), London: Bloomsbury.

de Haas, F. A. J. (1997), *John Philoponus' New Definition of Prime Matter: Aspects of Its Background in Neoplatonism and the Ancient Commentary Tradition* (Philosophia antiqua 69), Leiden – New York – Köln: Brill.

Dorandi, T., éd. (2012), *Porphyre, Sur la manière dont l'embryon reçoit l'âme*, texte grec révisé par –, travaux édités sous la responsabilité de L. Brisson (Histoire des doctrines de l'antiquité classique 43), Paris: Vrin, 2012.

qu'il le soit, puisque d'autres le font en étant animés par la croyance contraire; (2) ce n'est pas parce qu'ils vénèrent leur temples que les hommes qui les ont construits les croient impérissables; (3) c'est là une croyance seulement en la présence de la lumière divine.

[105] Ainsi, dans la *Physique* (8,1,251b14–9), Aristote appuie l'éternité du temps sur l'accord quasi unanime entre les physiciens – à l'exception de Platon. Simplicius juge l'argument valide (*In Ph.* 1329,7–10), car le nombre vaut comme expression et confirmation de la vérité, surtout que s'y ajoute la tradition commentariste unanime, que seule conteste son adversaire. Pour Philopon en revanche, en invoquant les Physiciens, Aristote parle tout au plus de cinq à dix personnes, ce qui affaiblit l'argument, surtout s'il faut jouer leur opinion contre celle de Platon (*CA* fr. 123 W = Simplicius, *In Ph.* 1164,7–30; cf. *CP* 5,4). Plus encore: si Aristote désire recourir à ce type d'arguments, il devrait s'interroger sur ses prises de position contre la majorité des Physiciens, notamment au sujet de la quintessence, que Philopon refuse.

[106] Simplicius, *In Ph.* 1155,20–6,3 et 1158,30–9,7.

Évrard, É. (1953), 'Les convictions religieuses de Jean Philopon et la date de son Commentaire aux *Météorologiques*', *Bulletin de l'Académie Royale de Belgique (Classe des Lettres)* 39: 299–357; repris dans É. Évrard (2020), *Études philoponiennes. Philosopher à l'École d'Alexandrie*, éd. M.-A. Gavray, Liège: Presses Universitaires de Liège, 21–69.

– (1961), *Jean Philopon, Contre Aristote. Fragments des livres I et II. Introduction, édition, traduction et commentaire*, repris dans É. Évrard (2020), *Études philoponiennes*, 197–334.

Gavray, M.-A. (2006), 'Être, puissance, communication: La *dunamis* dans le *Sophiste*', *Philosophie antique* 6: 29–57.

– (2018), 'Reconciling Plato's and Aristotle's Cosmologies: Attempts at Harmonization in Simplicius', in: *Die Kunst der philosophischen Exegese bei den spätantiken Platon- und Aristoteles-Kommentatoren: Akten der Tagung der Karl und Gertrud Abel-Stiftung vom 4. bis 6. Oktober 2012 in Trier*, éd. B. Strobel, Berlin – New York: De Gruyter, 101–25.

Golitsis, P. (2008), *Les Commentaires de Simplicius et de Jean Philopon à la* Physique *d'Aristote: Tradition et innovation* (Commentaria in Aristotelem Graeca et Byzantina 3), Berlin – New York: De Gruyter.

– (2016), 'Simplicius and Philoponus on the Authority of Aristotle', in: *Brill's Companion to the Reception of Aristotle in Antiquity*, éd. A. Falcon (Brill's Companions to Classical Conception), Leiden – Boston, MA: Brill, 419–38.

– (2019), 'μετά τινων ἰδίων ἐπιστάσεων: John Philoponus as an Editor of Ammonius' Lectures', in: *Aristotle and His Commentators: Studies in Memory of Paraskevi Kotzia*, éd. K. Ierodiakonou et P. Golitsis (Commentaria in Aristotelem Graeca et Byzantina 7), Berlin – New York: De Gruyter, 167–94.

Hadot, I. (2014), *Le néoplatonicien Simplicius à la lumière des recherches contemporaines: Un bilan critique* (Academia Philosophical Studies 48), Sankt Augustin: Academia Verlag.

Hoffmann, P. (1987), 'Sur quelques aspects de la polémique de Simplicius contre Jean Philopon: De l'invective à la réaffirmation de la transcendance du ciel', in: *Simplicius: Sa vie, son œuvre, sa survie. Actes du colloque international de Paris (28 sept. – 1ᵉ oct. 1985)*, éd. I. Hadot, Berlin – New York: De Gruyter, 183–221.

– (2012), 'Un grief antichrétien chez Proclus: L'ignorance en théologie', in: *Les Chrétiens et l'hellénisme: Identités religieuses et culture grecque dans l'Antiquité tardive*, éd. A. Perrot, Paris: Éditions rue d'Ulm, 161–97.

Mueller-Jourdan, P. (2011), *Gloses et commentaires du livre XI du* Contra Proclum *de Jean Philopon: Autour de la Matière première du monde* (Philosophia antiqua 125), Leiden – Boston, MA: Brill.

Rashed, M. (2016), 'Nouveaux fragments antiprocliens de Philopon en version arabe et le problème des origines de la théorie de l'"instauration" (ḥudut)', in: idem, *L'Héritage aristotélicien: Textes inédits de l'Antiquité*, Paris: Les Belles Lettres, 701–49.

Sorabji, R. (2015), 'Waiting for Philoponus', in: *Causation and Creation in Late Antiquity*, éd. A. Marmodoro et B.D. Prince, Cambridge: Cambridge University Press, 71–93.

– (2016), 'Dating of Philoponus' Commentaries on Aristotle and of His Divergence from His Teacher Ammonius', in: *Aristotle Re-Interpreted: New Findings on Seven Hundred Years of the Ancient Commentators*, éd. R. Sorabji, London – New York: Bloomsbury Academic, 367–92.

Soulier, P. (2014), *Simplicius et l'infini* (Anagôgé 7), Paris: Les Belles Lettres.
Verrycken, K. (1990), 'The Development of Philoponus' Thought and Its Chronology', in: *Aristotle Transformed: The Ancient Commentators and Their Influence*, éd. R. Sorabji, Ithaca, NY: Cornell University Press, 231–74.
Wildberg, C. (1987a), *Philoponus: Against Aristotle on the Eternity of the World*, translated by – (Ancient Commentators on Aristotle), London: Duckworth.
– (1987b), 'Prolegomena to the Study of Philoponus' *Contra Aristotelem*', in: *Philoponus and the Rejection of Aristotelian Science*, éd. R. Sorabji, London: Institute of Classical Studies, 239–50.
– (1988), *John Philoponus' Criticism of Aristotle's Theory of Aether* (Peripatoi 16), Berlin – New York: De Gruyter.
– (1991), *Simplicius: Against Philoponus on the Eternity of the World*, translated by – (Ancient Commentators on Aristotle), London: Duckworth.

From Eternal Life to the Word That Was in the Beginning

The Logic of Johannine Theology

Jörg Frey

Cosmology and Protology are underrepresented themes in the New Testament. In contrast with Jewish Apocalyptic writings, Hellenistic Jewish authors and works, or Christian and Christian Gnostic traditions from the second century onwards,[1] the New Testament is remarkably silent about the creation and material nature of the world and about the primordial origins of evil.[2] This is due to the primary focus on soteriology and eschatology. The main interest of New Testament authors is concerned with the restoration of Israel and the salvation of humans rather than with the nature of the created world. They focus on the hopes for the future (some of which are considered to have come true in Jesus Christ), rather than on explanations from the past. Only in the very late second-century text known as 2 Peter can we find a reasonable interaction with Hellenistic cosmological debates.[3] Even when the biblical accounts of the creation are referred to, the primary intention is not to discuss creation as such but to link the present state of salvation with creation or with the primordial will of God. In Christian theology, these texts have been adopted as *dicta probantia* for the themes of the divine predestination (thus in particular Ephesians 1) and for the pre-existence of Christ (thus the Gospel of John, esp. John 1:1–2; 17:5; and 17:24).[4] But according to the majority of interpreters, Christ's pre-existence is mentioned not due to a particular "speculative" interest in the primordial status of Christ, the Logos, or the world, but with the intention of forcefully proclaiming Christ's true dignity and to ensure readers of the message of their salvation. In the reception of the Fourth Gospel in the second century, the perspective changes, and the interest of the readers and interpreters is much more

---

[1] For the interpreters of the Johannine prologue (John 1:1–18, in particular 1:1–5) in the second century, see Frey 2015b.

[2] On the remarkable silence of New Testament texts about the origins of evil, see Götte 2016, 290–92.

[3] Cf. 2 Peter 3:5–13 where the author, probably around the middle of the second century, interacts with views about the immutability of the world in order to argue for the validity of the biblical expectation of an end of the world. See Frey 2015a, 327–38.

[4] For the interpretation of the statements about Christ's pre-existence, see Kunath 2016.

focused on the first five verses of the prologue (John 1:1–5) and the relations between the Logos and God, the Logos and the created world, or the Logos and the figure of Jesus. We can now find speculations about the mutual relation of the Logos, life, light, and other elements, or careful distinctions between an eternal divine Logos and another Logos which is capable of coming into the world or becoming incarnate. These changes are obviously due to a stronger interest in cosmology or protology, which dominates the reading of the Johannine prologue, introducing ideas and issues that are absent from the Gospel text.

It is an open question, however, whether theological interpretation, with its focus on the soteriological message of the Gospel, still neglects or underestimates the cosmological aspects in the New Testament. These elements are often regarded as "unnecessary" mythological elements that can be considered marginal for determining the theological meaning of the texts. Accordingly, in the scholarly debate about the motif of Jesus's pre-existence, there is a widespread tendency of downplaying the temporal or "mythological" elements of the Johannine view in favour of an atemporal or existential interpretation.[5] Only recently has scholarship rediscovered the temporal aspects in the Johannine narrative, including the pre-existence statements,[6] as a narrative feature deliberately chosen and carefully designed by the narrator.

Within this scholarly context, there is good reason to look afresh at the "protological" elements in the Fourth Gospel and at their connection with soteriology and eschatology. How are protology and eschatology related to each other? What comes first and what comes later, not only according to the temporal framework underlying the gospel narration but also historically, i. e., in the development of early Christian thought and according to the inner logic of Johannine theology?

In the present article, I will first present a survey of the various Gospel texts with a protological dimension and discuss some problems with their interpretation. Then, I will briefly discuss the reading strategy suggested in the gospel and the historical roots of the Johannine preaching in Messianism and eschatology. Finally, I will turn to the relationship between eschatology and protology and the theological thought logic of the Fourth Gospel.

---

[5] Cf. Bultmann [21]1984, 15: "ist nicht das erste Glied einer Zeitreihe, sondern liegt aller Zeit und damit aller Welt voraus"; similarly Weder 2008, 30, with the term "das Unvordenkliche"; but cf. Schnelle [4]2009, 36, who maintains that the phenomenon of the beginning necessarily implies the imagination of time; see also Kunath 2016, 332–34.

[6] Cf. Frey 1998 and 2014a, as well as Kunath 2016.

I. Protology in the Fourth Gospel

There is no need to begin with a "definition" of protology. Instead, in a preliminary survey, I will present a range of different texts referring to some state or event "before" or "beyond" the narrated story of the gospel. In which manner and for what purpose does the Fourth Gospel point "back" to a status or an action before or beyond the narrated story?[7] Here, we can include the classical passages that point to the pre-existence of Jesus or the Logos, which have been clearly defined on a linguistic basis in the recent work by Friederike Kunath.[8] To these we can add some other Johannine passages that refer to a prior act of God towards the world or towards Jesus, which provide the background or basis for the Jesus story narrated in the Gospel. We will, however, leave aside the Son-of-Man sayings[9] since the usage of this christological title does not, in every case, point to aspects of Jesus's pre-existence or to a concept of protology.

1. The Beginning

The first and perhaps most debated passage is the beginning of the gospel, the first verses of the prologue (John 1:1–5) and, in particular, the meaning of the words ἐν ἀρχῇ (John 1:1–2). It is sufficiently clear that this beginning, with the words ἐν ἀρχῇ, refers to the beginning of the Greek version of the Scriptures of Israel, Gen 1:1 LXX. Furthermore, the combination of word, life, light, and darkness adopts the cluster of terms used in the biblical creation account and a longer tradition of texts adopting and interpreting the creation.[10] With this reference, which links the origin of not only the Logos but also Jesus Christ to the context of creation or even beyond the beginning of the world, the Fourth Gospel begins with an openly protological statement. With such an opening, John goes much further back than the other gospels with their respective beginnings.

Mark also mentions the term ἀρχή, but only as a reference to the beginning of the gospel: this beginning is either a reference to the text of the written gospel or to the historical beginnings of the gospel message in the encounter between Jesus and the Baptiser, which is only preceded or "overshadowed" by a reference to the Scriptures that point to a divine act of sending (of the messenger to prepare the way of the Son).[11] Luke and Matthew use their genealogies to also point to a beginning within human history, related to the forefather Abraham (Matt

---

7 On the "analepses" of the Johannine narration, see the seminal narratological study by Culpepper 1983, 54–70.

8 Cf. the definition in Kunath 2016, 41–42.

9 A wider range of sayings and motifs linked with the aspect of the "pre-existence" of Jesus is, e.g., discussed in Hamerton-Kelly 1973 and Habermann 1990. Cf., however, Kunath 2016, 11–17.

10 See the comprehensive treatment in Endo 2002.

11 Cf. Frey 2011, 198–202; see also Klauck 1997.

1:1) or the primordial human Adam (Luke 3:38), whereas John, with his reference to the ἀρχή of Gen 1:1, goes beyond both beginnings. When John 1:3 πάντα δι' αὐτοῦ ἐγένετο refers to the genesis of the universe (πάντα), i.e., the creation work as described in Genesis 1, the status and reference of John 1:1–2 appears even more enigmatic: Is the ἐν ἀρχῇ of John 1:1–2 in a marked contrast with the aorist ἐγένετο used in John 1:3, thus referring to a kind of background or status behind the act of creation, which is mentioned thereafter in John 1:3?[12]

But regardless of the language used, the protological and cosmological questions posed by John 1:1–2 are difficult: Does John really want to refer to a time before the creation of time in his prologue? While some interpreters wanted to dismiss such an idea as naively mythological, others could take it as a starting point for an extensive speculation. Was there a status before the creation according to the views of the evangelist? And how is creation conceptualised if it is not a creation *ex nihilo*, but instead a creation from a former status or even stuff? Does John presuppose ideas such as the Stoic conflagration in which a former world is merely transformed into a new one by a process of collapse and regeneration? But nothing in the Gospel suggests an affinity with those concepts. From the reference to Gen 1:1, one could also conclude that such a former status is considered a kind of unstructured matter[13] which is, then, structured and formed in the creation? Or is it simply considered a status in which God and the Logos existed in a privileged co-ordination with nothing else in their company, since the universe only came into being through the act of creation narrated in v. 3? Later readers of the prologue have taken the verses as the point of departure for extensive speculations on the *pleroma* or on an emanation or a development within the divine sphere, but nothing in the text suggests that the gospel author already thought of further mediator figures apart from the divine Logos. Thus, a more extended cosmological speculation is certainly beyond the scope of John and his prologue, while the priority of the Logos – as being with God or oriented toward God – over against the whole universe is most clearly expressed.

This is, by the way, confirmed in John 17:24, the last one of the Johannine pre-existence statements, in which God's love for Jesus is dated back to a time or status "before the foundation of the world" (πρὸ καταβολῆς κόσμου). This is the only passage in John where the term κόσμος is clearly used with reference to the created world or the universe, not merely to humanity either as an object of God's love (as in John 3:16) or as a subject of unbelief and hostility against Jesus and his followers (cf. John 15:18). If the prologue and John 17 are not critically

---

[12] Concerning the remarkable contrast between the Greek tenses in John, see Frey 1998, 130–46. Concerning the aorist and imperfect in John 1:1–2, see in particular pages 92–93 and 157–58.

[13] Cf. the Hebrew expression *tohuwabohu* in Gen 1:2, which suggests the idea of a formless chaotic matter.

distinguished from the work of the evangelist,[14] these passages clearly show that the evangelist does not neglect the created world, but presupposes a view of the creation of the world as presented in the Scriptures, even though his focus is on humans and their salvation. But salvation is not conceptualised in an anti-cosmic manner.

2. *The Pre-existence of Christ*

This leads us to the explicit references to Christ's pre-existence in the Fourth Gospel. While previous scholarship has often discussed the motif by reference to a larger number of statements about Jesus as the Son of Man and his sending and commissioning, Friederike Kunath has recently made a helpful suggestion for more precisely defining the Johannine pre-existence expressions on the basis certain linguistic features. She describes a category of narrative phrases, wherein the narrator contrasts Jesus's temporal priority over against other narrative figures or the world. The changed temporal sequence in the text creates an irritation that draws the reader's attention.[15] In this category, she includes the passages that mention Jesus's temporal priority over against John the Baptist (John 1:15, 30), his being in a realm above "before" his coming (John 6:62), his existence prior to the genesis of Abraham (John 8:58), his possession of glory before the world was (John 17:5), and his love-relation with the Father before the foundation of the world (John 17:24). These explicit expressions of Jesus's pre-existence draw the reader's attention within their narrative context because they introduce a surprising temporal priority of Jesus over against the Baptiser, Abraham, or even the created world. Within the narrative sequence of the gospel, these sayings increasingly go back from the near past of Jesus's forerunner through the historical time of Israel's forefather until the pre-historical time before the creation of the world. The last phrase (John 17:24) is, then, most closely related to the beginning of the gospel and the ἀρχή imagined before the creation. The majority of the pre-existence phrases are also articulated in the imperfect tense, which links them with the "background status" marked by the imperfect ἦν in John 1:1–2.

Assembled in such a category, the Johannine pre-existence statements form a coherent web that pervades the whole Johannine narrative from chapter 1 to chapter 17 and is linked back to the opening of the prologue. But in spite of the temporal imagination created, these phrases are focused not on protology or

[14] Thus the result of the redaction-critical approach in Becker 1991, according to which the work of the evangelist is totally void of any reference to the creation because the prologue is considered a source used and reshaped by the evangelist and John 17 is considered part of a redactional expansion, the "Kirchliche Redaktion," in which the views of the evangelist are supplemented and changed from a different theological perspective. For criticism of this pattern, see Frey 1997, 274–87 and 2006, 3–15.

[15] Kunath 2016, 41–44.

cosmology, as such, but on Christology: Their main interest is in expressing Jesus's priority over against particular figures of history or even the world as a whole. This corresponds to the expression of the pre-existence of the Logos in communion with God in contrast with the created world in 1:1–3. The Gospel's interest is to claim Jesus's authority by means of a particular element of narrative design or even by the use of particular contrasting tenses. Jesus is given priority over against several figures of history and, ultimately, over against the world as a whole. This is an efficient means of expressing his supermundane, yet even divine authority.

3. The Sending, Commissioning, and Authorising of Jesus

In spite of the fact that the group of pre-existence statements can be clearly defined, the concept of the pre-existence of Jesus is linked with a number of other motifs of Johannine Christology which also emphasise Jesus's authority and the dignity of his revelation.

The first aspect or concept is the motif of Jesus or the Son being sent by the Father, which is utilised in the entire narration of the gospel.[16] The concept of the sending has even been suggested to be the dominant concept of Johannine Christology.[17] Others consider it an early Johannine concept[18] which was later overshadowed by "higher" concepts of Christology, such as the idea of the divine nature of Jesus or of his pre-existence. However, the attempts at reconstructing earlier strata of Johannine thought are methodologically problematic and have not led to convincing results. In earlier scholarship, the concept of the divine messenger was also linked with the reconstruction of a Gnostic redeemer myth, in particular with its aspects of the coming and the departure of the redeemer.[19] But the traditio-historical background of the concept can rather be found in Jewish traditions about Wisdom or the Messiah as a divine messenger,[20] and the idea of Jesus being sent or having come for a certain purpose is already expressed in a number of Synoptic sayings (Matt 10:40; Luke 10:16; cf. John 13:20) as well as in the Pauline tradition (Gal 4:4–5; Rom 8:3–4), and the form of those Pauline or rather pre-Pauline sending formulas has been adopted in the Johannine tradition (John 3:16 and 17; 1 John 4:9 and 4:10).[21] In any case, the idea of Jesus being sent is not an expression of his humility (and thus an element of a "low" Christology), but rather an element of his authorisation and

[16] Cf. the discussion in Miranda ²1976; Bühner 1977; Loader 1989; and Schnackenburg 1991.

[17] Thus Loader 1989, see also Loader 2017.

[18] Cf. Bühner 1977; other interpreters linked the motif with a possibly early prophet Christology, cf. Meeks 1972.

[19] Thus, in particular, Bultmann ²¹1984 (and in numerous earlier articles).

[20] Cf. Schimanowski 1985 and Hengel 2006.

[21] Cf. Hahn 2002, 606–08.

authority. Due to the cultural principle (not only attested in later Rabbinic sources) that the one being sent shares the authority of his sender,[22] the idea that Jesus is sent from the Father claims that his authority is given by the Father or that he acts and speaks with the authority of God. Therefore, belief in Jesus is belief in God (John 12:44–45; 14:1). Apart from the phrases using the words ἀποστέλλειν and πέμπειν (and in particular the formula about the Father ὁ πέμψας με [John 5:37; 6:44; 7:28; 8:16, 18, etc.]), the sending motif is linked with other expressions about Jesus's "coming" into the world, "coming" from heaven, or "descending" from heaven (cf. John 3:13; 6:33, 38, 41–42, 50). Thus, the links with the idea of Jesus's pre-existence are quite dense, but again, these motifs are used to express the authorisation of the one who is sent from the Father and thus authorised to bring the divine revelation.

A number of other aspects are linked with the motif of Jesus's sending: He "has seen" (John 3:32; 6:46) and thus can give testimony, or similarly, he "has heard" (John 3:32) and thus is able to proclaim and act accordingly. There is even the idea that Jesus continually "sees" the Father doing his works (John 5:19–20) or hears from the Father (John 5:30) so that when he acts accordingly, God himself is doing his works. But while this simultaneous acting of Jesus and the Father openly claims his unity with the Father during his ministry, the other passages mentioning a vision, audition, or authorisation in the aorist or in the perfect tense presuppose the idea that Jesus as the Son has been informed or authorised before his coming or his earthly appearance in the realm of the Father, or simply "above." Thus Jesus's commissioning or authorisation for his sending or ministry is imagined in connection with a time before or a realm above the narrated story. But the temporal imagination implied in those phrases, most prominently in the pre-existence phrase in John 6:62, also serves to authorise his ministry as the Son of God, sent into the world. The focus is not on the temporal or even cosmological aspects, but the phrases mentioned add some aspects to the mere idea of his sending.

One further aspect is to be added. Several passages mention that the Father "gave" (aorist) or "has given" (perfect) something to the Son: the possession of life in himself, the ability to communicate life (John 5:26), the authority to enact judgment (John 5:26), the words to reveal (John 17:8), and even the authority (ἐξουσία) over humans (John 13:3; 17:2), authority over their ability to believe, and authority over those who actually believe (cf. John 17:9). Such a bestowal of trust or authorisation is also to be imagined in a time before or reality before his sending or his coming into the world. In the Johannine view, the whole of Jesus's ministry is preceded by a multifaceted act of authorisation or bestowal of trust, and thus his whole work, his words and deeds, are authorised from a realm in which Jesus was "before" (John 6:62), and which is localised "above,"

22 Cf. the extensive treatment in Bühner 1977 and earlier Rengstorf 1933.

the realm of God. In this way, the ideas discussed here contribute to the cosmological imagination of John, even if their focus is not on cosmology but on soteriology.

The soteriological implication of the divine authorisation is also clearly expressed: What is given to Jesus by God himself cannot be taken away by someone else. Accordingly, humans who are given to Jesus belong to the flock of the Good Shepherd and cannot be snatched out of his hand (John 10:28). Thus, the protological confirmation of the salvation or the present communion with Jesus serves as an affirmation of eschatological perseverance. Believers are safe because their lives are not in their own hands, nor in the hands of someone else, but safely in the hands of Jesus, where God himself has placed them.

4. God's Love for His Son and for the World

From here, we come to the final dimension and the ultimate aims of "protology" in John. This dimension is not touched upon due to a particular interest in the material world or the universe, but rather due to the interest in ultimately anchoring and securing the relation between God and humans or God and Jesus. Therefore, the gospel takes up the idea from the beginning of the prologue that the Logos was πρὸς τὸν θεόν, i.e., in a close relation with God, and links it with unique expressions of divine love, not only towards the Son but also towards the world of humans. God's primordial love for the Son is expressed in the last of the Johannine pre-existence phrases, in John 17:24, where it is said that the Father loved Jesus "before the foundation of the world." This corresponds with the earlier statement in John 3:35: "The Father loves the Son, and has given all things into His hand." The bestowal of trust on and authorisation of Jesus is rooted in God's love, and this love is anchored in the primordial relation of unity between the Father and the Son, or between God and his divine Logos.

But the Son is not only the object of God's primordial and eternal love but also the world of humans, the realm into which the Son has been sent for the sake of salvation. Thus the statement in John 3:17 about the sending of Son for the salvation of the world and the kerygmatic summary in 3:16 that God "gave" his Son (not only into the world but also over to death) are equally preceded by the remarkable statement that God so loved the world.[23] God's love for the world and the love for the Son (3:16 and 3:35) are closely connected in this chapter and cannot be taken apart. Consequently, not only God's love for the Son, but also his love for the world, and thus his salvific will for humans, is rooted in the primordial state, before the creation, i.e., in protology.

This shows the real weight of protology in the Fourth Gospel: It is not focused on the origins of the world or its creation, nor on the origins of evil and its explanation. Nor is it merely interested in the pre-existence of Jesus as an

[23] On the motif of God's love in John, see in particular Popkes 2005 and also Frey 2008a.

expression of his divine authority or origin, but the ultimate focus is on the primordial roots of salvation. If salvation is rooted not only in a certain event in history, but in the loving intention of God the creator, and if such love even goes back to the very beginning, beyond the "world" of human history and suffering, if salvation ultimately springs from the love of the Father for his Son, it is assured to the utmost degree. Protology is thus articulated for the sake of eschatology.

Before we can draw further consequences from those insights, we have to discuss the relevance of protology with regard to the interpretation of the Gospel: How does protology affect the reading of the Gospel? Or which reading strategy is appropriate to the Johannine narrative?

II. Opposed Reading Strategies and the Theological Logic of the Fourth Gospel

Is the protological beginning the presupposition for reading the Johannine story of the earthly Jesus? Is the glory of the pre-existent one, his unity with God, and his superhuman nature the point of departure from which the whole narration has to be understood? This is a quite influential suggestion for reading the gospel, but we will have to discuss its implications and problems as well. This reading strategy was influentially advocated by the idealistic church historian and New Testament scholar Ferdinand Christian Baur in the nineteenth century,[24] and it was adopted by some authors around 1900 and in particular by Ernst Käsemann in the middle of the twentieth century.[25]

1. The Reading Perspective from the Eternal Logos and the Glory of the Pre-existent One

For Baur, the whole gospel narrative was simply a narrative exposition of the idea of the divine Logos, with the consequence that the Logos idea has priority, and the whole narrative is more or less an illustration of that idea. As a consequence, the history of the earthly Jesus becomes not only unimportant with regard to its historical source value, but also the whole earthly, bodily dimension of Jesus's ministry, and even his death are ultimately considered irrelevant and merely a mirror of the idea of the divine Logos and its glory. Such a devaluation of the earthly reality of Jesus is a consequence of Baur's idealistic view that idea precedes history.

Ernst Käsemann explicitly followed Baur's idealistic reading in critical rejection of Rudolf Bultmann's existential interpretation of the Fourth Gospel.

[24] On Baur's interpretation of John, see Frey 2017.
[25] See in particular Käsemann [4]1980; for discussion, see Frey 2008b.

Reading the Gospel from the premise of John 1:14b (ἐθεασάμεθα τὴν δόξαν αὐτοῦ), rather than 1:14a (ὁ λόγος σὰρξ ἐγένετο), and thus continuously presupposing the "glory" of the Pre-existent One, Käsemann could consider the Fourth Gospel a naively docetic or even Gnosticising writing.[26] If the Johannine story is read under the premise that the figure of Jesus is surrounded by his divine glory from the very beginning, then the traits of his true humanity, his emotions and thirst, his suffering and ultimately his death lose their weight. For Käsemann, therefore, the climax of John is in John 17, and the appended story of Jesus's passion can be considered almost obsolete and only adopted because of its place in the tradition. The earthly condition as presented in the gospel narrative is merely the stage set for the divine messenger to reveal his heavenly glory. In this reading, the sending motif, understood in terms of a mythological pattern, is the primary motif of Johannine Christology, whereas Jesus's death on the cross can no longer be considered the root of salvation. Consequently, John is accused of advocating a "theology of glory" in contrast with the Pauline (and truly Christian) "theology of the cross."

2. *The Problems of This Perspective and the Focus on Jesus's Death and Resurrection*

It is not our concern here to discuss Käsemann's concept of a "canon within the canon" and the implications for the canonical status of the Fourth Gospel. But we have to ask whether the reading suggested by Käsemann is textually appropriate or whether it unduly marginalises certain elements of the text, the references to Jesus's humanity, and in particular the passion narrative and the cross.[27] Why does John so strongly mark the fulfilment of the Scriptures and the fulfilment of the divine will in the scene of Jesus's death (John 19:28–30)[28] if those events have only marginal, if any, relevance? Why is the narration of Jesus's death so extensively prepared by preceding explanations in the Farewell Discourses? Why does John so frequently hint to the passion and resurrection of Jesus from the very beginning of his narration, by mentioning Jesus's hour (John 2:4), his exaltation as an act paralleled with the uplifting of Moses's serpent (John 3:14), the attempts of his adversaries to kill him, the mention of the one who was to "deliver" him, and so on?

The gospel obviously makes intense efforts to enable the readers to properly understand the events of Jesus's death by communicating its categories of inter-

[26] Thus, Käsemann rejects Bultmann's view (see Bultmann [21]1984) that the evangelist, while actually adopting sources (the Logos hymn and a source of revelation discourses) from a Gnostic milieu of baptiser groups, interpreted the coming of Jesus in an anti-Gnostic manner. On Käsemann's criticism of Bultmann, see Frey 1997, 160–70.

[27] For a critical interaction with Käsemann's views, see more extensively Frey 2002, 169–91 and 2009, 288–300.

[28] Cf. Frey 2007, 66–69.

pretation and further explanations in advance before the beginning of the passion narrative. In spite of the particular terms chosen for addressing Jesus's death, such as "departing" (ὑπάγειν), "being exalted" (ὑψωθῆναι), or "being glorified" (δοξασθῆναι), the gospel does not intend a euphemistic reading or a reduction of the notion of suffering in accord with the taste of a Hellenistic audience.[29] The aim is rather to avoid a misunderstanding of the cross as a defeat and to stimulate a reading of the passion in the light of the Easter events, i.e., as a victory (John 16:33), the enthronisation of the true king,[30] and the foundation of belief.

3. The Reading Perspective from the Presupposition of Jesus's Death and Resurrection

In John, not only the passion story but the whole Jesus story is programmatically narrated from a post-Easter perspective.[31] The narrative image of the earthly Jesus is consistently drawn from post-Easter insights. This is explicitly stated in some important narrative comments according to which the disciples and contemporaries of Jesus did not understand the events nor the words of Jesus during his lifetime, but only after his resurrection or glorification, they "remembered" and understood what the words and acts really meant (John 2:22; 12:16). Thus, the Gospel's image of Christ and its "high Christology" are explicitly explained from a post-Easter process of remembrance and reinterpretation, stimulated by the Spirit (John 14:25–26; 16:13). Herein the evangelist openly concedes that the true dignity or the glory of Jesus was not yet visible to the eyes of his contemporaries and that the narration in the gospel is not just a representation of the events "as they were." When, after the Cana episode, John 2:11 states that Jesus "revealed his glory," we cannot conclude that this glory was already revealed to his pre-Easter disciples or even to all his contemporaries seeing his deeds. Since even his miracles are obviously misconceived by many, the "signs" that really convey his glory are actually the narrated signs (i.e., the texts), designed as revelatory narratives by the evangelist and quite openly related to the events of Jesus's death and resurrection.[32] Thus, the glory of the earthly Jesus, as depicted in John, is actually the glory of the risen one, revealed to his followers in the post-Easter era.

This is confirmed by the fact that in the overwhelming majority of passages, Jesus's "glorification" is linked with the events of his "hour," i.e., his death and resurrection.[33] There is only one passage that points in another direction, John

---

[29] On the possible interpretational categories of a "noble death," see Frey 2007, 71–76.
[30] On the motif of kingship, see Frey 2014b, 385–89.
[31] Cf. Hoegen-Rohls 1996 and Frey 1998, 247–68; 2014a, 146–50, and 2018.
[32] On the interpretation of the semeia narratives, see Frey 2015c.
[33] Cf. Frey 2008b, 383–95.

17:5 (νῦν δόξασόν με σύ, πάτερ, παρὰ σεαυτῷ τῇ δόξῃ ᾗ εἶχον πρὸ τοῦ τὸν κόσμον εἶναι παρὰ σοί), where even Jesus's glory is linked with the communion between the pre-existent Jesus and the Father, and Jesus's glorification is said to be a renewal of the glory he had with the Father before the world was. But it seems more appropriate to read this most far-reaching idea as a logical consequence of the predominant idea of Jesus's glorification in his hour: When, in the post-Easter era, Jesus was considered glorified and being in the realm of the Father, his glory obtained in his resurrection or enthronisation could also be linked with the primordial communion and love between Jesus and the Father, or with the status of the pre-existent one. Thus, the idea only expressed in John 17:5 can be explained from the larger number of passages about Jesus's "glorification" that links them with his "hour."

The reverse explanation would provide serious problems. Most of the passages about Jesus's "glorification" link that that process with the events of his death and resurrection, whereas only one passage points to a premundane glory of the pre-existent one. If the idea of John 17:5 was presupposed in the whole Johannine narrative,[34] the idea of his "glorification" in the events of his "hour" (cf. John 13:31–32; 17:1 etc.) would be odds. In that case, such a glorification could only be a kind of restoration of a glory (temporarily) abandoned in his incarnation or veiled during his earthly ministry. This is how later theologians (in the Lutheran orthodoxy) actually discussed the status of Christ during his earthly ministry, either as a *kenosis* or as a *krypsis* of his divine glory and power. In John, however, there is no idea of any loss of dignity or glory in the incarnation. Only the later connection of the Johannine prologue with other biblical passages such as Phil 2:6 could suggest such a view, and later dogmatic debates actually draw on the combination of those passages.

But, historically, we should be clear how this idea could be developed: It is an ultimate consequence drawn from the insights of the post-Easter faith, not an ontological presupposition of the earthly appearance of Jesus.

4. The Necessity of Reading Backwards: From Eschatology to Protology

So, the later dogmatic construct of the divine Son abandoning or concealing his heavenly glory in the incarnation in order to be incarnate among humans is a reversal of the way the idea actually developed. Therefore, in contrast with the dogmatic narrative that goes from the divine glory through incarnation to the glorification, i.e., from protology to eschatology, *we have to read the gospel*

[34] The reference to John 1:14b does not help here because John 1:14 is definitely phrased from a post-Easter perspective, and it is at least unclear or ambiguous who is meant in the first person plural. The speakers claiming that they contemplated Jesus's glory are certainly not merely (and probably not primarily) the disciples from the time of Jesus, but rather the community of disciples looking back and commemorating the Jesus story as being taught by the Spirit-Paraclete (John 14:26; 16:13–15).

with a different perspective and according to a different strategy: from eschatology to protology, or from the events of Jesus's death and resurrection, understood as his glorification, back to the idea of his divine dignity, pre-existence, and primordial glory. Protology, as presented in the Fourth Gospel, is a consequence of eschatology, and it is inserted to affirm and ensure Jesus's function as the saviour and giver of eternal life.

III. From Early Messianism to John's High Christology: A Historical Perspective

This can be further explained by a very brief historical reconstruction of the making of Johannine Christology and Eschatology: Of course, such a reconstruction is hypothetical, and it works with patterns of a plausible development. Most of the former attempts at reconstructing Johannine Christology were based on the assumption of earlier sources or thought patterns, such as the Semeia source or a Jewish-Christian "Grundschrift," the patterns of a sending Christology or a prophet Christology etc. As scholarship has lost its former confidence in our capacity to determine and isolate pre-Johannine sources from the Fourth Gospel, all those hypothetical reconstructions of the thought development within the Johannine communities have lost their plausibility.[35] The only clearly perceptible source adopted in John is, apart from the Scriptures, the Gospel of Mark, which is presupposed and critically used at several points.[36] Furthermore, we can presuppose a number of sayings of Jesus which are attested elsewhere in the Synoptics, paralleled in the Johannine epistles or formed in a manner that suggests a previous existence in the Johannine community tradition.[37] But as it is difficult to locate those traditions in the Johannine or the wider early Christian tradition, we can only sketch the developments behind Johannine Theology in a more general manner.

1. The Development of Christology: From Early Messianism to High Christology

With regard to Christology, we have to start with a reconstruction of the message and ministry of Jesus of Nazareth, but the details and impasses of the debates related cannot be discussed in the present context.[38] A widely accepted consensus is that the earthly Jesus became known since the beginning of his

[35] Cf. Frey 2013, 17–21 and, more extensively, 1997, 266–97.

[36] Cf. Frey 2003.

[37] See the thorough overview in Theobald 2002.

[38] For overviews, cf. the works by Theissen and Merz 1996 and Hengel and Schwemer 2007.

ministry as an exorcist, healer, and preacher of the coming (and even imminent) kingdom of God. This is the activity that made him known to a larger number contemporaries, launched Messianic expectations at least in some of his sympathisers, and ultimately led to his denunciation as a Messianic pretender that brought him to death under Pontius Pilate. Whereas Mark (and John 1:19–34; cf. 3:22–26) plausibly located the historical origins of his ministry in the encounter with John the Baptist, the stories about his miraculous birth (in Matthew and Luke) are later supplements to the tradition, presupposing and developing earlier christological views about Jesus as the Messiah.

Even more so is the Johannine adoption of the motif of the divine Wisdom or Logos as a means of explaining Jesus's true origins in a realm of God and at a time before the creation of the world, a later expansion of christological thought towards protology. Pushing the origins of the Gospel message back from the beginning of Jesus's ministry to his birth, to the earlier history of Israel, or even to the creation of the world and beyond is part of the development of Christology within the first century CE. Christological thought developed from the perception and early Messianic interpretation of Jesus's ministry and the Paschal belief in his exaltation to divine glory toward the view that his ministry was prepared by earlier events such as the prodigies at his birth. Christological thought continued to develop views of Jesus's pre-existence in the Old Testament period, in the creation of the world, or in the divine reality beyond or before the world came into being.

The idea of such a christological development can be supported by numerous other observations. Although Mark prominently proclaims Jesus as "the Son of God" in several pivotal passages of his gospel, his Messianic identity must remain hidden until the open proclamation at his trial (Mark 14:61–62) or in the resurrection (cf. Mark 9:9). In contrast with this, the Gospel of John openly proclaims not only Jesus's Messianic identity but also his divine dignity from the very beginning.[39] Most of the important christological titles are already present in the first chapter. And while the christological titles used varies from "lower" titles (Messiah, prophet, the one who is sent…) to "higher" titles (Son of Man, Son of God, the Son, or even God), it is clear that for John the true identity and dignity of Jesus is expressed by the highest predications: Jesus is not just the Messiah – although he *is* (cf. John 4:26; 20:31) – and the predication as "prophet" (John 4:19; 6:26) is obviously insufficient. Instead, he is truly the Son who is one with the Father (John 10:30), and even God (John 1:18; 20:28). This is expressed most prominently in his I-am-sayings in which the formulaic self-presentation of the biblical God (cf. Exod 3:14 LXX and Isa 43:10–11 LXX or 45:12 LXX) is adopted in the mouth of the earthly Jesus so that the linguistic form of his sayings clearly serves the expression of his divine authority. As the

[39] On Johannine Christology, see Frey 2016.

divine messenger and the image of the one God (cf. John 14:7, 9), he has also been given the authority to communicate eternal life and to enact judgment (John 5:22–23, 26–27). Bringing the dead to life is a proper work of God, and thus his eschatological authority, which is most prominently demonstrated in the resurrection of Lazarus (John 11:1–45), is a consequence of his divine dignity.

2. The Development of Eschatology: Present-Oriented Eschatology as the Consequence of the Johannine Christology

From here, we can turn to the particular profile of Johannine eschatology, which has always been considered different from the eschatology in the Synoptics and in Paul.[40] Although there is no clear-cut contrast, and scholarship has too long underestimated the future-oriented aspects in the eschatology of the Fourth Gospel,[41] the focus of Johannine thought is obviously more on the present than on the future. Although the idea of Christ's return or "parousia" is presupposed in some passages of the gospel (and even more so in 1 John),[42] there is no image of his return on the clouds of the sky (Mark 14:62), and other elements of apocalyptic imagery are presented only in a strongly reduced manner. Furthermore, the main theological orientation is different in John: Salvation is not primarily expected in a future sequence of events, such as, e. g., the parousia, resurrection of the dead, and judgment, but according to a very prominent phrase in John (John 4:23 and 5:25), the hour originally expected is *now*. This hour is stunningly made present in the encounter with Jesus, in which the decision and division of humans, i. e., the judgment, happens (John 3:18) and the dead come to life when they hear Jesus's voice (John 5:25; cf. 11:43–44). Although the hope for the resurrection of the deceased believers is apparently presupposed (John 11:25–26; cf. John 6:39, 40, 44), the transfer from death to eschatological and eternal life already happens at present, in the faithful perception of the word of Jesus, which is the life-giving word of God.

Such a focus on the presence of the eschatological events in Jesus and in the proclamation of his word is to be explained as a consequence of Johannine Christology.[43] If Jesus truly represents the authority of God, life is given through him and in the encounter with him, and such life can be considered "eternal life," i. e., life in abundance and in eschatological validity.

John shares the conviction in Paul that eternal life is given through faith.[44] But, while Paul is still focused on the completion of salvation in the resurrection

---

[40] See the extensive study by Frey 2000.

[41] See the detailed history of research in Frey 1997 and the argument with regard to the Johannine texts in Frey 2000.

[42] Cf. John 21:22–23 and 16:16–19. In the epistles, see 1 John 2:28 and 3:2. Cf. Frey 2000, 14–22 and 83–94.

[43] Cf. Frey 2000, 321 and, in debate with Bultmann, Blank 1964, 38.

[44] This has been demonstrated convincingly by Ueberschaer 2017.

of the dead, and the final unification with Christ (cf. 1 Thess 4:17; 1 Cor 15:50–55; Rom 8:21–23 etc.), the Johannine focus is much more focused on eternal life as a present gift and possession (cf. John 3:18; 5:24 etc.). There is a marked difference between those concepts and other soteriological concepts in the New Testament, e.g., in Matthew, James, or 2 Peter: Eternal life, in the Johannine view, is not just a gift on probation, whereas the definitive appropriation still depends on appropriate conduct that is to be confirmed in a last and definitive judgment. Instead, life is considered a definitive eschatological gift that implies the resurrection in the case of physical death, but also the confirmation that the one who has been given life "will not die anymore" in the spiritual dimension (John 11:26).

Believers, therefore, are supposed to remain, to keep the word of Jesus, and to love each other, Jesus, and God, whereas they are loved by God and Jesus. Believing and staying in communion with each other and with God are considered so inseparable that the actual case of some community members separating themselves or not remaining with the community (cf. 1 John 2:18–22) can only be explained by the idea that those former members had never really belonged to the community. The practical problems of such a view cannot be further reflected upon in the present context. Theologically, the perseverance of believers has its ultimate reason in the fact that faith is a gift, which can be attributed to the activity of the Spirit, or even Jesus and God: Jesus promises that, after his exaltation, he will "draw all humans unto him" (John 12:32), and also the Father draws humans to Jesus (John 6:44). The divine activity of drawing humans to faith, or the idea that God has given Jesus his followers (John 6:39; 17:9), provides a firm basis for the promise of salvation: If they are "given" into the hands of the Good Shepherd by God himself, they cannot be dragged astray by anyone else; if the Father has given them into the hands of Jesus, they cannot fall out of his hands (John 10:28). Thus, Johannine eschatology and soteriology assure readers that their salvation is not in danger by the turmoil of human life and history, but firm and definitive, anchored in God himself and therefore eschatologically valid.

3. The Ultimate Reason for Salvation: The Love of God

Here, we arrive at the ultimate reason for salvation according to Johannine theology: It is God himself who, out of his love for the world, has sent his Son (John 3:16–17); it is God himself who has authorised the Son and his revelation; it is God himself who has given the Son authority over "all flesh;" and it is God himself who has drawn humans to Jesus and to faith.

In various Johannine passages, this is linked with the aspect of God's love – for the Son (John 3:35) but also for the world (John 3:16). God's love is mentioned as the ultimate reason for the sending of the only Son and his way into death for the forgiveness of sins (cf. 1 John 4:9–10). With this pivotal idea, salvation is ultimately anchored in a realm beyond the created world and beyond the uncertainties of history. Salvation is firm in that it is not dependent on further conduct, trials, or judicial acts; it is firm because it is rooted in the eternal, pre-mundane love of God himself, in the primordial relationship of love between the Father and the Son (John 17:24; cf. 3:35).

4. Protology as Affirmation of Salvation

This is the reason why John, unlike the other canonical gospels, goes back to protology. The dimension of the creation and even beyond is touched upon because it is the ultimate anchor for eschatological salvation and the confirmation of salvation as firm and eschatologically valid. Protology is, therefore, developed from eschatology and serves the interests of eschatology. But, whereas in the textual sequence of the Gospel, protology is touched upon at the very beginning, and eschatology only comes in view as the narrative unfolds, the historical development and the theological logic of Johannine thought follows the reverse direction: *from eschatology to protology.* At the beginning, there is an eschatological framework: the Messianic sending of Jesus, the eschatological salvation rooted in his death and resurrection. Protology is touched upon in order to express the ultimate assurance or the deepest reason of the eschatological confirmation of salvation. It is the dimension in which eschatological salvation has its primordial and therefore unshakeable foundations. In John, protology is not expressed in the interest of cosmology or philosophical speculation. Instead, it is expressed exclusively in the interest of soteriology and eschatology providing confirmation of salvation to a community in distress.

Bibliography

Becker, J. (1991), *Das Evangelium des Johannes*, 2 vols. (Gütersloher Taschenbücher Siebenstern 505–06; Ökumenischer Taschenbuchkommentar zum Neuen Testament 4/1–2), Gütersloh: Güterloher Verlagshaus Mohn; Würzburg: Echter.

Blank, J. (1964), *Krisis: Untersuchungen zur johanneischen Christologie und Eschatologie*, Freiburg i. Br.: Lambertus-Verlag.

Bühner, J.-A. (1977), *Der Gesandte und sein Weg im 4. Evangelium: Die kultur- und religionsgeschichtlichen Grundlagen der johanneischen Sendungschristologie sowie ihre traditionsgeschichtliche Entwicklung* (Wissenschaftliche Untersuchungen zum Neuen Testament [WUNT] II/2), Tübingen: Mohr (Paul Siebeck).

Bultmann, R. ([21]1984), *Das Evangelium des Johannes* (Kritisch-exegetischer Kommentar über das Neue Testament 2), Göttingen: Vandenhoeck & Ruprecht.

Culpepper, R. A. (1983), *Anatomy of the Fourth Gospels: A Study in Literary Design*, Philadelphia, PA: Fortress.

Endo, M. (2002), *Creation and Christology: A Study on the Johannine Prologue in the Light of Early Jewish Creation Accounts* (WUNT II/149), Tübingen: Mohr Siebeck.
Frey, J. (1997), *Die johanneische Eschatologie.* Vol. I: *Ihre Probleme im Spiegel der Forschung seit Reimarus* (WUNT 96), Tübingen: Mohr Siebeck.
– (1998), *Die johanneische Eschatologie.* Vol. II: *Das johanneische Zeitverständnis* (WUNT 110), Tübingen: Mohr Siebeck.
– (2000), *Die johanneische Eschatologie.* Vol. III: *Die eschatologische Verkündigung in den johanneischen Texten* (WUNT 117), Tübingen: Mohr Siebeck.
– (2002), '"Die *theologia crucifixi*" des Johannesevangeliums', in: *Kreuzestheologie im Neuen Testament*, ed. A. Dettwiler and J. Zumstein (WUNT 151), Tübingen: Mohr Siebeck, 169–238 (republished in Frey 2013, 485–554).
– (2003), 'Das vierte Evangelium auf dem Hintergrund der älteren Evangelientradition', in: *Johannesevangelium – Mitte oder Rand des Kanons? Neue Standortbestimmungen*, ed. T. Söding (Quaestiones disputatae 203), Freiburg i. Br: Herder, 60–118 (republished in Frey 2013, 239–94).
– (2006), 'Zu Hintergrund und Funktion des johanneischen Dualismus', in: *Paulus und Johannes: Exegetische Studien zur paulinischen und johanneischen Theologie und Literatur*, ed. D. Sänger and U. Mell (WUNT 198), Tübingen: Mohr Siebeck, 3–73 (republished in Frey 2013, 409–82).
– (2007), 'Edler Tod – wirksamer Tod – stellvertretender Tod – heilvoller Tod: Zur narrativen und theologischen Bedeutung des Todes Jesu im Johannesevangelium', in: *The Death of Jesus in the Fourth Gospel*, ed. G. Van Belle (Bibliotheca Ephemeridum Theologicarum Lovaniensium 200), Leuven: Peeters, 64–94 (republished in Frey 2013, 555–84).
– (2008a), '"God Is Love": On the Textual Tradition and Semantics of a Core Expression of the Christian Notion of God', in: *Divine Wrath and Divine Mercy in the World of Antiquity*, ed. R.G. Kratz and H. Spieckermann (Forschungen zum Alten Testament II/33), Tübingen: Mohr Siebeck, 203–27.
– (2008b), '"...dass sie meine Herrlichkeit schauen" (John 17,24): Zu Hintergrund, Sinn und Funktion der johanneischen Rede von der δόξα Jesu', *New Testament Studies* 54: 375–97 (republished in Frey 2013, 639–62).
– (2009), 'Leiblichkeit und Auferstehung im Johannesevangelium', in: *The Human Body in Death and Resurrection*, ed. T. Nicklas, F.V. Reiterer, and J. Verheyden (Deuterocanonical and Cognate Literature: Yearbook 2009), Berlin – New York: De Gruyter, 285–327 (republished in Frey 2013, 699–738).
– (2011), 'How Could Mark and John Do without Infancy Stories? Jesus' Humanity and His Divine Origins in Mark and John', in: *Infancy Gospels: Story and Identity*, ed. C. Clivaz, A. Dettwiler, L. Devillers, and E. Norelli (WUNT 281), Tübingen: Mohr Siebeck, 189–215.
– (2013), *Die Herrlichkeit des Gekreuzigten: Studien zu den Johanneischen Schriften I*, ed. J. Schlegel (WUNT 307), Tübingen: Mohr Siebeck.
– (2014a), 'Die Gegenwart der Vergangenheit und Zukunft Christi: Zur "Verschmelzung" der Zeithorizonte im Johannesevangelium', in: *Zeit* (Jahrbuch für biblische Theologie 28), Neukirchen-Vluyn: Neukirchener Verlag, 129–57.
– (2014b), 'Jesus und Pilatus: Der wahre König und der Repräsentant des Kaisers im Johannesevangelium', in: *Christ and the Emperor*, ed. G. Van Belle and J. Verheyden (Biblical Tools and Studies 20), Leuven: Peeters, 337–93.

– (2015a), *Der Brief des Judas und der zweite Brief des Petrus* (Theologischer Handkommentar zum Neuen Testament 15/2), Leipzig: Evangelische Verlagsanstalt.
– (2015b), 'The Johannine Prologue and the References to the Creation of the World in Its Second Century Receptions', in: *Les judaïsmes dans tous leurs états aux Ier–IIIe siècles (Les Judéeens des synagogues, les chrétiens et les rabbins): Actes du colloque de Lausanne 12–14 décembre 2012*, ed. C. Clivaz, S.C. Mimouni, and B. Pouderon (Judaïsme ancien et origines du christianisme 5), Turnhout: Brepols, 221–44.
– (2015c), 'From the *Sēmeia* Narratives to the Gospel as a Significant Narrative: On Genre-Bending in the Johannine Miracle Stories', in: *The Fourth Gospel as Genre Mosaic*, ed. K. Bro Larsen (Studia Aarhusia Neotestamentica 3), Göttingen: V&R unipress, 209–32.
– (2016), '"Wer mich sieht, der sieht den Vater": Jesus als Bild Gottes im Johannesevangelium', in: *Vermittelte Gegenwart: Konzeptionen der Gottespräsenz von der Zeit des Zweiten Tempels bis Anfang des 2. Jahrhunderts n. Chr.*, ed. A. Taschl-Erber and I. Fischer (WUNT 367), Tübingen: Mohr Siebeck, 179–208.
– (2017), 'Ferdinand Christian Baur and the Interpretation of John', in: *Ferdinand Christian Baur and the History of Early Christianity*, ed. M. Bauspiess, C. Landmesser, and D. Lincicum, trans. R.F. Brown and P.C. Hodgson, Oxford: Oxford University Press, 206–35.
– (2018), 'The Gospel of John as a Narrative Memory of Jesus', in: *Memory and Memories in Early Christianity: Proceedings of the International Conference Held at the Universities of Geneva and Lausanne (June 2–3, 2016)*, ed. S. Butticaz and E. Norelli (WUNT 398), Tübingen: Mohr Siebeck, 261–84.
Götte, M. (2016), *Von den Wächtern zu Adam: Frühjüdische Mythen über die Ursprünge des Bösen und ihre frühchristliche Rezeption* (WUNT II/426), Tübingen: Mohr Siebeck.
Habermann, J. (1990), *Präexistenzaussagen im Neuen Testament* (Europäische Hochschulschriften. Theologie 362), Frankfurt am Main: Lang.
Hahn, F. (2002), *Theologie des Neuen Testaments*. Vol. I: *Die Vielfalt des Neuen Testaments*, Tübingen: Mohr Siebeck.
Hamerton-Kelly, G. (1973), *Pre-Existence, Wisdom, and the Son of Man: A Study of the Idea of Pre-Existence in the New Testament* (Society for New Testament Studies. Monograph Series 21), Cambridge: Cambridge University Press.
Hengel, M. (2006), 'Der Sohn Gottes', in: idem, *Studien zur Christologie. Kleine Schriften 4* (WUNT 201), Tübingen: Mohr Siebeck.
Hengel, M. and Schwemer, A.M. (2007), *Geschichte des frühen Christentums*. Vol. I: *Jesus und das Judentum*. Tübingen: Mohr Siebeck.
Hoegen-Rohls, C. (1996), *Der nachösterliche Johannes: Die Abschiedsreden als hermeneutischer Schlüssel zum vierten Evangelium* (WUNT II/84), Tübingen: Mohr Siebeck.
Käsemann, E. (⁴1980), *Jesu letzter Wille nach Johannes 17*, Tübingen: Mohr Siebeck, 1966.
Klauck, H.-J. (1997), *Vorspiel im Himmel? Erzähltechnik und Theologie im Markusprolog* (Biblisch-theologische Studien 32), Neukirchen-Vluyn: Neukirchener Verlag.
Kunath, F. (2016), *Die Präexistenz Jesu im Johannesevangelium: Struktur und Theologie eines johanneischen Motivs* (Beihefte zur Zeitschrift für die neutestamentliche Wissenschaft 2012), Berlin – Boston, MA: De Gruyter.
Loader, W.R.G. (1989), *The Christology of the Fourth Gospel: Structure and Issues* (Beiträge zur biblischen Exegese und Theologie 23), Frankfurt am Main: Lang.

– (2017), *Jesus in John's Gospel: Structure and Issues in Johannine Christology*, Grand Rapids, MI: Eerdmans.
Meeks, W. A. (1972), 'The Man from Heaven in Johannine Sectarianism', *Journal of Biblical Literature* 91: 44–72.
Miranda, J. P. (²1976), *Der Vater, der mich gesandt hat: Religionsgeschichtliche Untersuchungen zu den johanneischen Sendungsformeln. Zugleich ein Beitrag zur johanneischen Christologie und Ekklesiologie* (Europäische Hochschulschriften. Theologie 7), Bern: Lang.
Popkes, E. E. (2005), *Die Theologie der Liebe Gottes in den johanneischen Schrifen* (WUNT II/197), Tübingen: Mohr Siebeck.
Rengstorf, K.-H. (1933), 'ἀποστέλλω κ. τ. λ.', in: *Theologisches Wörterbuch zum Neuen Testament* I, Stuttgart: Kohlhammer, 397–448.
Schimanowski, G. (1985), *Weisheit und Messias: Die jüdischen Voraussetzungen der urchristlichen Präexistenzchristologie* (WUNT II/17), Tübingen: Mohr Siebeck.
Schnackenburg, R. (1991), '"Der Vater, der mich gesandt hat": Zur johanneischen Christologie', in: *Anfänge der Christologie: Festschrift Ferdinand Hahn*, ed. C. Breytenbach and H. Paulsen, Göttingen: Vandenhoeck & Ruprecht, 275–92.
Schnelle, U. (⁴2009), *Das Evangelium nach Johannes* (Theologischer Handkommentar zum Neuen Testament 4), Leipzig: Evangelische Verlagsanstalt.
Theissen, G. and Merz, A. (1996), *Der historische Jesus: Ein Lehrbuch*, Göttingen: Vandenhoeck & Ruprecht.
Theobald, M. (2002), *Herrenworte im Johannesevangelium* (Herders biblische Studien 34), Freiburg i. Br.: Herder.
Ueberschaer, N. (2017), *Theologie des Lebens bei Paulus und Johannes: Ein theologisch-konzeptioneller Vergleich des Zusammenhangs von Glaube und Leben auf dem Hintergrund ihrer Glaubenssummarien* (WUNT 389), Tübingen: Mohr Siebeck.
Weder, H. (2008), *Ursprung im Unvordenklichen: Eine theologische Auslegung des Johannesprologs* (Biblisch-theologische Studien 70), Neukirchen-Vluyn: Neukirchener Verlag.
Zumstein, J. (2016), *Das Johannesevangelium* (Kritisch-exegetischer Kommentar über das Neue Testament 2), Göttingen: Vandenhoeck & Ruprecht.

Protology and Eschatology in Gnostic Thought*

Einar Thomassen

I. Eschatological and Protological Redemption in the *Gospel of Truth*

The *Gospel of Truth* opens with a celebration of the arrival of the Saviour:

The gospel of truth is joy for those who have received from the Father of truth the grace of knowing him, through the power of the Word that came forth from the Fullness, the one that was in the thought and the mind of the Father and who is called "the Saviour," because that is the name of the work he was to perform for the redemption of those who were ignorant of the Father (16,34–17,1).[1]

The passage describes an event of eschatological fulfilment: the Saviour, who until now has dwelt in the thought and the mind of the Father, has appeared among humans as the Word, making the Father known. A salvation historical scenario is suggested: throughout human history, the Father remained unknown; now, with the appearance of the Saviour, he has finally revealed himself.[2]

In the following paragraph, the scene changes. We are now given a description of the state of ignorance that reigned in the past. That may seem like a natural theme to follow at this point. What is surprising, however, is that the state of ignorance described is not that of humanity having been unaware of the existence of the divine Father from the time of creation until the present. Instead, a primordial scene is depicted, in which something called "the Entirety" is searching for the Father:

The Entirety went about searching for the one from whom they had come forth, and the Entirety was inside him, the incomprehensible and inconceivable one who is above all thought (17,4–9).

* In this article I build on previous work where I have discussed this theme, in particular Thomassen 2006a, 146–90, 315–29.

[1] I use the edition and translation by Harold W. Attridge and George W. MacRae in Attridge 1985, though I frequently modify the translation and occasionally provide my own.

[2] Biblical scholars will recognise in this text the "Revelations-Schema," or "Revelation Pattern," found especially in the letters of Paul: "Present from eternity – now revealed"; cf. Dahl 1957, esp. 4–5 and 1976, esp. 32–33. Further: Bornkamm 1967, 819–22; Bockmuehl 1990, esp. 208–10; Lang 2015.

"The Entirety" (τὸ ὅλον) is a normal Valentinian synonym for the *pleroma*, the Fullness of aeons that emanate from the Father. Though they are said here to have "come forth" from the Father, the aeons are nevertheless described as being still inside him, rummaging for the cause of their existence. Since the Father is boundlessly inconceivable, however, they remain ignorant. The ignorance gives rise to anguish and fear, which thicken into a blinding fog. In consequence, Error, *Planē*, takes hold; it produces a substitute for the truth, made from matter (17,10–20). We are here clearly in the realm of protology: this is a description of a primordial state existing before the creation of the world. It is a state of ignorance; the aeons stray about inside the unfathomable Father, and, not finding him, they succumb to a substitute, a simulacrum of the truth fabricated by Error. This simulacrum is clearly the material world.

After this protological scene, however, we are suddenly thrown back once more to recent history and the Saviour's revelation of the gospel:

> Through this gospel about that which they had been searching for, revealed through the mercy of the Father to those who have been made complete, the hidden mystery, Jesus, the Christ, enlightened those who were in darkness caused by oblivion.[3] He enlightened them and showed them a way, and that way was the truth that he taught them. For this reason, Error grew angry with him. It persecuted him, tormented him, and broke him (18,11–24).

The text continues with a description of the work and the passion of Jesus, all of which happened in order to bring to humans the knowledge about the unknown Father. In this way, the discourse of the *Gospel of Truth* continues to move on two levels simultaneously: history and protology. The story of the Saviour's mission to the world of humans to reveal the unknown Father consistently resonates with an account of the Entirety's primordial ignorance of the Father and how that ignorance as well was rectified by the Saviour. Thus, the Saviour saves not only earthly humans but the aeons of the *pleroma* also. His work of salvation seems to take place on both levels at the same time.

II. The Relationship of Protology and Eschatology

There are two ways of looking at this situation. One is to view the relationship between the protological and the eschatological narratives as a case of parallelism: the events taking place now, in the final phase of human history, are a mirror image of events that happened at the beginning. According to this perspective, the earthly career of Jesus may be understood as a symbolically charged restaging of protological events. The acts he performed and the events

[3] A complex construction. I take "revealed" and "the hidden mystery" to refer back to "this gospel," though other combinations are possible.

of his life were all designed to reveal things that had happened before the creation of the world, to serve the enlightenment of humans capable of perceiving the allusions to the protological myth. Valentinian texts provide many examples of such symbolic parallelism between the protological myth and the life of Jesus: the fall of the twelfth aeon is signified by the apostasy of Judas, for instance, or by the fact that Jesus suffered in the twelfth month, or by the woman who had had a haemorrhage for twelve years (Irenaeus, *Haer.* 1,3,3). "All these things are said to be counterparts of those things (above)" (πάντα γὰρ ταῦτα τύπους ἐκείνων εἶναι λέγουσιν), Irenaeus tells us in a similar context (*Haer.* 1,7,2). Or, as the *Gospel of Philip* says, "The Lord did everything in a mystery," meaning that, "everything the Lord did had a symbolic significance" (67,27–30).[4] From this point of view, the protological narrative serves as the mythological prototype of the eschatological events taking place in the life of Jesus.

The other point of view is to regard the protology and the eschatology as distinct episodes in a continuous narrative connecting them in a temporal sequence. From this perspective, the protology describes a situation or a process that still has to be concluded and whose conclusion will be reached only through the events taking place at the end of history. Interpreting the *Gospel of Truth* along such lines, we might say that the description of the confused aeons inside the Father represents a state where the aeons have not yet fully come into being. The fear, the oblivion, and the deceptive creation of Error are in fact said to be nothing (17,23–25); they are like fog, which dissolves once clarity of vision is achieved. By revealing the truth, the Saviour replaces this illusory reality with genuine being. A lengthy passage (27,11–28,16) describes how those who are within the Father are actually given birth once they learn to know him. By giving them a form and a name he brings them into existence:

> I do not say, then, that the ones who have not yet come into existence are nothing, but they are in him who will wish that they come into existence when he wishes. Just as the time that is to come, he knows all things he will bring forth before they are made manifest (27,34–28,4).

It may be observed from this passage that two distinct ideas are involved in the articulation of this second point of view. The first is the idea that the created world does not exist at all; it is a deception fabricated by Error. Being a product of ignorance it only has negative being: it exists merely as a lack of something and will disappear once that lack is filled, that is, when ignorance is replaced by knowledge.[5] Only when knowledge is produced will something real come into

[4] This passage is extensively discussed in Thomassen 2006b.

[5] "… for they were nothing, the anguish, the oblivion and the creature of deceit" (17,23–25); "Since the deficiency came into being because the Father was not known, therefore, when the Father is known, from that moment on the deficiency will no longer exist … as the darkness vanishes when light appears, so also the deficiency vanishes in the perfection" (24,28–25,3). Cf. 26,21–27; 28,24–32; 29,26–32.

being. Thus, the material world and whatever has taken place in it during its illusory temporal existence are bracketed out as having not really happened, so that it is only now, with the appearance of the Saviour, that the protological process can complete its course. The second idea involves the (Aristotelian) dichotomy of potentiality and actuality, and is presented as a qualification of the first: what has been until now is strictly speaking not simply nothing at all, but has existed in a potential state, as something that would come into being later. This idea is linked with the notion that the Entirety at first existed hidden inside the Father, like an embryo, and has now finally been made manifest and been born, receiving form and a name in the process.[6]

III. Different Interpretations of the Relationship in Valentinian Sources

The two ways of understanding the relationship of protology and eschatology – the eschatology as a copy of the protology or as a completion of the protology – stand in tension to one another and are developed differently in the various Valentinian sources. Here, as in several other respects, the *Gospel of Truth* and the *Tripartite Tractate* stand out against such versions of the Valentinian system as are found in Irenaeus and the anonymous *Refutatio omnium haeresium* (traditionally attributed to Hippolytus). In the *Tripartite Tractate*, just as in the *Gospel of Truth*, the idea that the Saviour's eschatological work of redemption completes the protological process and thereby also brings about the perfection of the Entirety and its aeons, is clearly articulated. A couple of quotations must suffice here to illustrate this point:[7]

> For not only earthly humans need the redemption, but the angels need the redemption as well ... and even the Fullnesses of the aeons and those marvellous luminous powers needed it ... (124,25–31).
> By hidden and inscrutable wisdom he guarded the knowledge until the end, until the members of the Entirety would have laboured in their search for God the Father ... And then he grants them to attain knowledge of this great gift of his ... (126,9–17).

In this vision of the salvific process, the ultimate formation of the *pleroma*, when the aeons will attain full knowledge of the Father, is deferred to the moment of eschatological consummation and will take place only after the Saviour has been sent down to earth to instruct the humans. The salvation of humanity and the completion of the *pleroma* thus happen simultaneously in the *eschaton*.

[6] "When the Father wishes, he manifests whomever he wishes by giving him form and giving him a name, and he gives a name to him and brings it about that those come into existence who, before they come into existence, are ignorant of him who fashioned them" (27,26–34).

[7] See also the discussion in Thomassen 2006a, 182–87.

In the sources used by Irenaeus and the *Refutatio*, on the other hand, this notion of a deferred protology is absent. There, the protology is completed already after the fall and restoration of Sophia. Sophia is brought back to the *pleroma* once she has been detached from her presumptuous passion. A new pair of aeons, Christ and the Holy Spirit, are brought forth to remedy the disturbance that has arisen within the *pleroma*, and to instruct the aeons about the Father. Through their actions, as well as through that of the Boundary, which shields the *pleroma* from the deficiency below, the *pleroma* is stabilised and attains perfect rest (Irenaeus, *Haer.* 1,2,5–6; cf. *Ref.* 6,31,2–6,32,1). The protology, which also is a process of redemption, thereby comes to an end. The *pleroma* is now fully formed. The remainder of the narrative is the distinct story of Sophia's passion, *enthymesis*, which was cut off from Sophia and is personified as Achamoth or the external Sophia. That story continues with the conversion of Achamoth, and her prayer for help, the bringing forth of the Saviour by the *pleroma* and his rescue mission to Achamoth, and Achamoth's begetting of the spiritual seed in response to the Saviour's manifestation. Then follow the creation of the world and of humanity, and finally the descent of the Saviour into the world to redeem Sophia's offspring. This is a separate story of redemption in which the *pleroma* is no longer involved. It is not the fulfilment of the protological process; instead, the already completed protology serves as the model for the Saviour's work at a lower level.

I shall not here discuss the question of which of the two versions is the more original one.[8] For present purposes it is more important to observe that the parallelism of protology and eschatology is present in both of them. I will now give some examples of this parallelism.

IV. Parallelism of Protology and Eschatology

In both contexts, a saviour figure plays an essential role. Just as the Saviour makes the Father known to humans in the course of his eschatological appearance, the Son reveals the Father to the aeons during the protological process. The attainment of knowledge, it may be recalled, is not just a cognitive operation, but has a formative effect; this is the case in both contexts:

> The cause of the Entireties' eternal being is the Father's incomprehensible existence, but that of their coming into being and of their formation is the Son (Irenaeus, *Haer.* 1,2,5).[9]

---

[8] The relative chronology of the various versions of the system is discussed in Thomassen 2006a, 248–68.

[9] καὶ τὸ μὲν αἴτιον τῆς αἰωνίου διαμονῆς τοῖς ὅλοις τὸ ἀκατάληπτον ὑπάρχειν τοῦ πατρὸς, τῆς δὲ γενέσεως καὶ μορφώσεως τὸ καταληπτὸν αὐτοῦ, ὅ δὴ υἱός ἐστί.

The end will come when all that is spiritual is given form and is perfected through knowledge, and that means spiritual humans who possess the perfect knowledge of God and are initiated into the mysteries of Achamoth (Irenaeus, *Haer.* 1,6,1).[10]

Thus, the Son plays the same role in the protology as the Saviour does in the eschatology. It is true that in Irenaeus, the Son is split into two figures, Monogenes, who is the condition for the formation of the *pleroma*, and Christ, who is emitted by Monogenes to instruct the aeons and implement their formation after the fall and restoration of Sophia, but this further elaboration of the figure of the Son, which is peculiar to the systems of Irenaeus and the *Refutatio*, need not further concern us here.[11]

Perhaps the most striking illustration of the parallelism between the protology and the eschatology is the appearance of the theme of the passion and the crucifixion of the Saviour in a protological context. In the *Tripartite Tractate*, we learn that, whereas the Father is ineffable and impassible (64,28–65,3), the Son, on the contrary,

extended himself and spread himself out. He is the one who gave firmness, location and a dwelling place to the Entirety – according to one of his names he is in fact 'Father of the Entirety' – through his constant suffering on their behalf (65,3–12).
… he stretched himself out to give birth and knowledge to the members of the Entirety (66,6–8).

The Son's spreading out in the generation of the *pleroma* is here described in terms of the crucifixion and the passion of the Saviour. Apparently, the generation of the multiplicity of aeons from the impassibility of the paternal oneness is regarded as a form of vicarious suffering and thus comparable to the salvific passion of the Saviour, who descended into the material world and let himself be nailed fast there, his limbs spread out on the Cross. The underlying ontological principle in both cases is that multiplicity implies passion and materiality. In Valentinianism, the crucifixion became a master symbol expressing this principle.[12]

In the system of Irenaeus, and cognate versions, the protological articulation of this idea is essentially deferred from the Son to the last of the aeons, Sophia. There, it is Sophia who extends herself, ever further into infinity, until she is halted by the Boundary. The Boundary, Horos, is also called the Cross.[13] In the course of her fall, Sophia is, in other words, crucified. The Boundary-Cross puts an end to her extension and splits her in two: Sophia is restored to the *ple-*

10 Τὴν δὲ συντελειαν ἔσεσθαι, ὅταν μορφωθῇ καὶ τελειωθῇ γνώσει πᾶν τὸ πνευματικὸν, τουτέστιν οἱ πνευματικοὶ ἄνθρωποι οἱ τὴν τελείαν γνῶσιν ἔχοντες περὶ θεοῦ καὶ <τὰ> τῆς Ἀχαμώθ μεμυημένοι μυστήρια.

11 Cf. Thomassen 2006a, 260.

12 Cf. Thomassen and Painchaud 1989, 305–07; Thomassen 2006a, 186–87, 276–77.

13 Irenaeus, *Haer.* 1,2,4; 1,3,1.5; 1,4,1; 1,7,2; Clement of Alexandria, *Exc. Theod.* 22,4; 42,1; [Hippolytus,] *Ref.* 6,31,7; 6,34,7.

roma while her passion, *enthymesis*, Achamoth, is cut off, left behind and becomes the substance of matter. Thus, the story of the Saviour's passion and crucifixion is transposed into the protological sphere to serve as a model for an account of the generation of matter.

This is even clearer in the older forms of the Valentinian Sophia myth, found in the system attributed (erroneously) to Valentinus himself in Irenaeus (*Haer.* 1,11), and in the *Excerpts from Theodotus* (23,2,32–33).[14] According to these versions, Sophia gives birth to Christ during her passion. Instead of Sophia herself being split in two, here Christ disengages from his mother and hastens back into the *pleroma*, while Sophia herself is left behind. Thus, in this clearly more original version of the story, Christ shares in the passion of Sophia, but subsequently separates from her and ascends. The model here is evidently the passion of Jesus, which ended with the separation of his spirit from his body, the former returning to the Father while his body was held back by the Cross.

The transposition of the crucifixion motif into a protological passion story is evidently embedded in a wider ontological framework according to which a single first principle extends and spreads itself out into infinite plurality and then withdraws or contracts after the imposition of a Boundary which leads to the excision of infinite materiality. In this ontology, the Christian theology of the crucifixion is fused with Neopythagorean theories of first principles.[15]

V. The Ritual Dimension

In addition to the protological ideas and the narrative of the Saviour's redemptive mission in the world, a third dimension should also be taken into account, namely ritual. Of central importance in this context is the ritual of baptismal initiation, which the Valentinians called the *apolytrosis* – the redemption. Performance of the ritual was, indeed, considered a necessary precondition for salvation, because it provided the mechanism by which the redemptive work of the Saviour could become efficient for each individual person. The Saviour had been baptised himself, of course, and that fact was as significant for the Valentinians as was his crucifixion. Those two crucial events in the Saviour's life on earth are complementary in that they together show the way for humans to be liberated from their material existence. The ritual is understood as a re-enactment of the Saviour's own baptism and as an appropriation of the redemptive power of its model. For the mechanism of appropriation to be effective, however, the Saviour must be conceived as having himself been redeemed by his baptism. Thus,

---

[14] Thomassen 2006a, 248–57.

[15] The terms "extension" (ἐκτείνειν, etc.) and "spreading out" (πλατύνειν, etc.) are used to describe the generation of the Dyad from the Monad in Neopythagorean physics, as I have argued in several publications; see previous note, and most recently Thomassen 20[illegible].

Valentinian theologians affirmed that having entered the material world of deficiency, the Saviour was redeemed by the Name that came down upon him while he was in the waters of the Jordan. Moreover, when the Saviour was sent out from the *pleroma*, he was accompanied by an entourage of angels, and we are told that the angels, too, were baptised together with the Saviour, "for our sake."[16]

The logic underlying this idea appears to be that the angels represent a multiplication of the Saviour that enables the baptismal candidates individually to share in the Saviour's redemptive baptism. This is why the ritual is also called "the bridal chamber": in it each baptismal candidate is married to an angel, who can be seen as a personalised avatar of the Saviour. Moreover, this multiplication of the Saviour was a necessary precondition for his descent into the cosmos, whose most basic characteristic is not matter as such, but rather division and fragmentation, stemming ultimately from the divisive action of Sophia.[17]

Thus it may be said that the Valentinian theory of baptism rests on the same logic as the protology and the theology of the crucifixion: the Saviour spreads himself out into multiplicity in order to collect the scattered spiritual elements and unite them into himself. This shared underlying logic explains why Valentinian protology employs not only language taken from the narrative of the passion and the crucifixion, but also vocabulary that belongs in the context of baptism. The *Tripartite Tractate* tells us that when the Son spreads himself out in order to give the Entireties a firm basis for their being by being united in him, he also illuminates them, clothes them, confirms them and lets them share in the Name of the Father.[18] This is all terminology that has its original *Sitz im Leben* in the baptismal ritual. Thus, the coming into being of the *pleroma*, mediated by the Son, is also conceived in terms of the rebirth taking place in baptism.

It might be pointed out that the coming into being of the aeons is not actually referred to as a "baptism" in the protological accounts. This may be because the Valentinians see the baptismal ritual as an image of the generation of the aeons, rather than, conversely, regarding the account of the generation of the eons as a projection of baptismal ideology into the protological sphere, as our modern analytical minds will be inclined to do. Towards the end of the *Tripartite Trac-*

[16] "They are baptised for our sake that we too may possess the Name and not be held back and hindered from entering the *pleroma* by the Limit and the Cross" (Clement of Alexandria, *Exc. Theod.* 22,4); Thomassen 2006a, 377–83.

[17] "It is, however, in unity that our angels were emitted, for they are one, having come forth from one single. Since we, however, were divided, Jesus was baptised, so as to divide the undivided, until he unites us with them in the *pleroma*, so that we who are many may become one and all be merged again with him who for our sake was divided" (Clement of Alexandria, *Exc. Theod.* 36); Thomassen 2006a, 382–83, 461–65.

[18] *Tri. Trac.* 65,4–67,34: "illumination" 65,20; 66,19–20; "clothing" 65,27; 66,31–32; "confirmation" 65,7; "Name" 65,9; 66,32; 67,33–34; Thomassen and Painchaud 1989, 305–06, 308.

tate, however, when the ritual of baptism as such becomes a theme, we read the following statement:

> As for the true baptism, into which the Entireties descend and where they come into being, there is no other baptism than the one – that is, the redemption – which takes place in God the Father, the Son, and the Holy Spirit, after confession has been made in those names, [which] are the single Name of the good tidings … (127,25–36).

It is peculiar that whereas the final part of the tractate (118,14–138,27) essentially deals with the eschatological redemption of humans, it is the Entireties, i. e. the aeons, that are brought into focus when baptism is introduced. This leaves the impression that the generation of the aeons described in the first part of the tractate is not actually a description of something that has already happened in a primordial moment of time, but takes place here and now, so that the redemption of humans and the unfolding of the *pleroma* are simultaneous and depend on one another. Thus, the notion that the eschatology entails a completion of the protology also applies to the ritual articulation of the redemption process.

A final remark on the use of ritual ideology in a protological context: the phenomenon is not restricted to Valentinianism, but seems to be more widespread. This is suggested by the following example. The *Tripartite Tractate*'s account of baptism includes a series of names that are given to this ritual (128,19–129,34). One of them is "silence." But why should baptism be called "silence"? The reason given in the text itself is certainly not illuminating: "It is called 'silence' because of its tranquillity and unshakability" (128,30–32). I think we get closer to an explanation for this name by taking a look outside Valentinianism, at the Hermetic text called *On Regeneration* (CH 13). There, "silence" is described as the womb from which the neophytes are born:

> – I do not know, Trismegistos, from which womb a human is born, and from what kind of seed.
> – My child, it is the intelligent wisdom in silence, and the seed is the truly good (CH 13,1–2).[19]

Now, "silence" is a frequent word in the Valentinian protological accounts, where Sigé often appears as the name of the Father's syzygic partner.[20] She is therefore the mother of the aeons. Thus, "silence" is another concept that serves to associate protological generation with baptismal rebirth by being conceived as the womb from which both take place.

---

[19] ἀγνοῶ, ὦ Τρισμέγιστε, ἐξ οἵας μήτρας ἄνθρωπος ἐγεννήθη, σπορᾶς δὲ ποίας. – Ὦ τέκνον, σοφία νοερὰ ἐν σιγῇ καὶ ἡ σπορὰ τὸ ἀληθινὸν ἀγαθόν.

[20] Irenaeus, *Haer.* 1,1,1; 1,2,1; 1,11,1; 1,14; Clement of Alexandria, *Exc. Theod.* 29; Epiphanius, *Pan.* 31,5,4; *Tri. Trac.* 57,3–8. Cf. Thomassen and Painchaud 1989, 280–81, 283–84, 444.

VI. A Brief Look at Non-Valentinian Gnostic Sources

At this point the question may be asked if the correspondences between protology, eschatology and ritual initiation made by the Valentinians can also be found in other forms of so-called Gnosticism. This is too vast a field of research to be entered here, especially because an answer to the question will have to be made through systematic analyses of the individual texts, a task that has not so far been undertaken. I should nevertheless like to offer a comment on the other main current of Gnostic thought, Sethianism.[21]

It seems to me that the observations that have been done above about the affinity of protology with initiation rituals may also be applicable to Sethian texts. Sethian protologies describe processes of generation that have unmistakable ritual elements. In the *Apocryphon of John*, for instance, Barbelo, the Father's Thought, comes into being in the luminous waters surrounding the Father, the Invisible Spirit (NHC II 4,19–5,11, and parallels). Correspondingly, at the end of the tractate a human person is "sealed in luminous water with Five Seals" (31,23–24). Clearly, the primordial waters from which Barbelo is brought into being have a baptismal character. Moreover, when Autogenes, the Self-generated Child, is in turn brought forth from the Invisible Spirit and Barbelo, we are told that he is anointed (6,23). Finally, after having come into being, the various spiritual entities invariably stand up to praise those who have brought them forth.[22] These are all ritual scenes. The primordial generation process can thus also be seen as a ritual process.

The correspondences between these primordial ritual processes and the rituals performed by humans on earth should, I think, be seen in the light of the principle stated at the end of the *Three Steles of Seth* (VII, 127), that "the way of ascent is the way of descent" (NHC VII, 127,20–21). This means that the elaborate descriptions of the architecture of the transcendental realm, with its many levels, is made in order to chart a topography that the Sethian initiate has to traverse in inverse direction in the course of a mystical ascent. This ascent is imagined as a series of initiations effecting successive ontological transformations of the ascending person, ultimately ending in the assimilation to the Barbelo aeon.[23]

With the depiction of the protological generation process in terms of initiation processes it may be claimed that the initiation ritual, which effects the eschatological salvation of the initiate, has been transposed to the protological sphere, which is also the aim of the initiation. Beginning and end become homologous, even ambivalently identical: salvation is a return to the beginning,

[21] On this topic, see also John D. Turner's contribution in this volume.
[22] 5,2–4.18–20.30–32, etc.
[23] See Turner 2001, 799, s.v. "visionary ascent."

but also in a sense the beginning itself, rebirth and birth coalescing in a protological process to which the redemptive ritual seeks to assimilate the initiate. There is a similarity between Sethianism and Valentinianism this regard. Valentinians hope to be assimilated to the *pleroma* by means of their ritual of redemption, just as the Sethians aspire to be assimilated to the Barbelo aeon by means of the ritual of the Five Seals, and both groups perceive the place where their initiation will take them as itself being constituted by acts and processes of initiation. On the other hand, there are also significant differences. For one thing, the Sethian ascent leads through a series of successive levels and transformations, whereas for the Valentinians it is a matter of a single relocation from one level, the cosmos, to another, the *pleroma*. Second, the Sethian ascent is essentially a journey of the solitary mystic, whereas redemption for the Valentinians is much more a collective affair: initiation takes place in the context of a congregation and leads to integration into a transcendent community of aeons. Third, and perhaps most importantly, Valentinian soteriology is Christocentric: redemption has been effected through the historical intervention and incarnation of the Saviour, through his baptism, passion and crucifixion, and this redemptive work provides a model to be ritually enacted and appropriated by the members of the community. There is nothing similar to this in Sethianism, as far as I can see. The successive descents of the Seth figure described in the Sethian descent texts are not comparable in function to the redemptive incarnation of the Saviour in Valentinianism.

VII. The Apocalyptical Background

In the last part of this contribution I will try to place these observations on the correlations of protology and eschatology in Gnostic texts in a wider historical context. It seems to me that the proper historical background for understanding these correlations should be sought in the area of Early Judaism and Early Christianity. In spite of the strong presence of Greek philosophical ideas in both Sethian and Valentinian theology, it is Judaism and Christianity that have provided the soteriologies of these theologies with the temporal dimension that makes it appropriate at all to speak about protology and eschatology and how they are correlated. It is well known that the correlations of *Urzeit* and *Endzeit* are a prominent topic in Early Jewish and Christian visions of salvation history, and particularly in the form of thought that goes under the name of apocalypticism.

More than fifty years ago, Jewish and Christian ideas about the correlations of the first and the last things were expertly surveyed by Nils A. Dahl in his contribution to the *Festschrift* for C.H. Dodd.[24] In the first place, Dahl says, we

[24] Dahl 1964.

find *analogy*, or parallelism: at the end, there will be a new creation, or, Christ is the new Adam. Secondly, we may find *contrast*, either in the form of a *restitution*: what was lost by the fall of Adam will be brought back, e.g. Adam's glory, or Paradise; or in the form of a *transformation*: the new creation will be much superior to the first – an idea found for example in the Book of Revelation. A third idea is that of *reservation*: that God has reserved some of the first things to be enjoyed by the righteous at the end of the world, for instance the light of the first day, or the sabbatical rest, as we hear in the Epistle to the Hebrews, chapter 4. Related to the idea of a reservation are ideas about pre-existence and pre-destination. Dahl sums up: "The main idea, which is common to the different forms of combining the last things with that which was at the beginning, is the idea that the end will bring the final realization of what from the beginning was the will of God the creator, who is himself the first and the last."[25]

It seems clear that these ideas developed within Jewish and Christian apocalypticism were appropriated by Valentinian soteriology. We have seen examples of *parallelism* between the beginning and the end in the way that events of the life of the Saviour have their counterparts in the protological accounts. The idea of *restitution* is also present: the end will be an *apokatastasis* and a return to the original unity, according to the *Tripartite Tractate*.[26] Finally, we have also seen that "the idea that the end will bring the final realization of what from the beginning was the will of God" is very much present, especially in the *Gospel of Truth* and the *Tripartite Tractate*. As was pointed out above, these texts make use of the so-called "Revelation Pattern" well known from Pauline literature: God's purpose has been hidden from eternity, as a mystery concealed in his wisdom, but now this mystery has been revealed to the saints.[27] We encountered this schema already in the opening words of the *Gospel of Truth*, which speak about "the Word that came forth from the Fullness, the one that was in the thought and the mind of the Father and who is called 'the Saviour'." Here are some more examples (the first was already partly quoted above):

> By hidden and inscrutable wisdom he guarded the knowledge until the end, until the members of the Entirety would have laboured in their search for God the Father, whom no one has found by his own wisdom and power. And then he grants them to attain knowledge of this great gift of his by means of that superior thought and that method which he has given them and which consists in ceaseless thanksgiving to him. Out of his immovable counsel, he then reveals himself for eternity to the ones who will prove themselves worthy of receiving, by his will, the knowledge about the Father, who is unknowable in his nature (*Tri. Trac.* 126,9–24).

---

25 Dahl 1964, 429.

26 *Tri. Trac.* 133,6–8: "The restoration (ἀποκατάστασις) back to that which was is unity." Cf. 123,19; 123,27–124,4. The term ἀποκατάστασις is frequent in Valentinian texts: Thomassen and Painchaud 1989, 437.

27 Above, n. 2.

For the Father produced the All like a little child, like a drop from a spring, like a blossom from a [vine], like a ... like a shoot ..., so that they needed [nourishment], growth, and perfection. He withheld the perfection for a time, having kept it in his mind from the beginning, possessing it from the beginning and gazing at it, but he <concealed> it for those who had come forth from him. This was not out of jealousy, but it was in order that the aeons should not receive their perfection from the beginning and thereby exalt themselves in glory as equal to the Father and think that they had achieved this perfection out of themselves (*Tri. Trac.* 62,6–26).

Although he kept within himself their perfection and did not give it to the Entirety, the Father was not jealous. What jealousy can there be between himself and his own members? For if this aeon had [received] their [perfection], they would not have attained [knowledge of] the Father. He keeps their perfection within himself, giving it to them as a return to him and as a perfect, unitary knowledge (*Gos. Truth* 18,36–19,7).

These texts show how Valentinians apply the apocalyptic idea that God has reserved the goods of salvation until the end. They are hidden in his mind in order to be revealed when his plan of salvation is implemented, which takes place with the sending of the Saviour. It may be observed how two distinct and logically conflicting notions of the salvation process are activated by this apocalyptic idea. One is the notion of a *return*: the Entireties and all other beings have strayed from the Father because they did not know him. Redemption will then take the form of restitution, an *apokatastasis* to a restored unity. The other notion is that the Entireties have until now not come into being at all – a point that was already made above. The implementation of the Father's purpose consists in letting the aeons be born as individual beings, though turned towards the Father and connected with him by knowledge. It will be seen that the idea of the Father's *mind* supports both an eschatological and a protological interpretation. Eschatologically the contents of the Father's mind and will are revealed at the end, protologically the mind of the Father is conceived as the womb from which the aeons are born as perfect spiritual beings. The concept of the Father's mind thus refers on the one hand to the hidden mystery of the divine plan of salvation in an apocalyptic context, and on the other hand to the *nous* as a source of intelligible realities in a philosophical sense, and thereby creates a coalescence of apocalyptic and philosophical thought.

A final remark: The inclusive soteriology represented by the *Gospel of Truth* and the *Tripartite Tractate* seems not to have been consistently maintained in all forms of Valentinianism. In the sources reported by the Church Fathers there is, as was already noted, a tendency to see the *pleroma* as complete and perfect after the restoration of Sophia. In these texts, the *pleroma* becomes a goal to be attained by spiritual humans here and now more than a process to be completed in the course of human history. Later Gnosticism, it seems to me, becomes on the whole less salvation historically oriented and more ritually oriented. The transcendent world is already there, as a perfected reality, and can be attained through ritual acts, mystical contemplation, and knowledge about its architecture and the words one needs to speak in order to reach it. This trend away from a temporally linear concept of the salvation process and towards a vertical concept of ascent towards the heavenly realities seems to be common to various forms of Gnosticism, but also to be part of a more general trend in the religions of Late Antiquity, one which may be observed in the transformation of Jewish apocalypticism to *Hekhalot* mysticism as well as in the weakening of eschatological thinking in mainstream Christianity.

Bibliography

Attridge, H.W., ed. (1985), *Nag Hammadi Codex I (The Jung Codex)* (Nag Hammadi Studies 22 and 23), Leiden: Brill.

Bockmuehl, M. (1990), *Revelation and Mystery in Ancient Judaism and Pauline Christianity* (Wissenschaftliche Untersuchungen zum Neuen Testament, II/36), Tübingen: Mohr Siebeck.

Bornkamm, G. (1967), ‘μυστήριον’, in: *Theological Dictionary of the New Testament* IV, Grand Rapids, MI: Eerdmans, 802–29.

Dahl, N.A. (1957), ‘Formgeschichtliche Beobachtungen zur Christusverkündigung in der Gemeindepredigt’, in: *Neutestamentliche Studien für Rudolf Bultmann*, ed. W. Eltester (Beihefte zur Zeitschrift für die neutestamentliche Wissenschaft 21), Berlin: Töpelmann, 3–9 (English translation: ‘Form-Critical Observations on Early Christian Preaching’, in Dahl 1976, 30–36).

– (1964), ‘Christ, Creation and the Church’, in: *The Background of the New Testament and Its Eschatology: In Honour of C.H. Dodd*, ed. W.D. Davies and D. Daube, Cambridge: Cambridge University Press, 422–43 (reprint in Dahl 1976, 121–40).

– (1976), *Jesus in the Memory of the Early Church: Essays*, Minneapolis, MN: Augsburg.

Lang, T.J. (2015), *Mystery and the Making of a Christian Historical Consciousness: From Paul to the Second Century* (Beihefte zur Zeitschrift für die neutestamentliche Wissenschaft 219), Berlin – Boston, MA: De Gruyter.

Thomassen, E. (2006a), *The Spiritual Seed: The Church of the “Valentinians”* (Nag Hammadi and Manichaean Studies 60), Leiden – Boston, MA: Brill.

– (2006b), ‘*Gos. Philip* 67:27–30: not “in a mystery”’, in: *Coptica – Gnostica – Manichaica: Mélanges offerts à Wolf-Peter Funk*, ed. L. Painchaud and P.-H. Poirier (Bibliothèque copte de Nag Hammadi. Section “Études” 7), Québec: Presses de l’Université Laval; Leuven – Paris: Peeters, 925–39.

– (2017), ‘Gnosis and Philosophy in Competition’, in: *PHILOSOPHIA in der Konkurrenz von Schulen, Wissenschaften und Religionen: Zur Pluralisierung des Philosophiebegriffs in Kaiserzeit und Spätantike*, ed. C. Riedweg (Philosophie der Antike 34), Boston, MA – Berlin: De Gruyter, 61–74.

Thomassen, E. and Painchaud, L. (1989), *Le Traité Tripartite* (Bibliothèque copte de Nag Hammadi. Section “Textes” 19), Québec: Presses de l’Université Laval.

Turner, J.D. (2001), *Sethian Gnosticism and the Platonic Tradition* (Bibliothèque copte de Nag Hammadi. Section “Études” 6), Québec: Presses de l’Université Laval; Leuven – Paris: Peeters.

"Where the Beginning Is, There Shall Be the End"

Protology and Personal Eschatology in the Platonizing Sethian Apocalypses *Zostrianos* and *Allogenes*

John D. Turner †

Jesus' pronouncement in saying 18 of the *Gospel of Thomas*, "Where the beginning is, there shall be the end," is a proposition echoed in many sources, for example as "*En ma Fin gît mon Commencement*" embroidered on Mary Queen of Scot's estate cloth, or the incipit "In my end is my beginning" of the second of T.S. Eliot's *Four Quartets*, and perhaps even implied in the "As it was in the beginning, is now, and ever shall be" of the *Gloria Patri*. This frequent theme of eschatological myths of salvation, especially in apocalyptic literature, was classically first expressed by Hermann Gunkel as "Endzeit gleicht Urzeit," a dictum borrowed from the *Epistle of Barnabas* 6:13, "behold I make last things as the first."[1] This dictum expresses the age-old attempt to escape the burdens of temporal existence, whether by the undoing of history by a divine intervention, or simply by an imaginative although temporary return to its beginnings by an act of vision or contemplation that presumes to unwind, undo or simply transcend the temporal flux of phenomenal experience.

Two of the questions raised for this volume are: "How is the initial order restored, both in its overall ontological structure and in the more particular case of human beings? Is this restoration a return to the exact same state that is described in protology?" I would like to pursue these questions, not so much in the domain of cosmic eschatology as in the domain of personal eschatology, indeed the experience of personal salvation as reflected in the Platonizing Sethian apocalypses *Zostrianos* and *Allogenes*. These treatises are essentially ascent apocalypses, charting the progress of an exemplary seer or visionary during an ascent from earth into the transcendent domain, the receipt of various revelations of the nature of that domain, and a return to earthly existence, an experience summarized by the concluding dictum of a closely related Sethian treatise, the *Three Steles of Seth*: "The way of ascent is the way of descent."[2]

[1] Gunkel 1895, 369.

[2] NHC VII 127,20–21: ϯ<ϩι>ⲏ ⲛ̄ ⲃⲱⲕ ⲉϩⲣⲁï ⲡⲉ ϯ<ϩι>ⲏ ⲛ̄ ⲉⲓ ⲉⲡⲉⲥⲏⲧ', in apparent imitation

The salvific eschatology of these three ascent apocalypses is that of an atemporal personal transformation rather than a linear or cyclic cosmic transformation. But while *Zostrianos* (and the *Three Steles of Seth*) portrays the ascending visionary as a figure distinct from and *external* to the object of his vision with which he enters into a *communion*, in *Allogenes* the ascent to divine realities initially conceived as external to the self leads to an actual mystical *union*, that is, to an *internal* contemplative withdrawal into one's prefigurative self coincident with the supreme source of all reality. Here protology and eschatology coincide: both origin and eschaton are entirely transcendental, and the eschaton is realized through a mystic aspirant's apparently non-temporal contemplative reabsorption into his or her primordial origin.

I. Realized Eschatology as the Coincidence of Beginning and End

The apocalyptic vision of a coming new age and new creation to replace the present evil order is a well-attested biblical motif, as in Isa 65:18: "For behold, I create new heavens and a new earth; and the former things shall not be remembered or come into mind." Typically this new creation – often portrayed as a cosmic transformation involving the destruction of the present world order and a return to a prelapsarian Paradise – is to be expected at an unknown time in the future, whether imminent or distant, putting an end to the present evil age, which will endure only a very short time until the advent of a heaven-sent deliverer, the resurrection of the dead, and the last judgment. Among Christian authors, perhaps because of the delay in the expected parousia of the Messiah, certain cosmic events associated with the eschaton became prefigured or even experientially realized in the present moment through ritual actions. Thus in 2 Cor 5:18 Paul could say if anyone has been baptized in Christ, "he is a new creation; the old has passed away, behold, the new has come," implying that the prelapsarian condition of Adam as the image of God is being restored in the days of the Messiah's coming. So too the fourth evangelist can maintain that the final judgment has already occurred for those who believe in the name of God's only Son (John 3:17–18; 12:31). An even more extreme statement of realized eschatology is offered by the *Gospel of Thomas*, where those who search for the eschaton are told that the end is present already.[3] Indeed, according to saying 18,

of Heraclitus' own dictum "the way up and the way down are one and the same," fr. DK B60: ὁδὸς ἄνω κάτω μία καὶ ὡυτή.

[3] As Davies 1992 argues, the major perspectives of the *Gospel of Thomas* are: 1. The eternal light of Gen 1:3 through which the world was created persists in the world and in people. 2. Jesus physically came and informed people of the possibility of actualizing that light. 3. People who actualize their light perceive the world and themselves to be at the condition of the primordial seven days. 4. Such people are in their primordial unisexual state of immortal rest and dominion as images of God prior to religious requisites. 5. They are as Jesus is and live in

from which the title of this essay is taken, when asked about the end, Jesus responds in terms of the beginning:

Gos. Thom. 18: The disciples said to Jesus, "Tell us how Our end will be." Jesus said, "*Have you discovered, then, the beginning, that you look for the end? For where the beginning is, there will be the end.* Blessed is he who will take his place in the beginning: he will know the end and will not experience death."

In the development of the early Church, this telescoping or collapsing together of both beginning and the end with the present was often expressed in ritual actions such as baptism and the common meal. By this means, apparently unattainable realities – whether of a primordial or final or utterly transcendent nature – become present in the performance of ostensibly everyday acts, concentrated into a special ritual occasion. In these acts, the participant could experience or imagine being transported, whether it be back to the beginning of creation or forward to a final consummation or elevated to the transcendent realm of the origin and destiny of one's soul, and perhaps even beyond that realm to the primal principle and source of all, the supreme deity.

Among such rites, of especial interest are initiatory rituals such as immersionary baptism, especially in an early Christian context, where the descent into and ascent out of water becomes associated not only with cleansing and enlightenment, but also with burial and revival from the grave, death and resurrection, or entry into and rebirth from the watery womb. Throughout the first four centuries, the notions of cleansing and the washing away of sins, inherited from John the Baptist and other pre-Christian water rites, continue to play a role in the interpretation of Christian baptism. Particularly relevant for this essay are the notions of rebirth or regeneration (παλινγεννησία and ἀναγέννησις) and the association of baptism with enlightenment and the vision of God in both Justin and Clement of Alexandria.[4]

---

the kingdom of God. For the *Gospel of Thomas*, the kingdom of God is already present; it is the indwelling of light in all things and people: *Gos. Thom.* 3, "the kingdom of the father is spread out upon the earth, and men do not see it"; *Gos. Thom.* 113, "the kingdom of God is within you and outside of you." *Gos. Thom.* 24: "His disciples said, 'Show us the place where you are, since it is necessary for us to seek it'; He said to them, 'Whoever has ears, let him hear. There is light within a man of light, and it lights up the whole world. If it does not shine, it is dark'" (a play on φῶς, "light" and the Homeric form φώς, for "man"; cf. Clement of Alexandria, *Paed.* 1,28,3); *Gos. Thom.* 49. Blessed are the solitary and elect, for you will find the kingdom. For you are from it, and to it you will return"; *Gos. Thom.* 50. Jesus said, "If they say to you, "Where did you come from?" say to them, "We came from the light, the place where the light came into being on its own accord and established [itself] and became manifest through their image." *Gos. Thom.* 51: "His disciples said to him, 'When will the rest for the dead take place, and when will the new world come?' He said to them, 'What you are looking forward to has come, but you don't know it'."

4 For references, see Einar Thomassen's unpublished essay "Christian Initiation in Antiquity: A Synopsis." For enlightenment and the vision of God, see Justin, *1 Apology* 61,12: "And this washing (λουτρόν) is called illumination, because they who learn these things are illumi-

II. From Exterior to Interior Ritual in Sethian Literature

Now in several of the so-called Sethian or Classic Gnostic treatises in the Nag Hammadi corpus, much the same symbolism appears in connection with a baptismal ritual called the "Five Seals." A comparison of three Sethian texts – the *Apocryphon of John*, the *Trimorphic Protennoia*, and the *Holy Book of the Invisible Spirit* – with the ascent apocalypses *Zostrianos* and *Allogenes* seems to reveal a general line of development in which the objective acts of earthly baptismal ritual become displaced by the verbal performances of a heavenly liturgy by which the participant is elevated to angelic status and to increasingly silent acts of visionary imagination culminating in acts of self-reflexive cognition and assimilation to the divine reality itself.[5]

This ritual seems to have originally featured a renunciation of worldly life, an invocation of spiritual powers, a water baptism by multiple immersions in the name of various Sethian divine figures, and perhaps also acts of anointing, investiture, and enthronement, symbolizing the new status conferred upon the participant.[6] Eventually the original earthly water ritual was transformed into

nated in their thinking (καλεῖται δὲ τοῦτο τὸ λουτρὸν φωτισμός, ὡς φωτιζομένων τὴν διάνοιαν τῶν ταῦτα μανθανόντων). And in the name of Jesus Christ ... he who is illuminated is washed." See also Clemens Alexandrinus, *Paed.* 1,6,26,2: "Being baptized, we are illuminated (βαπτιζόμενοι φωτιζόμεθα); illuminated, we become sons; being made sons, we are made perfect; being made perfect, we are made immortal (τελειούμενοι ἀπαθανατιζόμεθα)." "I," says He, "have said that you are gods, and all sons of the Highest. This work is variously called grace, illumination, perfection, and washing: ... illumination, by which that holy light of salvation is beheld, that is, by which we see God clearly" (φώτισμα δὲ δι᾽ οὗ τὸ ἅγιον ἐκεῖνο φῶς τὸ σωτήριον ἐποπτεύεται, τουτέστιν δι᾽ οὗ τὸ θεῖον ὀξυωποῦμεν); *Paed.* 1,6,27,3: "And he who is only regenerated – as the name necessarily indicates – and is enlightened, is delivered forthwith from darkness, and on the instant receives the light" (Καὶ ὁ μόνον ἀναγεννηθείς, ὥσπερ οὖν καὶ τοὔνομα ἔχει, φωτισθεὶς ἀπήλλακται μὲν παραχρῆμα τοῦ σκότους, ἀπείληφεν δὲ αὐτόθεν τὸ φῶς); and notably the Valentinian Theodotus (*Exc. Theod.* 78): "Until baptism, they say, Fate is real, but after it the astrologists are no longer right. But it is not only the washing that is liberating, but the knowledge (γνῶσις) of/who we were, and what we have become, where we were or where we were placed, whither we hasten, from what we are redeemed, what birth is and what rebirth (ἀναγέννησις)."

[5] Of the four Platonizing Sethian treatises, *Zostrianos*, *Allogenes*, and *Marsanes* commemorate the ecstatic ascent of a *single* exceptional individual, such as the ancient figures of Zostrianos, the alleged uncle or grandfather of Zoroaster, or Allogenes, the "one of another kind," or the biblical son of Adam Seth, or even a contemporary Sethian prophet such as Marsanes. On the other hand, the *Three Steles of Seth* presupposes an entire *community* of aspiring visionaries by providing for their use a set of exemplary doxological prayers long ago uttered by Seth in the course of his own spiritual ascent to the supreme deity. Analysis of the mythemes and literary composition of the Sethian treatises suggest that, while elements of both patterns are present throughout the entire corpus, as one moves from what seem to be relatively early treatises to the relatively later ones, there is a noticeable trend away from the descent pattern towards the ascent pattern. See my introduction and commentary to *Zostrianos* in Barry 2000, 139–48, and Turner 2001, 292–301; 720–22.

[6] In terms of van Gennep 1961's model. Of such "rites of passage" with their successive phases of separation, liminality, and reincorporation, the acts of renunciation, stripping, and

the practice of visionary and contemplative ascent depicted in *Zostrianos*, where baptismal imagery still occurs, or in *Allogenes*, where such imagery is entirely absent.

What we seem to have is a process of "ritual internalization," a term that Mircea Eliade applied to the emergence of yogic practices from the sacrificial ritual of ancient Vedic religion, wherein yogic asceticism amounts to an internal sacrifice in which subjective psycho-physiological states and processes replace external ritual acts and objects such as the sacrificial fire and various libations.[7] Guy Stroumsa points to an analogous process in post-second-temple Judaism, where the ritual action of sacrifice in the ancient temple lives on in the form of prayer and verbal liturgy in which "*telling* has replaced the *doing* to such a point that the recitation of sacrificial injunctions in a synagogue was now equivalent to their former practice in the temple."[8] In the subsequent Merkavah mysticism that developed in the wake of Ezekiel's vision of the divine throne, prayer – when accompanied by intense concentration (*kavvanah*) – is the means that effects the ascent to the divine chariot (*Yordei Merkavah*) and the direct vision of the divine glory (*kavod*). Thus we seem to have a general line of development from ritual action through verbal liturgy and prayer that culminates in silent contemplation and adoration of God and his attributes.

III. The Sethian Baptismal Rite of the Five Seals

According to the Sethian *Apocryphon of John*, the baptism of the Five Seals separates one from ignorance, servitude to hostile powers, and the prospect of bodily reincarnation, and reincorporates one into the elect seed of the Mother

---

disrobing denote *separation* from the profane condition of ignorance and mortality. Through immersion in and reemergence from the baptismal waters, the baptizand passes through a *liminal* state of death, burial, and rebirth wherein one is "neither this nor that, and yet is both." Here, one is neither enlightened nor unenlightened, but inhabits a liminal state of literal or figurative nakedness and loss of customary distinctions, with no claim to status or special knowledge. But there follows a third phase of ritual *reincorporation* into a new social status or group such as the seed of Seth – or in terms of individual consciousness, into a new identity or state of self-awareness.

[7] Eliade 1969, 111. The term "ritual interiorization" bears a multitude of meanings: a mental performance of the ritual; replacement of the ritual with a continuous process of life, such as breathing or eating; a particular way of life, such as renunciation; an actual performance with an inner interpretation; the replacement of the external ritual with an internal one, and so on (see Bodewitz 1973).

[8] Stroumsa 2009, 68–71. The link between the divine and human is realized no longer in *ex opere operato* ritual actions, but in an inward focus on maintaining the link between the individual's interior conscience and a God who is even more invisible and incomprehensible than when the temple was still standing, a focus whose outward counterpart became directed to the heavenly temple depicted by Ezekiel as the true palace of the invisible God.

Barbelo, that is, into an awareness of one's immortal and divine identity. The divine Mother, who is herself the divine Providence (πρόνοια) as well the instrument of its "remembrance," calls on those who hear her to "arise from the deep sleep" of forgetfulness and ignorance and to "remember that you have heard and trace your root, which is I." The rite culminates in being sealed in the "light of the water" (NHC II 31,22–25), understood as a reentry into primordial aqueous luminosity from which the supreme Invisible Spirit generated the divine realm, in effect undoing the soul's primordial descent into mortality.

The *Trimorphic Protennoia* (NHC XIII 49,22–50,12) portrays the Five Seals as a sequence of five ritual actions (investiture, baptism, enthronement, glorification, and rapture) that strip away and replace bodily and emotional preoccupations with an enlightenment that protects one from the deceptive influence of the Archons, resulting in the ascent of the baptizand to the primordial light; he becomes a light in light, reabsorbed into his protological condition.[9]

In the *Gospel of the Egyptians* (NHC III 62,25–63,23 = IV 74,9–75,11), whose baptismal liturgy closely resembles that practiced by other Christian groups, the emphasis seems to lie on the *descent* of the holy powers upon the baptizand.[10] Here, Seth descends in the guise of Jesus to institute a baptism in which a renunciation of the lower world and invoking its symbolic reconciliation with the upper world results in the rebirth of the "saints" conceived as ineffable wombs[11] for the Father's preexistent light:

---

[9] In the *Trimorphic Protennoia* (NHC XIII 48,7–33; cf. 45,12–20), the Five Seals are interpreted as a sequence of acts administered by the divine Mother Barbelo, apparently consisting of a stripping away of the initiate's psycho-somatic nature, followed by investiture in a luminous garment, baptism in living water, enthronement, glorification, rapture into the light, and induction into the mystery of knowledge: NHC XIII 45,12–20: "I am inviting you into the exalted, perfect Light. Moreover, (as for) this (Light), when you enter it, you will be glorified by those [who] give glory, and those who enthrone will enthrone you. You will accept robes from those who give robes and the Baptists will baptize you and you will become gloriously glorious, the way you first were when you were (Light)." NHC XIII 48,7–33: "I gave him the Water [of Life, which strips] him of the thought of [the corporeal] and psychic [faculty] ... I put upon him a shining Light ... I handed him over to those who [covered] him with a robe of Light ... he was baptized ... he was immersed in the spring of living water ... he was enthroned in glory ... he was glorified with the glory of the Fatherhood ... he was raptured into the light-[place] of his Fatherhood ... he received the Five Seals ... he partook of the mystery of knowledge, and he became a light dwelling in light." NHC XIII 49,28–35: "He who possesses the Five Seals of these particular names has stripped off (the) garments of ignorance and put on a shining Light."

[10] In the *Gospel of the Egyptians* (NHC III 64,9–68,1), the recipient of the Five Seals offers an invocation (ἐπίκλησις) of the aeonic powers and certain renunciations (ἀπόταξις, ἀποταγή), undergoes baptism in the spring of truth in which one receives the name and a vision of Autogenes, followed by an extension of one's arms to symbolize inclusion in the "circle of light" and the receipt of the ointment (or perfume) of life.

[11] I.e., on analogy with Plato's receptacle, the initiated person becomes a receptacle for the divine light just as the divine mother Barbelo served as a receptacle for the supreme Father's light at the origin of her self-generated Child; cf. *Trimorphic Protennoia* (NHC XIII 45,6–8): "I am the Womb [that gives shape] to the all by giving birth to the Light that [shines in] splen-

A1. Gos. Egypt. (NHC III 62,25–63,23 = IV 74,9–75,11): The great Seth was sent … to save the errant race … through a baptism … for the rebirth (IV 74,29) of the saints by the Holy Spirit through invisible secret symbols in a unification (ϩⲱⲧ̄ⲡ̄; IV 75,3 has ϩⲱⲧ̄ⲃ̄, killing) of worlds through the renouncing of the world and the god of the thirteen aeons, and the invocations of the holy and ineffable ones, even the incorruptible wombs and the Father's great light that preexisted with his Pronoia.

In the hymnic section that concludes the *Gospel of the Egyptians*, the baptizand acknowledges that he has become one with the supreme deity's primordial light, from which he or she originated.[12]

IV. From Exterior to Interior Ritual

In the course of time, such ritual acts can become interiorized as techniques of mental transformation, conceptual refinement and abstraction, and entrance into a higher state of consciousness, techniques which could be practiced either while participating in a physical water ritual or quite apart from it. The soul's successive divestiture of its psychic and somatic accretions reappears "internalized" as an ascending scale of mental states by which the self, while still in the body, might reunite with its originally pristine naked state as an immanent, even if temporary, condition that prefigures and guarantees its final post-mortem return to the divine realm, perhaps even to unite once again with God. As Hans Jonas once argued,[13] by such transposition of a ritual action into the in-

dor"; *Apocryphon of John* (NHC II 6,10–18): "And he gazed intently into Barbelo with the pure light surrounding the Invisible Spirit and its radiance, and she conceived from him. And he begot a luminous spark …. This was an Only-begotten of the Mother-Father who came to appearance; he is his sole [offspring], the Only-begotten of the Father, the pure light."

[12] *Gos. Egypt.* (NHC III 66,22–67,10): "This great name of yours is upon me, O indivisible self–begotten one, who are not outside of me. I see you, you who are invisible before everyone… Now that I have recognized you, I have mixed myself with the immutable; I have armed myself with an armor of light; I have been made light…. I was given shape (*morphē*) in the circle of the wealth of the light that is in my bosom…"

[13] Jonas 1969, 291–304 observed that mystical philosophies like that of Plotinus or Origen may have originated when the dualism between the evil cosmos and the transcendent god reflected in the dramatic antagonisms between the actors that populate much early gnostic mythology was gradually replaced by a monistic emanative scheme in which a continuum of greater or lesser degrees of perfection extends downwards and upwards throughout the entire chain of being. Simultaneously, external ritual practices gradually gave way to self-performable interior rituals of self-reflexive contemplation whose ascending stages inversely replicate the original descending order of emanations. In this way, the aspiring mystic can experience as an internal pilgrimage already in this life what earlier gnostic myth had portrayed as an external and often *post mortem* return of the soul to its native realm of light. According to Jonas, the culminating, soteriology of most typical Gnostic myths and rituals offer only a preparation for deliverance from the world and its governing powers, since the actual deliverance will take place only after death. Nevertheless, it is precisely at this point that gnostic myth and ritual can develop into a mystical philosophy by which this ultimate deliverance can

wardness of the person and the concomitant translation of its objective stages into a structured sequence of increasingly self-reflexive acts of cognition, external ritual performance can pass into an internal discipline of contemplative acts culminating in mystic union. It seems to me that the same process is visible in the Nag Hammadi Sethian Platonizing treatises *Zostrianos* and *Allogenes*. To see how this works, we first have to take a detour through the ontogenetic metaphysics of emanation adopted by these treatises.

V. The Metaphysics of the Sethian Platonizing Treatises

The metaphysical hierarchy of the Platonizing Sethian treatises is headed by a supreme and pre-existent Unknowable One who, as in Plotinus, is clearly beyond being and is therefore conceivable only through negative predication and cognitive vacancy. Below the supreme One, at the level of determinate being, is the Barbelo Aeon, conceived along the lines of a Middle Platonic tripartite divine Intellect.[14] It contains three ontological levels, conceived as sub-intellects

be in some way experienced already in this life. But before mystic philosophy can fully develop, the gnostic myth and ritual on which it is based must first be "rationalized" by transforming the beings who had appeared as actors in the original mythical drama into a sequence of impersonal entities that spontaneously emanate from a supreme source, and by replacing their generative and salvific actions by some kind of automatic process that determines the necessary order of these emanations. When the dualism of the evil cosmos and the transcendent god reflected in the original mythical drama is transformed into monism, the cosmos is no longer god's adversary but simply his "other." The proactive antagonisms and conflicts of earlier myth are replaced by a continuum of greater or lesser degrees of perfection extending downwards and upwards throughout the entire chain of being. Similarly, external ritual practices must be transformed into a self-performable interior ritual of self-reflexive contemplation whose ascending stages inversely replicate the original descending order of emanations. In this way, the aspiring mystic can experience as an internal pilgrimage already in this life what the gnostic myth had described as an external and often *post mortem* journey. Here speculation and theory are the anticipation, not the projection, of experience; they actually make experience possible. Myth and ritual coalesce into mysticism; gnosis has turned into contemplative philosophy like that of Origen or Plotinus. "Thus, in order that certain experiences may become possible and even conceivable as valid anticipations of an eschatological future, or as actualizations of metaphysical stages of being, speculation must have set the framework, the way, and the goal, long before the subjective experience has learned to walk the way" (329).

[14] Cf. Bechtle 2000, 393–414, esp. n. 74: "Barbelo really is equivalent to mind. It is the first thought of the Invisible Spirit and it has, principally speaking, three levels: Kalyptos, the hidden One, Protophanes, the first appearing One, Autogenes, the selfbegotten One. At first this triad is an emanative triad: it represents the stages of the unfolding and proceeding of the aeon of Barbelo from its source in the Invisible Spirit. In the beginning Barbelo is hidden as purely potential intellect in the Invisible Spirit. Once Barbelo is constituted, Kalyptos will represent the realm of that which truly exists, i.e. the ideas. Next, Barbelo first appears as the male intelligence which is then conceived of as those which exist together, those which are unified (perhaps mind and ideas which are unified through intellection), represented by Protophanes who thinks the ideas of Kalyptos, on the one hand, and acts on the individuals, on the other hand. Finally, Barbelo becomes the selfbegotten demiurgical mind which can be

or subaeons of the Barbelo Aeon: first, one that is contemplated (νοῦς νοητός), called Kalyptos or "hidden" and contains the intelligible authentic existents (τὰ ὄντως ὄντα) or forms; second, one that contemplates those intelligibles (νοῦς θεωρῶν), called Protophanes Nous or "first appearing" Mind; and a third, a demiurgic intellect (νοῦς διανοούμενος) that governs the realm of Nature, called Autogenes or "self-generated."

As a reader and critic of *Zostrianos* and *Allogenes*, Plotinus recognized that this tripartition of the divine intellect is based on a reading of Plato's *Tim.* 39e3–40a2: "According, then, as Intellect perceives (καθορᾷ) Forms existing in the Living–Thing–that–Is (ὅ ἔστι ζῷον), such and so many as exist therein did He decide (διενοήθη) that this Cosmos also should possess." In the Sethian implementation, Kalyptos corresponds to the paradigmatic Living-Thing-that-Is,[15] Protophanes to the contemplating demiurge, and Autogenes to the resulting world soul that governs the cosmos.[16]

Although these names presently designate the intellectual and ontological levels of the Barbelo Aeon, it is likely that they originally designated a dynamic process of ontogenesis by which the Barbelo Aeon itself gradually unfolds from the Invisible Spirit: at first "hidden" (καλυπτός) or latent in the Spirit as its prefigurative intellect, then "first appearing" (πρωτοφανής)[17] as the Spirit's sepa-

identified with the rational part of the world soul. As an established ontological level it is the individuals represented by Autogenes who has the demiurgic role of a world soul. Thus Barbelo corresponds to Numenius' second mind. Insofar as the second mind is participated in and used by the first, i.e. insofar as the second mind is prefigured in the first and thus is the first in a certain way, we have Kalyptos. Insofar as the Numenian second mind is identical with the third and acts through the third it can be compared to Autogenes. *Stricto sensu* the second mind as second mind is comparable to the Protophanes level of the Sethians."

[15] *Zost.* NHC VIII 117,1–4: "It is there (i.e., in Kalyptos) that all the living things are, individually yet joined together." Cf. Plato, *Tim.* 30c2–5: "We shall affirm this [cosmos] to be most similar to that [living] thing of which all other living things are parts, both individually and according to species. For that one has all intelligible living things (νοητὰ ζῷα πάντα) by comprising them within itself."

[16] *Ennead* 2,9[33],6,14–21:"And the (Gnostics') making of multiplicity among the intelligibles – Being, and Intellect, and another Demiurge, and the Soul – has been taken from what is written in the Timaeus: for he [Plato] says about it, "The one who made this All thought that it should contain the Forms which the Intellect surveys in the 'living thing that is.' But they [the Gnostics] did not understand, and took it to mean that there is one [intellect] in a state of quietude having within it all the things that are, and another intellect different from that one that contemplates [the intelligibles] in the former, and yet another [intellect] that deliberates – but frequently, according to them, the Soul is the demiurge instead of the deliberating intellect." I owe this insight to Mazur 2014.

[17] Cf. Phanes, *Orphicorum Hymni* 52,5–6; *Papyri Graecae Magicae* 4,943–44; cf. Orphic *Argonautica*, line 16 (Dottin 1930): Φάνητα … καλέουσι Βτοτοί· πρῶτος γὰρ ἐφάνθη. Note the use of φαίνειν in the following Gnostic testimonia: Simon Magus *apud* Hippolytus, *Refutatio* 6,18: "For Thought (ἔννοια) that subsists in unity processing forth became two, being rendered manifest to itself from itself (φανεῖς αὐτῷ ἀπό ἑαυτοῦ), the Father passed into a state of duality.); Marcus *apud* Hippolytus, *Refutatio* 6,42:"The self-existent Father opened His mouth, and sent forth a Logos similar to himself and it stood by him and showed him who he

rately-existing thought or intellect, and finally "self-generated" (αὐτογενης) as a distinct demiurgical mind that operates on the physical world below in accordance with its vision of the archetypal ideas emerging in the divine intellect, Protophanes. [18]

VI. The Noetic Triad of Being-Life-Mind in Plotinus and the Sethian Platonizing Treatises

On a still higher level, the dynamic process by which the Barbelo Aeon itself gradually unfolds from the Invisible Spirit, the Platonizing Sethian treatises employed a completely different and distinctive terminology, namely the noetic or "intelligible" triad of Being, Life, and Mind. Indeed, Plotinus too employed the terms of this triad mostly to describe the activity of his second hypostasis, intellect, in which Mind (νοῦς) denotes the thinking subject, Being (τὸ ὄν) denotes the object of its thinking, and Life (ζωή) denotes the thinking activity itself, but also on occasion to designate phases in the emanation of Intellect and Being as a trace of Life from the One.[19]

By contrast with Plotinus, the Platonizing Sethian treatises conceive the intelligible triad as the Invisible Spirit's Triple Power, a quasi- or inter-hypostatic triad of powers that functions as the means by which the supreme Invisible Spirit gives rise to the Aeon of Barbelo.[20] Since the Invisible Spirit and its pow-

was, that he himself had been manifested as a form of the Invisible One" (ὃς παραστὰς ἐπέδειξεν αὐτῷ ὃ ἦν, αὐτὸς τοῦ ἀοράτου μορφὴ φανείς). Cf. Codex Bruce, *Untitled* 242,24–253,2 [Schmidt and MacDermot 1978]: "Moreover the power that was given to the forefather is called first-visible because it is he who was first manifest (πρωτοφανής). And he was called unbegotten because no one has created him. And he was called the ineffable and the nameless one. And he was also called self-begotten (αὐτογενής) and self-willed because he had revealed himself by his own will." The Orphic associations of the names Kalyptos and Protophanes has been persuasively confirmed by Thomassen 2013, calling attention to their occurrence in one or another form as appellations of the deity Eros in an erotic spell from the great Paris magical papyrus *PGM* 4, The "Sword of Dardanos" *PGM* 4,1716–1870: πρωτοφανῆ at line 1791, πρωτόγονε at 1755, and in lines 1757–1758 "[you] who conceal reasonable thoughts beneath a shroud (ὁ τοὺς σώφρονας λογισμοὺς ἐπικαλύπτων). Thomassen sees here evidence of a prior philosophical interpretation of an Orphic theogony that would have informed both this magical text and the Platonizing Sethians.

[18] In *Ad Candidum* 14,11–14, Victorinus hints at a similar progression: "For what is above ὄν is hidden (cf. Kalyptos) ὄν; indeed the manifestation (cf. Protophanes) of the hidden is generation (cf. Autogenes), since ὄν in potentiality generates ὄν in act."

[19] See *Ennead* 6,7[38],17,6–43.

[20] While *Zostrianos* tends to portray this entity as the Invisible Spirit's inherent three-fold power, *Allogenes* (and *Marsanes*) tends to hypostatize the Triple Power as a quasi-hypostatic "Triple Powered One" or "Triple-Powered Invisible Spirit" interposed between the supreme Unknowable One and the Aeon of Barbelo by identifying it in terms of its median processional phase (e.g., Vitality, Life, Activity; NHC XI 66,30–38: "From the One who constantly stands, there appeared an eternal Life, the Invisible and Triple Powered Spirit, the One that is

ers or acts are beyond the realm of determinate being, the triad of powers can no longer be represented by substantive nouns, but only by abstract terms: Existence (ὕπαρξις or "beingness" ὀντότης) rather than Being (τὸ ὄν), Vitality or "livingness" (ζωότης) rather than Life (ἡ ζωή), and Mentality or "mentation" (νοότης, in *Zostrianos* rendered as μακαριότης, Blessedness) rather than Intellect (ὁ νοῦς). Each of its powers designates a distinct phase in the emanation of the Barbelo Aeon: (1) In its initial phase as a purely infinitival Existence, the Triple Power is latent within and identical with the supreme One; (2) in its emanative phase it is an indeterminate Vitality that proceeds forth from One; and (3) in its final phase it is a Mentality [or Blessedness] that contemplates its prefigurative source in the supreme One and, thereby delimited, takes on the character of determinate being as the intellectual Aeon of Barbelo.[21] It thus appears that the authors of *Zostrianos* and *Allogenes* further interpreted the *Tim.* 39e passage by reasoning that the *activities* of *being* and *living* that comprise the Living-Thing-that-Is (ὅ ἔστιν ζῷον), which they identified with Kalyptos, and the *intellection* of the observing Intellect, which they identified with Protophanes, must have pre-existed on an even higher, supra-noetic level. They conceived these activities as a distinct triad of activities that they elevated to the level of the hyper-transcendent first principle of Sethian theology, the "Invisible Spirit" or Unknowable One. Now called the "*Triple-Powered* Invisible Spirit," its three powers were

in all existing things and surrounds them all while transcending them all"), although in its initial and final phases it actually *is* these two.

[21] E.g., *Zost.* NHC VIII 81,6–20: "She (Barbelo) [was] existing [individually] [as cause] of [the declination]. Lest she come forth anymore or get further away from perfection, she knew herself and him (the Invisible Spirit), and she stood at rest and spread forth on his [behalf] ... to know herself and the one that pre-exists"; *Allogenes* NHC XI 45,22–30: "For after it (the Barbelo Aeon) [contracted, it expanded] and [spread out] and became complete, [and] it was empowered [with] all of them, by knowing [itself in the perfect Invisible Spirit]. And it [became an] aeon who knows [herself because] she knew that one"; XI 48,15–17: "It is with [the] hiddenness of Existence that he provides Being, [providing] for [it in] every way, since it is this that [shall] come into being when he intelligizes himself"; XI 49,5–26: "He (the Triple Powered One) is endowed with [Blessedness] and Goodness, because when he is intelligized as the Delimiter (D) of the Boundlessness (B) of the Invisible Spirit (IS) [that subsists] in him (D), it (B) causes [him (D)] to revert to [it (IS)] in order that it (B) might know what it is that is within it (IS) and how it (IS) exists, and that he (D) might guarantee the endurance of everything by being a cause for those who truly exist. For through him (D) knowledge of it (IS) became available, since he (D) is the one who knows what it (IS; or he, D?) is. But they brought forth nothing [beyond] themselves, neither power nor rank nor glory nor aeon, for they are all eternal." Cf. *Apocryphon of John* (NHC II 4,19–28): "For it is he (the Invisible Spirit) who looks at himself in his light which surrounds him, the Fount of living water ... the Fount of pure luminous water surrounding him, and his thought became actual and she [Barbelo] appeared"; rather like Narcissus, the Invisible Spirit sees his reflected image and unites with it, but rather than ending in self-annihilation, the visionary act is here productive. The living waters of the baptismal rite have become a transcendent emanation of luminous, living, and self-reflective thinking.

identified as the source of the substantive being, life and thought that become externally instantiated in the Aeon of Barbelo.[22]

Let us now see how this ontogenetic metaphysics plays a role in the visionary ascent described in *Zostrianos* and *Allogenes*.

VII. Angelification and Celestial Liturgy: Zostrianos

Among the Sethian treatises, the transformation of earthly ritual to heavenly liturgy is most clearly noticeable in the Sethian Platonizing treatise *Zostrianos*. Here, the baptismal ritual of the Five Seals has been entirely transcendentalized, since the baptisms occur, not on the earthly plane but in the course of a visionary ascent into the supramundane world.

Having ascended from earth to the heavenly regions and entering the realm of the Self-generated Aeons at the lowest reaches of the divine Intellect or Barbelo Aeon, Zostrianos is baptized five times in the name of the divine Autogenes. At the first four baptisms, he becomes a different kind of angel (contemplative, masculine, holy, and perfect), and upon the fifth, he becomes divine.[23]

B1. Zost. NHC VIII 6,7–7,22: I was baptized in the [name of] the divine Autogenes [by] those powers that preside [over the] living water, Michar and Mi[cheus.] I was purified by [the] great Barpharanges. I was [glorified] and inscribed in glory. I was sealed by those who preside over these powers, [Michar], Micheus, Seldao, Ele[nos] and Zogenethlos. I [became] a [contemplative] angel and stood upon the first – that is the fourth – aeon together with the souls....
[7] I was [baptized for the] second time in the name of the divine Autogenes by these same powers. I became an angel of masculine gender. I stood upon the second – that is the third – aeon along with the children of Seth, and I blessed these same ones.
And I was baptized for the third time in the name of the divine Autogenes by these same powers. [I] became a holy angel and stood upon the third – that is the second – [aeon], and I [blessed] these same ones.
And I was baptized for the fourth time by these [same] powers. I became [a] perfect [angel and stood upon] the fourth – [that is the first] – aeon, and [blessed these same ones]....

[22] I owe this observation to Mazur 2014.

[23] Upon each of the first four baptisms, Zostrianos "stands" upon each of four aeons, in all probability defined by the Four Sethian Luminaries in ascending order, Eleleth, Daveithe, Oroiael, and Armozel (7,1b–22a).These angelic qualities may be intended to characterize the traditional Sethian inhabitants of these aeons; e.g., in the *Apocryphon of John* (NHC II 8,28–9,24): the repentant souls, the seed of Seth (the male race), the holy Seth, and the perfect Adam. Zostrianos successively becomes a "[contemplative] angel" (6,17–18), an "angel of masculine gender" (7,4–6), a "holy angel" (7,13), and a "perfect angel" (7,18–19). Some 46 pages later, when he is baptized the fifth time in the name of Autogenes, he becomes "divine" and stands upon the "fifth" aeon, presumably upon the entire assemblage of the Self-generated Aeons (53,15–24). Finally standing before the Protophanes, Zostrianos is baptized in "living water" and becomes "truly existing" (61,14).

Zost. NHC VIII 53,15–24: [When I was] baptized the fifth [time] in the name of the Autogenes by these same powers, I became divine. [I] stood upon the [fifth] aeon, a habitation for all [of them]; I saw all those belonging to [the] Autogenes, [those] who truly exist.

Zostrianos' transformation into angelhood likely draws on motifs well-known in Jewish ascent apocalypses and mystical literature, in which visionaries not only witness but actually participate in the heavenly liturgy, where they acquire angelic status.[24] In a similar vein, the Sethian elect probably saw themselves as ritually angelified and saved in this lifetime, albeit as a proleptic experience of the final salvation that would come with death and the escape from the cycle of reincarnation.

After having undergone his five baptisms in the name of Autogenes in the lowest level of the Barbelo Aeon or divine intellect, Zostrianos must now ascend through its three major levels comprised by the intellectual triad Autogenes, Protophanes, and Kalyptos, here conceived as aeons, each of which is

---

[24] Thus in the Enochic apocalypses, Enoch is elevated to the divine throne, receives priestly investiture and is transformed into an angel: *1 Enoch* 22:8–10: "And the LORD said to Michael, 'Go, and extract Enoch from [his] earthly clothing. And anoint him with my delightful oil, and put him into the clothes of my glory'. And so Michael did, just as the Lord had said to him. He anointed me and clothed me. And the appearance of that oil is greater than the greatest light, and its ointment is like sweet dew, and its fragrance myrrh; and it is like the rays of the glittering sun. And I looked at myself, and I had become like one of his glorious ones, and there was no observable difference." In *3 Enoch* 3–16, Enoch is invested, crowned with inscribed crowns, named, enthroned in heaven, transformed into the angel Metatron and worshipped by the angels. Rather than baptism, Enochic celestial angelification focuses on priestly anointment as the occasion for the acquisition of angelic, priestly vestments. In the Qumran *Songs of the Sabbath Sacrifice*, angels are described as heavenly priests in luminous robes, and in the "Self-Glorification Hymn," the author, extolling himself as one who has been reckoned among the gods (4Q471C, 6 & 11; Eshel et al. 1998): "I shall be reckoned with the gods and my dwelling place is in the holy congregation") becomes angelified in a liturgical *communion* (*unio liturgica*) with God and his angels, yet there is no mention of an actual mystical union (*unio mystica*). According to the Hekhalot text *Ma'aseh Merkabah*, a similar series of attributes is acquired by the Jewish mystic who descends to the divine chariot: "R. Akiba said to me: Were uprightness and righteousness in your heart then you would know how many measures are in heaven. He said to me: When I was in the first palace I was righteous, in the second palace I was pure, in the third palace I was upright, in the fourth palace I was perfect, in the fifth palace I arrived holy before the king of kings, blessed be he" (*Ma'aseh Merkabah* 9, cited in Janowitz 1989, 41. In *2 Baruch* and the *Ascension of Isaiah*, the righteous, having become angels through the acquisition of the heavenly garment, are to become even *greater* than the angels. See Schäfer 2009, 349–50 citing Alexander 2006, 105: "Where does Qumran stand on this issue [the question of a mystical union with God]? The position there seems to be unequivocal: there is no absorption into God. The highest transformation that the mystic can undergo is into an *angel*, not into God, and angels are definitely not God. The scrolls do indeed use language which at first sight dangerously blurs the boundary between God and angels (e.g., by applying the same term Elohim apparently indiscriminately to both), but closer inspection shows that in fact the distinction is rigidly maintained: our authors evince a deep consciousness of the difference between God and the Angels, even the highest of the Angels. The Angels are outside the Godhead."

imbued with its own special baptismal water. Each level is distinguished by the degree of enlightenment it conveys as well as by the nature of the knowledge appropriate for cognitive assimilation to the ontological character of its aeonic level:[25]

B2. Zost. NHC VIII 24,28–25,22: [For each] of the aeons [there is] a baptism [of this sort]. Now if [one] strips off the world **25** and lays aside [nature], whether one is a sojourner, without dwelling place or power, following the practices of others, or whether one repents, having committed no sin, being satisfied with knowledge (and) without concern for anything (worldly), baptisms are appointed respectively for these; it is the path into the Self-generated ones. (There is) the one (in the name of Autogenes) in which you have now been baptized each time, which is appropriate for seeing the [perfect] individuals; it is a knowledge of everything, having originated from the powers of the Self-generated ones. (There is) the one you will perform when you transfer to the all-perfect aeons (of Protophanes). When you wash in the third baptism, [then] you will learn about those [that] truly [exist] in [that] place (i. e., of Kalyptos).

The originally ontogenetic function of these intellectual sub-aeons becomes apparent in their association with three grades of baptismal water whose ultimate source is the supreme intelligible triad of Existence, Vitality and Blessedness by which all reality subsequent to the supreme One is generated:

B3. Zost. NHC VIII 15,1–18: And [there exists] a water for [each] of them. Therefore they are [three] perfect waters: It is the water of Life hat belongs to Vitality in which you now have been baptized in the Autogenes. It is the [water] of Blessedness that [belongs] to Knowledge in which you will be [baptized] in the Protophanes. It is the water of Existence [which] belongs to Divinity, that is, to Kalyptos. And the water of Life [exists with respect to] Power, that of [Blessedness] with respect to Essence, and that of [Divinity] with respect to [Existence]. But all [these] [are likenesses and forms of the] Triple Powered One.

B4. Zost. NHC VIII 22,4–12: And the universal intelligence joins in when the water of Autogenes is complete. When one knows it and all these, one has to do with the water of Protophanes; when one unites with him and all these, one has to do with Kalyptos.

The passages B2 and B4 from *Zostrianos* suggest that the metaphysical connection between the ontogenetic Existence-Vitality-Mentality/Blessedness triad and the intelligible Kalyptos-Protophanes-Autogenes triad arose in the ritual context of the Sethian baptismal rite. Here, the ascent has become an intellectual act of contemplation whose stages are symbolized by an ascending series of transcendental baptisms in which the various baptismal waters are isomorphically associated, not only with each term of the lower triad of intellects com-

[25] Baptism is interpreted in epistemological categories essentially similar to those in Plato's *Symposium* 210–11, where the vision of absolute beauty is achieved by progressive shift of attention away from individual instances of beauty, to the ideal beauty of all forms, and finally to absolute beauty itself, which then discloses itself as a sudden (ἐξαίφνης) and immediate intuition. The next higher stage is therefore achieved by a purifying and unifying synthesis of the experience of the lower stage.

prising the Barbelo Aeon – Autogenes, Protophanes, and Kalyptos – but also with the higher noetic triad of powers – Existence, Life, and Blessedness – by which the Invisible Spirit gave rise to the intelligible world.

Baptism into each successive level enables ascending degrees of spiritual enlightenment or knowledge. Such enlightenment is a progression from awareness of discrete individuality characteristic of ordinary perception toward a vision of the unity of all things including one's own unity with the eternal principles:

B5. Zost. NHC VIII 23,17–24,1: According to each locale one has a portion of the eternal ones [and] ascends [to them. As] one [becomes pure and] simple, just so one continually [approaches] unity. Being [always] pure and [simple], one is filled [with Mentality,] with Existence [and Essence] and a holy Spirit. There is **24** nothing of him outside of him.

Zostrianos portrays an erstwhile earthly liturgy transposed to a celestial liturgy, yet one in which the visionary becomes ontologically transformed.[26] Although Zostrianos has been transformed into an angel or even into an aeonic being, he nevertheless remains distinct from and external to the supreme One. Having become "truly existing" (*Zost.* NHC VIII 61,14) he remains only within the Barbelo Aeon, the realm of determinate being.

But the treatise *Allogenes* offers an even further shift from external ritual *communion* to internal mystical *union* in which a visionary ascent to divine realities conceived as external to oneself leads to a contemplative, internal self-reflexive withdrawal into one's primordial self coincident with the supreme source of all reality.

[26] As a rite of passage, *Zostrianos* clearly interprets baptism as a series of cognitive acts by which one's perception of self and world undergoes a shift in awareness from multiplicity and fragmentation to unity. The separation phase is achieved Zostrianos' abandonment of his earthly body and successive baptisms in the various realms between earth and the Self-generated Aeons. As a stripping away of worldly preoccupations and ways of thinking, these baptisms broadly resemble the purgative function of the ritual of the Five Seals, such as the stripping away of one's psycho-somatic nature described in the *Trimorphic Protennoia* and the renunciations in the *Gospel of the Egyptians*. The liminal phase consists in a gradual loss of the self conceived as a center of awareness of entities outside of oneself; all the powers have become an indistinguishable inner unity lacking any determination. The phase of reincorporation is not so much an integration into a new community such as the seed of Seth as it is into a new supra-personal state of awareness of the unity of one's intellect with the intelligible world, conceived along Platonic lines. This conception stands in contrast to the more apotropaic conception of baptism in the *Gospel of the Egyptians* and the *Trimorphic Protennoia*, where receipt of the divine Living Water enables one to escape the influence of the hostile cosmic powers by entering a community that possesses insight into the existence and nature of the superior powers that govern the true world beyond this one.

VIII. From External Communion to Internal Assimilation: *Allogenes*

Allogenes presents a sequence of ascending cognitive states similar to those of *Zostrianos*, but without any reference to baptismal ritual or imagery. While Zostrianos *ascends* up to and enters the lower *intellectual* triad of Autogenes, Protophanes, and Kalyptos, Allogenes first achieves an *earthly vision* of this intellectual triad, and only then is suddenly raptured beyond this lower triad to the *peak* of the Barbelo Aeon which coincides with Mentality, the lowest level of the higher ontogenetic triad of Existence, Vitality, and Mentality. His subsequent contemplative ascent toward actual union with the supreme One consists of an ontological assimilation with each successive power, from Mentality to Vitality to pure Existence. The progress of this assimilation is marked by his transfer from firm self-knowledge to uncertain instability to firm "standing."

Allogenes' ascent is described as a sequence of centripetal self-withdrawals from determinate self-knowledge leading to a loss of awareness and annihilation of self that ends in a cognitively vacant union with the self's original prefiguration still resident in the supreme One:

C1. Allogenes NHC XI 60,14–61,22: There was within me a stillness of silence, and I heard the Blessedness whereby I knew <my> proper self. And I withdrew to the Vitality as I sought <myself> (ⲚⲤⲰ<ï>; cod. ⲚⲤⲰⲤ; cf. 59,14 "seeking yourself"). And I joined it and stood, not firmly but quietly. And I saw an eternal, intellectual, undivided motion, all-powerful, formless, undetermined by determination. And when I wanted to stand firmly, I withdrew to the Existence, which I found standing and at rest. Like an image and likeness of what had come upon me; by means of a manifestation of the Indivisible and the Stable I was filled with revelation; by means of an Originary Manifestation **61** of the Unknowable One, [as though] incognizant of him, I [knew] him and was empowered by him. Having been permanently strengthened, I knew that [which] exists in me, even the Triple-Powered One and the manifestation of his uncontainableness. And by means of a Originary Manifestation of the First who is unknowable to them all – the god who is beyond perfection – I saw him and the Triple-Powered One who exists within them all. I was seeking the the ineffable and unknowable god – whom if one should know him, one would absolutely 'unknow' him – the mediator of the Triple–Powered, the one who abides in stillness and silence and is unknowable.

In *Allogenes*, these withdrawals constitute a series of reflexive reversions towards his inner self, as if the entire triad comes to abide within the mystical aspirant. First perceiving the quiet Blessedness that conveys self-knowledge, Allogenes next penetrates the boundary of his own self by withdrawing into and joining with the more indeterminate and unstable level of Vitality. His third and final withdrawal is made towards the completely stable level of Existence, which he finds "standing and at rest." At this point all cognition fades into a complete unknowing, whether of self or of other than self. Having himself become "like an image and likeness" of the stability "that has come upon" him, Allogenes is "filled" by the primordial unity and stability that preceded his very own existence, where all cognition and awareness are absent.[27] These withdrawals are essentially acts of vanishing self-cognition in which a product retreats into the precognitive emptiness of its "originary manifestation," that is, its own pre-existent prefiguration still latent in the source from which it originally emanated.[28]

The process of contemplative union with the Unknowable One is the exact inverse of the process by which the Barbelo Aeon emanates from the supreme One's Triple Power; the two processes are mirror images of one another. In other words, the power by which even the divine Intellect attains its own union with the supreme principle is the same as that by which it was originally generated, and is a power that is also present to human aspirants either jointly or individually. The ascending human seeker thus assumes identity, not just with the divine Intellect, but with its primordial prefiguration, which eternally subsists as the supreme One's own initial moment of self-apprehension.[29] The primordial instant of emanation and the penultimate instant of mystical self-reversion thus coincide.

[27] Similarly Plotinus, *Ennead* 5,8,10,40–44: "One must transport (μεταφέρειν) what one sees into oneself (εἰς αὑτὸν), and look at it as oneself, as if someone possessed by a god, Phoebus or one of the Muses, could bring about the vision of the god in himself."

[28] A notion found also in Plotinus, *Ennead* 3,8,[30],9,29–39: "What is it, then, which we shall receive when we set our intellect to it ? Rather, the Intellect must first return ["withdraw"], so to speak, backwards, and give itself up, in a way, to what lies behind it (δεῖ τὸν νοῦν οἷον εἰς τοὐπίσω ἀναχωρεῖν καὶ οἷον ἑαυτὸν ἀφέντα τοῖς εἰς ὄπισθεν αὐτοῦ ἀμφίστομον ὄντα) – for it faces in both directions; and there, if it wishes to see that First Principle, it must not be altogether intellect. For it is the first life, since it is an activity manifest in the way of outgoing of all things (Ἔστι μὲν γὰρ αὐτὸς ζωὴ πρώτη, ἐνέργεια οὖσα ἐν διεξόδῳ τῶν πάντων; cf. *Allogenes* NHC XI 48,34–38: 'But when they (passively) apprehend (i. e., through a preconception), they participate in the previtality [ⲧϣⲟⲣ̄ⲡ̄ ⲙ̄ ⲙ̄ ⲛ̄ ⲧ̀ⲱⲛ̄ ⲉ̄ = ζωὴ πρώτη], even an indivisible activity [ἐνέργεια], a reality [ὑπόστασις] of the first One, of the One that truly exists'); outgoing not in the sense that it is now in process of going out, but that it has gone out (οὐ τῇ διεξιούσῃ, ἀλλὰ τῇ διεξελθούσῃ). If, then, it is life and outgoing and holds all things distinctly and not in a vague general way – for [in the latter case] it would hold them imperfectly and inarticulately – it must itself derive from something else, which is no more in the way of outgoing (ἐν διεξόδῳ), but is the origin of outgoing, and the origin of life and the origin of intellect and all things" (ἀρχὴ διεξόδου καὶ ἀρχὴ ζωῆς καὶ ἀρχὴ νοῦ καὶ τῶν πάντων) (transl. A. H. Armstrong). Cf. 6,7,15,31–32: δεῖ δὲ ἑαυτὸν ἐκεῖνο γενόμενον τὴν θέαν [ἑαυτὸν] ποιήσασθαι.

[29] The contemplator's acts of self-withdrawal (ἀναχωρεῖν) are equivalent to the self-contraction that precedes the emanation of all subsequent reality from the One's Triple Power. Compare *Allogenes* NHC XI 45,21–37: "[O] Triple-Powered One who [truly exists]! For after it [contracted] [it expanded], and [it spread out] and became complete, [and] it was empowered [with] all of them by knowing [itself] [and the perfect Invisible Spirit], and it [became an] aeon. By knowing [herself] she (Barbelo) knew that one, [and] she became Kalyptos. [Because] she acts in those whom she knows, she is Protophanes, a perfect, invisible Intellect, Harmedon. Empowering the individuals, she is a triple male (Autogenes)."

IX. From Baptism to Mystical Union

In this essay, I have suggested that the Sethian treatises exhibit a development from exterior to interior ritual, especially in the ritual context of the baptism of the "Five Seals." In this process, the tactual, auditory and visionary actions of an external physical rite become transformed into a visionary ascent. *Zostrianos* represents a penultimate stage, where the visionary is angelified or even divinized as a heavenly being, yet remains distinct from the supreme principle. The ultimate stage is represented by *Allogenes*, where the ascent has become completely interiorized as a sequence of contemplative states culminating in one's actual, even if temporary, assimilation to the supreme deity itself.

In the *Apocryphon of John*, the *Trimorphic Protennoia*, and the *Gospel of the Egyptians*, speculation on the nature and source of the baptismal waters – called the Living Water[30] – has come to conceive them as the transcendent emanative medium of radiant life and thought flowing from the supreme deity that gave rise to his First Thought, the divine mother Barbelo. As Barbelo's epithet "womb of the all"[31] suggests, immersion in and reemergence from such waters is tantamount to a rebirth, a reentry and reemergence from the supra-cosmic womb, in which the old self is extinguished and the new self is reborn.[32] To be immersed in this luminous water is to be set free from bondage to the body and the powers and limitations that control it and be reborn by being reabsorbed into the self's own primordial point of origin as a portion of the Mother's light. Such rebirth is in effect to retrace or rewind – or indeed to unwind – the very process by which, not only the transcendent world, but ultimately all levels of reality, came into being. While *Zostrianos* portrays this process as an entirely transcendentalized baptismal ritual ending in angelification, *Allogenes* presents it as an act of contemplative imagination leading to a temporary annihilation of the individuated self and its reabsorption into the single principle and source of all reality. Here protology and eschatology coincide: both origin and eschaton are entirely transcendental, and the eschaton is realized through an apparently non-temporal contemplative reabsorption of the mystic aspirant into his or her primordial origin.

---

[30] I.e., flowing, Life-giving water (Gen 21:19) whose analogue is the ritually pure water used in the temple and its cleansing rituals (Lev 14:5, 6, 50, 51; Num 5:17; 19:17). Significantly, Zech 14:8 uses the expression to describe the water which flows out from Jerusalem to renew the land in the last days (cf. Rev 7:15–17; 21:6; 22:1–2, 17; John 4:7–15 and 7:37–39).

[31] Cf. *Ap. John* NHC II 5,5; *Trim. Prot.* NHC XIII 38,11–16; *Gos. Egypt.* NHC III 43,1; Codex Bruce, *Untitled* ch. 13, and the references in note 11.

[32] Cf. Nicodemus' literalistic interpretation of Jesus' injunction that one must be reborn/born from above (γεννηθῇ ἄνωθεν) in John 3:3: "Can a man enter his mother's womb a second time and be born?"

Bibliography

Alexander, P. (2006), *The Mystical Texts: Songs of the Sabbath Sacrifice and Related Manuscripts* (Library of Second Temple Studies 61), London: T&T Clark.

Barry, C., Funk, W.-P., Poirier, P.-H., Turner, J.D. (2000), *Zostrien (NH VIII, 1)* (Bibliothèque copte de Nag Hammadi. Section "Textes" 24), Québec: Presses de l'Université Laval; Leuven – Paris: Peeters.

Bechtle, G. (2000), 'A Problem concerning the Question of Being in 2./3. Century Platonism', *Ancient Philosophy* 20: 393–414.

Bodewitz, H.W. (1973), *Jaiminiya Brahmana 1.1–65: Translation and Commentary, with a Study of Agnihotra and Pranagnihotra*, Leiden: Brill.

Corrigan, K. and Rasimus, T., eds. (2013), *Gnosticism, Platonism, and the Late Ancient World: Essays in Honour of John D. Turner* (Nag Hammadi and Manichaean Studies 82), Leiden: Brill.

Davies, S. (1992), 'The Christology and Protology of the Gospel of Thomas', *Journal of Biblical Literature* 111: 663–82.

Dottin, G. (1930), *The Orphic Argonautica – Les Argonautiques d'Orphée.* Texte et traduction par –, Paris: Les Belles Lettres.

Eliade, M. (1969), *Yoga: Immortality and Freedom* (Bollingen Series), Princeton, NJ: Princeton University Press.

Eshel, E. et al. (1998), *Qumran Cave 4.VI: Poetical and Liturgical Texts, Part 1* (Discoveries in the Judaean Desert 11), Oxford: Clarendon.

Gunkel, H. (1895), *Schöpfung und Chaos in Urzeit und Endzeit: Eine religionsgeschichtliche Untersuchung* über *Gen. 1 und Ap. Joh. 12*, Göttingen: Vandenhoeck & Ruprecht.

Janowitz, N. (1989), *The Poetics of Ascent: Theories of Language in a Rabbinic Ascent Text*, Albany, NY: SUNY Press.

Jonas, H. (1969), 'Myth and Mysticism: A Study of Objectification and Interiorization in Religious Thought', *The Journal of Religion* 49: 315–29 (reprint in idem, *Philosophical Essays: From Ancient Creed to Technological Man*, Englewood Cliffs, NJ: Prentice Hall, 1974, 291–304).

Mazur, Z. (2014), 'Intimations of the Pre-Plotinian Gnostic Use of the Noetic (Existence–Life–Intellect) Triad in Chapter 6 of Plotinus' Treatise Against the Gnostics, II.9[33]'. Unpublished paper presented at Université Laval, Québec, 4 March 2014.

Schäfer, P. (2009), *The Origins of Jewish Mysticism*, Tübingen: Mohr Siebeck.

Schmidt, E. and MacDermott, V. (1978), *The Books of Jeu and the Untitled Text in the Bruce Codex* (The Coptic Gnostic Library), Leiden: Brill.

Stroumsa, G.G. (2009), *The End of Sacrifice: Religious Transformations in Late Antiquity*, translated by S. Emanuel, Chicago, IL – London: University of Chicago Press.

Thomassen, E. (2013), 'Sethian Names in Magical Texts: Protophanes and Meirotheos', in: *Gnosticism, Platonism, and the Late Ancient World: Essays in Honour of John D. Turner*, ed. K. Corrigan and T. Rasimus (Nag Hammadi and Manichaean Studies 82), Leiden: Brill, 63–77.

– (unpublished), 'Christian Initiation in Antiquity: A Synopsis', unpublished essay on *Academia* <https://www.academia.edu/34165308>.

Turner, J.D. (2001), *Sethian Gnosticism and the Platonic Tradition* (Bibliothèque copte de Nag Hammadi. Section «Études» 6), Québec: Presses de l'Université Laval; Leuven – Paris: Peeters.

van Gennep, A. (1961), *The Rites of Passage*, Chicago, IL: University of Chicago Press, 1961 (original: *Les rites de passage*, Paris: Nourry, 1909).

"Above the Starry Canopy"

Spatial and Non-spatial Patristic Perspectives on the Christian Hope for Afterlife

Benjamin Gleede

Where are we going to stay after death? Will there be yet any room or place for us? Jesus himself promises "many mansions in my father's house" (John 14:2), but how and especially where are we to imagine those? If Christians hope to be resurrected in the flesh, according to the mainstream tradition in the very same earthly, spatially circumscribed flesh we carry in this life,[1] they also have to answer the question where those spatially circumscribed bodies are going to stay in eternity, which space is going to circumscribe them and where.

Considering the immense amount of ink spilled in Christian antiquity on the exact nature of the resurrection body, it is astonishing how rarely this question is actually asked, let alone discussed in more detail. Already St. Paul had to face the Platonist bias that the earthly remains of this body, primary substrate of all our decay, cannot play any permanent role in the postexistence of a human individual (cf. 1 Cor 15:35–49). If the body is *per definitionem* a conglomeration of matter and changing natural qualities,[2] the Pauline affirmation of an imperishable body has to sound like an outright *contradictio in adiecto*, especially as it implies a continuity between perishability and imperishability which is very hard to reconcile with the fact that the earthly body undoubtedly perishes and plays its unavoidable part in the natural recycling process.

The extensive debate about the resurrection body in Christian apologetic literature thus focusses almost exclusively on the very nature of this continuity, on the "how" of resurrection,[3] yet mostly neglects the "where." Confronted with the rather obvious consequence that bodily remuneration and punishment

---

[1] When Rufinus' orthodoxy was challenged at the occasion of his Origen-translations, he had to defend himself primarily by emphasizing that no other flesh is to be resurrected instead of the one we have, "sed hanc ipsam, nullo omnino ei membro amputato uel aliqua corporis parte desecta, sed cui nihil omnino ex omni natura sua desit, nisi sola corruptio" (*Apologia ad Anastasium* 4; CCL 20,26). For the background and the earlier apologetic discussions cf. Setzer 2004.

[2] Cf. Plotinus, *Ennead* 6,3(44),8.

[3] Cf. e.g. Kiel 2015, 208–335.

would also imply some spatial arrangements where they are supposed to take place, most authors of Christian antiquity would probably have reacted like Aphrahat or John Chrysostom: with deep hesitation or quite indignantly. For the Persian sage, the whereabouts of reward and punishment can never be fixed with any certainty, as the divine power on the one hand lets the sons of Corah enter hell through a hole in the Palestinian desert (Num 16:32–33) and thus seems to establish a spatial continuity between this life and the afterlife, but on the other hand promises to remodel heaven and earth in their entirety before realizing the final judgement (Isa 51:6).[4] According to the "gold mouthed" patriarch of Constantinople, however, Christians should concentrate on the very fact of eternal remuneration and punishment rather than scrutinize its circumstances, i.e. the whole point of preaching heaven and hell is an ethical, not a cosmological one. This is why the patriarch dismisses the Christian lore about an entry to hell in the valley of Josaphat (cf. Joel 4:2) and points to some mysterious place beyond this cosmos where in his opinion the eschaton is most likely to be taking place.[5]

To be sure, Chrysostom does not intend a consequent reduction of the Christian faith to an ethical or existential attitude without any cosmological implications, but wants to keep those implications as abstract as possible. Obviously, he is unwilling to engage in the same end- and fruitless discussions about nature which had been keeping the philosophers busy for about one millennium in Chrysostom's time, but apparently had not yielded really unequivocal results in any respect.[6] Although this relative cosmological indifferentism was widely held also in the context of growing Christian intellectual dominance and

[4] *Homily* 22,24 (PS 1, 1035–36).

[5] *Homiliae in Epistulam ad Romanos* 31,3 (PG 60, 673–74): Καὶ ποῦ, φησὶ, καὶ ἐν ποίῳ χωρίῳ αὕτη ἔσται ἡ γέεννα; Τί γάρ σοι τούτου μέλει; τὸ γὰρ ζητούμενον, δεῖξαι ὅτι ἔστιν, οὐχ ὅπου τεταμίευται καὶ ἐν ποίῳ χωρίῳ. Τινὲς μὲν γὰρ μυθολογοῦντές φασιν, ὅτι ἐν τῇ κοιλάδι τοῦ Ἰωσαφὰτ, ὃ περὶ πολέμου τινὸς εἴρηται παρελθόντος, καὶ νῦν τοῦτο εἰς τὴν γέενναν ἕλκοντες· ἡ δὲ Γραφὴ οὐ τοῦτό φησιν. Ἀλλ' ἐν ποίῳ τόπῳ, φησὶν, ἔσται; Ἔξω που, ὡς ἔγωγε οἶμαι, τοῦ κόσμου τούτου παντός. Καθάπερ γὰρ τῶν βασιλείων τὰ δεσμωτήρια καὶ τὰ μέταλλα πόῤῥω διέστηκεν, οὕτω δὴ καὶ τῆς οἰκουμένης ταύτης ἔξω που ἔσται ἡ γέεννα. On the historical context cf. Guinot 2012, 117–18. On Chrysostom's eschatology in general cf. the extensive analysis of Schiwietz 1914, esp. 201–15.

[6] For Chrysostom's biblicistic distrust in philosophical cosmological speculations cf. *De incomprehensibli Dei natura* 2,473–89 (SC 28, 154–55): Καὶ ἵνα μάθῃς ὅτι τοῦτό ἐστιν ἀληθές, μηδὲν περὶ τῶν ἄνω διαλεχθῶμεν, ἀλλ' εἰ βούλει κάτω πρὸς τὴν ὁρωμένην κτίσιν τὸν λόγον ἀγάγωμεν. Οὐχ ὁρᾷς τουτονὶ τὸν οὐρανόν; ὅτι μὲν καμάρας εἰκόνα διασῴζει ἴσμεν, καὶ τοῦτο αὐτὸ οὐκ ἀπὸ λογισμῶν, ἀλλ' ἀπὸ τῆς θείας Γραφῆς μαθόντες· καὶ ὅτι πᾶσαν περιλαμβάνει τὴν γῆν, καὶ τοῦτο ἴσμεν, ὁμοίως παρ' ἐκείνης ἀκούσαντες· τίς δὲ τὴν οὐσίαν ἐστὶν ἀγνοοῦμεν. Εἰ δέ τις διϊσχυρίζοιτο καὶ φιλονεικοίη, λεγέτω τί τὴν οὐσίαν ἐστὶν ὁ οὐρανός· ἆρα κρύσταλλος πεπηγώς; ἆρα νέφος πεπυκνωμένον; ἆρα ἀὴρ παχύτερος; Ἀλλ' οὐδεὶς ἂν ἔχοι σαφῶς οὐδὲν εἰπεῖν. Ἔτι οὖν ἀποδείξεως, εἰπέ μοι, δεῖσθε πρὸς τὸ μαθεῖν τὴν μανίαν τῶν τὸν Θεὸν εἰδέναι λεγόντων; Τοῦ οὐρανοῦ τοῦ ὁρωμένου καθ' ἡμέραν τὴν φύσιν οὐκ ἔχεις εἰπεῖν, καὶ τοῦ ἀοράτου Θεοῦ μετὰ ἀκριβείας ἐπαγγέλλῃ τὴν οὐσίαν εἰδέναι; Καὶ τίς οὕτως ἀναίσθητος ὡς μὴ τὴν ἐσχάτην τῶν ταῦτα λεγόντων καταγινώσκειν μανίαν;

self-consciousness in the times of Theodosius,[7] many Christian thinkers went one step further and were no longer satisfied with a Christian theology and cosmology which would receive from pagan science the more or less non-controversial aspects and did not care about the rest.

I. 'Antiochene' Biblicism

Already Chrysostom's teacher Diodore of Tarsus had detected several rather clear contradictions between the conception of the world presupposed in some passages of the OT and the standard image among pagan intellectuals which pictured the cosmos as a spherical earth surrounded by nine planetary spheres.[8] In contrast, the prophet Isaiah clearly seems to describe the sky as a vault and both the creation account of Genesis 1 and Ps 103:2–3 speak of a firmament between heaven and earth which apparently stores vast additional amounts of water upon its back. If one takes this seriously, one actually has to abandon the spherical, Ptolemean picture in favor of a giant dome with the earth as its flat basis and the firmament as intermediate ceiling separating the upper waters from the lower ones.[9] As Diodore and his most famous pupil Theodore were heavily compromised as "Nestorian" heretics in the christological controversies to follow,[10] we unfortunately do not have enough of their works left to reconstruct more exactly their cosmological position and their reasons for the deviation from the scientifically established consensus. The first text which expounds these Christian deviations in more detail[11] and which is obviously heavily influenced by the theological tradition originated by Diodore and Theodore stems from the middle of the sixth century and was attributed in the later manuscript tradition to a certain Cosmas the India traveller.[12]

In sharp contrast to Chrysostom and the theological mainstream of the centuries before him, this author opposes any attempt to downplay the cosmological implications of the Christian faith. Instead, he is writing a Christian topog-

---

[7] Cf. e.g. Makarios Magnes, *Apokritikos* 4,2–3 (TU 169, 314).

[8] Cf. Wolska 1978, 173–77.

[9] Cf. esp. Photius' summary of Diodore's *De fato* (Cod. 223 220b5–19): δύο μὲν οὐρανοὺς λέγει γεγενῆσθαι, ἕνα μὲν τοῦ ὁρωμένου ἀνώτερον, ὃν καὶ συνυφεστάναι τῇ γῇ, θάτερον δὲ τὸν ὁρώμενον· δύο δὲ ὄντων τὸν μὲν ὀροφῆς ἐπέχειν λόγον, τὸν δὲ ὡς μὲν τὴν γῆν ὀροφῆς ὡσαύτως, ἐδάφους δὲ καὶ βάσεως ὡς τὸν ὑπερέχοντα. Καὶ γῆν δὲ μίαν. Καὶ τὰ μὲν οὐράνια ταῖς κρείττοσιν ἀπονενεμῆσθαι δυνάμεσι, τοῖς ὁρωμένοις δὲ τὰ ὑπουράνια. Μὴ σφαῖραν δὲ τὸν οὐρανὸν εἶναι, ἀλλὰ σκηνῆς καὶ καμάρας διασῴζειν σχῆμα. Καὶ ταύτης τῆς ὑπολήψεως γραφικάς, ὡς οἴεται, προβάλλει μαρτυρίας, οὐ μόνον περὶ τοῦ σχήματος, ἀλλὰ καὶ περὶ δύσεως καὶ περὶ ἀνατολῆς ἡλίου. Αἰτιολογεῖ δὲ καὶ τὴν τῶν ἡμερῶν καὶ νυκτῶν αὐξομείωσιν, καὶ ἄλλα τινὰ τοιαῦτα πολυπραγμονεῖ, ὡς ἔμοιγε δοκεῖ, τὸ ἀναγκαῖον οὐκ ἔχοντα, εἰ καὶ τοῖς ἱεροῖς λογίοις προσφύεται.

[10] Cf. Abramowski 1955–56; Chazelle 2007.

[11] Cf. the relevant surveys by Inglebert 2001, 27–108 and Krüger 2000.

[12] On the "Einleitungsfragen" to the *Topography* cf. now Uthemann 2005.

raphy which aims exactly at demonstrating that the basic tenets of his faith, especially the resurrection of the body, only work within a world conceived exactly in line with the indications of Holy Scripture, not within the one pictured according to pagan astronomy. If God the creator and the redeemer are to be identical and the purpose of creation is nothing but mankind and its redemption, creation also must have been designed accordingly from the very beginning and the structure of the cosmos must reflect God's plan for salvation in all of its aspects – an idea Cosmas finds pronounced by Jesus himself in Matt 25:34. If Jesus himself promises to the believers a kingdom prepared for them at the very foundation of the cosmos, we should expect a description of this preparatory act in the Genesis *Hexaemeron*, and in fact Cosmas finds such a description in Gen 1:6–7, the creation of the firmament on the second day. Apart from separating the upper waters from the lower ones, this firmament is supposed to create two different habitats within the world, the lower, earthly one between earth and firmament which is characterized by constant change and mutual affection, and the upper, heavenly one between firmament and first heaven, which transcends every kind of change and is reserved for immutable entities.[13]

This duality of habitats is made necessary by the peculiar nature of the finite, created spirits. In contrast to the infinite spirit of their creator, they do not possess any skill or knowledge by their very essence, but have to acquire those in a process of free and fallible learning, of trial and error, of constant comparison between good and bad experiences. A permanent and immutable realization of ethical perfection in contemplation of the divine is thus for the finite spirit only achievable via experiencing its opposite, the constant temptation, mutability and fallibility below the firmament. Hence, the finite spirit needs two habitats in order to achieve perfection, and the firmament had to be created in order to separate and establish the two.[14] As God foresaw, however, that the finite spirit

[13] For Cosmas' basic cosmographical pattern cf. next to the extensive exposition in *Topography* 2,6–23 the concise summaries in 4,4–6 and 7,83–86. For the significance of Matt 25:34 in making it theologically relevant cf. *Topography* 1,1; 5,254; 6,28 et al.

[14] Cf. esp. *Topography* 6,29 (SC 197, 45–46): Ἅπας οὖν ὁ σκοπὸς τῆς οἰκονομίας τοῦ Θεοῦ οὗτός ἐστι· δεῖ γὰρ ὡς ἐν ἀνακεφαλαιώσει συντομώτερον αὐτὸν ἐξειπεῖν· ἠβουλήθη ἐξ ἀγαθότητος ἑτέροις μεταδοῦναι τοῦ εἶναι, δυνάμεώς τε καὶ λόγου καὶ γνώσεως· ἐπειδὴ δὲ οἱ ἐκ μετοχῆς τούτων τυγχάνοντες ἀδυνάτως ἔχουσιν ὑφ' ἓν γνῶναι καὶ ἔχειν πάντα – ἐπείπερ τοῦτο μόνον ἴδιον Θεοῦ, τὸ δίχα μαθήσεως καὶ πείρας ταῦτα πάντα εἰδέναι, αὐτόχρημα ὢν καὶ δύναμις καὶ λόγος καὶ γνῶσις, γενητῶν δὲ τὸ ἐκ τοῦ πεποιηκότος μετέχειν τούτων ἁπάντων – , πεποίηκεν ἅμα τὰς δύο ταύτας καταστάσεις, τὴν πρώτην μὲν θνητὴν καὶ τρεπτὴν πείρας ἕνεκα καὶ παιδεύσεως τῶν λογικῶν, ἵνα τῇ ποικιλίᾳ τοῦ παντὸς καὶ τῇ παραθέσει τῶν ἐναντίων γυμναζόμενοι πειραθῶμεν ἡδέων καὶ λυπηρῶν, τὴν δευτέραν δὲ ἀθάνατον καὶ ἄτρεπτον εἰς ἀπόλαυσιν τῆς χάριτος αὐτοῦ, πρὸς τὸ διακριτικῇ ἕξει, λόγῳ καὶ πείρᾳ καὶ γνώσει, τῶν καλῶν παραθέσει, τῶν πρώτων τὴν μετουσίαν δέξασθαι ἡμᾶς. Cosmas resumes here a core motive from Theodore of Mopsuestia's theology (cf. Wolska 1962, 54–61 and n. 38) which is – probably via Origen's mediation – of Neoplatonic origin: Already Plotinus explains the descent of the souls into the corporeal world by their need for "comparison" (παράθεσις) between the two worlds: ἱστορίαν ὧν ἐνταῦθα εἶδέ τε καὶ ἔπαθε προσλαβούσῃ καὶ μαθούσῃ, οἷον ἄρα ἐστὶν ἐκεῖ εἶναι, καὶ τῇ παραθέσει τῶν οἷον ἐναντίων

would not directly acquire the perfect learning success, but would rather go astray completely and get hopelessly entangled in his failure and sin, he also foresaw the necessity of a high priest, who would show mankind the right way and lead them to their heavenly destination through the curtain of the firmament – a conception of Jesus Christ which is primarily inspired by the letter to the Hebrews. Thus, the entire world had to be designed as a temple, and according to the model of the Exodus tabernacle: We need two chambers, the outer or lower one and the inner or upper one, which have to be separated by a curtain, the firmament, through which Jesus entered heaven as our forerunner according to Heb 6:19–20 and paved us the "new, living way and access" according to Heb 10:20.[15] Just as the upper habitat, this point of access has to be topographically localizable for Cosmas: it is exactly that point where the ascending body of Jesus penetrated the firmament and entered the upper habitat, thus concretely and locally providing access for all the finite spirits and resurrected bodies below the firmament. We even find a quite imaginative description of the problems the ascending body of Christ would have encountered in a spherical world: If he had entered the lunar sphere in doing that, he would have either had to join the moon in its retrograde movement and thus oppose the motion of the entire cosmos like a fish swimming against the current, or he would have had to move against his own sphere being forced by the movement of the cosmos. If he had entered, however, some higher sphere, this would contradict the apostolic description in the letter to the Hebrews which has him transgress exactly one curtain.[16]

The cosmological allegorization of the tabernacle is thus one of the most important foundations of Cosmas' argument. Small wonder, he also wants the details of the lower habitat to be modelled according to the design laid out for the outer chamber of the tabernacle in the OT. To him, this may have seemed even more obvious, as he can rely on an age-old tradition of allegorical exegesis there which goes back at least to Philo of Alexandria.[17] He firstly points to the seven armed candle holder: Just as in the tabernacle the seven lights are ignited and extinguished according to the liturgical year, the world had to be equipped with seven heavenly lights, the planets, the ignition and extinction of which brings us not only day and night, but also the cycle of the week structured according to the seven planets.[18] Even more important is, however, the rectangular showbread table, which was realized cosmologically as the inhabited earth itself: The

---

οἷον σαφέστερον τὰ ἀμείνω μαθούσῃ. Γνῶσις γὰρ ἐναργεστέρα τἀγαθοῦ ἡ τοῦ κακοῦ πεῖρα οἷς ἡ δύναμις ἀσθενεστέρα (*Ennead* 4,8[6],7,12–16).

[15] Cf. esp. *Topography* 3,85 (SC 141, 525–26); 7,11–17 (SC 197, 67–75).

[16] *Topography* 7,90–91 (SC 197, 159–60).

[17] Cf. Conway-Jones 2014, 35–46; Wolska 1962, 113–43. Cosmas exposes his version of this allegory four times (*Topography* 2,35–36; 3,51–53; 5,33–47; 9,8–11). We will mostly rely on the third, most extensive version.

[18] Cf. esp. *Topography* 5,33 (SC 159, 59–60). The interpretation is traditional and occurs

twelve breads on the table symbolize the twelve months during which the earth carries the fruits of human labor and exhibits them in honor of the Divine, and the wavelike decorative strip around it stands for the waters of the Okeanos which surrounds the inhabited earth and separates it from the paradise in the east.[19] That the inhabited earth is actually more or less rectangular in shape is to be demonstrated empirically: Cosmas points to the experiences of his own travels, first of all to an inscription copied by himself in Southern Ethiopia where Ptolemaeus Euergetes claims to have seen the end of the world only a small distance south from this point.[20] Moreover, locating the showbread table in the north and the candle holder in the south of the tabernacles' front yard indicates the northbound elevation of the earth and its being illuminated by the sun from the south. This way, night and day is explained by an archaic tradition according to which the sun during the night is hidden by some giant mountain range up north,[21] the so-called Ῥίπαια ὄρη already mentioned by Aristotle in his *Meteorology*.[22] Insisting consequently on spelling out every cosmological consequence of the Christian faith in the most concrete detail thus seems to lead back to an awkwardly naive and archaic conception of the world, which was not only despised by educated Christian contemporaries like John Philoponus,[23] but still gave rise to anti-Christian bias in 1955, when Arno Schmidt's novel *Kosmas oder vom Berge des Nordens* tried to denounce Christianity in its entirety as ignorant and anti-scientific.[24]

before Theodore of Mopsuestia (*Collectio Coisliniana* frg. 21; TEG 10, 38–39) already in Philo (*De vita Mosis* 2,103).

[19] Cf. esp. *Topography* 5,34 (SC 159, 63). The details of this interpretation might be Cosmas' original contribution. In Theodore, the showbread table only symbolizes the earth inasmuch its four corners stand for the four seasons and the twelve showbreads for the twelve months (*Collectio Coisliniana* 21; TEG 10, 38–39).

[20] Cf. *Topography* 2,37–82 (SC 141, 343–401).

[21] Cf. esp. *Topography* 2,31–36 (SC 141, 337–43).

[22] *Meterologia* 2,1,354a27–32: περὶ δὲ τοῦ τὰ πρὸς ἄρκτον εἶναι τῆς γῆς ὑψηλὰ σημεῖόν τι καὶ τὸ πολλοὺς πεισθῆναι τῶν ἀρχαίων μετεωρολόγων τὸν ἥλιον μὴ φέρεσθαι ὑπὸ γῆν ἀλλὰ περὶ τὴν γῆν καὶ τὸν τόπον τοῦτον, ἀφανίζεσθαι δὲ καὶ ποιεῖν νύκτα διὰ τὸ ὑψηλὴν εἶναι πρὸς ἄρκτον τὴν γῆν. For an extensive and penetrating discussion of this subject cf. Kiessling 1920.

[23] On Philoponus' *De opificio mundi* and its criticism of archaic cosmography cf. Scholten 1996, 45–72.

[24] Cf. e.g. Schmidt 1990, 33: "Nee mein Junge, wer die Erde als Scheibe ansieht, weil eine 1000 Jahre alte verworrene Chronik das verlangt, mit dem gibt es keine Verständigungsmöglichkeit! Schon daß man an das Vorhandensein eines von Gott diktierten unfehlbaren Schmökers glaubt, zieht eben den Strich! Unfehlbar ist nichts, und Gott schon gleich gar nicht: die traurige Beschaffenheit einer Welt, deren lebende Wesen dadurch bestehen, daß sie einander auffressen, ist wohl nur im Witzblatt als das Meisterstück kombinierter Allmacht, -weisheit und -güte zu bezeichnen."

II. Platonizing Origenism

Would it thus have been more advisable for a Christian theologian of antiquity to follow the path of John Chrysostom and treat the cosmological problems imposed by some Christian tenets with relative indifference rather than attempting an original solution on the basis of the new Christian premises? Or was there a real alternative which would have both adequately addressed the cosmological component of the Christian faith and taken into account the actually undeniable facts established by ancient natural science? At the very least a promising attempt at such an alternative is in fact provided by Origenism. At a closer look, this theological tradition seems to advocate the exact opposite of what we heard from Cosmas in all three of the problem areas which had provided the theological motives for rejecting the spherical image of the world: eschatology (spatial nature of the resurrection body), Christology (spatial character of the ascension and the glorified body of Christ) and protology (interpretation of the Genesis account, especially regarding the firmament and the upper waters).

As regards eschatology, especially Gregory of Nyssa teaches us an entirely different conception of the resurrection body in his *De mortuis non esse dolendum* which completely disposes of the need for localizing it. On the basis of 1 Cor 15:42 ("sown in corruption, raised in incorruptibility") he postulates a complete transformation of the body analogous to the one of the grain: Transformed from corruptibility into incorruptibility the body loses every single trait connected to corruptibility or mutability and acquires divine immutability instead. The basic presupposition for movement and change of the bodies is, however, their spatial circumscription which Gregory exactly for this reason explicitly excludes from the realm of incorruptibility. Inspired by the closing myth of Plato's *Gorgias*, where the souls stand naked before their judge Radamanthys and can no longer hide within their bodies (523e), he postulates the eschatological annulment of the difference between inside and outside, soul and body and thus a metaphorical dissolution of the bodily into the spiritual element itself, just as the body of Jesus is dissolved into the infinite sea of his divinity and also everything else returns into the father according to 1 Cor 15:28.[25]

As regards Christology, i.e. Christ's heavenly priesthood and his ascension, neither Origen nor his pupils share the interpretation of the letter to the Hebrews proposed by Diodore, Theodore and their followers. For them, the tabernacle is to be interpreted strictly ecclesiogically, as structural anticipation of the Church of Christ without any cosmological implication.[26] Accordingly, the ascension for them neither has the same soteriological nor any cosmological rele-

[25] Cf. Gleede 2011, 525–28.

[26] Cf. Conway-Jones 2014, 43–46 and 96–115.

vance. Origen even sympathizes with an entirely allegorical interpretation of it: The event is not about a bodily translocation, but about Christ's exaltation to being the heavenly, spiritual teacher of his believers' souls, and his inauguration as high priest of heaven is to be understood as a return to full spiritual power and efficacy, not as spatially defined liturgical action at a heavenly place.[27] Also for Gregory, the statement of the angel in Acts 1:11, that the ascended Christ is going to return in the very same shape in which the pupils had just seen him ascending, cannot actually mean that Christ's return is going to take place in finite human shape. Instead, Gregory insists that according to 2 Cor 5:16 we will no longer know Christ according to the flesh and that the shape in which he is going to return at the end of days and call to judgement has to be void of all mutability related traits including spatial confinement: According to Matt 24:23ff. par. the παρουσία of Christ is not going to take place here or there, but like sudden lightning from one end of heaven to the other.[28]

Accordingly, neither Origen nor Gregory or his older brother Basil have any problems with the spherical shape of earth or heaven. The only cosmological problem they actually have is the exact function of the firmament and the division between upper and lower waters, which is both clearly testified to in the books of Genesis (1:6–7) and Psalms (103:3; 148:4 LXX) and, as we have seen, serves as most important biblical starting point for the Christian opposition against the spherical world view. At this point, Basil is suspicious towards too far-reaching allegorizations and wants to interpret the firmament as a fine membrane surrounding the earth which both stores the lighter water necessary for rain- and snowfall and at the same time cools down heaven in order to pre-

---

[27] Cf. e.g. *De oratione* 23,2 (GCS 3, 350): οὐχὶ δέ γε ταῦτα τοπικῆς μεταβάσεως νοουμένης περὶ τὸν πατέρα καὶ τὸν υἱὸν πρὸς τὸν ἀγαπῶντα τὸν λόγον τοῦ Ἰησοῦ γίνεται, οὐδ' ἄρα τοπικῶς ταῦτα ἐκδεκτέον· ἀλλ' ὁ λόγος τοῦ θεοῦ, ἡμῖν συγκαταβαίνων καὶ ὡς πρὸς τὴν ἰδίαν ἀξίαν, ὅτε παρὰ ἀνθρώποις ἐστὶ, ταπεινούμενος, μεταβαίνειν λέγεται "ἐκ τοῦ κόσμου τούτου πρὸς τὸν πατέρα," ὅπως καὶ ἡμεῖς ἐκεῖθι τέλειον αὐτὸν θεασώμεθα, ἀπὸ τῆς παρ' ἡμῖν κενότητος, ἣν "ἐκένωσεν ἑαυτὸν," ἐπὶ τὸ ἴδιον "πλήρωμα" παλινδρομοῦντα· ἔνθα καὶ ἡμεῖς, αὐτῷ ὁδηγῷ χρώμενοι, πληρωθέντες πάσης κενότητος ἀπαλλαγησόμεθα. ἀπιέτω τοίνυν "πρὸς τὸν πέμψαντα" αὐτὸν ἀφεὶς τὸν κόσμον ὁ τοῦ θεοῦ λόγος, καὶ "πρὸς τὸν πατέρα" πορευέσθω. καὶ τὸ ἐπὶ τέλει δὲ τοῦ κατὰ Ἰωάννην εὐαγγελίου· "μή μου ἅπτου· οὔπω γὰρ ἀναβέβηκα πρὸς τὸν πατέρα μου" μυστικώτερον νοῆσαι ζητήσωμεν· τῆς ἀναβάσεως "πρὸς τὸν πατέρα" τοῦ υἱοῦ θεοπρεπέστερον μετὰ ἁγίας τρανότητος ἡμῖν νοουμένης, ἥντινα ἀνάβασιν νοῦς μᾶλλον ἀναβαίνει σώματος. On Origen's understanding of the ascension cf. further Davies 1958, 90–94.

[28] Cf. *Antirrheticus* (GNO III/1, 222–23); *Contra Eunomium* 3,4,20 (GNO II, 141: Οὐδε γὰρ ὁμοίως ἐμάθομεν παρὰ τοῦ ἀποστόλου γινώσκειν Χριστὸν νῦν τε καὶ πρότερον, οὕτως εἰπόντος τοῦ Παύλου ὅτι Εἰ καὶ ἐγνώκαμέν ποτε κατὰ σάρκα Χριστόν, ἀλλὰ νῦν οὐκέτι γινώσκομεν, ὡς ἐκείνης μὲν τῆς γνώσεως τὴν πρόσκαιρον οἰκονομίαν δηλούσης, ταύτης δὲ τὴν ἀΐδιον ὕπαρξιν) and the exegesis of John 20:17 in *De tridui spatio* (GNO IX, 304): Μή μου ἅπτου, ἀλλ' ὅταν ἀναβῶ πρὸς τὸν πατέρα, τότε σοι ἔξεστιν ἅπτεσθαι, τουτέστιν μηκέτι τὴν σωματώδη καὶ δουλικὴν μορφὴν ἐν τῇ σεαυτοῦ πίστει ἀνατυπώσῃ, ἀλλὰ τὸν ἐν τῇ δόξῃ τοῦ πατρὸς ὄντα καὶ ἐν μορφῇ θεοῦ ὑπάρχοντα καὶ θεοῦ ὄντα λόγον τοῦτον προσκύνει, μὴ τὴν τοῦ δούλου μορφήν. For the background cf. Gleede 2011, 536–37.

vent the cosmos from being dried out by the heat of the stars.[29] This strange theory is one of the few points where Gregory criticizes his brother in his apology for the latter's *Hexaemeron Homilies* and explicitly returns to Origen's allegorical exegesis which had been rejected by Basil: Apparently, Origen had realized that in the framework of the Aristotelian conception of the four elements and their natural places within the cosmos it makes absolutely no sense to postulate an amount of "lighter water" stored above some membrane up in heaven. For that reason, he resorted once again to allegory in his understanding of the Genesis account. If according to Ps 148:4–5 the upper waters praise God, for Origen and his disciple Gregory the OT cannot refer by this term to an actual amount of water. The expression rather stands allegorically for the intelligible world, the bands of angels, which were separated from the corporeal beings on the occasion of preparing the earth to be inhabited by the latter, i.e. the angels were made unavailable for direct perception by corporeal senses. The firmament is thus nothing like an intermediary ceiling between the earth and the first heaven, but the non-spatial boundary between intelligible and perceptible being, the limit of knowledge for all beings limited to sense-perception, animals and non-philosophical human beings.[30]

III. Theodore's Antiplatonism

If one compares this Origenist tradition with the biblicistic one going back to Diodore, one will have to admit that avoiding Cosmas' naive archaic cosmological consequences comes at a very high price, clearly too high for the Christian theological mainstream from the fifth century onwards. Bodily resurrection just as bodily ascension and return of Christ is not denied, but heavily reinterpreted almost as a mere metaphor, the 'starry canopy' of the OT becomes the Platonic intelligible world, and in the end everything strives for the purely intelligible unity of the ἀποκατάστασις πάντων, for the assertion of which Origen was condemned by Justinian,[31] whereas Gregory luckily got away with it.[32]

Hence, it is understandable that at the end of the fourth century there was a growing tendency for dissimilation from paganism among Christian theologians, which by no means necessarily amounted to a rejection of secular knowledge as such, but primarily targeted the ideological and religious components of the spherical conception of the world and expected new insights from intensi-

[29] Cf. Köckert 2009, 374–90.

[30] Cf. Köckert 2009, 481–87.

[31] Cf. *Edictum contra Origenem* (ACO III, 205–06). The current discussion of this subject is dominated by I. Ramelli's numerous and very extensive publications on the subject (esp. Ramelli 2013).

[32] Cf. Tóth 2011.

fied studies of Holy Scripture. The later reports on Diodore's relevant works, especially the catalogue of his writings in the *Suda*, testifies to an intense engagement with pagan astronomy,[33] and this primarily for the sake of refuting the belief in the eternity of celestial motion and the fate-determining forces of stars and planets, which he apparently identified as the very basis of the Ptolemean system.[34] His primary target was thus pagan astrology, not astronomy. Theodore of Mopsuestia in contrast does not seem to have targeted pagan science directly, but rather the destructive influence it tended to exert on Christian theologians who try to prove it in full agreement with Christian faith. In the fragments of especially the introduction to his Genesis commentary, his enemy is undoubtedly none other than Origen and the Platonizing type of Christian theology following him. Their lack of understanding for Holy Scripture starts for Theodore already at its very first verse and from there penetrates the entirety of their exegesis and dogmatics. According to the bishop of Mopsuestia, "In the beginning God created heaven and earth" is misunderstood by Origenism at least in a twofold way: Firstly, this "beginning," the date of material creation, can for Origen never be the absolute beginning of God's actions, as qua eternal intelligible cause God has to have equally eternal effects. Thus, the eternal creation of the spiritual cosmos has to precede the temporal one of the material world.[35] Secondly, if God's creation of the material heaven and earth are not conceived as the primordial act of the divine condescension towards something other than God himself, they equally do not provide the ultimate framework for the divine work of creation and redemption, in which it all has to take place. Exactly this, however, is the point of Gen 1:1 for Theodore, which is why he insists over several pages on the absolute priority of the circumscribing element over the circumscribed one, of the container over the contained: Just as the human soul according to Gen 2:7 could not have been created without shaping the circumscribing body from earth before, the angels and spiritual beings could not have been created without establishing heaven and earth first, which circumscribe those and give them place, support and boundary.[36] Thus Theodore transfers the microcosmic relationship between soul and body to the macrocos-

---

[33] *Suda* Δ 1149. On the different catalogues of Diodore's works cf. Abramowski 1960, 498–500.

[34] Cf. Amand 1945, 469–79.

[35] Cf. esp. *De principiis* 1,4,3 (GCS 22, 65–66). On the background cf. Ketteler 1969. Theodore's counter-arguments against the creation of angels and spiritual beings prior to creation are extensively refuted by John Philoponus, *De opificio mundi* 1,8–22.

[36] Sachau 1869, 3–6 (lat.)/4–9 (syr.). Cf. Theodore apud Philoponum, *De opificio mundi* 1,16: θαυμαστὸν μὲν οὖν ἔμοιγε φαίνεται τό τινας οἴεσθαι πρὸ οὐρανοῦ τε καὶ γῆς τὰς ἀοράτους καὶ λογικὰς οὐσίας ὑπὸ θεοῦ γεγονέναι, ἃς ἔνδον τε τούτων εἶναι καὶ περιγεγράφθαι ὑπ' αὐτῶν διὰ πάσης παιδευόμεθα τῆς θείας γραφῆς. ποῖος γὰρ δὴ παραδέξεται λόγος τὰ ἐντὸς πρὸ τῶν ἐκτὸς ὑπάρχειν καὶ πρὸ τῶν περιεχόντων εἶναι τὰ περιεχόμενα; ἀνάγκη δὴ ἄρα κἀκεῖνο ζητεῖν ὅπου τότε ἦσαν αἱ νῦν τῷδε περιγεγραμμέναι τῷ τόπῳ. For the Platonic counter-arguments against conceiving of the body as "container" of the soul cf. Plotinus, *Ennead* 4,3(27),20–24.

mic one between the world-body consisting of heaven and earth and the angels which thus function as some kind of world-soul keeping all the processes within their body going. He consciously and polemically inverts the priority relationship between the two in the light of Gen 2:7: The soul is no longer preexistent master, let alone creator of the body,[37] but is created by God for a preexisting body both in order to keep it alive and to find place and shape in it.

Qua being created, spiritual beings for Theodore cannot have the structural eternity and transcendence towards time and place which characterizes the Platonic world of ideas, but first of all need a place in order exert its actions, a place which God assigns to them in order to give them the possibility to learn and develop their potentials.[38]

Unfortunately, Theodore's extant works do not tell us, what the necessity of such a place entails for the structure of the cosmos in the *Eschaton*. According to the Eastern Syriac mystics of the eighth and ninth century, he apparently did not just assign the space above firmament to the believers and the earth as place of eternal punishment to the unbelievers like Cosmas, but seems to have postulated a final return of all created spirits to their divine origin in a way similar to Origen's and Gregory's.[39] That he was actually able to conceive of a relationship between spirit and matter which would avoid both the *aporiai* of a naive materialism and a Platonic intellectualism can be doubted. With all the justified criticism against the predominant Platonic intellectualism with the Origenist tradi-

---

[37] According to Plotinus, *Ennead* 4,3(27),9–12 the world soul creates its body and the *logoi* of the world soul create the images of the individual souls attracting the latters' descent.

[38] Cf. *In Epistulam ad Romanos* 11:15 (Staab 1933, 156–57): Τίνος ἕνεκεν τῇ πάντων διορθώσει τὴν ἀνάστασιν ἡγεῖται ὁ ἀπόστολος ἔψεσθαι πάντων, ἀναγκαῖον εἰπεῖν. τοῖς μὲν ἀλόγοις φυσικῶς ἅπαντα πρόσεστι, [...] τοῖς δὲ λογικοῖς πᾶν τοὐναντίον· [...] οὐδὲ γὰρ ἀδίδακτον ἔχειν ἡμᾶς τῆς ἀρετῆς ἐνεδέχετο τὴν ἕξιν λογικοὺς γεγονότας τὴν φύσιν, ἐπείπερ αὕτη σαφὴς λογικῶν τε καὶ ἀλόγων διάκρισις, τῷ τὰ μὲν ἐν τῇ φύσει παντὸς οὗτινος οὖν ἔχειν τὴν εἴδησιν περαιτέρω δυνάμενα μανθάνειν οὐδέν, τοὺς δὲ τοῦ χρόνου προϊόντος τὰ πλείονα μανθάνειν ὧν οὐκ ἠπίσταντο πρότερον. τούτου ἕνεκεν θνητοὺς μὲν ἡμᾶς κατὰ τὸν παρόντα τουτονὶ πεποίηκε βίον, νόμους δὲ ἔδωκεν ἱκανοὺς εἰς ὑπόμνησιν ἡμᾶς ἄγειν τῆς τοῦ καλοῦ διορθώσεως, ὡς ἂν ἐντελῆ τῆς ἀρετῆς οὕτως τὴν μάθησιν κομισαίμεθα. [...] ἐπειδὴ δὲ οὐχ ὥσπερ ἴσμεν τὸ καλόν, οὕτω καὶ ποιεῖν αὐτὸ ῥᾳδίως δυνάμεθα, ἄχρις ἂν ἐπὶ τῆς θνητότητος διαμένωμεν, δεύτερόν τινα βίον τὸν μέλλοντα ἡμῖν διὰ τῆς ἀναστάσεως ὁ ποιητὴς δεδώρηται, κατὰ πολὺ τοῦ παρόντος ἀμείνω, ἀθάνατόν τε καὶ ἀπαθῆ καὶ πάσης ἁμαρτίας ἀπηλλαγμένον. [...] εὐθὺ μὲν ἡμᾶς ἐν ἐκείνοις καταστῆσαι οὐ καλῶς ἔχειν ἡγησαμένου τοῦ σοφοῦ τῶν ψυχῶν οἰκονόμου, ὡς ἂν μὴ ἄλογόν τινα καὶ ἀδιάκριτον ἐνοῦσαν ἡμῖν ἔχοιμεν τοῦ καλοῦ τὴν ἕξιν, ἐγγενομένης δὲ ἡμῖν ἐπὶ τοῦ παρόντος βίου καθ' ὃν ἔφην τρόπον τῆς τοῦ καλοῦ μαθήσεως, εὐκαιρότατα καὶ μάλα γε ἀναγκαίως τῶν μελλόντων παρέχεται τὴν κατάστασιν· τοῦτο μέν, ἵνα κατὰ παράθεσιν τῶν παρόντων ἀκριβῶς εἰδέναι τῶν τότε τὸ διάφορον ἔχωμεν, τοῦτο δέ, ὡς ἂν λογικῇ πρεπόντως φύσει τῆς τοῦ καλοῦ κατορθώσεως αἰσθανώμεθα, ὧν ἐνταῦθα κατὰ τὴν ἀπόρρητον τοῦ θεοῦ σοφίαν ποικίλως τὴν εἴδησιν ἐδεξάμεθα, ταῦτα τότε πόνων ἐκτὸς τῇ τοῦ πνεύματος χάριτι κατορθωμένα ἐν ἡμῖν ὁρῶντες, καίτοιγε ἐπὶ τοῦ παρόντος οὐδὲ μετὰ πόνων παραπλησίως τοῖς τότε καθαρεύειν τῆς τῶν ἀτόπων δυνάμενοι πράξεως. On the background and reception of this idea cf. above n. 14.

[39] That Theodore – against prior research (e.g. Bruns 1995, 396–401) – actually advocated this doctrine in his treatise against original sin is strongly suggested by the later Theodore reception (cf. Kavvadas 2010).

tion, it should, however, not be overlooked that Paul in 1 Corinthians 15 lays more emphasis on the discontinuity within the eschatological transformation process – a fact which is correctly emphasized especially by Gregory of Nyssa, but downplayed by the entire theological mainstream from Tertullian onwards,[40] which lays much more weight on the continuity and postulates a resurrection in the very flesh we carry in this life.[41] From a Pauline perspective, the problem with Origenism is not the metaphorical understanding of the resurrection body as such, but the way in which it is spelled out. If Christian theology wants to take the act of creation seriously, it is ill advised to postulate a universal return of all the relative creatures into the absolute, intelligible divine self. If the absolute spirit of the Divine from eternity made room for something other than itself, the relative spiritual and material creation, a simple reabsorption of all of this at the end of days would make of the entire creation and salvation a rather meaningless episode. However, localizing the untransformed earthly, three dimensional bodies on the icy back of the cosmic firmament makes actually even less sense, not only from the modern perspective. Perhaps it would have been best to reconsider the soul-body-relationship as such far more carefully in order to figure out which of the bodily elements are actually essential to the relative, finite self and which are not. That the body is in a way *das Andere meiner selbst*, the element of me which on the hand I constantly have to rely on and on the other hand I cannot control in most of its aspects, could be interpreted as a remaining structural trait of the finite self without having to localize this self in the sense of assigning GPS coordinates to it. The overall lesson Christian theology could learn from this controversy between Origenists and Theodorians would then be not so much a cosmological, but an anthropological one: Notwithstanding all the affinities between the Platonic and the Christian faith, the latter needs more differentiated reflection on the nature of the created, body-bound spirit which can be neither a part of the world soul nor embodied by a merely accidental, secondary lapse from the original unity with the divine spirit.

Bibliography

Abramowski, L. (1955–56), 'Der Streit um Diodor und Theodor zwischen den beiden ephesinischen Konzilien', *Zeitschrift für Kirchengeschichte* 67: 252–82.

– (1960), 'Diodore de Tarse', *Dictionnaire d'histoire et de géographie ecclésiastiques* 14: 496–504.

Amand, D. (1945), *Fatalisme et liberté dans l'antiquité grecque* (Recueil de travaux d'histoire et de philologie 3/19), Louvain: Bibliothèque de l'Université.

[40] Cf. *De resurrectione mortuorum* 52–62 (CSEL 47, 107–23) and Gleede 2011, 527–28.

[41] Cf. above n. 1.

Bruns, P. (1995), *Den Menschen mit dem Himmel verbinden: Eine Studie zu den katechetischen Homilien Theodors v. Mopsuestia* (Corpus Scriptorum Christianorum Orientalium. Subsidia 549), Leuven: Peeters.

Chazelle, C. (2007), *The Crisis of the "oikoumene": The Three Chapters and the Failed Quest for Unity in the Sixth-century Mediterranean* (Studies in the Early Middle Ages 14), Turnhout: Brepols.

Conway-Jones, A. (2014), *Gregory of Nyssa's Tabernacle Imagery in Its Jewish and Christian Contexts* (Oxford Early Christian Studies), Oxford: Oxford University Press.

Davies, J. G. (1958), *He Ascended into Heaven: A Study in the History of Doctrine*, London: Lutterworth Press.

Gleede, B. (2011), 'Der eine Christus vor, in und nach dem Fleisch: Einige Überlegungen zu Gregor von Nyssas *Ad Theophilum adversus Apollinaristas*', in: *Gregory of Nyssa: The Minor Treatises on Trinitarian Theology and Apollinarism*, ed. V. Drecoll et al. (Vigiliae Christianae. Supplements 106), Leiden – Boston, MA: Brill, 519–40.

Guinot, J. (2012), 'Eschatologie et Écriture en milieu antiochien à partir du IIe siècle', in: idem, *Théodoret de Cyr: Exégète et théologien*, vol. II, Paris: Cerf, 87–125.

Inglebert, H. (2001), *Interpretatio christiana: Les mutations des savoirs (cosmographie, géographie, ethnographie, histoire) dans l'antiquité chrétienne* (Collection des Études augustiniennes. Série Antiquité 166), Paris: Institut d'Études Augustiniennes.

Kavvadas, N. (2010), 'On the Relations between the Eschatological Doctrine of Isaac of Nineveh and Theodore of Mopsuestia', *Studia Patristica* 45: 245–50.

Ketteler, F.-H. (1969), 'Die Ewigkeit der geistigen Schöpfung nach Origenes', in: *Reformation und Humanismus: Robert Stupperich zum 65. Geburtstag*, ed. M. Greschat and J. F. G. Goeters, Witten: Luther-Verlag, 272–97.

Kiel, N. (2015), *Ps-Athenagoras'* De Resurrectione*: Datierung und Kontextualisierung der dem Apologeten Athenagoras zugeschriebenen Auferstehungsschrift* (Vigiliae Christianae. Supplements 133), Leiden – Boston, MA: Brill.

Kiessling, A. (1920), ''Ῥίπαια ὄρη', *Paulys Realencyclopädie* II/1: 846–916.

Köckert, C. (2009), *Christliche Kosmologie und kaiserzeitliche Philosophie: Die Auslegung des Schöpfungsberichtes bei Origenes, Basilius und Gregor von Nyssa vor dem Hintergrund kaiserzeitlicher Timaeus Interpretationen* (Studien und Texte zu Antike und Christentum 56), Tübingen: Mohr Siebeck.

Krüger, R. (2000), *Eine Welt ohne Amerika*. Vol. II: *Das Überleben des Erdkugelmodells in der Spätantike (ca. 60 v.u.Z. – ca. 550)*, Berlin: Weidler.

Ramelli, I. L. E. (2013), *The Christian Doctrine of "Apokatastasis": A Critical Assessment from the New Testament to Eriugena* (Vigiliae Christianae. Supplements 120), Leiden – Boston, MA: Brill.

Sachau, E. (1869), *Theodori Mopsuesteni fragmenta syriaca*, Leipzig: Engelmann.

Schiwietz, S. (1914), 'Die Eschatologie des hl. Johannes Chrysostomus und ihr Verhältnis zur origenistischen', *Der Katholik* 13: 45–63, 200–16, 271–81, 436–48.

Schmidt, A. (1990), *Kosmas oder Vom Berge des Nordens*, Frankfurt am Main: Fischer.

Scholten, C. (1996), *Antike Naturphilosophie und christliche Kosmologie in der Schrift "De opificio mundi" des Johannes Philoponos* (Patristische Texte und Studien 45), Berlin – New York: De Gruyter.

Setzer, C. (2004), *Resurrection of the Body in Early Judaism and Early Christianity: Doctrine, Community, and Self-definition*, Leiden – Boston, MA: Brill.

Staab, K. (1933), *Pauluskommentare aus der griechischen Kirche* (Neutestamentliche Abhandlungen 15), Münster: Aschendorff.

Tóth, J. (2011), 'Interpretation and Argumentation in *In illud tunc et ipse filius*', in: *Gregory of Nyssa: The Minor Treatises on Trinitarian Theology and Apollinarism*, ed. V. Drecoll et al. (Vigiliae Christianae. Supplements 106), Leiden – Boston, MA: Brill, 427–43.

Uthemann, K. (2005), 'Kosmas Indikopleustes' Leben und Werk: Eine Übersicht', in: idem, *Christus, Kosmos, Diatribe: Themen der frühen Kirche als Beiträge zu einer historischen Theologie*, Berlin – New York: De Gruyter, 497–561.

Wolska, W. (1962), *La topographie chrétienne de Cosmas Indicopleustès: Théologie et science au VI*[e] *siècle* (Bibliothèque byzantine. Études 3), Paris: Presses Universitaires de France.

– (1978), 'Geographie', *Reallexikon für Antike und Christentum* 10: 155–222.

"Mind the (Ontological) Gap!"

The Collateral Loss of the Pauline-Stoic Creation "From God" in the Joint Attack of the Arian-Nicene Creation "From Nothing" on the Platonic Creation "From Disorderly Matter"

George van Kooten

I. Introduction: The Endurance of Ancient Philosophical Cosmologies into the 1960s

In this contribution, I will address the views espoused in the corpus of Pauline writings on the origin and the end of the cosmos and will contextualize them in the context of contemporary Graeco-Roman thought.[1] By way of a starting point, however, I would like to briefly draw attention to the fact that most, if not all of the relevant categories of thought from this phase in the history of cosmological ideas were still very much on the table fifty to seventy years ago. Although Edwin Hubble (1889–1953) had discovered in the 1930s that the cosmos is expanding, cosmologists responded differently to this finding, and in Cambridge in the 1950s and 1960s, for instance, the following debate raged: On the one hand, there were those who propounded a so-called "steady state cosmology," the idea of an eternal cosmos that was never generated, but existed without beginning from all eternity and, in the process of expanding, was creating new matter in a kind of continuous creation – a view articulated by such scholars as Fred Hoyle (1915–2001) at the Cambridge Institute of Astronomy. On the other hand, there were those who extrapolated the expanding cosmic movement backwards to an original singularity and inferred from the detection of the so-called "cosmic microwave background radiation," which decreases in temperature whilst the cosmos expands, that the cosmos had been generated via an immensely hot "big bang," so that the cosmos did have a beginning and will prob-

[1] This piece is dedicated to Dr. E. P. Meijering, Reader Emeritus in Patristics at the University of Leiden, on the occasion of his 80th birthday, out of gratitude for all his lectures on Tertullian and Athanasius, and above all for sowing the seeds of a deep suspicion against Adolf von Harnack's historiography in my mind, as well as his encouragement over the years to explore the alternative path of scholars such as A. Lasson and C. Weizsäcker.

ably, because of its expansion, also experience an end – a view expressed by such scholars as Martin Ryle (1918–84) of the Cavendish Radio Astronomy Group. The latter view assumed that through the big bang, the cosmos was generated from a minute, infinitely dense, and (due to the absence of space and time) still invisible nucleus – thus, in a sense, from nothing. Fred Hoyle resisted the idea of a non-eternal cosmos generated from nothing because of its (allegedly) pseudo-scientific argument for a beginning and its resemblance to arguments in support of the existence of a (Judeo-Christian) creator.[2]

It is fascinating that this debate between steady state and big bang cosmologies still shares so much of the terminology and concepts of the debate about the cosmos conducted in Graeco-Roman antiquity, among all kinds of different philosophical schools and between Greeks, Jews, and Christians, none of whom coincided with any particular school. In the philosophical schools of the Graeco-Roman period, there were four options which, each in a different way, share key terminology with recent modern cosmological thinking.

1. Creation from the Disorder of Pre-existing Matter

The Platonic school followed Plato's view, expressed in his cosmological dialogue *Timaeus*, that the Demiurge, the creator-god, took pre-existing, disorderly matter and "brought it into order from disorder" (εἰς τάξιν αὐτὸ ἤγαγεν ἐκ τῆς ἀταξίας, 30a).[3] Within the Platonic school, however, the issue of whether Plato really believed that the cosmos had a beginning, or whether he used this imagery for didactic, pedagogical purposes – to explain the principle and function of cosmic order and the cosmos's ontological dependence upon God – was a matter of dispute. Some Platonists took Plato literally and believed that the cosmos had temporal beginnings. Other Platonists took his account to be didactic and considered the cosmos to be without temporal beginnings, but rather "sempiternal."[4]

Many of the early Christians who adopted Plato's explanation in their interpretations of the creation account in Genesis 1 agreed with the former, literal Platonic interpretation that the cosmos was created in time; with Plato's *Timae-*

---

[2] Smith 1992, 217–37.

[3] Greek texts have been searched with the aid of and quoted from the online *Thesaurus Linguae Graecae: A Digital Library of Greek Literature* (hereafter TLG), unless otherwise indicated. Translations of classical writings, the Bible, and early Christian writings are normally derived from the digital Loeb Classical Library (LCL), Long and Sedley 1987 (LS); Boys-Stones 2018 (GBS), the New Revised Standard Version (NRSV), the electronic edition of the New English Translation of the Septuagint (NETS), and the Ante-Nicene Fathers (ANF) and Nicene and Post-Nicene Fathers (NPNF) series, unless otherwise indicated, with small modifications where necessary. Pertinent chronological and biographical information is usually derived from the online *Oxford Classical Dictionary* (OCD), *Brill's New Pauly*, and *The Cambridge Dictionary of Christianity*.

[4] Boys-Stones 2018, 195–97, sub 1–3.

us, they believed that this was not a creation from nothing, but a creation from pre-existing, disorderly matter which was put in order. These early Christians include Justin and Athenagoras.[5] Interestingly, their interpretation of the account in Genesis 1 as an explanation how chaotic, disorderly, pre-existing matter was organized in creation has been vindicated by many modern exegetes of Genesis 1, who are of the opinion that Genesis 1 does *not* reflect the notion of a creation from nothing, but that the depiction of how "the earth was a formless void and darkness covered the face of the deep" (Gen 1:2) describes the preliminary situation, which is changed by the creation that is already announced in the opening line of the book of Genesis (Gen 1:1) and subsequently described in what follows the description of preliminary chaos.

However, there were Jews, such as Philo of Alexandria, who seem to have disagreed with this idea of such a temporal approach to creation in the book of Genesis and Plato's *Timaeus*, and agreed with those Platonists who believed that Plato spoke of a temporal creation only didactically, but in fact believed in an "eternal creation" of the cosmos – that is, in its ontological dependence upon God. In line with their interpretation, and on this understanding, Philo interpreted the opening statement of the book of Genesis not in a temporal sense, as a reference to "the beginning" of creation, but as a reference to "the (ontological) principle" of creation (Philo, *On the Creation* 26–28).[6]

Regardless of the different interpretations Platonists developed of the (descriptive, literal or merely didactic, non-literal) mode of Plato's protological thinking, with regard to eschatology, it is clear that Plato believed that the cosmos would never come to an eschatological end; although it could, because the cosmos is a frail, composite entity, it never would, because God in his goodness had bound the cosmos together with bonds. As the Demiurge tells the created astral gods, whilst looking back on his creation of the cosmos:

> Gods of gods, those works whereof I am framer and father are indissoluble save by my will. For though all that is bound may be dissolved, yet to will to dissolve that which is fairly joined together and in good case were the deed of a wicked one. Wherefore ye also, seeing that ye were generated, are not wholly immortal or indissoluble, yet in no wise shall ye be dissolved nor incur the doom of death, seeing that in my will ye possess a bond greater and more sovereign than the bonds wherewith, at your birth, ye were bound together (*Tim.* 41a–b).

Whereas Plato's concept of creation from the disorder of pre-existing matter is theistic, in the sense that it is the Demiurge, the creator-god, who implements order in matter, there are also non-theistic variants of this belief in pre-existing

[5] Boys-Stones 2018, 116 sub 7(a), cf. 196 sub 3(a).

[6] Boys-Stones 2018, 196 sub 2(e). Cf. David T. Runia (2001, 156–62, esp. 156–57), who understands Philo's view as a "*creatio simultanea*," in which creation takes place "as a temporal *event*" involving "a beginning, not *in time*, but *of time*," whereas Gregory E. Sterling takes Philo's view in the sense of a "*creatio aeterna*" (Sterling 1992, 15–41).

matter or atoms, including the view of Democritus and Epicurus, who believed that pre-existing material was organized by chance.[7]

2. An Eternal Cosmos without Protological Beginnings

Whereas the status of Plato's remarks about *the beginnings* of the cosmos were disputed (Was he speaking literally or merely didactically?), the views of his pupil Aristotle were unambiguous. In a way comparable with Hoyle's steady state theory,[8] Aristotle believed that the cosmos had no temporal beginnings, that it had always existed in a steady, eternal state, and would do so eternally (Aristotle, *Physics*, esp. book 8).[9]

3. A Dynamic Cosmos with Protological Beginnings and Eschatological Endings

The Stoics, in stark contrast to both Aristotle's view and a sempiternal understanding of Plato's view on the matter, were of the opinion that the cosmos was generated and will come to an end, and is hence embedded in a constant cosmic process. In their view, this process will continue even through the endless cycles of new cosmic ordering (διακόσμησις) and reconstitution (ἀποκατάστασις) that follow upon each eschatological conflagration (ἐκπύρωσις). However, they did not believe that the cosmos was created "from nothing," as the modern big bang theory has it; rather, they believed that the nucleus from which the cosmos emerged was God himself, into whom the cosmos will also return and be reabsorbed.

4. Creation from Nothing

In contrast to what many scholars believe, the argument of creation from nothing is not a distinctively Jewish-Christian invention, but was also propounded in Graeco-Roman thought. Although many philosophers (notably the materialistic Epicureans) explicitly denied the possibility that something could evolve from nothing, some indeed proposed the concept of creation from nothing. For instance, a Pseudo-Aristotelian interpretation of one of the oldest Greek poems – Hesiod's *Theogony* – argued that ultimately the cosmos had indeed arisen from nothing (Pseudo-Aristotle, *On Melissus* 1,975a4–17, ed. L.C. Apelt, LCL).

---

[7] See LS 8 on the Epicurean notion of atoms, and LS 13 on Epicurean cosmology without teleology.

[8] On the "steady state" theory, see Islam 1983, 115–17.

[9] See Aristotle, *Physics*, esp. book 8, on the necessity of *eternal* and constant motion, the existence of one eternal primary unmoved mover (i.e., God), and the eternal, constant, and rotational movement of the heavens as being primarily and directly moved by such a mover, to be distinguished from other forms of movement. Cf. *Metaphysics*, book 12, about God as the *eternal* object of the love of the heavenly spheres.

This fourth and last option of Greek cosmological views, the *creatio ex nihilo* theorem, was adopted by some Christians from the second century onwards and finally, after the fourth century, became the default Christian position. However, in this article, I will show (albeit not precisely in the following order) that (a) the "creation from nothing" theorem had not yet been contemplated in the New Testament writings; that (b) the New Testament writings evince either a Stoic or a Platonic conceptualization; and that (c) the notion of creation from nothing became an increasingly popular position because it was very effective (i) in explaining the conceivability of the resurrection of the dead, and (ii) in responding to the Platonic concept of creation from pre-existing matter that was seen as an infringement upon God's omnipotence. I will proceed as follows, in four steps.

Firstly, due to the present contribution's focus on the Pauline writings among early Christian literature, I will centre my exploration on the Pauline literature and argue that Paul's own cosmology is deeply Stoic. This becomes clear in his use of so-called "prepositional metaphysics," in which – in line with Stoic theology and physics – God is seen as the one "from whom," "through whom," and "into whom" all things develop. This basically Stoic tenet is not an isolated notion in Paul's thought, but is fully consistent with and supported by other expressions of Paul's views. Secondly, I will show how Paul's Stoic inclinations in his cosmology were further promulgated among his pupils in the Pauline School, as becomes clear in the Pauline Letter to the Ephesians. Thirdly, however, other pupils in the Pauline School instead championed a Platonization of Paul's cosmological views, as transpires in the Pauline Letter to the Colossians. Through these first three steps, I will demonstrate that Pauline cosmological thought oscillated between Stoicizing and Platonizing positions, with Stoicization being the stronger tendency. Regardless of this oscillation, however, in every case the cosmos – whether in its beginning, its end, or its present stability – is seen as closely related to God. Its cosmology is either basically panentheistic (inasmuch as the cosmos, throughout all of its phases, is encompassed by and ultimately rests in God) or, alternatively, assumes an uninterrupted "chain of being," according to which the visible world "reflects" or is "grounded in" an invisible reality. Fourthly, in a final step, I will argue that this changed entirely when the Pauline wavering between Stoic and Platonic cosmologies came to a halt and was replaced with the advancement of the new *creatio ex nihilo* theorem, which cut the close ontological ties between creation and God that had characterized the Platonic and Stoic conceptualizations of God and the cosmos, and placed the latter's origins "nihilistically" in "the nothingness" of creation, thus creating an ontological gap between creation and its creator. It is from this observation that my contribution takes its title: "Mind the (ontological) gap!"

II. Paul's Stoic Proto- and Eschatology: The Cosmos is "from, through, and to God" (Rom 11:36; 1 Cor 8:6)

That Paul's cosmology is basically Stoic is made clear in two main passages in his Letter to the Romans and his First Letter to the Corinthians. In the first of these – in solemn, doxological, credo-like style – he expresses the relation between God and the cosmos as follows: "from him and through him and to him are all things (ἐξ αὐτοῦ καὶ δι' αὐτοῦ καὶ εἰς αὐτὸν τὰ πάντα). To him be the glory for ever. Amen" (Rom 11:36). As Gregory Sterling has clearly shown,[10] these expressions, which are often dubbed "liturgical," are (at the same time) not without technical meaning. They find their background in so-called "prepositional metaphysics," in which the relation between both the cosmos and human beings vis-à-vis God is stipulated through the use of specific prepositions. In this passage from Romans, the ontological grounding of "all things" in God, from whom (ἐξ αὐτοῦ) the cosmos originates and to whom (εἰς αὐτόν) it will return, bears clearly Stoic overtones (as we shall see below when we focus on the relevant Stoic texts, contrasting them with comparable Platonic texts which favour a different set of propositions). The expression of the cosmos's emergence from, mode of creation and current subsistence through, and future return to God in Rom 11:36 is not an isolated view in Paul's Letter to the Romans. It is entirely consistent with the views on the cosmos and nature with which Paul opens his letter – that is, with his "natural theology," according to which "the unseens" or "the invisibles," meaning the invisible qualities (τὰ ἀόρατα) of God – namely "his eternal power" (ἀΐδιος αὐτοῦ δύναμις) and "divinity" (θειότης) – "when reflected upon (νοούμενα) by the human mind," can be "insightfully deduced" (καθορᾶται) from the things that have been created (τοῖς ποιήμασιν) (1:20). So, to some extent, the distinctively divine qualities of eternity and deity are also transferred to visible creatures, who become the bearers of these qualities – apparently sharing in them in some real, ontological sense – and in this way render these invisible qualities visible.

Such a perception of visible creatures in the light of eternity and divinity inspires the search for a divine natural law with which human ethics can comply. For this reason, according to Paul, even those (non-Jewish) nations unacquainted with the (Mosaic) law can do by nature what the (divine natural) law requires – namely, treating other creatures in the light of their eternal, divine, "sacrosanct" qualities: "Whenever nations that do not have a law do by nature the things that the law requires, they, despite not having a law, are [in the positive sense of the word] a law to themselves" (ὅταν [...] ἔθνη τὰ μὴ νόμον ἔχοντα φύσει τὰ τοῦ νόμου ποιῶσιν, οὗτοι νόμον μὴ ἔχοντες ἑαυτοῖς εἰσιν νόμος, 2:14). In line with these opening statements about the interconnectedness of both the cosmos

[10] Sterling 1997, 219–38.

and human beings with their creator-God, it comes as no surprise that Paul, in his doxological statements about God, heralds God as the one "from whom, through whom, and into whom all things exist" (11:36). In fact, one could argue that the entire letter is one extensive, prolonged argument for how the human mind, which is theoretically able to reflect upon creation and discern its divine qualities (1:20), has in practice suffered many setbacks (1:28; 7:23–25) from which it needs to be restored (12:2) by aligning itself with the divine mind, the "mind of the Lord" (11:34 = Isa 40:13 LXX; cf. 14:5–6),[11] "from whom, through whom, and into whom all things exist" (11:36). This statement about the origins of the cosmos "from within" God and about its final destiny in God is thus not an isolated occurrence in Rom 11:36, but is consistent with Paul's "divine" views on creation and nature.

The same holds true for the other main occurrence of prepositional metaphysics in Paul's own letters, in the First Letter to the Corinthians. In this letter, in the passage in 8:6, we encounter a variant of the expression in Rom 11:36. Whereas the passage in Romans was "theological" in the proper sense – in its concentration on God – the Corinthian passage differentiates between God's and Christ's perspectives. In the latter passage, Paul says: "for us there is one God, the Father (εἷς θεὸς ὁ πατήρ), from whom are all things (ἐξ οὗ τὰ πάντα) and to whom we exist (καὶ ἡμεῖς εἰς αὐτόν), and one Lord, Jesus Christ (εἷς κύριος Ἰησοῦς Χριστός), through whom are all things and through whom we exist (δι' οὗ τὰ πάντα καὶ ἡμεῖς δι' αὐτοῦ)" (1 Cor 8:6). There are small variations here as compared to the passage in Romans.

To begin with, whereas all things are indeed "from" the divine Father, they are now said to be "through" his divine Son instead of "through" God himself. The Son here assumes the function of the Stoic Logos, which in Stoicism proper is identical with God and permeates the cosmos, inasmuch as the Logos-Reason, as the active principle in the cosmos, is inherent "throughout" the passive principle of matter so that it becomes shaped by him: "there are two principles of the universe, that which acts and that which is acted upon. That which is acted upon is unqualified substance, i.e. matter; that which acts is the Logos in it, i.e., God. For this, since it is everlasting, constructs every single thing throughout all matter" (διὰ πάσης αὐτῆς, Diogenes Laertius, *Lives of Eminent Philosophers* 7,134 = *SVF* 2,300 and 2,299 = LS 44B; transl. LS, with minor changes). According to the Stoic view, God or Zeus (Δία) is the cause "*through* which" (δι' ὅν) all things have been generated by pervading "*through* all things" (διὰ πάντων):

He is the creator of the whole and, as it were, the father of all (εἶναι δὲ τὸν μὲν δημιουργὸν τῶν ὅλων καὶ ὥσπερ πατέρα πάντων), both generally and, in particular, that part of him

[11] A mindset that can also be depicted as "the mind of Christ," as the parallel quotation of Isa 40:13 LXX in 1 Cor 2:16 shows.

which pervades *through all things* (τὸ μέρος αὐτοῦ τὸ διῆκον διὰ πάντων), which is called by many descriptions according to his powers. For they call him Zeus (Δία) as the cause (δι' ὃν) *through* which all things are (Δία μὲν γάρ φασι δι' ὃν τὰ πάντα) (*SVF* 2,1021 *apud* Diogenes Laertius, *Lives of Eminent Philosophers* 7,147 = LS 54A; transl. LS, with minor changes).

We also find this view expressed in Philo, according to whom "the Logos" is that "through which (δι' οὗ) the whole cosmos was created (λόγος [...], δι' οὗ σύμπας ὁ κόσμος ἐδημιουργεῖτο)" (Philo, *On the Special Laws* 1,81). It is also similar to the Stoicizing expressions in the Pseudo-Aristotelian treatise *On the Cosmos*: "all things are from God (ὡς ἐκ θεοῦ πάντα) and are constituted by God (καὶ διὰ θεὸν συνέστηκεν)" (Pseudo-Aristotle, *On the Cosmos* 397b14–15). That Paul models the cosmic Christ here on the Stoic creator – from whom, *through* whom, and to whom all things exist – may well be confirmed by the fact that Paul can easily alternate between the versions of 1 Cor 8:6 and Rom 11:36, so that Christ is indeed seen as a function of God. According to Gregory Sterling, however, the preposition "through" should be taken not so much in a Stoic sense, but in a Platonic sense. Sterling emphasizes the development of instrumental agency in Middle Platonism since the first century BCE and suggests that 1 Cor 8:6 "used the Stoic formula for God [εἷς θεὸς ὁ πατήρ, ἐξ οὗ τὰ πάντα] and then balanced it with the Platonic formula for Christ [εἷς κύριος Ἰησοῦς Χριστός, δι' οὗ τὰ πάντα]."[12] Yet as we shall see shortly, a distinctively Platonic "through" refers to God's goodness because of which the cosmos was created. Paul thus seems to use Stoic prepositions both in order to depict God himself as the agent through whom the cosmos emerged from God himself (Rom 11:36) and to single out Christ as his instantiation or intermediary through whom this was accomplished (1 Cor 8:6). Although Paul never depicts Christ explicitly as the Logos in his letters, the depiction of his function in creation here comes very close.

Furthermore, an additional variation between the prepositional metaphysical passages in Romans and 1 Corinthians lies in the fact that, whereas the "from" and the "through" statements focus on the origins and creation (and perhaps the current preservation) *of the cosmos* (it is the divine Father "*from* whom are *all things*" and his Son "through whom are *all things*," as are "we" too), the "to" statements that express the final destiny now centre not on the destiny *of the cosmos*, but on that *of human beings*: it is the divine Father "*to* whom *we* exist" (καὶ ἡμεῖς εἰς αὐτόν). Nevertheless, despite these variations, the same basic prepositional metaphysics shines through.

In addition to the important passage from 1 Cor 8:6, I would like briefly to mention another, shorter, subsidiary passage from this letter, which nevertheless illustrates the degree to which Paul is persistent and consistent in his cos-

[12] Sterling 1997, 227 (with reference to "the through which" [τὸ δι' οὗ] in Philo, *On the Cherubim* [124–27]), 229, 233, and 235–36 (with application to 1 Cor 8:6).

mological use of the preposition "from." In 1 Cor 11:11–12, a passage in which he discusses gender relations, Paul writes the following: "in the Lord woman is not independent of man or man independent of woman. For just as woman came *from* man (ὥσπερ γὰρ ἡ γυνὴ ἐκ τοῦ ἀνδρός), so man comes *through* woman (οὕτως καὶ ὁ ἀνὴρ διὰ τῆς γυναικός); but all things come *from* God (τὰ δὲ πάντα ἐκ τοῦ θεοῦ)." The prepositions known to us from their previous occurrences in 1 Cor 8:6 are almost graphically assigned to the different genders: women come "from" (ἐκ) men, from male, paternal seed, just as the first woman, Eve, was created from Adam (1 Cor 11:8; cf. Gen 2:23 LXX); men, in their turn, come "through" (διά) women, "through" the female, maternal birth canal. In this sense both genders are interdependent, whereas the cosmos is additionally fully dependent upon God, as it is "from" (ἐκ) him. It is rather interesting that in a context in which Paul differentiates between the genders (1 Cor 11:2–16), this sub-section emphasizes their interdependence, as well as the cosmos's close relation with and origins "from" God.

Before I go on to show how these Corinthian passages are also consistent with other expressions in the same letter, I will briefly assert the basically Stoic nature of both of the main Pauline instances of prepositional metaphysics that we have seen thus far. The prepositions that occur in both passages are "from / out of / forth from" (ἐκ), "through / by" (διά), and "into / to" (εἰς). The first and the last terms in particular are distinctively Stoic prepositions, suitable to express the kind of processual dynamics characteristic of Stoic cosmology, according to which the cosmos has a beginning and an end. These prepositions are different from the prepositional phrases used in Platonic metaphysics, which employs a set of prepositions which are terminologically distinct or have another meaning, as we shall see shortly.

The meaning of Stoic prepositional metaphysics is aptly illustrated by the following passage from Diogenes Laertius, according to which the Stoics regard God as

> the peculiarly qualified individual consisting of all substance (τὸν ἐκ τῆς ἁπάσης οὐσίας ἰδίως ποιόν), who is indestructible and ingenerable, since he is the manufacturer of the world-order (δημιουργὸς [...] τῆς διακοσμήσεως), at set periods of time (κατὰ χρόνων ποιὰς περιόδους) consuming all substance *into himself* (ἀναλίσκων εἰς ἑαυτὸν τὴν ἅπασαν οὐσίαν) and reproducing it again *from himself* (καὶ πάλιν ἐξ ἑαυτοῦ γεννῶν) (Diogenes Laertius, *Lives of Eminent Philosophers* 7,137 = *SVF* 2,526 = LS 44F; transl. LS).

The cosmos is thus generated by God "from himself" (ἐξ ἑαυτοῦ) and finally again absorbed back "into himself" (εἰς ἑαυτόν). This is the notion of the cosmos's origins from God, and of the final destiny of the cosmos and human beings in God, that we find in Paul's applications of these Stoic prepositional metaphysics. The prepositional phrases used here are indeed different from the Platonic variants, as I will show by drawing on one of the *loci classici*, the passage from Plato's *Tim.* 28a–30a – not only for the benefit of illustrative contrast, but also because it will help us recognize the Platonizing tendency of the Pauline Letter to the Colossians when we encounter it below. In this passage from Plato's *Timaeus*, the distinctively Stoic prepositional phrases "*from* God" and "*into* God" are absent. Instead, attention is focused on (1) what is generated "*through* (ὑπό) some cause (ὑπ' αἰτίου τινός)" (28a, c) – through God as "the artificer" (28a), "the Maker and Father of this cosmos" (28c), "the Architect" (28c). Furthermore, attention is drawn to (2) the paradigmatic model (παράδειγμα) "to" (πρός) which this creator looked when generating the cosmos (28a, c), so that the cosmos is in fact a copy (εἰκών) of that paradigm (29b) – to generate the cosmos, the creator looked to "that which is apprehensible by reason and thought" (29a), to what is ungenerated, to the eternal (29a). Moreover, this passage also focuses our attention on (3) the cause because of (διά) which the cosmos was created, namely God's goodness (29d–30a). Finally, if the notion of "creation from" occurs, it is – as we have already seen in the introduction – in the sense of creating the cosmos "from disorder" (ἐκ τῆς ἀταξίας), from the disorder of pre-existing matter, which is arranged into order: when God "took over all that was visible, seeing that it was not in a state of rest but in a state of discordant and disorderly motion, He brought it *into* order *from* disorder" (εἰς τάξιν αὐτὸ ἤγαγεν ἐκ τῆς ἀταξίας, 30a). But in contrast to Stoicism, the cosmos is certainly not perceived as having emerged "from God" himself. This classic passage of Platonic prepositional metaphysics from Plato's *Timaeus* is much commented upon in later Platonism.[13]

From these brief samples of Stoic and Platonic prepositional metaphysics, as found in the passages from Diogenes Laertius and Plato, it is clear that they differ greatly. The Stoics favour the prepositions "from" (ἐκ) and "into" (εἰς) in order to sketch the full cosmic process that starts from within God and also ends in him, whereas the Platonists employ the prepositions "through" (ὑπό) – since they understand God as an architect, an artificer through whom the cosmos is made – and "to" (πρός) in order to introduce the paradigm to which this architect looks in his construction of the visible cosmos. In this way, it also becomes clear that Paul – in his statements that the cosmos is "from" (Rom 11:36; 1 Cor 8:6) God and is also destined to revolve back "into" God (Rom 11:36), just as human beings also find their final destination "in" God (1 Cor 8:6) – is in profound agreement with a Stoic mode of expression. The notion that the cosmos and human beings are also "through/by" (διά) God might either refer to the moment of their creation or to their present preservation by the Stoic Logos, through which creation unfolded and which also currently permeates the cosmos and is present in human reasoning. As we have seen, Paul's assertion in his

[13] Plato, *Tim.* 28a–30a. Cf. Dörrie and Baltes 1996, no. 111.0 ("Die Lehre von den Prinzipien"), nos. 111–22; and no. 111 ("Die präpositionale Umschreibung").

Letter to the Romans that the cosmos emerged from, is preserved by, and will return into God was not an isolated view, but rather fully consistent with the letter's grand overture, with the theme of the cosmos's embodiment of God's own eternal power and divinity, and with the subsequent recognition that, however difficult, it is (at least theoretically) possible to follow the law of nature. As we shall now see, this instance of prepositional metaphysics in Paul's Corinthian passage is neither isolated nor insignificant, but is in fact part of an entirely coherent worldview.

1. *The Stoic "Scheme" of the Cosmos (1 Cor 7:31)*

First of all, the statement that there is only one God, from whom the cosmos has emerged and to whom human beings, together with the entirety of the cosmos, are due to return (1 Cor 8:6), is entirely consistent with the view, expressed in the letter a few lines earlier, that "the form (σχῆμα) of this [present] cosmos is passing away (παράγει [...] τὸ σχῆμα τοῦ κόσμου τούτου)" (1 Cor 7:31). Paul expresses this view in a passage that encourages his readers to adopt an "indifferent" attitude towards all worldly roles and emotions – an indifference grounded in this awareness of the passing away of the present cosmic "form."[14] In view of this certainty of cosmic finitude, it is best to live one's life in this temporary, transient cosmos "as though" this life, this particular worldly function, this particular emotion, is not absolute, but relativized to the point of indifference:

> I mean, brothers and sisters, the appointed time has grown short (ὁ καιρὸς συνεσταλμένος ἐστίν); from now on, let even those who have wives be as though they had none (ὡς μὴ ἔχοντες), and those who mourn as though they were not (ὡς μὴ) mourning, and those who rejoice as though they were not (ὡς μὴ) rejoicing, and those who buy as though they were not (ὡς μὴ) enjoying their possessions, and those who make use of the cosmos as though they were not (ὡς μὴ) consuming it. For the form of this cosmos is passing away (παράγει γὰρ τὸ σχῆμα τοῦ κόσμου τούτου) (1 Cor 7:29–31).

This notion that the cosmos "passes by," "passes on its way," and is thus involved in a process and progresses towards its end, is entirely compatible with the view that, after its emergence from God, it is again on its way back to him (1 Cor 8:6; Rom 11:36). This "form" of the cosmos is the current form, the current appearance the cosmos takes on as part of the (multi-phased) "scheme" in which it is embedded.

This is the meaning that the term "form" (σχῆμα) acquires in Stoic thought, as we see in Marcus Aurelius's *Meditations*. Whereas Platonists prefer the terminology of paradigm and copy, the term "scheme" conveys the sense of dynamics that propel the cosmos and structure its development. According to the Stoic emperor-philosopher, the human "rational soul," which is part of "the soul of all rational things, which is but one" (4,29,1; cf. 5,34,1), is able to discern the

[14] On Paul and (Stoic) indifference, see van Kooten 2017, 133–64.

"scheme" or the "plan" of the cosmos in its entire process, including its periodic regeneration:

[I]t [the rational soul] goes about the whole cosmos and the void surrounding it (ἔτι δὲ περιέρχεται τὸν ὅλον κόσμον καὶ τὸ περὶ αὐτὸν κενόν) and traces its plan (καὶ τὸ σχῆμα αὐτοῦ) and stretches forth into the infinitude of Time, and comprehends the periodic regeneration of all things, and takes stock of it (καὶ τὴν περιοδικὴν παλιγγενεσίαν τῶν ὅλων ἐμπεριλαμβάνει καὶ περινοεῖ) (Marcus Aurelius, *Meditations* 11,1,2).

So this cosmic "scheme," the "scheme of this cosmos," is part of the so-called "orderly arrangement of the cosmos," the διακόσμησις, which according to the Stoics, as we saw above, involves the generation of the cosmos from within God and its dissolution and absorption into him:

God himself, the peculiarly qualified individual consisting of all substance, [...] is indestructible and ingenerable, since he is the manufacturer of the world-order (διακόσμησις), at set periods of time consuming all substance into himself (εἰς ἑαυτόν) and reproducing it again from himself (ἐξ ἑαυτοῦ) (Diogenes Laertius, *Lives of Eminent Philosophers* 7,137 = *SVF* 2,526 = LS 44F; transl. LS).

In Stoicism, this insight into the cosmic process goes together with the same indifference that we encountered in Paul's reasoning: the passing away of the form of this cosmos renders us indifferent to worldly functions and human emotions (1 Cor 7:29–31). When the Stoic sage encounters difficulties, he models himself on God, who, at the dissolution of the cosmos, retreats into himself:

His life will be like that of Jupiter, who, amid the dissolution of the world (*cum resoluto mundo*), when the gods are confounded together (*et dis in unum confusis*) and Nature rests for a space from her work, can retire into himself and give himself over to his own thoughts (*sibi cogitationibus suis traditus*). In some such way as this the sage will act; he will retreat into himself (*in se reconditur*), and live with himself (Seneca, *Letters* 9,16 = *SVF* 2,1065 = LS 46O).

Seen in this light, Paul's assertions about the passing scheme of the cosmos and the indifference to one's personal circumstances that this causes are fully consistent with a Stoic worldview and support a Stoic understanding of Paul's prepositional metaphysics. Of course, there is also an important difference between Paul and the Stoics, insofar as the latter believed that this cosmic process of generation and dissolution recurs eternally, whereas in Paul's view this process takes place only once. But both cosmic processes are cyclical in the sense that they come full circle, and the cosmos that emerged from God returns back into him. The distinction is between an endlessly repeated cycle and a cycle executed only once. The "theologically grounded" structure of the cosmos in God as the origin and the end of the cosmos, however, is one and the same. At least so far as Paul is concerned, it is incorrect to say that the Christian understanding of time is linear; his understanding of time is cyclical, in the sense that the cosmos returns to its beginning – to God.

2. The Stoic Identification of God with the Final State of the Cosmos (1 Cor 15:28)

Later in the same Corinthian letter, in the section about Christ's resurrection and eschatology, Paul brings up the status of the cosmos in the interval between resurrection and the end. According to Paul, as Christ's resurrection is the beginning of his exalted, heavenly status, enthroned at the right hand of the divine Father, it is from this position that Christ fights the cosmic principles, powers, and forces, which leads to the total submission of the cosmos to God (1 Cor 15:24–28). The final purpose of this subjection is "that God may be all in everything" (ἵνα ᾖ ὁ θεὸς [τὰ] πάντα ἐν πᾶσιν, 1 Cor 15:28). This means that God is in the end identical with the cosmos, and this is an apt rendition of the notion expressed in the prepositional metaphysical statement in 1 Cor 8:6 that the cosmos has not only emerged from the single, one-and-only God, the divine Father (εἷς θεὸς ὁ πατήρ, ἐξ οὗ τὰ πάντα καὶ ἡμεῖς εἰς αὐτόν), through the intermediary activity of Christ in creation and preservation, but that human beings (as part of and together with the cosmos, as we have seen in Rom 11:36) will also return "into him" (εἰς αὐτόν) – that is, into God. Because of this return into God as the origin of all things, God, in the final state of the cosmos, is now said to *be* "all in everything" (1 Cor 15:28). As I have argued elsewhere, the phrase "all in everything" is a well-known idiom construed by the early Greek philosopher Anaxagoras to explain the coherence of the cosmos,[15] and Paul uses it here to describe the eschatological identification of God with the cosmos in a Stoic sense, which had already found expression in the metaphysical statement that all things, after they have emerged from God, will also finally return into God.

The similarity of Stoic and Pauline cosmology on this point is confirmed by the fact that the Platonists, the competing philosophical school, criticized them both for precisely this identification of God with the cosmos. According to the Platonists, such an equation of God with the fate of the cosmos amounts to sacrilege. The Middle-Platonic philosopher Plutarch criticizes the Stoics for this. In Plutarch's criticism, the Stoic theological view that God, in his manifestation as the god Apollo, sweeps down on the cosmos in fire at the moment of the conflagration and destroys what has been created is considered "irreverent" even to listen to:

> And as for his vagaries and transformations when he sends forth fire that sweeps his own self along with it (ἐκστάσεις δ' αὐτοῦ καὶ μεταβολὰς <εἰς> πῦρ ἀνιέντος ἑαυτὸν ἅμα τοῖς πᾶσιν), as they [the (Stoic) theologians] say, and again when he forces it down here [at the conflagration of the cosmos] and directs it upon the earth and sea and winds and living creatures, and, besides, the terrible things done both to living creatures and to growing vegetation – to such tales it is irreverent even to listen (οὐδ' ἀκούειν ὅσιον); else will the god be more futile than the Poet's fancied child [cf. Homer, *Iliad* 15,362], playing a game

[15] See van Kooten 2003, 104–07.

amid the sand that he heaps together and then scatters again, if the god indulges in this game with the universe constantly, fashioning the cosmos that does not exist, and destroying it again when it has been created (ταύτῃ περὶ τὰ ὅλα χρώμενος ἀεὶ καὶ τὸν κόσμον οὐκ ὄντα πλάττων εἶτ' ἀπολλύων γενόμενον) (Plutarch, *The E at Delphi* 393e–f).[16]

Earlier in his treatise, Plutarch had already introduced these (Stoic) theologians, who emphasize God's participation in the vicissitudes of the cosmos and understand the cosmic process as an expression of transformations that God experiences in his own person:

Now we hear the theologians affirming and reciting, sometimes in verse and sometimes in prose, that the god is deathless and eternal in his nature (ὡς ἄφθαρτος ὁ θεὸς καὶ ἀίδιος πεφυκώς), but, owing forsooth to some predestined design and reason (ὑπὸ δή τινος εἱμαρμένης γνώμης καὶ λόγου), he undergoes transformations of his person (μεταβολαῖς ἑαυτοῦ χρώμενος), and at one time enkindles his nature into fire and makes it altogether like all else (ἄλλοτε μὲν εἰς πῦρ ἀνῆψε τὴν φύσιν πάντα ὁμοιώσας πᾶσιν), and at another time he undergoes all sorts of changes in his form, his emotions and his powers (ἄλλοτε δὲ παντοδαπὸς ἔν τε μορφαῖς καὶ ἐν πάθεσι καὶ δυνάμεσι διαφόροις γιγνόμενος), even as the cosmos does today (Plutarch, *The E at Delphi* 388e–f).

Over against these Stoic theologians, Plutarch maintains that God is eternal and unchangeable, and takes care that the cosmos does not disintegrate:

For, on the contrary, so far as he is in some way present in the world, by this his presence does he bind together its substance (τοὐναντίον γὰρ ὃ θεῖον ἁμωσγέπως ἐγγέγονε τῷ κόσμῳ, τοῦτο συνδεῖ τὴν οὐσίαν) and prevail over its corporeal weakness, which tends toward dissolution (καὶ κρατεῖ τῆς περὶ τὸ σωματικὸν ἀσθενείας ἐπὶ φθορὰν φερομένης). And it seems to me right to address to the god the words "Thou art," which are most opposed to this account, and testify against it, believing that never does any vagary or transformation take place near him (ὡς οὐδέποτε γινομένης περὶ αὐτὸν ἐκστάσεως καὶ μεταβολῆς) (Plutarch, *The E at Delphi* 393f–394a).

In the same vein in which Plutarch criticized the Stoics, the anonymous pagan Platonic critic of Christianity in Macarius Magnes's *Apocriticus*, who was formerly commonly identified as Porphyry, finds fault with Paul's assertion in 1 Cor 7:31, which we have discussed above, that "the scheme of this cosmos is passing away." Similarly to Plutarch, this critic believes that it is wrong to regard the cosmos as destructible because this would reflect badly on the creator-God, and therefore it cannot be true:

What does Paul mean by saying that *the form of the world* passes away? [...] Or how can the form of this world pass away? What is it that passes away, and why does it do so? For if the creator were to make it pass away, he would incur the charge of moving and altering that which was securely founded. Even if he were to change the form into something better, in this again he stands condemned, as not having realised at the time of creation a fitting and suitable form for the world, but having created it incomplete, and lacking the

[16] For Plutarch's critique of Stoic philosophy, see Opsomer 2014, 88–103. Cf. also Opsomer 2006, 147–70.

better arrangement. In any case, how is one to know that it is into what is good that the world would change if it came to an end late in time? And what benefit is there in the order of phenomena being changed? And if the condition of the visible world is gloomy and a cause for grief, in this, too, the creator hears the sound of protest, being reduced to silence by the sound of reasonable charges against him, in that he contrived the parts of the earth in grievous form, and in violation of the reasonableness of nature and afterwards repented, and decided to change the whole (Anonymous *apud* Macarius Magnes, *Apocriticus* 4,1; transl. T.W. Crafer 1919).[17]

This anonymous criticism is comparable to the standard Platonic critique of the Stoic view of the destructibility of the cosmos and of God's identification with its last phase; both criticisms involve the negative implications that such a cosmology would have for one's theology. This confirms that Paul's views on these issues are comparable to a Stoic position, even if the anonymous critic does not formally acknowledge that Paul's argument is Stoic – probably because he wishes to present Paul as altogether unphilosophical, despite this similarity with Stoic thought. The very contents of his criticism, however, are rather similar to the kind of Platonic criticism that Plutarch expressed against the Stoics, and thus this passage offers extra confirmation that Paul's position is indeed Stoic.

3. The Stoic "Spiritual Body" (σῶμα πνευματικόν) *(1 Cor 15:44)*

Finally, the consistency of Paul's Stoic prepositional metaphysics with his wider thought is also evident in his description of the kind of materiality of the eschatological world, when the cosmos has returned into God (1 Cor 8:6; Rom 11:36) and God is all in everything (1 Cor 15:28). Paul describes this kind of eschatological materiality in the same section as his assertion about God's identity with the final phase of the cosmos, which we have discussed above; both statements are part of his passage on the eschatological resurrection of the human body. According to Paul, whereas human beings currently possess a "psychological body" (σῶμα ψυχικόν), after the resurrection they will receive a "pneumatic body" (σῶμα πνευματικόν) (1 Cor 15:44). In this terminology of the "pneumatic body," Paul's fundamentally Platonic anthropology and his basically Stoic cosmology overlap, as I will now briefly indicate.

In the immediate context of this section on the resurrection, the "pneumatic body" is differentiated from the "psychological body" (15:44) and the "flesh" (σάρξ, 15:39), and this differentiation between *pneuma*, psyche, and flesh (cf. 1 Thess 5:23) follows the tripartite Platonic anthropological definition of human beings as consisting of mind/*pneuma* (i.e., the guiding principle or dominant part of the soul), soul (i.e., the lower soul of the emotions), and the body.[18] De-

[17] This text is included in the digital "Early Church Fathers – Additional Texts" collection, edited by Roger Pearse and available online at: www.tertullian.org/fathers. Cf. Cook 2000, 220–22.

[18] Van Kooten 2008, 269–312.

pending on which layer human beings are determined by as their highest functional principal, the three constituents can also indicate three distinct classes of human beings. This kind of classification was undertaken by contemporary Platonists – such as Philo of Alexandria, Plutarch, and Plotinus[19] – and we also encounter it in this very letter. Earlier in the text, Paul differentiated between the pneumatic, the psychological, and the merely fleshly types of human beings: the *pneumatikoi* (πνευματικοί), the *psychikoi* (ψυχικοί), and the *sarkikoi* (σαρκικοί or σαρκίνοι; see 1 Cor 2:1–3:3). So when Paul uses the term "pneumatic body" in contrast with "psychological body" (15:44), in one sense this must be understood as part of his attempt to use a tripartite Platonic anthropology to qualify the human body after the eschatological resurrection: a "pneumatic body" is a body that is fully determined by the *pneuma* to an unprecedented degree; it is a *fully* pneumatic body. To a Platonist, however, this phrase must appear to be a contradiction *in terminis*. Although Platonists would entirely agree with the appropriateness of a differentiation between mind/*pneuma*, psyche, and body, and would moreover recognize such a differentiation as Platonic anthropology, they would always maintain a hierarchical relation between these anthropological constituents. As we have seen above, Plutarch's Platonic god is certainly willing to prevent the disintegration of the cosmic *body* by binding its substance together, and in this way he "prevail[s] over its bodily weakness, which tends toward dissolution" (καὶ κρατεῖ τῆς περὶ τὸ σωματικὸν ἀσθενείας ἐπὶ φθορὰν φερομένης, Plutarch, *The E at Delphi* 393e–f). However, from a Platonist perspective, *the body* – whether that of the cosmos or of human beings – could never lose its fundamental weakness and become a totally "pneuma-dominated" corporeality. For this reason, a fully "pneumatic body" is a Platonic impossibility, and its non-Platonic character is confirmed by the provenance of the phrase.

Despite the fact that the phrase "pneumatic body" appears in Paul's creative application of a *Platonic* tripartite anthropology that helps him to differentiate between a pre-resurrection "psychological body" and a post-resurrection "pneumatic body," the latter phrase is *Stoic*, whilst Paul coins the former phrase by way of contrast. Whereas Paul applies the Stoic phrase for *anthropological* reasons here (though in a wider cosmological context), in Stoic thought, the "pneumatic body" is a *cosmological* phrase describing the last phase of the cosmos – when the cosmos is taken back into God and fully coincides with God's *pneuma*, and is thus rendered into a σῶμα πνευματικόν, a "pneumatic body." We know this from its occurrence in Origen's *Commentary on the Gospel of John*, in a passage in which Origen takes issue with this view. Commenting on Jesus's statement in John's Gospel that "God is *spirit*, and that those who worship him

[19] Cf. Dillon 1989, 69–76, repr. Dillon 1991, 69–76. For Plutarch, see his *On the Sign of Socrates* 591d–92c, with Dillon 2001, 35–44.

must worship *in spirit* and truth" (John 4:24), Origen criticizes those who maintain that God has an ethereal, pneumatic *body* and ascribes this view to the Stoics:

(125) [...] for few have had an understanding concerning the nature of bodies, and especially of bodies fitted out by reason and providence. **And yet they [the Stoics] assert as a general definition that the body that provides [the "providential," divine body] has the same essence as those that have been provided.** The body that provides is perfect, but nevertheless it resembles that which has been provided. Those who wish God to be a body (οἱ θέλοντες εἶναι σῶμα τὸν θεόν) accept the absurd conclusions that present themselves to their argument because they are incapable of opposing those arguments that reason clearly presents. (126) But I make the following remarks as a refutation of those who say there is a fifth nature of bodies in addition to the [four] elements. (127) If every material body has a nature that is without quality in its characteristic disposition, and is mutable and subject to variation and change in general, and contains whatever qualities the creator may wish to bestow on it, God too, if he is material, must be mutable and subject to variation and change (ἀνάγκη καὶ τὸν θεὸν ὑλικὸν ὄντα τρεπτὸν εἶναι καὶ ἀλλοιωτὸν καὶ μεταβλητόν). (128) Those who hold this view are not ashamed to say **that since God is a body he is also subject to corruption (ὅτι καὶ φθαρτός ἐστι σῶμα ὤν), but *they say his body is pneumatical* and like ether, *especially in his commanding-faculty* (σῶμα δὲ πνευματικὸν καὶ αἰθερῶδες μάλιστα κατὰ τὸ ἡγεμονικὸν αὐτοῦ). Furthermore, they say that although God is subject to corruption he is not corrupted, because no one exists who might corrupt him** (Origen, *Commentary on the Gospel of John* 13,21,125–28, containing in bold the Stoic fragment of *SVF* 2,1054; transl. R. Heine, with minor changes).[20]

Thus, according to the Stoics, God has a body not in the gross material sense, but in the sense of a "pneumatic, ethereal body" (σῶμα πνευματικὸν καὶ αἰθερῶδες), a status that particularly applies to God's *hēgemonikon* (ἡγεμονικόν) – which, in Stoic philosophy, is the commanding-faculty of the cosmos, particularly after the cosmos has been taken back into God and no gross materiality remains, except God's *hēgemonikon*. At the moment of the eschatological conflagration, the entire substance of the cosmos is consumed into God (cf. *SVF* 2,526 = LS 44F), entirely coinciding with his commanding-faculty, so that God is fully coextensive with the cosmic substance. In contrast, during the periods of world-order before and after the conflagration, God is only present in part of the cosmic substance:

The god of the Stoics, inasmuch as he is a body, sometimes has the whole substance as his commanding-faculty (Ἀλλὰ καὶ ὁ τῶν Στωϊκῶν θεός, ἅτε σῶμα τυγχάνων, ὁτὲ μὲν ἡγεμονικὸν ἔχει τὴν ὅλην οὐσίαν); this is whenever the conflagration is in being (ὅταν ἡ ἐκπύρωσις ᾖ); at other times, when the world-order exists, he comes to be *in a part* of the substance (ὁτὲ δὲ ἐπὶ μέρους γίνεται αὐτῆς, ὅταν ᾖ διακόσμησις) (Origen, *Against Celsus* 4,14 = *SVF* 2,1052 = LS 46H; transl. LS).[21]

[20] *Origen: Commentary on the Gospel of John* (The Fathers of the Church 80, 89), Washington, DC: The Catholic University of America Press, 1989–1993, 2 vols.

[21] Cf. Plutarch, *On Stoic Self-Contradiction* 1053b = *SVF* 2,605 = LS 46F: "When the cos-

At the moment of conflagration, God is a fire, and in view of the world-order that will emerge again from him when he reproduces the cosmic substance out of himself (cf. *SVF* 2,526 = LS 44F), this fire is called "a designing fire" (πῦρ τεχνικόν), which consists of God's Logos (the collective *spermatikoi logoi* or "seminal principles") and Pneuma:

The Stoics make God out to be intelligent, a designing fire which methodically proceeds towards creation of the world, and encompasses all the seminal principles (ἐμπεριειληφὸς πάντας τοὺς σπερματικοὺς λόγους) according to which everything comes about according to fate, and a breath (Pneuma) pervading the whole cosmos (καὶ πνεῦμα μὲν ἐνδιῆκον δι' ὅλου τοῦ κόσμου) (Aëtius, *Placita* 1,7,33, in H. Diels, *Doxographi graeci* 305,14–306,6 = *SVF* 2,1027 = LS 46A; transl. LS, with minor changes).[22]

It is at the moment of conflagration, when the cosmic body is subsumed into God and entirely coextensive with God's commanding-faculty, that God has a "*pneumatic* body" (σῶμα πνευματικόν). It is in this sense that the Stoics say, "his body is pneumatic and like ether, especially in his commanding-faculty" (Origen, *Commentary on the Gospel of John* 13,21,128 = *SVF* 2,1054).

Thus, Paul argues that the status which human bodies will attain after the resurrection is that of the divine pneumatic body itself. This makes sense in the broader context of Paul's resurrection chapter, in which he already said that at the end of time, which is also the moment of the (spiritual, pneumatic) resurrection of all human beings, God will be identical with *the cosmos*, as God will then *be* "all in everything" (1 Cor 15:28) – the passage we discussed above. We find a similar transition from a human-centred argument about the resurrection towards a broader cosmological argument in Paul's Letter to the Philippians, when he says that Christ "will transform the body of our humiliation so that it may be conformed to the body of his glory, by the power that also enables him to make all things (τὰ πάντα) subject to himself" (Phil 3:21). The power by which the body is transformed into a new type of body – into a "pneumatic body" (1 Cor 15:44), we may add – is the same power by which the transformation of the cosmos takes place. This is the same connection that is made between eschatological resurrection and the eschatological fate of the cosmos in chapter 15 of his First Letter to the Corinthians. In the eschatological *resurrection*, which coincides with the identification of God with *the entire cosmic whole* (including human beings), when all things will revert back into God – at that moment,

mos is fiery through and through, it [the cosmos] is directly both its own soul and commanding faculty" (διόλου μὲν γὰρ ἂν ὁ κόσμος πυρώδης <γένηται>, εὐθὺς καὶ ψυχή ἐστιν ἑαυτοῦ καὶ ἡγεμονικόν; transl. LS, with minor changes).

[22] Cf. Aristocles *apud* Eusebius, *Preparation for the Gospel* 15,14,2 = *SVF* 1,98 = LS 46G: "At certain fated times the entire cosmos is subject to conflagration, and then is reconstituted afresh. But the primary fire is as it were a sperm which possesses the principles (*logoi*) of all things" (τὸ μέντοι πρῶτον πῦρ εἶναι καθαπερεί τι σπέρμα, τῶν ἁπάντων ἔχον τοὺς λόγους; transl. LS, with minor changes).

human beings will find their bodily existence subsumed in God's pneumatic body, with which they, along with the entire cosmic reality, will be fully identified. At that moment, for the first time, their bodies will be totally determined by the divine *pneuma*. This is a masterly, innovative, and consistent merger of Paul's Platonic anthropology with his Stoic cosmology, protology, and eschatology.

It is interesting to note that what Paul does *not* say is that this final phase of God's identification with all and everything will result in a new cosmic ordering, beyond and after this identification. This would be the normal Stoic view – according to the Stoics, this cosmic process is (eternally) recurrent, so that every destruction of the cosmos by fire (ἐκπύρωσις), which leads to the subsumption of the cosmos *into* God's *hēgemonikon*, will subsequently lead to the emergence of a new cosmos *from* God (*SVF* 2,526 = LS 44F; *SVF* 2,1052 = LS 46H) and thus to a full reconstitution of the cosmos (ἡ τοῦ παντὸς ἀποκατάστασις or ἡ ἀποκατάστασις πάντων). But it is here that Paul abandons his Stoic protology and eschatology, switching to a Platonic view of the soul's eternal afterlife in the transcendent heavenly realm. As he says in his other Corinthian letter, in a passage known for its Platonic view of the afterlife (2 Cor 4:16–5:10), the Platonic "inner human being" (ὁ ἔσω ἄνθρωπος, 2 Cor 4:16; cf. ὁ ἐντὸς ἄνθρωπος in Plato, *Republic* 9,588b–589d) gains its full strength in heaven, when the "tent" (σκῆνος, 2 Cor 5:1; cf. Plato, *Spuria* 366a) of its body, "the outer human being" (ὁ ἔξω ἡμῶν ἄνθρωπος, 2 Cor 4:16), will have been dissolved, and human beings will receive "an *eternal* […] dwelling in the heavens" (οἰκία […] αἰώνιος εν τοῖς οὐρανοῖς, 2 Cor 5:1), in the realm of the invisible (2 Cor 4:18), where they will enjoy the opportunity "to be away from the body and to be at home with the Lord" (ἐκδημῆσαι ἐκ τοῦ σώματος καὶ ἐνδημῆσαι πρὸς τὸν κύριον, 2 Cor 5:8). This future existence is the spiritual, pneumatic existence of the Lord, Christ, and the Spirit, into which they are already being transformed through a gradual metamorphosis over the course of their earthly existence:

> Now the Lord is the Spirit (ὁ δὲ κύριος τὸ πνεῦμά ἐστιν), and where the Spirit of the Lord (τὸ πνεῦμα κυρίου) is, there is freedom. And all of us, with unveiled faces, seeing the glory of the Lord as though reflected in a mirror, are being transformed (μεταμορφούμεθα) into the same image from one degree of glory to another; for this comes from the Lord, the Spirit (καθάπερ ἀπὸ κυρίου πνεύματος) (2 Cor 4:17–18).

This Spirit prepares them for their final transformation in heaven (2 Cor 5:5), when their earthly body is destroyed and taken off (2 Cor 5:1–3) and their "naked" selves (2 Cor 5:3; cf. Plato, *Cratylus* 403b, *Gorgias* 523e) are clothed with their heavenly, spiritual existence (2 Cor 5:4) – that is, if we may adduce the notion from 1 Cor 15:44 here, when their earthly bodies are transformed into a "pneumatic body," entirely determined by the divine *pneuma*. This heavenly existence, when the cosmos will have been subsumed in the identity of God himself, is thus clearly the end of the human and cosmic trajectories, when the cosmos which has emerged from God turns full circle and returns into God. Paul's protology and eschatology are thus clearly part of a full Stoic cycle, but once this cycle has reached its end point in God and the cosmos is subsumed in him, this subsumption is not temporary, as in Stoicism. Instead, human beings remain in this "heavenly" state forever, face to face with God, in his eternal presence.

It is here that Paul's Stoicism turns in a Platonic direction, though without becoming entirely Platonic, as we shall see in due course. For Paul, the transformation and subsumption of the cosmos into the pneumatic body of God, when God identifies himself with the cosmos entirely and without reserve (probably – along Stoic lines – by admitting the cosmos into God's *hēgemonikon*),[23] indicates *the end* of the cosmic journey. There is thus no subsequent re-emergence of the cosmos from God, as there is in Stoicism. Paul's cosmology is Stoic insofar as it is cyclical, with the end returning to its beginning in God, but this cycle is a one-time only rather than an eternally recurrent event. Moreover, in Paul's thinking, there is no "new heaven and earth"; the phrase "a new creation" (2 Cor 5:17; Gal 6:15) is used only as a moral metaphor, signalling the need for a transformation of one's current existence. For Paul, there is no reconstitution of the physical cosmos (ἀποκατάστασις πάντων). There could have been, if Paul had been more Stoic and had not synthesized his Stoic cosmology with his Platonic anthropology. The author of the Second Letter of Peter, for instance, follows a more completely Stoic path when he indicates that the conflagration of the cosmic elements (2 Pet 3:7, 10, 12) will be followed by the creation of "new heavens and a new earth, where justice is at home" (2 Pet 3:13; cf. Isa LXX 65:17, 66:22),[24] just as in Stoic thought the conflagration serves the moral renewal of the earth at the dawn of a new cycle: "Whenever they [the Stoics] subject the cosmos to conflagration, no evil at all remains, but the whole is then prudent and wise" (Plutarch, *Against the Stoics on Common Conceptions* 1067a = *SVF* 2,606 = LS 46N; transl. LS, with minor changes). For Paul, however, there is no such reconstitution of the physical cosmos.

That also means that, for Paul, there will be no physical resurrection in this new, re-established cosmos. There could have been, as indeed, according to some Christians, the resurrection (ἀνάστασις) is part of the ἀποκατάστασις – the new cosmic reality that follows the end. Gregory of Nyssa (ca. 330–95 CE), for instance, argues this point in his *On the Soul and the Resurrection*. In an attempt to answer "the objections of the outsiders to the resurrection" (τὰ περὶ τῆς ἀναστάσεως παρὰ τῶν ἔξωθεν προφερόμενα, 129,4–5), he defines resurrection as

[23] See *SVF* 2,1054; *SVF* 2,1052 = LS 46H, as discussed above.

[24] For the interpretation of 2 Pet 3:3–7 and 10–13 in the light of the Stoa, see Adams 2007, 200–35.

the (re-)constitution of life that results from the re-assemblage of the bodily elements around the same individual soul when the cosmos has completed its full revolution:

[T]he inspired Writings, both in the New and in the Old Testament, declare most emphatically not only that, when our race has completed the ordered chain of its existence as the ages lapse through their complete circle (κατὰ τὴν παροδικὴν τοῦ χρόνου κίνησιν), this current streaming onward as generation succeeds generation will cease altogether, but also that then, when the completion of the cosmos (τὸ πᾶν) no longer admits of further increase, all the souls in their entire number will come back out of their invisible and scattered condition into tangibility and light, the identical elements (belonging to each soul) reassembling together in the same order as before (τῶν αὐτῶν στοιχείων κατὰ τὸν αὐτὸν εἱρμὸν πρὸς ἄλληλα πάλιν ἀναδραμόντων); *and this (re-)constitution* of human life *is called*, in these Writings which contain God's teaching, *the resurrection* (Ἡ δὲ τοιαύτη τῆς ζωῆς κατάστασις, περὶ τῶν τῆς θείας διδασκαλίας Γραφῶν ἀνάστασις λέγεται), the entire movement of the elements receiving the same term as the raising up of that which is actually prostrate on the ground (Gregory of Nyssa, *Dialogus de anima et resurrectione*, PG 46, 129,8–23).

Accordingly, Gregory defines the resurrection as "the reconstitution (*apokatástasis*) of our nature in its original form": ἀνάστασίς ἐστιν ἡ εἰς τὸ ἀρχαῖον τῆς φύσεως ἡμῶν ἀποκατάστασις (*Dialogus de anima et resurrectione*, PG 46, 148,1–2; cf. 156,30–32), a definition which we also find in Eusebius of Caesarea's *Commentaries on the Psalms*: ἡ γὰρ ἀνάστασις εἰς τὸ ἀρχαῖόν ἐστιν ἀποκατάστασις (Eusebius, *Commentaria in Psalmos*, PG 23, 1285,55–56).[25]

Indeed, also according to the Stoics themselves, the reconstitution (ἀποκατάστασις) of the cosmos would bring with it the re-appearance of Socrates and Plato in the next world. This becomes clear from a Stoic fragment (*SVF* 2,625) preserved in *On the Nature of Man* by Nemesius, bishop of Emesa in Syria (fl. ca. 400 CE). The passage first sets out the Stoic view on the conflagration and the subsequent reconstitution of the cosmos, and then illustrates the fully restorative nature of this *apokatástasis* by stating that "Socrates and Plato will exist again (ἔσεσθαι [...] πάλιν Σωκράτην καὶ Πλάτωνα), and each person with the same friends and fellow-citizens," subsequently remarking that this

[25] See further Gregory of Nyssa, *In Ecclesiasten* (homiliae 8), vol. V, 296,16–18, ed. P. Alexander: οὐδὲ γὰρ ἄλλο τι ἐστιν ἡ ἀνάστασις, εἰ μὴ πάντως ἡ εἰς τὸ ἀρχαῖον ἀποκατάστασις. Cf. also his *Great Catechism* (*Oratio catechetica*), ch. 16: "And this is the resurrection, namely the return, after they have been dissolved, of those elements that had been before linked together, into an indissoluble union through a mutual incorporation" (Καὶ τοῦτό ἐστιν ἡ ἀνάστασις, ἡ τῶν συνεζευγμένων μετὰ τὴν διάλυσιν ἐπάνοδος εἰς ἀδιάλυτον ἕνωσιν ἀλλήλοις συμφυομένων, *Oratio catechetica* 16,59–62). Cf. also Pseudo-Justin Martyr, *Quaestiones et responsiones ad orthodoxos* 472c,5–7: Βασιλείαν θεοῦ οἶδεν ἡ θεία γραφὴ ὀνομάζειν οὐ τὴν ἀνάστασιν ἁπλῶς, ἀλλὰ τὴν μετὰ τὴν ἀνάστασιν ἀποκατάστασιν. For a treatment of the early Christian interpretations of the *apokatástasis*, see Ramelli 2013; for its connection with the resurrection, see Ramelli's subject index, s.v. "resurrection."

pattern of destruction and exact reconstitution will be eternally recurrent.[26] The full fragment reads as follows:

The Stoics say that *the planets are reconstituted* (ἀποκαθισταμένους) into the same sign according to magnitude and longitude in which each was in the beginning when the cosmos first was formed (ὅτε τὸ πρῶτον ὁ κόσμος συνέστη), and at set revolutions of time they bring about the conflagration and destruction of what exists (ἐκπύρωσιν καὶ φθορὰν τῶν ὄντων ἀπεργάζεσθαι) *and again reconstitute the cosmos in the same state* (καὶ πάλιν ἐξ ὑπαρχῆς εἰς τὸ αὐτὸ τὸν κόσμον ἀποκαθίστασθαι), and, as the stars travel once again in the same way, each of the things that came to be in the previous cycle is brought to be unchanged (ἕκαστον <τῶν> ἐν τῇ προτέρᾳ περιόδῳ γενομένων ἀπαραλλάκτως ἀποτελεῖσθαι). *For Socrates and Plato will exist again* (ἔσεσθαι γὰρ πάλιν Σωκράτην καὶ Πλάτωνα), *and each person with the same friends and fellow-citizens*, and they will have the same experiences, meet with the same events and undertake the same activities, and every city and village and field will be reconstituted as before. *The reconstitution of the cosmos occurs not once but many times* (γίνεσθαι δὲ τὴν ἀποκατάστασιν τοῦ παντὸς οὐχ ἅπαξ, ἀλλὰ πολλάκις), or rather, to infinity, and *the same things will be reconstituted without end* (μᾶλλον δὲ εἰς ἄπειρον καὶ ἀτελευτήτως τὰ αὐτὰ ἀποκαθίστασθαι). But, they hold, the gods who are not subject to this destruction [i.e., Zeus],[27] having observed one cycle, know from [112] it everything that will come about in the following cycles. For there will be nothing foreign beyond what happened before, but everything will be the same without change even in the least detail (Nemesius, *On the Nature of Man*, section 38, 111,14–112,3 = *SVF* 2,625 = LS 52C; transl. Sharples and van der Eijk 2008, with minor changes).[28]

The Stoics even take "reconstitution" (ἀποκατάστασις) and "resurrection" (ἀνάστασις) as (near) synonyms, as we see in the following Stoic text from the Augustan period, written by the philosopher Arius Didymus of Alexandria and preserved in Eusebius's *Preparation for the Gospel*:

Universal Logos (ὁ κοινὸς λόγος) having advanced thus far, or universal nature (κοινὴ φύσις) having grown and increased, it finally dries up all things (τέλος ἀναξηράνασα πάντα) and *takes it up into itself* (καὶ εἰς ἑαυτὴν ἀναλαβοῦσα), *and comes to be in the whole substance* (ἐν τῇ πάσῃ οὐσίᾳ γίνεται). *It returns* to the so-called primary Logos (ἐπανελθοῦσα εἰς τὸν πρῶτον ῥηθέντα λόγον) and *to that resurrection* (καὶ εἰς τὴν ἀνάστασιν ἐκείνην) *which creates the greatest year, in which the reconstitution from itself alone into itself recurs* (καθ' ὃν ἀπ' αὐτῆς μόνης εἰς αὐτὴν πάλιν γίνεται ἡ ἀποκατάστασις). Having returned because of the order from which it began to create the cosmos (διακοσμεῖν [...] ἤρξατο) in just such a way, it manufactures the same way of life again according to reason, since such periods occur everlastingly without ceasing (Arius Didymus *apud* Eusebius,

[26] Cf. Long 2006a, 256–82, with an analysis of the recurrence of Socrates on pp. 274–76 and 280. Long concludes that there is not "a succession of Socrateses and a succession of his lives," but that there is "one and only one Socrates," "the self-same Socrates, time and again" (280).

[27] See Long and Sedley 1987, 2:307, commentary on 52C, lines 12–13.

[28] Sharples and van der Eijk 2008. For similar views on the reappearance of individuals in the same shape after death and the rebirth of "the same I" in the "recreation" in other Stoic fragments, see Lactantius, *Divine Institutes* 7,23 = *SVF* 2,623 = LS 52B; Simplicius, *On Aristotle's Physics* 886,12–16 = *SVF* 2,627 = LS 52E; and Alexander, *On Aristotle's Prior Analytics* 180,33–36 and 181,25–31 = *SVF* 2,624 = LS 52F.

Preparation for the Gospel 15,19,1–2 = *SVF* 2,599 = LS 52D; transl. LS, with minor changes).

God, the universal Logos and nature, is said to take the cosmos back up "into itself" and to start the "resurrection" (ἀνάστασις) and the "reconstitution" (ἀποκατάστασις) of the cosmos. Clearly the resurrection and reconstitution of the cosmos are (nearly) synonymous here, and A. A. Long has argued that the term "resurrection" should not be regarded as Eusebius's Christian intrusion into the Stoic fragment that he preserves. As Long argues, "If [...] the next Stoic world includes individual persons numerically identical to those in this world, it seems quite credible that Stoics themselves may have called the initial conditions of the next world 'resurrection'."[29]

Not only did the Stoics themselves apparently use the term "resurrection" in order to depict the cosmic reconstitution, but they (or other pagans) also acknowledged that the Christians made this equation. The Nemesius passage quoted above not only states that "Socrates and Plato will exist again" in the re-established cosmos, but the immediate continuation of this passage goes on as follows: "Some say that the Christians imagine the resurrection because of this reconstitution (καὶ διὰ [LSJ III. Causal III.1 *by aid of*; III.2 *through*] ταύτην τὴν ἀποκατάστασιν, φασί τινες, τοὺς Χριστιανοὺς τὴν ἀνάστασιν φαντάζεσθαι [LSJ φαντάζω I. Med., *place before one's mind, picture an object to oneself, imagine*])." According to Nemesius, this is "far wide of the truth. For the sayings of Christ foretell that the resurrection will occur once and not periodically" (εἰς ἅπαξ [...] καὶ οὐ κατὰ περίοδον, Nemesius, *On the Nature of Man*, section 38, 112,3–6). Of course Nemesius is partly correct in saying that the Christian understanding of the resurrection differs from the Stoic perception of cosmic reconstitution, as the latter is indeed eternally recurrent, whereas the former occurs only once.[30] Yet Nemesius is also partly wrong, as the Pauline and the Stoic positions do indeed resemble one another in their fundamentally cyclical (though not periodical) understanding of protology and eschatology: both regard the relation between beginning and end not as linear but as cyclical, as the cosmos returns to and is subsumed in God. This holds true not only for Paul, but also for the author of the Gospel of Luke and the Acts of the Apostles.

In Acts, Luke not only uses (1) the Stoic notion of the reconstitution of the cosmos (ἀποκατάστασις πάντων), which Peter applies whilst walking in the Stoa (!) of Solomon in the Jerusalem temple (Acts 3:19–21), but also (2) the (related) Stoic (and even more widely applied ancient philosophical) notion of divine-human-cosmic kinship (συγγένεια),[31] supported by Paul's quotation of a relevant

[29] Long 2006a, 273 n. 67.

[30] Sharples and van der Eijk (2008, 194 n. 947) refer for this difference to Origen, *Against Celsus* 5,20–23.

[31] These notions are interrelated because, insofar as the entire cosmos (including human beings) originates from, returns to, and is reconstituted by God, human beings "live, move,

verse from the Stoic Aratus: "For we too are his kin" (Τοῦ γὰρ καὶ γένος ἐσμέν, 17:28 = Aratus, *Phaenomena* 5; cf. also Cleanthes, *Hymn to Zeus* = *SVF* 1,537 = LS 54I). In addition, Luke also portrays (3) the open-mindedness of the Stoics, who are present at Paul's trial in the Areopagus in Athens, towards Paul's message regarding the resurrection (ἀνάστασις). Whereas the Epicureans contemptuously ridicule Paul when he talks about the resurrection (17:31; cf. 17:18), their counterparts – the Stoics – suspend their discussion until another, more suitable moment: "When they heard of the resurrection of the dead, some (οἱ μέν) scoffed; but others (οἱ δέ) said, 'We will hear you again about this'" (17:32). Given the relation between the notions of cosmic reconstitution and resurrection, it is not difficult to see why Luke portrays them as open for further discussion. It seems that, contrary to what is often thought, there is no fundamental difference between the Stoics and Christians such as Paul and Luke in their ontology. Although the Stoics might be surprised about the Christians' notion of the resurrection of a particular individual prior to the reconstitution of the cosmos, the equation of this reconstitution and universal resurrection with the reappearance of all individuals in the next cosmos is attested in the Stoic fragments from Nemesius and Arius Didymus which we have seen above: "Socrates and Plato will exist again, and each person with the same friends and fellow-citizens." In this sense, Paul's and Luke's ontologies are not fundamentally different, and the Stoics accept their terminology and notion of resurrection. The difference between their eschatologies is not that between a cyclical Stoic and a linear Jewish-Christian eschatology; the Stoic and Pauline-Lukan eschatologies are both cyclical, as the cosmos, together with all human beings, issues from God as his offspring and experiences reconstitution. As we have seen, the author of the Second Letter of Peter even shares the Stoic views of "new heavens and a new earth" that come after the conflagration of the cosmic elements. The only difference is that, according to the Stoics, the pattern of protology and eschatology is eternally recurrent, whereas according to Paul, Luke, and Peter, it is not.

As we have seen, however, Paul actually does not affirm the reconstitution of the cosmos that would follow its destruction and assumption into God. For him, there is no gross-physical resurrection in a new cosmos, but rather a fine-spiritual resurrection of the body in heaven, as the body will be rendered pneumatic. There is some lack of clarity between the different Pauline letters regarding the timing of the resurrection: Does it take place at the end of time, concomitantly with the transformation of the then-living (1 Thess 4:15–17; 1 Cor

and exist" in God (17:28a), whose offspring they are (17:28c; cf. also the direct genealogy of Adam from God in Luke 3:38, as well as the parable of the prodigal son who, even in his self-chosen exile, carries with him – in Luke's consciously ambiguous terminology – his share of the "substance/property" [οὐσία] and "life/livelihood, property [βίος] of the [divine] Father, according to Luke 15:12 and 30).

15:51–53), or immediately after death, as a re-clothing of the naked human being in heaven (2 Cor 4:16–5:10)? What is clear is that none of the resurrected will receive a gross-physical 2.0 version of life on a new 2.0 version of earth, but will rather ascend from the earth into the air in order to be with God "for ever" (1 Thess 4:17). Moreover, the resurrected are fundamentally changed in this process, acquiring "a pneumatic body" (1 Cor 15:44) as well as imperishability and immortality (1 Cor 15:52–53; 2 Cor 5:4). Indeed, for Paul there is no physical resurrection in a new cosmos, but the resurrection of the body takes place as a "pneumatic body" in a heavenly, transcendental realm in the eternal presence of God, from whom no new physical reality emerges. It is as if, after the destruction and conflagration of the present cosmos and its subsequent subsumption into God, the cosmic process comes to an eternal standstill in this identification of the former cosmos with God in the form of his pneumatic, ethereal body, now reduced or compressed into the commanding-faculty (τὸ ἡγεμονικόν) of God himself. This is how Paul's basically Stoic cosmology (with its characteristic protology and eschatology) merges with his Platonic anthropology to form a new, innovative synthesis.

I gather from the individual Pauline passages that we have discussed, as well as from their mutual coherence, that Paul did indeed participate in such a philosophical discourse with Stoics and Platonists.[32] Although it is impossible to confirm Paul's authorial intention, it does not seem that the proposed reading of his passages reflects only my own intention. As Umberto Eco has argued, between the intention of the author (*intentio auctoris*) and the intention of the interpretative reader (*intentio lectoris*), there is also the intention of the text (*intentio operis*).[33] According to Eco, one can check whether one's conjectures about the text's intention are correct by drawing upon the text "as a coherent whole" and examining "the internal textual coherence": "any interpretation given of a certain portion of a text can be accepted if it is confirmed by, and must be rejected if it is challenged by, another portion of the same text."[34] What we have seen, I believe, is that a reading of the relevant passages from Paul's Corinthian (and other) correspondence within the context of a Stoic discourse works very well. To adapt Eco's phraseology, "[I]f [...] I read [this Pauline literature] according to the [Stoic] encyclopedia, it appears textually coherent in each of its parts."[35] In this reading, both Paul's agreements *and* his disagreements within this contemporary philosophical discourse become evident. Both his participation in and his departure from this discourse, and hence also the nature of his innovation,

---

32 For a debate with colleagues on this disputed issue, see van Kooten, Wischmeyer, and Wright 2015, 239–53.

33 Eco 1992a, 25.

34 Eco 1992b, 64–65, quoting from 65.

35 Eco 1992b, 65.

become apparent. He allows for "propaedeutic" overlap with other schools, but also offers something distinctive.[36]

Paul's discourse is Stoic in its depiction of the cosmic process as an emergence from (1 Cor 8:6; 11:12) and return and subsumption into God (1 Cor 8:6) – the full identification of the cosmos with God in its post-destruction state (1 Cor 15:28) and its rendition into a "pneumatic body" (1 Cor 15:44). But it is un-Stoic insofar as there is no new physical cosmic order (διακόσμησις) after the disappearance of the form of the present cosmos (1 Cor 7:31), and no reconstitution (ἀποκατάστασις) of the cosmos after its rendition into a "pneumatic body" and its subsumption into and identification with God. It is Platonic in its post-mortem, eternal beatific vision of God in a heavenly transcendental realm (1 Cor 15:52–53; 2 Cor 4:16–5:10), but un-Platonic in the total disappearance of the physical cosmos, which the Platonists deemed to be without end. Paul clearly participates in a Stoic cosmological discourse (as the individual passages and their mutual consistency show beyond reasonable doubt), but eventually suspends it in a Platonizing mode. The permanent end of this process consists in one's existence as a "pneumatic body" and in one's identification with God's guiding principle, a status that becomes eternally established in heaven, and in that sense becomes Platonic: the final prospect is acquiring an eternal home in heaven (2 Cor 5:1), not on a new, re-established earth. Paul complies with the dynamics of Stoic cosmology and ontology, with its distinctive protology and eschatology (including its cyclical thinking, though without eternal recurrence), but eventually settles for a Platonic eternity, though with a Stoic twist: humans are not merely in God's presence, but are actually identified with God.

It seems that Paul's discourse with Stoicism and Platonism is furthered in his letters to the Ephesians and the Colossians, which we will briefly explore in the next two sections. I take the common view that these two letters are Pseudo-Pauline, each written by a different author, and understand them as products of ongoing discussions in the Pauline School. As I will argue, the Pseudo-Pauline author of the Letter to the Ephesians follows Paul's Stoicizing discourse, whereas the author of the Letter to the Colossians tries to foreground a Platonic understanding of reality – not only with regard to the transcendental afterlife, as Paul himself did, but also, in contrast to Paul, as regards the present cosmos. I will comment briefly on how these letters continue Paul's debate about the cosmos before raising the question of how this particular proto- and eschatological discourse subsequently disappeared from the agenda almost entirely.

[36] For a view of "propaedeutic" relations between the ancient philosophical schools, see Boys-Stones 2019.

III. The Furtherance of Paul's Stoic Debate in Pseudo-Paul's Letter to the Ephesians

In many respects, the author of the Letter to the Ephesians simply furthers the kind of Stoic views on the cosmos (regarding its origins from and return to God) that we have seen in Paul's letters, notably in his Corinthian correspondence and his Letter to the Romans. This becomes clear from the fact that the author of Ephesians also states that the cosmos emerged from God. This will prove to be the most notable difference between these letters and the protology of the Pseudo-Pauline author of the Letter to the Colossians, who, in what seems to be a Platonic worldview, does not follow Paul in this protological view of the emergence of the cosmos from God, and only entertains a very "weak" eschatology. The author of Ephesians, however, remains fully Pauline in the sense that he entirely shares Paul's proto- and eschatological views, and even enriches the expression of Paul's Stoicizing views on the issue. According to the author of Ephesians, it is "the [divine] Father *from whom* every 'fatherhood' in heaven and on earth takes its name" (τὸν πατέρα, ἐξ οὗ πᾶσα πατριὰ ἐν οὐρανοῖς καὶ ἐπὶ γῆς ὀνομάζεται, Eph 3:14–15). Similarly to Paul, this Pseudo-Pauline author sees God as the origin "from whom" (ἐξ οὗ) the cosmos emerges and the congeniality (one might even say the "consubstantiality") of the paternal creator with his creation is shown in the fact that the entire cosmos can be called a πατριά, a "paternal descent" (in the sense of a πάτρα, a "fatherhood," a "descent from a common father" [see LSJ πατριά II; LSJ πάτρα II]), when one recognizes that it emerges from this heavenly πάτρη (father).

Further on in the letter, in good Pauline-Stoic fashion, this Father is subsequently described as the "one God and Father of all, who is above all and through all and in all" (εἷς θεὸς καὶ πατὴρ πάντων, ὁ ἐπὶ πάντων καὶ διὰ πάντων καὶ ἐν πᾶσιν, Eph 4:6). Interestingly, the following Stoic fragment similarly depicts God as "the Father of all" (πατὴρ πάντων) and sees him as pervading "through all things" (διὰ πάντων):

> They [the Stoics] say that God is a living being which is immortal and rational or intelligent, perfect in happiness, not admitting of any evil, provident towards the world and its occupants, but not anthropomorphic. He is the creator of the whole and, as it were, *the father of all* (εἶναι δὲ τὸν μὲν δημιουργὸν τῶν ὅλων καὶ ὥσπερ πατέρα πάντων), both generally and, in particular, that part of him which pervades *through all things* (τὸ μέρος αὐτοῦ τὸ διῆκον διὰ πάντων), which is called by many descriptions according to his powers. For they call him Zeus (Δία) as the cause (δι' ὃν) of all things (Δία μὲν γάρ φασι δι' ὃν τὰ πάντα) (*SVF* 2,1021 *apud* Diogenes Laertius, *Lives of Eminent Philosophers* 7,147 = LS 54A; transl. LS, with minor changes).

Thus the letter's protology is basically Stoic and portrays the same views that we have seen in Paul's own letters, as the cosmos has come about "through" God (Rom 11:36) and has emerged "from" him (1 Cor 8:6; Rom 11:36).

This protology matches the corresponding eschatology, which regards God not only as the source, but also as the end of this cosmic process. It is the letter's explicit intention to understand the mystery that the divine Father (ὁ θεὸς καὶ πατήρ, Eph 1:3) intends to make known (Eph 1:8–9), which consists of the "recapitulation of all things" (Eph 1:10):

With all wisdom and insight he has made known to us the mystery of his will, according to his good pleasure that he set forth in Christ, as a plan for the fullness of time (εἰς οἰκονομίαν τοῦ πληρώματος τῶν καιρῶν), to *recapitulate* all things in Christ (ἀνακεφαλαιώσασθαι τὰ πάντα ἐν τῷ Χριστῷ), things in heaven and things on earth (Eph 1:8–10).

Judging from what follows in a later passage in the letter, the community is somehow involved in this cosmic recapitulation. This passage in Eph 4:15 should not be translated as the New Revised Standard Version (NRSV) translates it: "speaking the truth in love, we must grow up *in every way* into him who is the head, into Christ" (Eph 4:15), but rather as "speaking the truth in love, we must *cause all things* to grow up towards him who is the head, Christ": ἀληθεύοντες δὲ ἐν ἀγάπῃ αὐξήσωμεν (taken as a transitive rather than an intransitive verb, with τὰ πάντα as its object) εἰς αὐτὸν τὰ πάντα (taken as the object of the transitive verb rather than adverbially), ὅς ἐστιν ἡ κεφαλή, Χριστός (Eph 4:15).[37] Like the Stoic philosophers who, together with the cosmos, constitute the Stoic cosmopolis, the Christian community is aware of the cosmos[38] and – in a further, rather un-Stoic move – considers itself to be playing an active role in the unfolding cosmic process by speaking the truth, and resisting and combating the planetary forces that rule the cosmos (κοσμοκράτορες, 6:12) by speaking out in truth, performing justice, and spreading peace and trust (Eph 6:10–16). Of course this resistance against the planets is very un-Stoic, because in Stoic thinking, as we have seen above, it is the planets and stars that determine the onset of the conflagration and destruction of the present cosmos by returning to their original positions at the beginning of the so-called "greatest year" and by finishing their full cycle, thus leading to the reconstitution of the cosmos (see *SVF* 2,599 = LS 52D; *SVF* 2,625 = LS 52C, both discussed above).[39] Yet the author's main view on this cosmic process is thoroughly Stoic in its emergence from and ending in God. The author of Ephesians sees this process as one of recapitulation (ἀνακεφαλαίωσις) in which Christ, also by means of the Christian community (Eph 1:22–23; 3:10; 4:15), increasingly fills the cosmos with himself (Eph 4:10). As we will see in the other Pseudo-Pauline letter below, the author of the Letter to the Colossians, by contrast, does *not* reckon with such a progressive cosmic

[37] For the full argument, see van Kooten 2003, 183–91 and 192, esp. 186–87, with n. 71.

[38] For the relevance of the Stoic notion of the cosmopolis here, see van Kooten 2003, 175–79. See further Schofield 1991, repr. 1999.

[39] On Stoic astral determinism, see Long 2006b, 128–52.

process, but believes that the cosmos as it is, is fundamentally static and is also already full of God and Christ. According to the author of Ephesians, however, the cosmos is involved in a process that stretches from its emergence from God (Eph 3:14–15), through its present permeation by God (as God is also the one ὁ ἐπὶ πάντων καὶ διὰ πάντων καὶ ἐν πᾶσιν, "who is above all and through all and in all," Eph 4:6), to its full eschatological recapitulation (Eph 1:10) and fulfilment through the activities of Christ and the cosmopolitan Christian community (Eph 4:10; 1:22–23).

Given the clearly Stoic terminology, notions, and overtones in the general thrust of Ephesians, it is not surprising that an early Christian reader such as Gregory of Nyssa, whose equation of the cosmic reconstitution and the resurrection we have noted above, understands the letter's *recapitulation* (ἀνακεφαλαίωσις) of the cosmos as just such a *reconstitution* (ἀποκατάστασις). In his reflections on the ascension of Christ, Gregory quotes Psalm 23 LXX and answers the question this Psalm raises with the following references to Christ as the one who *recapitulates* and *reconstitutes* the cosmos:

> "Who is this King of glory?" (Ps 23[24]:8a, 10a LXX) The answer to this question is then no longer: "The one who is strong and powerful in war" (Ps 23:8b–c LXX), but: "The Lord of powers" (Ps 23:10b LXX), the one who has clung on to his power over the cosmos (ὁ τοῦ παντὸς ἐξημμένος τὸ κράτος), who *recapitulated all things within himself* (ὁ ἀνακεφαλαιώσας τὰ πάντα ἐν ἑαυτῷ, Eph 1:10), who is the first in everything (ὁ ἐν πᾶσι πρωτεύων, Col 1:18), who *reconstituted all things back into the first creation* (ὁ εἰς τὴν πρώτην κτίσιν ἀποκαταστήσας τὰ πάντα). "This one is the King of glory" (Ps 23:10c) (Gregory of Nyssa, *In ascensionem Christi* 9,326,26–327,4, ed. E. Gebhardt).

Although "recapitulation" is not a Stoic term, Gregory senses the implications of Ephesians' terminology and associates cosmic *recapitulation* (ἀνακεφαλαίωσις) with the *reconstitution* (ἀποκατάστασις) of the cosmos. Strictly speaking, recapitulation seems rather to point at the destruction and subsumption of the cosmos within Christ, as there is no hint of a subsequent reconstitution of a physical cosmos; nevertheless, the equation of recapitulation and cosmic reconstitution is understandable. It shows how the author's notion of recapitulation can be understood as his expression for the return of the cosmos into God, and in this sense, the author of Ephesians, in both his protology and his eschatology, remains true to Paul's Stoic cosmology. The cosmos emerges from the divine Father (Eph 3:14–15) and is recapitulated back to him in Christ (Eph 1:10). However, in these terms of origin and destination, such a cosmic process is absent from the Pseudo-Pauline Letter to the Colossians, which expounds a very different, Platonic cosmology.

IV. The Shift to a Platonic Discourse in Pseudo-Paul's Letter to the Colossians

The difference between Paul's writings and Ephesians on the one hand and the Letter to the Colossians on the other is very clear when we note that the notion of the emergence of creation from God, which characterizes Pauline protology, is absent from Colossians. There is no "from God" (ἐκ τοῦ θεοῦ) phraseology in the Letter to the Colossians. Rather, the letter invites us to read the text in a Platonic context. As we have seen in the introduction, the notion of creation "from God" is also absent from Plato's *Timaeus*. When Plato uses the preposition "from" in this dialogue about creation, it is in the sense of creation "from disorder" (ἐκ τῆς ἀταξίας), the disorder of pre-existing matter that is arranged into order: when the creator "took over all that was visible, seeing that it was not in a state of rest but in a state of discordant and disorderly motion, he brought it *into* order *from* disorder" (εἰς τάξιν αὐτὸ ἤγαγεν ἐκ τῆς ἀταξίας, 30a). Furthermore, as we will see below, it is this Platonic notion of creation from disorderly matter that triggers the subsequent Christian critique of Plato from the second century onwards, because it implies that this disorderly matter is coeval with, and therefore an infringement upon (the omnipotence of) God.

Compared with Pauline-Stoic cosmology, not only is the notion of a creation "from God" absent from Colossians, but so too is the notion of the return of creation "into God" (εἰς τὸν θεόν). As such, the preposition "into" (εἰς) does occur in Colossians, in the author's statement that "all things have been created through him [the cosmic Christ] and *into / in regard to* him" (τὰ πάντα δι' αὐτοῦ καὶ εἰς αὐτὸν ἔκτισται, Col 1:16), but it seems more likely that the preposition εἰς bears a Platonic meaning here, as expressing a relation in the sense of "in regard to" (LSJ εἰς IV.1a) him rather than a movement "into" (LSJ εἰς I.1a) him; it indicates the paradigm *to which* God looked when creating the cosmos. This is the sense in which the preposition occurs in Plato's *Timaeus*, together with its equivalent πρὸς, indicating the perspective a creator ought to take on the paradigmatic model whilst creating his material, artistic object:

> But when the creator of any object (ὅτου μὲν οὖν ἂν ὁ δημιουργός), in forming its shape and quality, keeps his gaze fixed *upon* (πρός) that which is uniform (πρὸς τὸ κατὰ ταὐτὰ ἔχον βλέπων ἀεί), using a paradigm of this kind (τοιούτῳ τινὶ προσχρώμενος παραδείγματι), that object, executed in this way, must of necessity be beautiful; but whenever he directs his gaze *towards* (εἰς) that which has come into existence (οὗ δ' ἂν εἰς γεγονός) and uses a created model (γεννητῷ παραδείγματι προσχρώμενος), the object thus executed is not beautiful (Plato, *Tim.* 28a–b).

This is clearly not the Stoic εἰς, but the paradigmatic Platonic εἰς, which is *directed towards* the immaterial paradigm (παράδειγμα) "*to*" (πρός) which the creator looked when generating the cosmos (28a, c), so that the cosmos is in fact a copy (εἰκών) of that paradigm (29b) – to generate this, the creator looks to "that which is apprehensible by reason and thought" (29a), to what is ungenerated, to the eternal (29a).

I believe this paradigmatic sense that the Platonic εἰς and πρός carry is also the meaning of the statement in Colossians that "all things were created through him and *unto him / in regard to him*" (τὰ πάντα δι' αὐτοῦ καὶ εἰς αὐτὸν ἔκτισται, Col 1:16) – that is, with an eye to the divine paradigm. This creational statement about the cosmic Christ is followed by a statement about the incarnate Christ, when the author says that "in him [the incarnate Christ] all the fullness of God was pleased to dwell (ἐν αὐτῷ εὐδόκησεν πᾶν τὸ πλήρωμα κατοικῆσαι), and through him God was pleased to reconcile all things *to himself* (δι' αὐτοῦ ἀποκαταλλάξαι τὰ πάντα εἰς αὐτόν), whether on earth or in heaven, by making peace (εἰρηνοποιήσας) through the blood of his cross" (Col 1:19–20). But even here the preposition "to himself" (εἰς αὐτόν) does not acquire an eschatological Stoic meaning, because the cosmic appeasement has already been fully realized on the cross (cf. Col 2:9–15); this is more comparable with the cosmic pacification of the unruly cosmos by the Middle-Platonic gods.[40] This is all in marked contrast to Ephesians, where the cosmos emerges "from" God (3:14–15) and is involved in a process of gradual recapitulation (1:10), by which it will finally be brought back into him (4:15) at the end of time.

In Colossians, however, the present cosmos is entirely static and fully stabilized, as it is (1) an indirect image that, via the cosmic Christ, is a creational reflection of God; (2) entirely filled with God; (3) stable; (4) coherent because it has been firmly bound together; and (5) operating as part of a vertical, hierarchical order of paradigm and corresponding image, an order that encourages human beings to look upwards to the heavenly, paradigmatic reality. This language is thoroughly Platonic, as I will briefly demonstrate.

Firstly, the language of image is found at the end of Plato's *Timaeus*, where the cosmos is depicted as "a perceptible God made in the image of the Intelligible (εἰκὼν τοῦ νοητοῦ θεὸς αἰσθητός), most great and good and fair and perfect in its generation" (*Tim.* 92c). In Colossians, the same language is applied to the pre-incarnate, pre-existent cosmic Christ, in whom the entire cosmos is subsequently created: the cosmic Christ is "the image of the invisible God (εἰκὼν τοῦ θεοῦ τοῦ ἀοράτου), the first-born of all creation, for in him all things in heaven and on earth were created, things visible and invisible (πρωτότοκος πάσης κτίσεως, ὅτι ἐν αὐτῷ ἐκτίσθη τὰ πάντα ἐν τοῖς οὐρανοῖς καὶ ἐπὶ τῆς γῆς, τὰ ὁρατὰ καὶ τὰ ἀόρατα)" (Col 1:15–16). Hence the cosmic Christ, together with the cosmos that was created "in him," are the (increasingly) visible, tangible expressions of the invisible divine paradigm, exemplar, or ideas in heaven on which the image, the copy is modelled (cf. Plato, *Tim.* 28c–29b and *Republic* 592b; Aris-

[40] Cf. van Kooten 2003, 129–35.

totle, *Metaphysics* 991a21–991b3). As Plutarch summarizes Plato's views, "the intelligibles are patterns, that is ideas, of which the perceptibles are as images or reflections" (παραδείγματα καὶ ἰδέας τὰ νοητὰ τῶν αἰσθητῶν ὥσπερ εἰκόνων ἢ ἐμφάσεων, Plutarch, *Platonic Questions* 3,1001e). According to both Plato and Colossians, the cosmos is thus grounded in God's divine paradigmatic reality as a copy of that model.

Secondly, according to Plato's *Timaeus*, since it is the "perceptible God made in the image of the Intelligible," this cosmos is entirely complete and fulfilled: "this our Cosmos has received the living creatures both mortal and immortal and been thereby fulfilled (συμπληρωθεὶς ὅδε ὁ κόσμος οὕτω); it being itself a visible Living Creature embracing the visible creatures (ζῷον ὁρατὸν τὰ ὁρατὰ περιέχον), a perceptible God made in the image of the Intelligible" (Plato, *Tim.* 92c). The same sense of the fulfilment and completeness of the cosmos is found in Colossians, although again mediated through the cosmic Christ, as it is the cosmic Christ who is the head of all cosmological powers, in whom "the whole fullness of deity" takes the form of a cosmic body (Col 2:9–10).[41]

Thirdly, according to Colossians, the present cosmos not only fully reflects the divine fulness, but is also entirely stable, as "in him all things hold together" (τὰ πάντα ἐν αὐτῷ συνέστηκεν, 1:17):

> He is the image of the invisible God (ὅς ἐστιν εἰκὼν τοῦ θεοῦ τοῦ ἀοράτου), the first-born of all creation (πρωτότοκος πάσης κτίσεως); for in him all things in heaven and on earth were created, things visible and invisible (ὅτι ἐν αὐτῷ ἐκτίσθη τὰ πάντα ἐν τοῖς οὐρανοῖς καὶ ἐπὶ τῆς γῆς, τὰ ὁρατὰ καὶ τὰ ἀόρατα) [...], in him all things hold together (τὰ πάντα ἐν αὐτῷ συνέστηκεν) (Col 1:15–17).

The cosmos's coherence is thus due to the fact that it has been created in Christ, who, as the image of the invisible God, grounds creation in God himself. In addition to this strong Platonic imagery of copy and paradigm, there might even be a trace of Stoicism left in this reasoning, as Christ is not only seen as an image, but also as "the first-born of all creation" (πρωτότοκος πάσης κτίσεως, Col 1:15b), a notion that seems to suggest that the cosmic Christ and the ensuing creation are both born from God. It is the cosmic Christ who is begotten as God's "first-born" (from God),[42] "in whom" subsequently the rest of creation takes place as a birth (from God). But this Stoic notion of creation from God is understated here and remains merely implicit.

---

[41] Cf. van Kooten 2003, 23–27.

[42] This is indeed how Athanasius (*Defence of the Nicene Definition* [*De decretis Nicaenae synodi*] 26,6) understands Col 1:15b, stating (against the Arians): "And one may say to them: 'O reckless men, is he a work, who is "the first-born of all creation" (Col 1:15b), who is "born from the womb before the morning star" (Ps 109[110]:3 LXX), who said, as Wisdom, "Before all the hills He begets me" (Prov 8:25)?'" (πρὸς οὓς καὶ εἴποι ἄν τις· ὦ ῥιψοκίνδυνοι ἄνθρωποι, ποίημα ὁ πρωτότοκος πάσης κτίσεως, ὁ ἐκ γαστρὸς πρὸ ἑωσφόρου γεννηθείς, ὁ εἰπὼν ὡς σοφία· ‹πρὸ δὲ πάντων βουνῶν γεννᾷ με›).

Fourthly, the coherence and stability of the present cosmos is also described using the imagery of bonds which bind it together. In the *Timaeus*, Plato uses this imagery to state that the body of the cosmos has been securely bound together with bonds (*Tim.* 31b–32c); the cosmos became indissoluble except to God, who had bound this body together (συνδεῖν, 32b–c). The author of Colossians also employs this imagery; according to him, the divine fulness dwells in the cosmic Christ and in him takes on the form of a cosmic body (Col 2:9; cf. 1:15–17), which is bound together with bonds (σύνδεσμοι, 2:19).[43] In a passage in his *The E at Delphi*, which we have already discussed above, and which was a criticism of the Stoic identification of God with a cosmic process of emergence from and dissolution back into God, Plutarch argues as follows:

For, on the contrary, so far as he is in some way present in the world, by this his presence does he bind together its substance (τοὐναντίον γὰρ ὅ θεῖον ἀμωσγέπως ἐγγέγονε τῷ κόσμῳ, τοῦτο συνδεῖ τὴν οὐσίαν) and prevail over its corporeal weakness, which tends toward dissolution (καὶ κρατεῖ τῆς περὶ τὸ σωματικὸν ἀσθενείας ἐπὶ φθορὰν φερομένης) (Plutarch, *The E at Delphi* 393f).

The Colossian Christ is very much depicted in terms of such a Platonic understanding of God's stabilizing influence on the present cosmos; this view of Christ's triumph over the cosmos is modelled on the notion of the subjugation of cosmological forces and elements in (Middle-)Platonic philosophy.[44] In contrast to the Pauline-Stoic view, however, God is never involved in a cosmic process that extends from and returns into God: "never does any vagary or transformation take place near him" (ὡς οὐδέποτε γινομένης περὶ αὐτὸν ἐκστάσεως καὶ μεταβολῆς, Plutarch, *The E at Delphi* 393f–394a).

Finally, this view of a present, essentially stable cosmos is also expressed in the conviction that the cosmos is embedded in a vertical, hierarchical order, thus differentiating between "the [real] things above" (τὰ ἄνω), which one should contemplate (Col 3:1–2; Plato, *Phaedrus* 249d), and "the things below" (τὰ κάτω, Plato, *Phaedrus* 249d), "the things that are on earth" (τὰ ἐπὶ τῆς γῆς, Col 3:2). The present cosmos is thus not involved in an ongoing process that carries it back to its origins in God, but is stabilized in an enduring hierarchical relation, as that between copy and paradigm.

In these ways, Colossians is indeed very different from the Pauline-Stoic views of Paul himself and of the author of Ephesians. The author of Colossians clearly prefers a Platonic understanding of the cosmos over a Stoic one; he de-Stoicizes and Platonizes Paul's cosmology. Although we have dealt with Ephesians in direct succession to Paul's letters, prior to addressing Colossians, we should remember that Ephesians is probably a response to Colossians,[45] so

43 See van Kooten 2003, 30–53, esp. 39–40.
44 Cf. van Kooten 2003, 129–35.
45 See van Kooten 2003, 147–203.

that the author of Ephesians actually de-Platonizes, re-Stoicizes, and in that sense, re-Paulinizes the cosmological views found in Colossians by re-introducing a Stoic protology and eschatology. In his view, the cosmos has been created "from" the divine Father, and the entire current cosmic process is seen as Christ's recapitulation (ἀνακεφαλαίωσις) of the cosmos, which leads the cosmos back to God.

These cross-border oscillations between Stoicism and Platonism within the Pauline School are by no means extraordinary. There is indeed evidence for de-Stoicizing, Platonizing Stoics and de-Platonizing, Stoicizing Platonists, also in the areas of protological and eschatological views. Examples of the first category – of de-Stoicizing Stoics who did not believe in the eschatological conflagration and subsequent reconstitution of the cosmos – include two Stoic philosophers from the second century BCE: Boethus of Sidon, a pupil of Diogenes of Babylon who had begun to doubt the conflagration and suspended his views on this; and Panaetius of Rhodes, also a pupil of Diogenes of Babylon. According to Philo of Alexandria,

> Thus Boethus of Sidon and Panaetius, powerful supporters of the Stoic doctrines, did under divine inspiration abandon the conflagrations and regenerations (τὰς ἐκπυρώσεις καὶ παλιγγενεσίας καταλιπόντες) and deserted to the more religious doctrine that the whole world was indestructible (πρὸς ὁσιώτερον δόγμα τὸ τῆς ἀφθαρσίας τοῦ κόσμου παντὸς ηὐτομόλησαν). It is said too that Diogenes in his youth subscribed to the doctrine of the conflagration but in later years felt doubts and suspended judgement (Philo of Alexandria, *On the Eternity of the World* 76–77 = LS 46P).

Although Panaetius became head of the Stoa after the death of Antipater of Tarsus, he was apparently able to express non-orthodox views on issues such as the conflagration and reconstitution of the cosmos. The positions of Boethus and Panaetius within Stoicism are comparable to the stance that the author of Colossians took within the Pauline School as he de-eschatologized and Platonized its cosmology.

Examples of the second category – of de-Platonizing, Stoicizing Platonists and Peripatetics – include Pseudo-Aristotle, who, contrary to his school, adopted the Stoic view that the cosmos is "from God" (ἐκ θεοῦ) in his *On the Cosmos*. In a discussion "about the cause that holds the cosmos together" (περὶ τῆς τῶν ὅλων συνεκτικῆς αἰτίας), he writes:

> It is indeed an ancient idea, traditional among all mankind, that *all things are from God* (ὡς ἐκ θεοῦ πάντα) and are constituted by God (καὶ διὰ θεὸν συνέστηκεν), and nothing is self-sufficient if deprived of his preserving influence. So some of the ancients were led to say that all the things of this world are full of gods (πάντα ταῦτά ἐστι θεῶν πλέα) (Pseudo-Aristotle, *On the Cosmos* 397b9–18).

Similarly against the tenets of their school, the Platonist philosophers Atticus and Severus, both of whom lived in the second century CE, offered a Stoicizing interpretation of a particular passage from Plato. According to Atticus, the quotation of the ancient (probably Orphic) statement in Plato's *Laws* that "that God who […] holds the beginning, the end, and the centre of all things that exist (ὁ μὲν δὴ θεός […] ἀρχήν τε καὶ τελευτὴν καὶ μέσα τῶν ὄντων ἁπάντων ἔχων), completes his circuit by nature's ordinance in straight, unswerving course" (Plato, *Laws* 715e–716a) needs to be understood in the following, Stoicizing way, with regard to its protology:

> Plato sees all things in relation to God and as derived *from God* (μὲν Πλάτων εἰς θεὸν καὶ ἐκ θεοῦ πάντα ἀνάπτει), for he says that God "holds the beginning and middle and end of all things (Φησὶ γὰρ αὐτὸν ἀρχήν τε καὶ μέσα καὶ τελευτὴν τῶν ὄντων ἔχοντα), and accomplishes his purpose directly as he revolves" [*Laws* 715e–716a] (Atticus, fr. 5,3–10, ed. J. Baudry 1931; fr. 3, ed. É. des Places 1977 = Eusebius, *Preparation for the Gospel* 15,5,2, 7–9).[46]

This passage clearly demonstrates that a Stoicizing interpretation of Plato is possible, based on the Orphic statement about God as the beginning, middle, and end of all things in Plato's *Laws*.

Similarly, Severus refers to the notion of cosmic cycles in the tale of the Eleatic Stranger in Plato's *Statesman* (272b–274e), as Proclus indicates in his commentary on Plato's *Timaeus*:

> Severus […] says that the cosmos *simpliciter* is sempiternal, but that this present cosmos, moving in the way that it is, was generated. For there are two cycles, as the Eleatic Stranger showed: the one which the universe presently follows, and its opposite. So the cosmos is generated and had a beginning insofar as it is revolving in this cycle; *simpliciter*, though, it is not generated (Severus, fr. 6t, ed. A. Gioè 2002 = Proclus, *On the Timaeus* 1,289,6–1; transl. Boys-Stones 2018, 201, 7G).

These examples clearly indicate that there was much cross-border traffic between the philosophical schools, also with regard to the issues of protology and eschatology. Stoics such as Boethus of Sidon and Panaetius of Rhodes became Platonic in abandoning their eschatological views, whereas a Peripatetic philosopher such as Pseudo-Aristotle and Platonic philosophers such as Atticus and Severus adopted Stoic views on the beginning (and end) of the cosmos, in two cases with the emphatic assertion that all things are "from God." The Stoicizing and Platonizing tendencies within the Pauline School are hence in full accord with the "lived philosophy" of the contemporary schools.

Regardless of whether the Pauline School is more Stoically or Platonically coloured, both forms of Paulinism assume a close, ontological relation between creator and creation. Either because the cosmos has emerged from God or because it is a copy of the invisible paradigm, there is an ontological continuity between creator and cosmos. However, this changed as soon as some Christians began to criticize one of the specifics of Platonic cosmology: its notion of crea-

---

46 Transl. Boys-Stones 2018, 334, text 11A.

tion from disorderly matter. As we shall see, this anti-Platonic response also eclipsed the strongly Stoic nature of Paul's cosmology.

V. The Rise of the "Creation from Nothing" Theorem

The question we need to address at this point is: Why didn't Paul's Stoic concept of creation from God remain influential in post-Pauline Christianity, despite his own frequent and consistent use of this theorem? It seems that the alternative view of creation from nothing became successful for two reasons. Firstly, it seems to have been particularly helpful in explaining the resurrection: if God was able to create the cosmos from nothing, then he is certainly also able to resurrect the dead. Secondly, the *ex nihilo* theorem also effectively responded to Christian concerns about the inadequacy of the Platonic concept of creation from pre-existent, disorderly matter or "from disorder" (ἐκ τῆς ἀταξίας, Plato, *Tim.* 30a), as the apparently independent existence of matter seemed to suggest that matter was almost a god alongside God, coeval with him and independent from him, thus infringing on God's omnipotence. For these two reasons, the "nihilistic" theorem of creation "from nothing" rose to dominance, defeating the Platonic model of creation "from matter" and eclipsing the Stoic model of creation "from God" himself. I will elaborate on this in some detail, distinguishing seven different phases or aspects of this prolonged debate, in the course of which the Stoic concept of creation from God became increasingly marginalized and was finally almost entirely eclipsed.

1. The Explanatory Force of the "Creation from Nothing" Theorem for Understanding the Resurrection

In Second Maccabees, part of the literature that narrates the martyrdom of Jews during the Maccabean revolt against the Hellenization of Antiochus IV Epiphanes in 168–67 BCE, the "creation from nothing" theorem is introduced to instil hope via the possibility of resurrection. This is evident in the exhortation which the mother of the Jewish martyrs gives to her youngest son after his brothers have already been martyred:

> I beg you, my child, to look at the heaven and the earth and see everything that is in them, and recognize that God did *not* make them *from things that are* (οὐκ ἐξ ὄντων ἐποίησεν αὐτὰ ὁ θεός). And in the same way the human race came into being. Do not fear this butcher, but prove worthy of your brothers. Accept death, so that in God's mercy I may get you back again along with your brothers (2 Macc 7:28–29).

Clearly the recognition that God did "not" make the cosmos "from things that are" (οὐκ ἐξ ὄντων) implies a view on creation from nothing that grounds the mother's hope in resurrection. Precisely this argument occurs frequently in

Christian writings from the late second century CE onwards and throughout the third and fourth centuries, in treatises on the resurrection, in exhortations of Christian martyrs, and in other writings. It occurs in the writings of Christian authors such as Tertullian, Minucius Felix, Cyprian, Methodius, Macarius Magnes, and the author of *The Apostolic Constitutions*.[47] Tertullian, for instance, in his *On the Resurrection of the Flesh*, puts it concisely: "if God produced all things whatever *from nothing*, He will be able to draw forth *from nothing* even the flesh which had fallen into nothing" (*On the Resurrection of the Flesh* 11). Cyprian, in his *Exhortation to Martyrdom*, actually quotes the passage from 2 Macc 7:28–29 to encourage Christian martyrs via the hope of resurrection.[48] Based on many *ex nihilo* passages in Christian literature, it becomes clear that the *ex nihilo* view is grounded in a strongly voluntaristic picture of God. Tertullian, for example, in his *Apology*, states that the dead "come into being again from nothing, *at the will of* the same creator whose will created you from nothing at the first" (Tertullian, *Apology* 48).

2. Early Attestations of the "Creation from Nothing" Theorem beyond Discussions of Resurrection

Whilst many early Christians such as Tertullian, Minucius Felix, and Cyprian indeed fall into line with the Hellenistic-Jewish author of 2 Maccabees in applying the notion of creation from nothing to strengthen the expectation of resurrection, other Christians in the mid-second century CE use this notion to ground their views on (a) salvation, (b) divine judgement, or (c) more speculative issues.

Pseudo-Clement, the author of the *Second Letter of Clement to the Corinthians*, uses the creation from nothing theorem to elucidate the salvation of human beings by intimating a parallel between their creation and their salvation: "we had not the slightest hope of being saved, unless it came through him. For he called us while we did not exist (ἐκάλεσεν γὰρ ἡμᾶς οὐκ ὄντας), and he wished us to come into being *from what does not exist* (καὶ ἠθέλησεν ἐκ μὴ ὄντος εἶναι ἡμᾶς)" (*2 Clem.* 1:7–8). At face value, this seems rather similar to what Paul says when he uses the same language of "calling" in Romans, writing of "God" as the one "who gives life to the dead and calls into existence the things that do not exist" (θεοῦ τοῦ ζῳοποιοῦντος τοὺς νεκροὺς καὶ καλοῦντος τὰ μὴ ὄντα ὡς ὄντα, Rom 4:17). Yet the essential, telling difference here is that Paul does not use the phrase "*from* what does not exist" (ἐκ μὴ ὄντος); even the "into" (in "into exist-

[47] Apart from the passages from Tertullian and Cyprian (still to be mentioned), see also Tertullian, *Apology* 48; Tertullian, *Five Books against Marcion* 5,19; Tertullian, *Against Hermogenes* 34; Minucius Felix, *The Octavius* 34; Methodius, *Discourse on the Resurrection* 1,14; Macarius Magnes, *Apocriticus* 30; and *The Apostolic Constitutions* 5,1.

[48] See Cyprian, *Exhortation to Martyrdom, Addressed to Fortunatus* 11.

ence") is an addition in the NRSV translation, as the text does not say that "God [...] calls *into* existence the things that do not exist," but literally that he "calls the things that are non-existing (τὰ μὴ ὄντα) *as if*, *as*, *in the belief that* (ὡς; LSJ C.III.1–2) they are existing" (καλοῦντος τὰ μὴ ὄντα ὡς ὄντα) – that is, "as if already existing." Paul mentions two distinct categories here, "the things that are" and "the things that are not," and inverts their relative value, without saying anything about *how* they come about, as that question is answered in his frequently expressed view that all things emerge *from* God (Rom 11:36; 1 Cor 8:6; 11:12; cf. Eph 3:14–15). The language of *calling* that Paul and Pseudo-Clement employ here must derive from the vocative language used in the creation account in Genesis 1, in which God is continuously calling (see Gen 1:5, 8, 10 LXX). We see this also in Philo's use of this vocative language of calling in his creation account. According to Philo, God "called the non-existent into being (τὰ γὰρ μὴ ὄντα ἐκάλεσεν εἰς τὸ εἶναι) and produced order from disorder (τάξιν ἐξ ἀταξίας [...] ἐργασάμενος)" (Philo, *On the Special Laws* 4,187). He inadvertently uses the phraseology of calling creation "into being," but like Paul, and in contrast to Pseudo-Clement, he does not say that creation was accomplished "from what does not exist" (ἐκ μὴ ὄντος). This is because he takes the Platonic view that creation was accomplished "from disorder" (ἐξ ἀταξίας, Plato, *Tim.* 30a). I suggest that where Philo is Platonic, Paul is Stoic; Philo, Paul, and Pseudo-Clement all use the preposition "from" (ἐκ), but in decisively different senses: in a Platonic sense of "from disorder" (ἐξ ἀταξίας, as in Philo); in the Stoic sense of "from God" (ἐκ τοῦ θεοῦ, as in Paul); or in the "nihilistic" sense of "from what does not exist" (ἐκ μὴ ὄντος, as in Pseudo-Clement). Despite the superficial similarities between Pseudo-Clement and Paul, their views are diametrically opposed.

This difference between Pseudo-Clement and Rom 4:17 is further confirmed if we take another Pauline passage into account. In 1 Corinthians, instead of the vocative-creational language of "calling the things that do not exist as if they (already) exist," Paul uses the *elective* language of "choosing the things that are not":

> But *God chose* (ἐξελέξατο ὁ θεός) what is foolish in the world to shame the wise; *God chose* (ἐξελέξατο ὁ θεός) what is weak in the world to shame the strong; *God chose* (ἐξελέξατο ὁ θεός) the uncreated [i.e., in a metaphorical sense, the ignoble] things of the cosmos (τὰ ἀγενῆ τοῦ κόσμου) and the things that are set at naught (τὰ ἐξουθενημένα), *the things that are not* (τὰ μὴ ὄντα), *to reduce to nothing the things that are* (ἵνα τὰ ὄντα καταργήσῃ), so that no one might boast in the presence of God, *from whom you are* (ἐξ αὐτοῦ δὲ ὑμεῖς ἐστε) in Christ Jesus, who became for us wisdom from God, and righteousness and sanctification and redemption (1 Cor 1:27–30).

Here also, it is neither stated nor implied that "the things that are" (τὰ ὄντα) have been created *from nothing*. Rather, in full compliance with what we have seen extensively above, the only "from" Paul knows of is the "from God," as he refers to "the god, *from whom* you are" (τοῦ θεοῦ, ἐξ αὐτοῦ δὲ ὑμεῖς ἐστε, 1:29–30).

Even if the focus is soteriological here, the parallelism with subsequent cosmological statements in the same letter – that "for us there is one God, the Father, *from whom* are all things" (ἡμῖν εἷς θεὸς ὁ πατήρ, ἐξ οὗ τὰ πάντα, 8:6), and that "all things are *from God*" (τὰ δὲ πάντα ἐκ τοῦ θεοῦ, 11:12) – is noteworthy. Clearly, the soteriological view that when one is saved, one is (metaphorically speaking) "a new creation" (2 Cor 5:17; cf. Gal 6:15) automatically brings with it the cosmological notion of being created "from" God. Paul thus remains entirely consistent, and even when he talks about "the things that are" (τὰ ὄντα) and "the things that are not" (τὰ μὴ ὄντα), he never even suggests that the former have been created from the latter.

Of course, in Greek, "the things that are" (τὰ ὄντα) and "the things that are not" (τὰ μὴ ὄντα) are simply ways of indicating what is and what is not, regardless of their relation. Hence, in a non-cosmological context, these phrases can even simply mean "facts" (τὰ ὄντα) and "fictions" (τὰ μὴ ὄντα). Xenophon, for instance, states that a certain Democrates of Temnus "enjoyed the reputation of having made accurate reports in many previous cases of the same sort, describing what were *facts as facts* and what were *fictions as fictions*" (τὰ ὄντα τε ὡς ὄντα καὶ τὰ μὴ ὄντα ὡς οὐκ ὄντα, Xenophon, *Anabasis* 4,4,15–16). In a philosophical sense, the antithesis occurs in a quotation from the sophist Protagoras: "Of all things the measure is man: of those that are, that they are; and of those that are not, that they are not" (πάντων χρημάτων μέτρον ἐστὶν ἄνθρωπος, τῶν μὲν ὄντων ὡς ἔστιν, τῶν δὲ οὐκ ὄντων ὡς οὐκ ἔστιν, LCL Early Greek Philosophy 8: Protagoras, *Testimonia*, part 2, doctrine D9 = Sextus Empiricus, *Against the Logicians* [*Adversus mathematicos*] 7,60–61).[49] Thus Paul's use of the contrastive pair "the things that are" (τὰ ὄντα) and "the things that are not" (τὰ μὴ ὄντα) says nothing about their interrelation and is no evidence that he believed in a creation from nothing. Rather, it is Pseudo-Clement who derives human existence from creation from nothing, and he does so out of soteriological interest: "we had not the slightest hope of being saved, unless it came through him. For he called us while we did not exist (ἐκάλεσεν γὰρ ἡμᾶς οὐκ ὄντας), and he wished us to come into being *from what does not exist* (καὶ ἠθέλησεν ἐκ μὴ ὄντος εἶναι ἡμᾶς)" (*2 Clem.* 1:7–8).

In a substantially different manner, Pseudo-Clement's contemporary, the author of *The Shepherd of Hermas*, applies the notion of creation from nothing out of his interest in the divine judgement, as becomes evident in two passages. In the first, the author describes the following complaint of one human being against another, which is based on the principle that God sees everything because he has created all things (from nothing): "God, who dwells in the heavens,

---

[49] Cf. also LCL Early Greek Philosophy 8: Protagoras, *Testimonia*, part 2, doctrine D38 = Plato, *Theaetetus* 166d: "each of us is the measure of the things that are and of those that are not" (μέτρον γὰρ ἕκαστον ἡμῶν εἶναι τῶν τε ὄντων καὶ μή).

and made from that which does not exist the things that exist (ὁ θεὸς ὁ ἐν τοῖς οὐρανοῖς κατοικῶν καὶ κτίσας ἐκ τοῦ μὴ ὄντος τὰ ὄντα) [...] is angry with you for having sinned against me" (*The Shepherd of Hermas* 1:6). A similar view is then repeated in the second passage, which consists of a moral exhortation based on the same principle: "believe that there is one God who created and finished all things (εἷς ἐστιν ὁ θεός, ὁ τὰ πάντα κτίσας καὶ καταρτίσας), and made all things from that which does not exist (καὶ ποιήσας ἐκ τοῦ μὴ ὄντος εἰς τὸ εἶναι τὰ πάντα). He alone is able to contain the whole, but himself cannot be contained. Have faith therefore in him, and fear him; and fearing him, exercise self-control" (*The Shepherd of Hermas* 26:1).

Yet another second-century application of the creation from nothing theorem beyond the topic of the resurrection is found in the works of Basilides of Alexandria, who lived during the reigns of the emperors Hadrian and Antoninus Pius (117–161 CE). In Gerhard May's well-known, now classic monograph on creation from nothing, Basilides is depicted as the first Christian to use the notion in a fully developed, technical sense, and May makes much of the fact that he is a Christian Gnostic.[50] However, as my developmental sketch shows, the accuracy and relevance of this seems quite questionable, as we have seen that – ever since 2 Maccabees – the notion is consistently applied to explain the resurrection, and the difference between such a use and a more developed notion (though May strongly emphasizes this and underpins his argument with a stark antithesis between "biblical" and "philosophical" domains) seems rather fluid. Moreover, Basilides's application of the notion of "creation from nothing" is very idiosyncratic. He does say that God created "from things that are not" (ἐξ οὐκ ὄντων), but he expresses this view in conjunction with his apophatic understanding of God, whom he understands as a "non-existent God" (οὐκ ὢν θεός, Basilides *apud* Pseudo-Hippolytus, *Refutation of All Heresies* 7,21,4). In this he follows Plato's view that "the Good is not being (οὐκ οὐσίας ὄντος τοῦ ἀγαθοῦ), but reaches even farther beyond being (ἐπέκεινα τῆς οὐσίας) in rank and power" (Plato, *Republic* 509b) – a view that subsequently resonates throughout the works of early Christian authors, such as Justin Martyr, Origen, and Eusebius, as well as Neoplatonists, such as Plotinus, Iamblichus, and Porphyry.[51] Importantly, Basilides connects his reflections on God as "non-existing," in the sense of being "beyond being," with his explorations of creation as created from non-being:

So when there was nothing [...] (Ἐπεὶ οὐδέν <ἦν>), then the non-existent God (whom Aristotle calls "thinking of thinking," and what these people call "Non-existent") want-

---

[50] May 1994, 62–84.

[51] See Justin Martyr, *Dialogue with Trypho* 4,1; Origen, *Against Celsus* 6,64; Eusebius, *Preparation for the Gospel* 11,17,10; 11,21,5–7; and *Proof of the Gospel* 5,1,25; as well as the Neoplatonists (Plotinus, *Enneads* 1,7,1; 1,8,6; 5,1,8; 5,4,2; 5,6,6; 6,7,40; 6,8,16; 6,8,19; 6,9,11; Iamblichus, *De mysteriis* 1,5; Porphyry, fr. 12,22–29 [ed. P. Hadot]). For a discussion of Plato's "beyond being," see Krämer 2014, 122–48.

ed to make the world [...] (<ὁ> οὐκ ὢν θεός – ὃν Ἀριστοτέλης καλεῖ νόησιν νοήσεως, οὗτοι δὲ οὐκ ὄντα [...] κόσμον ἠθέλησε ποιῆσαι). [...] (4) In this way, then, the non-existent God made the non-existent cosmos from things that are not (Οὕτως <ὁ> οὐκ ὢν θεὸς ἐποίησε κόσ(μ)ον οὐκ ὄν<τα> ἐξ οὐκ ὄντων) (Basilides *apud* Pseudo-Hippolytus, *Refutation of All Heresies* 7,21,1, 7,21,4; text and transl. Litwa 2016, with minor changes).

Due to this conjunction between the notions of the non-existent God and his creation from nothing, the latter notion seems to take on quite a different meaning from the conventional one, as we can see in his further reflections. On the one hand, in an anti-Platonic fashion and in accordance with conventional interpretations of the notion of creation from nothing, Basilides denies that God made the cosmos from pre-existing matter (7,22,2) and instead develops the view that creation was created from nothing, as is clear in the instance of the light, which came into being "from nothing" (ἐξ οὐδενός) by God's speech (7,22,3), just as "the cosmic sperm," from which the rest of the cosmos develops, also "came to be from what does not exist" (Γέγονε [...] ἐξ οὐκ ὄντος τὸ σπέρμα τοῦ κόσμου, 7,22,4). On the other hand, however, Basilides simultaneously transforms his argument by stating that God the creator is himself also non-existent: "The one who spoke [...] did *not* exist" (ὁ δὲ λέγων [...] οὐκ ἦν, 7,22,3). Moreover, he states that what was contained in, and subsequently arose in three eruptions from the cosmic sperm, namely a "triple Sonship," is "in every respect *consubstantial with the non-existent God* and born from things that are not" (κατὰ πάντα τῷ οὐκ ὄντι θε<ῷ> ὁμοούσιος, γεν<ν>ητὴ ἐξ οὐκ ὄντων, 7,22,7).

Basilides's interpretation of the notion of creation from nothing thus takes on a very specific meaning, one coloured by his understanding of God as non-existent, which then challenges the real meaning of his creation from nothing. What does creation from nothing really mean if God himself is also non-existent? This might even be read as creation from God himself, from God's own non-existence. Incidentally, this would be consistent with Basilides's use of the Stoic notion of the cosmic sperm, which is equivalent to God's Logos or Pneuma (cf. *SVF* 2,1027 = LS 46A and *SVF* 1,98 = LS 46G, discussed above), and (the content of) which, according to Basilides, is indeed "consubstantial (ὁμοούσιος) with the non-existent God." In that case, Basilides's critique of the emanationist terminology of "projection" (προβολή) and the equally emanationist imagery of God emanating the cosmos from himself as a spider does its threads (7,22,2) would make his own view rather incoherent. The basically Stoic inclinations of Basilides's thought, however, seem to be confirmed by the fact that the third sonship, which is contained in the cosmic sperm, ends in a Stoic reconstitution (*apokatástasis*) and return to God (7,25,1; 7,26,2; 7,27,4–5 and 10–11). Thus the irony is that, although Basilides uses the notion of a creation from nothing, his view of God as a "non-existent God" actually propagates a form of creation from God himself.

3. Hermogenes's Theorization of All Three Major Models (Stoic, "Nihilistic," and Platonic)

A full Christian comparison between and theorization of all three major models (the Platonic notion of creation from disorder, the Stoic notion of creation from God, and the "Nihilistic" notion of creation from nothing) was offered by Hermogenes around the last quarter of the second century CE, when this Syrian painter from Antioch was resident and worked in Carthage (ca.175–205 CE). During this time, Hermogenes began to attract Tertullian's criticism because, in contrast to Tertullian, he opted for the first, Platonic theorem. Interestingly, Hermogenes expressed his choice of the Platonic model in a concomitant critique of the Stoic and Nihilistic alternatives. Indeed, as Tertullian indicates in his *Against Hermogenes*, Hermogenes himself opened his discussion of creation by

> laying down the premise, that the Lord made all things either a) from himself [i. e., the Stoic model], or b) from nothing [i. e., the Nihilistic position], or c) from something [i. e., the Platonic position]; in order that, after he has shown that it was impossible for him to have made them either from himself [i. e., the Stoic view] or from nothing [i. e., the Nihilistic view], he might thence affirm the residuary proposition that He made them from something, and therefore that that something was matter [i. e., the Platonic view] (Hermogenes *apud* Tertullian, *Against Hermogenes* 2).

The arguments Hermogenes brings forward against the Stoic view that the cosmos was created from God are clearly Platonic in style: "He could not have made all things, he says, from himself; because whatever things God made from himself would have been parts of himself; but he is not dissoluble into parts, because, being God, he is indivisible, and unchangeable, and always the same" (Hermogenes *apud* Tertullian, *Against Hermogenes* 2).

The criticism of God's changeability is clearly a Platonic disapproval of a dynamic Stoic understanding of God, as we have already seen above in our discussion of Plutarch's critique of Stoicism and of Paul's anonymous pagan critic in Macarius Magnes. Whereas Hermogenes's argument against the Stoics is Platonic in nature, his subsequent criticism of the Nihilistic notion of creation from nothing is theodicean. In Hermogenes's view, creation from nothing would make God responsible for the evil that we find in created things; hence the blame for this must be redirected, away from God to something else – to the disorderly matter from which God created creation (Hermogenes *apud* Tertullian, *Against Hermogenes* 2). In Hermogenes's theodicy, evil is an attribute of pre-existing matter, not of the creator. As Tertullian puts it, Christians such as Hermogenes "set up matter with the creator, in order that they may derive evil from matter, not from the creator" (Tertullian, *Against Hermogenes* 10). In this way, Hermogenes arrives at his Platonic position as an alternative to the Stoic and Nihilistic views that he criticizes. What is rather interesting, as we will shortly confirm, is that Tertullian, in his critique of Hermogenes's Platonic position, is actually free-riding on the criticism that Hermogenes already levelled against the Stoic position. According to Tertullian, Hermogenes has already shown that the Stoic position is not viable: "according to the position of Hermogenes, nothing could have been produced from God" (Tertullian, *Against Hermogenes* 15). This is a pattern that we shall see elsewhere: the Stoic theorem of creation from God is simply eclipsed by the attack that the Nihilistic position launches against the Platonic concept of creation from disorderly matter. This critique of the Platonic position is undertaken shortly after 180 CE by Theophilus of Antioch in his *To Autolycus*, and then again around the turn of the century (from ca. 203 CE) by Tertullian in his *Against Hermogenes*, as we will now see in more detail.

4. The Critique of the Platonic Model

Although Christian Platonists such as Hermogenes accuse Christian promulgators of the creation from nothing theorem of infringing on God's *goodness* by making God responsible for evil, the Christian critics of the Platonic creation from pre-existing matter theorem charge the Platonists with undermining God's *omnipotence*. According to these critics, the main problem with the Platonic concept of creation from pre-existing, disorderly matter is the coevality of matter with God, and hence its competition with and infringement on God's supremacy and omnipotence. Theophilus of Antioch is aware of the fact that it is the Platonists who assert that matter is coeval with God: "But Plato and those of his school acknowledge indeed that God is uncreated, and the Father and Maker of all things; but then they maintain that matter as well as God is uncreated, and aver that it is coeval with God" (*To Autolycus* 2,4). But according to Theophilus, "God made all things from nothing; for nothing was coeval with God," and as he explicitly states: "matter, from which God made and fashioned the world, was in some manner created, being produced by God" (Theophilus of Antioch, *To Autolycus* 2,10).

This anti-Platonic criticism is continued in Tertullian's *Against Hermogenes*. Whereas Theophilus raises objections against the coevality of matter with God, Tertullian stresses the limitations this would place on God's omnipotence. Against Hermogenes's Platonic position, which we have outlined above, Tertullian argues that if God made all things from pre-existing matter, God would thereby be subject to matter, which would be an infringement upon his power; however, he is powerful enough to have created all things from nothing (Tertullian, *Against Hermogenes* 8). According to Tertullian, "even if matter had previously existed [i. e., temporarily, prior to the actual creation of the cosmos], we must have believed that it had been really made by God, since we maintained (no less) when we held the rule of faith to be, that nothing except God was uncreated" (*Against Hermogenes* 33). Tertullian expresses a similar criticism of the Platonic position in his *On the Resurrection of the Flesh*, in which he criticizes fellow Christians who do not argue from God's omnipotence, but "will rather have it, after the philosophers, that the cosmos was in the beginning made by God from underlying matter" (*On the Resurrection of the Flesh* 11). In his *Against Marcion*, he also accuses Marcion of entertaining such a view: "He [Marcion] too has fabricated a world from some underlying material which is unbegotten, and unmade, and contemporaneous with God" (Tertullian, *Five Books against Marcion* 1,15).

Whereas Theophilus was very aware that the position he criticized was the Platonic concept of creation from matter, Tertullian sometimes blends his critique of the Platonic view with a critique of the Stoics. According to Tertullian, Hermogenes was equally inspired by Platonism and Stoicism. Depicting them according to a metaphor of the distinctive buildings they used in Athens, the Platonic "Academy" and the Stoic "Porch," Tertullian says the following:

> he [Hermogenes] takes from Him everything which is God, since he will not have it that He made all things of nothing. For, turning away from Christians to the philosophers, from the Church to the Academy and the Porch, he learned there from the Stoics how to place matter (on the same level) with the Lord, just as if it too had existed ever both unborn and unmade, having no beginning at all nor end, from which, according to him, the Lord afterwards created all things (Tertullian, *Against Hermogenes* 1).[52]

At some level this is correct, as the Stoics indeed argue that matter is the passive principle upon which God, the active principle, acts,[53] and that the elements evolve out of this matter as a result of God's actions.[54] But in contrast to the Platonists, the Stoics held that matter was not coeval with God, but had arisen from God himself: God is "the manufacturer of the world-order (διακόσμησις), at set periods of time consuming all substance into himself (εἰς ἑαυτόν) and reproducing it again *from himself* (ἐξ ἑαυτοῦ)" (Diogenes Laertius, *Lives of Eminent Philosophers* 7,137 = *SVF* 2,526 = LS 44F; transl. LS). In this sense, Tertullian's critique of the Stoics is incorrect and highly tendentious.

Alongside Theophilus and Tertullian, there is another early critique of non-nihilistic views on creation contained in Pseudo-Hippolytus's *Refutation of All Heresies*, which is dated to the early third century CE, not long after 222 CE.[55] In book 10 of his *Refutation*, Pseudo-Hippolytus sketches the cosmologi-

---

[52] With regard to Marcion, cf. Tertullian, *Against Marcion* 5,19: "Moreover, from the porch of the Stoics he [Marcion] brings out matter, and places it on a par with the divine creator."

[53] See Diogenes Laertius, *Lives of Eminent Philosophers* 7,134 = *SVF* 2,300; 2,299 = LS 44B, as discussed above.

[54] See further Sextus Empiricus, *Against the Professors* 9,75–76 = *SVF* 2,311 = LS 44C; Diogenes Laertius, *Lives of Eminent Philosophers* 7,135–36 = *SVF* 1,102 = LS 46B; and Diogenes Laertius, *Lives of Eminent Philosophers* 7,142 = *SVF* 1,102 = LS 46C.

[55] See Litwa 2016, xl–xli.

cal views of the Greek philosophers (10,6,2–10,8,1) – including those of the Platonists (10,7,7), but also those of the Stoics (10,6,4) and many other philosophical positions – and of the leading Christian heresies (10,9,1–10,29,3), including Hermogenes (10,28,1). Subsequently, Pseudo-Hippolytus sets forth his own notion of creation from nothing, stating that the elements of the cosmos have been made "from things that are not" (ἐξ οὐκ ὄντων, 10,33,4) and that "the cosmos has been made from nothing (ὁ δὲ κόσμος ἐξ οὐδενός), and so it is not God. It is susceptible to dissolution when the creator wills (οὗτος ἐπιδέχεται καὶ λύσιν, ὅτε βούλεται ὁ κτίσας)" (10,33,8; cf. Plato, *Tim.* 41a–b). Although he takes up Plato's view of the (theoretical) dissolvability of the cosmos, he clearly disagrees with Plato's view of the pre-existence (and disorderly nature) of matter. Yet in this book, Pseudo-Hippolytus simply juxtaposes his own idea of creation from nothing with the alternative views and does not engage in an argument against Plato, the Stoics, or any other position.

What is most striking is that when most early Christian authors develop an argument against non-nihilistic positions, they mainly address the Platonic concept of creation from matter, not the Stoic position. This is particularly clear in the case of Tertullian, who simply free-rides on the criticism that Hermogenes, as a Platonist Christian, had already levelled against the Stoic position. It seems to be chiefly the Platonic position that triggers a Nihilistic response, because it is especially this position – in contrast to the Stoic position – that is seen as an undue limitation of God's omnipotence, due to its assumption of the coevality of matter with God. As a result of this primary front between the Nihilistic position and the Platonic concept of creation, the Stoic theorem of creation from God is simply eclipsed, so that the triumph of the Nihilistic position is, among other things, certainly also due to its efficiency in responding to the Platonic view. The Nihilistic theorem of creation from nothing thus triumphs over the Platonic concept of creation, but then becomes even more radical in its nihilism when, according to the Christian Arius, it is not only creation that has been created from nothing, but the divine Son as well.

5. The Cosmologically and Christologically "Nihilistic" Position of Arius: Widening the Ontological Gap Even Further

According to Arius, not only creation, but also the divine Son was created from nothing, "from the things that are not."[56] As he says in a letter to Eusebius of Nicomedia (ca. 318 CE) with regard to the Son:

Before he was begotten, or created, or defined, or founded (καὶ πρὶν γεννηθῇ ἤτοι κτισθῇ ἢ ὁρισθῇ ἢ θεμελιωθῇ; cf. Prov 8:22–25), he did not exist (οὐκ ἦν). For he was not unbegotten. But we are persecuted because we have said the Son has a beginning but God has no beginning. We are persecuted because of that *and for saying he came from things that are*

[56] One of the few studies on this statement by Arius is Stead 1998, 671–84.

not (ἐξ οὐκ ὄντων ἐστίν). But we said this since he is not a portion of God nor of anything in existence (οὐδὲ μέρος θεοῦ ἐστιν οὐδὲ ἐξ ὑποκειμένου τινός) (Theodoret, *Church History* 1,5,5, ed. L. Parmentier and F. Scheidweiler, p. 27,1–5 = H.-G. Opitz, *Urkunden*, Urk. no. 1/Dok. no. 15: Arius to Eusebius of Nicomedia [ca. 318 CE]; transl. FCC).[57]

Arius thus believes in the creation of the cosmos by God from nothing, but here he also applies this notion of creation to the relation between God and the divine Son, and as a result, the ontological gap between creator and creation is fully maximized, as even the Son is on the side of creation, which has been created from nothing. On the basis of the christological prooftext in Prov 8:22–25 – in which "begotten," "created," and "founded" are seen as equivalents, the exegesis of which sparked the Arian controversy[58] – Arius believes that when the Son is called "begotten," that means he is created, and created means to be created *from things that are not* (ἐξ οὐκ ὄντων). This is not to say that Arius believes that there is no difference between the Son and the rest of creation, as he is indeed of the opinion that, although the (begotten) Son is not coeval with the (unbegotten) divine Father, he came into being *before* (the rest of) creation, and that creation was even created by God through him.

Arius and his followers explained this to Alexander of Alexandria, the bishop who had excommunicated him, as follows:

We acknowledge One God, alone unbegotten [...], who begat an only-begotten Son *before time and the ages* (γεννήσαντα υἱὸν μονογενῆ πρὸ χρόνων αἰωνίων), *through whom he made both the ages and all that was made* («δι' οὗ καὶ τοὺς αἰῶνας καὶ τὰ ὅλα πεποίηκε," Heb 1:2); who begot him not in appearance, but in reality; and that he made him subsist at his own will, unalterable and unchangeable, the *perfect* creature of God (κτίσμα τοῦ θεοῦ τέλειον), *but not as one of the creatures* (ἀλλ' οὐχ ὡς ἓν τῶν κτισμάτων); offspring, *but not as one of the other things begotten* (γέννημα, ἀλλ' οὐχ ὡς ἓν τῶν γεγεννημένων); [...]. (4) [...] And God, being the cause of all that happens, is absolutely alone without beginning; but the Son, begotten apart from time by the Father, and *created and founded before the ages* (ὁ δὲ υἱὸς ἀχρόνως γεννηθεὶς ὑπὸ τοῦ πατρὸς καὶ πρὸ αἰώνων κτισθεὶς καὶ θεμελιωθείς; cf. Prov 8:22–25), was not in existence before his generation, but was begot-

[57] For the edition of the documents of the early Arian controversy, see *Athanasius Alexandrinus: Werke*. Vol. III,1: *Urkunden zur Geschichte des Arianischen Streites 318–328* (Documents on the History of the Arian Conflict) 3,1,1 (1934) nos. 1–18; 3,1,2 (1935) nos. 19–34; 3,1,3 (2007) nos. 1–44, including a German translation of the *Urkunden* under their new document number; 3,1,4 (2014). Reference is made to the Urkunde number ("Urk.") in H.-G. Opitz 1934–35, vols. III,1,1–III,1,2; and the corresponding revised document number ("Dok.") in H.C. Brennecke et al. 2007, vol. III,1,3. English translations are adapted, with minor modifications where necessary, from the collection of the complete set of English translations of the *Urkunden* on the website dedicated to Fourth-Century Christianity (FCC), founded and directed by Dr. Glen L. Thompson, sponsored by the History Department of Wisconsin Lutheran College and by Asia Lutheran Seminary, available online at: https://www.fourthcentury.com/documents-of-the-early-arian-controversy/.

[58] See Eusebius of Caesarea, *Vita Constantini* 2,69,1, ed. F. Winkelmann 1975 (= Opitz 1934–1935, Urk. no. 17/Dok. no. 19: Emperor Constantine to Alexander of Alexandria and Arius [October 324 CE]).

ten apart from time *before all things* (ἀλλὰ ἀχρόνως πρὸ πάντων γεννηθείς), and he alone came into existence by the Father (μόνος ὑπὸ τοῦ πατρὸς ὑπέστη) (Athanasius, *On the Synods* 16,2–5 = Opitz, *Urkunden*, Urk. no. 6/Dok. no. 1: Arius and his followers to Alexander of Alexandria [ca. 320 CE]; transl. FCC).

And it is indeed with reference to this declaration by Arius that Eusebius of Caesarea, in a letter to Alexander of Alexandria from circa 320 CE, tells him:

(2) Your letters have misrepresented them [the Arians] as though they were saying that since the Son came into being from that which does not exist, he must therefore be *just like the rest of creation* (Κατηγορεῖ αὐτῶν τὰ σὰ γράμματα ὡς λεγόντων, ὅτι ὁ υἱὸς ἐκ τοῦ μὴ ὄντος γέγονεν ὡς εἷς τῶν πάντων). But they have brought forth their own document, which they have written for you, in which they explain their faith, confessing it with these very words: "The God of the Law and of the Prophets and of the New Testament begat an only begotten Son *before time began, through whom he also made the ages* [Heb 1:2] *and all things*, begetting him not in appearance but in reality, causing him to exist by his own will. He is unchanging and unchangeable, God's perfect creation, *but not a creation in the same way like one of God's other creations.*" And so surely indeed their writings speak the truth, since these opinions are certainly held by you also when they confess that the Son of God existed before time began, that *God also made the ages through him*, that he is unchanging, God's perfect creation, *but not like God's other creations.* (3) But your letter surely misrepresents them as saying that *the Son is the same as the other created things.* They are not saying this! But they clearly draw a distinction, saying that *he is "not like one of the created things"* (ἡ δὲ σὴ ἐπιστολὴ κατηγορεῖ αὐτῶν ὡς ἂν λεγόντων, ὅτι ὁ υἱὸς γέγονεν ὡς ἓν τῶν κτισμάτων. αὐτῶν τοῦτο μὴ λεγόντων, ἀλλὰ σαφῶς διορισαμένων, ὅτι «οὐχ ὡς ἓν τῶν κτισμάτων») (Eusebius, *Epistula ad Alexandrum Alexandrinum* 2–3, ed. H.-G. Opitz = Opitz, *Urkunden*, Urk. no. 7/Dok. no. 9: Eusebius of Caesarea to Alexander of Alexandria [ca. 320 CE]; transl. FCC).

Yet, despite this gradual, temporal difference between the Son and (the rest of) creation – which allows (the rest of) creation to be created through him – from an ontological perspective, in Arius's view, the Son and creation are *both* created from nothing.

That this is indeed Arius's view is confirmed by both his supporters and his opponents. In a letter from the Arian sympathizer Athanasius of Anazarbos to Alexander of Alexandria, written in about 322 CE, Athanasius complains to him as follows:

Why do you find fault with Arius' men when they say, "The Son of God has been made, *a creation from things that are not* (ἐξ οὐκ ὄντων κτίσμα πεποίηται ὁ υἱὸς τοῦ θεοῦ), and is one with all other things (καὶ ἓν τῶν πάντων ἐστίν)?" (Athanasius, *On the Synods* 17,4 = Opitz, *Urkunden*, Urk. no. 11/Dok. no. 11: Fragment of a letter from Athanasius of Anazarbos to Alexander of Alexandria [ca. 322 CE]; transl. FCC).

Furthermore, Alexander of Alexandria's encyclical letter on Arius's deposition, which was sent to all the bishops (ca. 318 CE), confirms that it is this view of the creation of the Son from nothing that they found unacceptable. Alexander first lists this view among Arius's other, directly related views:

The dogmas which, going beyond Scripture, they [the Arians] have invented and asserted, are the following: "God was not always the Father, but there was once when God was not the Father. The Logos of God was not always in existence, *but came into being from things that are not* (οὐκ ἀεὶ ἦν ὁ τοῦ θεοῦ λόγος, ἀλλ' ἐξ οὐκ ὄντων γέγονεν), *for 'the God who is' made 'him who did not previously exist' from that which does not exist* (ὁ γὰρ ὢν θεὸς τὸν μὴ ὄντα ἐκ τοῦ μὴ ὄντος πεποίηκε)" (Athanasius, *Defence of the Nicene Definition* [*De decretis Nicaenae synodi*] 35,7 = Opitz, *Urkunden*, Urk. no. 4b / Dok. no. 2.2: Alexander of Alexandria's encyclical letter on Arius's deposition, to all bishops [ca. 318 CE]; transl. FCC).[59]

And as Alexander subsequently makes clear in his letter, he himself believes that there is scriptural support for the opposite view: that the Son did not come forth from nothing, but from the divine Father. From the Septuagint, the Jewish Scriptures in Greek, he quotes passages that – if read from the perspective of God, and if his locutions are imbued with christological significance – suggest that the Son has indeed been brought forth "from" within the divine Father, a procedure that is described with the graphic preposition "from" (ἐκ):

And how could he [the Son] come into existence *from things that are not* (πῶς δὲ ἐξ οὐκ ὄντων ἂν εἴη) when the Father has said, "My heart has 'vomited *forth*' a good word" (ἐξηρεύξατο [LSJ ἐξερεύγομαι, I. *vomit forth*] ἡ καρδία μου λόγον ἀγαθόν) (Ps 44[45]:2 LXX); and "I begot you *from the womb* before the morning star" (ἐκ γαστρὸς πρὸ ἑωσφόρου ἐγέννησά σε) (Ps 109[110]:3 LXX)? (Athanasius, *Defence of the Nicene Definition* [*De decretis Nicaenae synodi*] 35,12 = Opitz, *Urkunden*, Urk. no. 4b / Dok. no. 2.2; transl. FCC).

Arius had already expressed his disapproval of such metaphors as the Son being vomited forth from God. In his letter to Eusebius of Nicomedia (quoted above), he complained about such figures as

Philogonius [of Antioch] and Hellanicus [of Tripolis] and Macarius [of Jerusalem], unlearned heretics some of whom say that the Son was *"a vomit"* (τὸν υἱὸν λεγόντων οἱ μὲν ἐρυγήν), others that he was a "projection" (οἱ δὲ προβολήν) (Theodoret, *Church History* 1,5,3, ed. Parmentier and Scheidweiler, p. 26,15–16 = Opitz, *Urkunden*, Urk. no. 1 / Dok. no. 15: Arius to Eusebius of Nicomedia [ca. 318 CE]; transl. FCC).

---

[59] Cf. also the description of the Arian position by Athanasius himself in his *On the Synods* (*De synodis Arimini in Italia et Seleuciae in Isauria*) 15,1 "Arius and those with him thought and professed thus: 'God made the Son *from things that are not* (ἐξ οὐκ ὄντων πεποίηκε τὸν υἱὸν ὁ θεός), and called him his Son (καὶ κέκληκεν ἑαυτῷ υἱόν)'; 'The Word of God is one of the creatures'; and 'Once He was not'; and 'He is alterable; capable, when it is his Will, of altering'." Cf. *On the Synods* 36,4–5: "'But', they say, 'all this is not written: and we reject these words as unscriptural'. But this, again, is an unblushing excuse in their mouths. For if they think everything must be rejected which is not written, wherefore, when the Arian party invent such a heap of phrases, not from Scripture, '*From things that are not* (τὸ 'ἐξ οὐκ ὄντων')', and 'the Son was not before his generation', and 'Once He was not', and 'He is alterable', and 'the Father is ineffable and invisible to the Son', and 'the Son knows not even his own substance'."

According to another of Arius's writings, his opponents had made use of several scriptural passages containing the preposition "from" in support of their view that the Son had been generated from God, rather than from nothing. Not only had they used the quotation from Ps 109[110]:3 LXX about the divine begetting of the Son "*from the womb*" (ἐκ γαστρός), but they had also used quotations from the Johannine and Pauline writings, including the statement about God in Rom 11:36, which we have dealt with extensively in this contribution: "*from him* (ἐξ αὐτοῦ) and through him and to him are all things," which indeed brings us right to the heart of our subject matter.

In the confession of faith he sent to Alexander of Alexandria in about 320 CE, Arius seriously objects to the application of these passages to the generation of the Son "from" the divine Father. Moreover, his objections seem to bear the anti-Stoic overtones of a Platonic critique of the Stoic notion of creation from God:

But if the expressions "*from him*" (εἰ δὲ τὸ «ἐξ αὐτοῦ») [Rom 11:36] and "*from the womb*" (καὶ τὸ «ἐκ γαστρὸς») [Ps 109[110]:3 LXX] and "I came *from the Father*, and I have come" (καὶ τὸ «ἐκ τοῦ πατρὸς ἐξῆλθον καὶ ἥκω») [John 16:28], are understood by some to mean that he is part of him [the Father], one in substance or as a projection (ὡς μέρος αὐτοῦ ὁμοουσίου καὶ ὡς προβολὴ ὑπό τινων νοεῖται), then the Father is, according to them, compounded and divisible and alterable and material (σύνθετος ἔσται ὁ πατὴρ καὶ διαιρετὸς καὶ τρεπτὸς καὶ σῶμα κατ' αὐτούς), and, as far as their belief goes, the incorporeal God endures a body (καὶ τὸ ὅσον ἐπ' αὐτοῖς τὰ ἀκόλουθα σώματι πάσχων ὁ ἀσώματος θεός) (Athanasius, *On the Synods* 16,5 = Opitz, *Urkunden*, Urk. no. 6/Dok. no. 1: Confession of faith from Arius and his followers to Bishop Alexander of Alexandria [ca. 320 CE]; transl. FCC).

Interestingly, the anti-Arians use the Pauline phrase "from him," which in Rom 11:36 – as we have seen repeatedly above – denotes a *cosmological* event, in a *christological* context.

This is also confirmed in a letter that a particular priest named George wrote to the Arians. This George – who, according to Athanasius of Alexandria, "now is in Laodicea, but was at that time a priest of Alexandria, and was spending time in Antioch,"[60] and who, in different letters, addressed both the Arian and the anti-Arian faction,[61] and seems to have tried to mitigate between them – shows how anti-Arians made use of such Pauline prepositional "from"-passages and renders the rationale behind the use of cosmological "from"-passages for christological ends explicit in the following way:

And [George] wrote to the Arians: "Why do you find fault with Bishop Alexander [i.e., the anti-Arian Alexander of Alexandria] for saying that the Son is *from the Father* (ἐκ τοῦ

[60] Athanasius, *On the Synods* 17,5 = Opitz, *Urkunden*, Urk. no. 12/Dok. no. 6: A fragment of a letter of priest George to Alexander of Alexandria.

[61] See Opitz, *Urkunden*, Urk. no. 12/Dok. no. 6 (Athanasius, *On the Synods* 17,5), addressed to the anti-Arians; and Opitz, *Urkunden*, Urk. no. 13/Dok. no. 7 (Athanasius, *On the Synods* 17,6), to the Arians.

πατρὸς τὸν υἱόν)? For you also should not be afraid to say that the Son is *from God* (ἐκ τοῦ θεοῦ τὸν υἱόν). For if the Apostle wrote 'All things are *from God*' [1 Cor 11:12], though all things have clearly been made *from things that are not* (εἰ γὰρ ὁ ἀπόστολος ἔγραψε· 'τὰ δὲ πάντα ἐκ τοῦ θεοῦ', καὶ ἔστι δῆλον ἐξ οὐκ ὄντων πεποιῆσθαι τὰ πάντα), and if also the Son is a creature (κτίσμα), and he too was made, then the Son can be said to be '*from God*' (ἔστι δὲ καὶ ὁ υἱὸς κτίσμα καὶ τῶν πεποιημένων εἷς), just as all things are said to be '*from God*' (λεχθείη ἂν καὶ ὁ υἱὸς ἐκ τοῦ θεοῦ οὕτως, ὥσπερ καὶ τὰ πάντα λέγεται ἐκ τοῦ θεοῦ)" (Athanasius, *On the Synods* 17,6 = Opitz, *Urkunden*, Urk. no. 13 / Dok. no. 7: Fragment of a letter from Priest George to the Arians [ca. 322 CE]; transl. FCC).

George's argument is of course very formal and in fact crypto-Arian, as he only urges the Arians to accept the christological applicability of the phrase "from God" because the phrase is also applied to the cosmos; he suggests, however, that we know this is *not* literally true because "all things have clearly been made from nothing." By this time in the early fourth century, both the Arians and the anti-Arians shared the dominant (but not yet exclusive and officially authorized) view that, despite Paul's assertions, the cosmos had not been created "from God," but "from nothing." Hence, according to both Arians and anti-Arians, the Pauline phrase "from God" must mean something other than its original, Stoic, "literal" meaning.

This is indeed also the view of Athanasius of Alexandria, according to whom it is against the Epicureans, who deny God's involvement in creation, that Paul asserts that creation is "from God," indicating that it was created by his will, rather than from his substance (Athanasius, *On the Synods* 35–36). This profound confusion that has arisen over the meaning of Paul's view on a creation "from God" – now that its literal, Stoic, ontological meaning is no longer acknowledged – allows George to tempt the Arians to agree with the applicability of this phrase, understood metaphorically, to Christ. Thus in Arian thought, not only creation, but also the divine Son emerges from nothing, accompanied by a strong emphasis on both God's voluntaristic relation to creation and his omnipotence: creation does not emerge from God's substance, in the Stoic sense; neither does the divine Son. Rather, creation is brought about by God's will, as the instrument of his omnipotence. Although the anti-Arians agree that God's will was instrumental in creation, they resist its application to the generation of the divine Son. Hence the regional Synod of Antioch in 325 CE, immediately prior to the oecumenical Council of Nicea, felt the need to criticize this extreme voluntarism vis-à-vis the divine Son, as follows:

He has not been begotten or come into being merely *by the Father's will*, nor has this status been placed upon him, which would make him appear to be *from nothing*. But he was begotten as was fitting for him (*Letter of the Synod of Antioch*, ed. E. Schwartz 1905 and F. Schulthess 1908 = Opitz, *Urkunden*, Urk. no. 18 / Dok. no. 20: *Letter of the Synod of Antioch* [early 325 CE]; transl. FCC).

By this time, however, for both Arians and anti-Arians, creation had become a matter of God's will rather than something which, in the Pauline-Stoic sense, emerges from God. Arianism, as I understand its development, represents the further de-Stoicizing and extremely nihilistic position of a creation from nothing, which affects not only cosmology, but also Christology, as the divine Son has not been generated "from" God, but has been created "from nothing." This christological position in turn has profound consequences for cosmology, as Frances Young has also suggested in her 1991 article on creation from nothing. She argues from the other side – from cosmology to theology and Christology – but she notes the same intrinsic relation between cosmology and Christology: "But creation out of nothing was not just a doctrine about the world. It was doctrine about God. For it meant that God was no longer conceived as ontologically intertwined with the world, as he was in Stoicism, in Pseudo-Aristotle's *De Mundo*, and most other contemporary cosmologies."[62] She could have added Paul's Stoic views here to illustrate this point. Subsequently, Young implies that Arianism is the further radicalization of the "de-ontologization" and "nihilization" of creation (ascribing creation to its origins from nothing, rather than from God) and the "volutarization" of God:

> Christological discussions from Arianism on were the result of pressing this theology of God as the sole *arche-*, the one *agene-tos* being, who created *gene-ta* from nothing. Logos-theology had tempered the dichotomy, bridged the gulf between creator and created: for God's own Reason containing his Ideas produced the material world which the Logos then pervaded as its immanent order and rationality while remaining the Reason of God himself. But the tendency to regard this Logos as a mediating being [...] led to the old "creation" question re-surfacing now in relation to this "mediator": is the Logos "out of God" or "out of nothing"?[63]

As we will shortly see, although the Nicene Creed authorized the idea of creation from nothing for the first time, it also mitigated this "nihilistic" development by maintaining that the divine Son himself, "through whom all things were generated," was generated from God, from his substance. In this way, by implication, it was suggested that at least some of God's intrinsic qualities might be reflected in creation, because creation was not just created by "the Father almighty, creator of all things," but also "through" the one who is "from" his substance.[64] Only in this way can the creed avert the radical "nihilization" of creation that is characteristic of the Arian position – according to which, as we have seen, the Son is also created from nothing. Arianism pushes the ontological gap between God and creation to its extreme limits, so that the Arian position could not be further removed from Paul's view on creation.

---

62 Young 1991, 150.
63 Young 1991, 151.
64 Denzinger [43]2012, no. 125, with minor changes in P. B. Kotter, translation.

From a history of religions viewpoint, especially with regard to the development of the so-called Abrahamic religions and their proto- and eschatological views, it is most intriguing that the full Arian "nihilization" of creation, via its "nihilistic Christology," might have inspired early Islam, including the Qur'an. This link between Arianism and Islam was suggested by John of Damascus (650/675?–ca. 750 CE), who was the third generation of his family to serve the Arab caliph in Damascus before he became a monk in Jerusalem, "in the shadow of the newly built mosques on the Temple mound."[65] In the final chapter of his *On Heresies* (*De haeresibus*) – the title of which clearly indicates his inclusion of Islam as a (heretical) form of Christianity – he comments on Islam and its relation with Arianism as follows:

From that time on a false prophet appeared among them [the "Ishmaelites"], surnamed Mameth (Μάμεδ), who, having casually been exposed to the Old and the New Testament (ὅς τῇ τε παλαιᾷ καὶ νέᾳ διαθήκῃ περιτυχών) and supposedly encountered an Arian monk (ὁμοίως ἀρειανῷ προσομιλήσας δῆθεν μοναχῷ), formed a heresy of his own (ἰδίαν συνεστήσατο αἵρεσιν). [...] He says that there exists one God maker of all, who was neither begotten *nor has he begotten* (Λέγει ἕνα θεὸν εἶναι ποιητὴν τῶν ὅλων, μήτε γεννηθέντα μήτε γεγεννηκότα). He says that Christ is the Word of God, and his Spirit, *created* and a servant (Λέγει τὸν Χριστὸν λόγον εἶναι τοῦ θεοῦ καὶ πνεῦμα αὐτοῦ, κτιστὸν δὲ καὶ δοῦλον), and that *he was born without a seed from Mary* (καὶ ὅτι ἐκ Μαρίας [...], ἄνευ σπορᾶς ἐτέχθη) [...]. For, he says, the Word of God and the Spirit entered Mary and she gave birth to Jesus (Ὁ γὰρ λόγος, φησί, τοῦ θεοῦ καὶ τὸ πνεῦμα εἰσῆλθεν εἰς τὴν Μαρίαν, καὶ ἐγέννησε τὸν Ἰησοῦν) who was a prophet and a servant of God (John of Damascus, *De haeresibus* 100,10–13 and 17–22, ed. P.B. Kotter = PG 94,764b–765b; transl. Sahas 1972).[66]

Thus, according to John of Damascus, Muhammad had encountered an Arian monk, whose influence is subsequently visible in Muhammad's view that Christ was not begotten (from God), but entered Mary as the (created) Logos and Pneuma, created (from nothing), even without paternal human seed. Little scholarly attention has been paid to the implications of this early, contemporary view on the origins of Islam,[67] yet this might change, as there is an increasing awareness that the Qur'an was familiar with and was engaging trends from the late antique world.[68]

Indeed, it is clear in the Qur'an itself that the text takes an Arian, anti-Nicene perspective. The Qur'an challenges the Nicene Creed directly, asserting that

65 A. Louth, "Ioannes Damascenus," OCD online, consulted 7 June 2019.

66 Kotter 1981, 4:19–67. See Sahas 1972, with a full translation of John of Damascus's *De haeresibus* in appendix 1. For Sahas's comment on the relation between Islam and Arianism, see pp. 68 and 73–74.

67 Cf., however, Mayer and Neil 2013, esp. Neil, 215–28; and Reynolds 2008.

68 I am greatly indebted here to Dr. Clare Wilde (University of Groningen) for sharing her expertise in early Islam and Islamic-Christian relations with me. For the growing awareness of the late-antique context of early Islam, see Fowden 2014; Donner 2012; Hoyland 2012, 1053–77; Neuwirth 2010; Cotton, Hoyland, Price, and Wasserstein 2009; Hawting 1999.

"God is one" and "he does not beget nor is he begotten" (Q [Qur'an] 112:3),[69] a text also inscribed on the Dome of the Rock in Jerusalem.[70] According to early Islamic tradition, as represented by Abd al-Jabbār, an Islamic theologian who lived and worked in Baghdad and Rey (Teheran) in the period between 935–1025 CE, Constantine and the Council of Nicaea played a major role in the corruption of Christianity.[71] Moreover, it is of prime interest for our argument that the Qur'an also seems to agree with the Arian view of the creation of Jesus from nothing, as it compares Jesus's creation to that of Adam. God need only say "be," and something becomes: "In God's eyes Jesus is just like Adam: He created him from dust, said to him, 'Be', and he was" (Q 3:59; transl. A. Haleem). These simultaneous statements in the Qur'an – that (1) Jesus is not begotten (from God), but (2) that he has been created, not like other human beings from their parents, but directly (from nothing) by God, like Adam was – seem to confirm John of Damascus's view that early Islam engages with early Christianity and sides with the extremely nihilistic Arian views of creation from nothing, both with regard to the world and with regard to Christ. There is of course a slight difference between Arianism and Islam here, inasmuch as, according to Arius, the (created) Son is still chronologically prior to (the rest of) creation, and creation has been created by God through him, whereas Islam only picks up on the incarnation of Jesus. Nevertheless, both Arianism and early Islam see him not as begotten from God but as created from nothing, and share a radical understanding of creational nihilism with an accompanying emphasis on divine voluntarism and divine omnipotence. As we shall now see, the Nicene Creed mitigated this radical creational nihilism, although it did not revert to the fully emanationist position of the Pauline-Stoic concept of creation from God.

6. The Anti-Arian Response of the Nicene Creed and Its Semi-nihilistic Position: Reducing the Ontological Gap

As briefly indicated above, the Nicene Creed is quite ambiguous in its concept of creation. On the one hand, the creed is part of the movement towards creational nihilism, as it also, together with the Arians, asserts that the cosmos was created from nothing. Although this is not its prime focus, nevertheless, by virtue of its being a document arising out of the first oecumenical council of the Christian church, it authorizes this notion of creation from nothing for the first time. Its implicit affirmation of creation from nothing is evident in its denial that the Son was created from nothing. In this way, it forges a contrast between

[69] See *Corpus Coranicum – Textdokumentation und historisch-kritischer Kommentar zum Koran*, available online at http://www.corpuscoranicum.de/kontexte/index/sure/112/vers/3); and cf. Kropp 2011, 247–64.

[70] Cf. Grabar 2006.

[71] Reynolds and Samir 2010. Cf. Reynolds 2004.

this erroneous christological view that *the Son* has been created "from nothing" and the correct christological view that he was generated "from God" – thus implying that the cosmos was indeed created from nothing. As the creed itself indicates, it affirms:

one Lord Jesus Christ, the Son of God, the Only-Begotten, generated *from* the Father (γεννηθέντα ἐκ τοῦ πατρός), that is *from* the substance of the Father (τουτέστιν ἐκ τῆς οὐσίας τοῦ πατρός), God *from* God (θεὸν ἐκ θεοῦ), light *from* light, true God *from* true God, *begotten, not made* (γεννηθέντα οὐ ποιηθέντα), one in substance with the Father (ὁμοούσιον τῷ πατρί) [...]. However, those who say: "There was a time when he [the divine Son] was not" and "Before he was begotten he was not" and that he came into being *from nothing* (καὶ ὅτι 'ἐξ οὐκ ὄντων ἐγένετο') [...] <such persons> the Catholic Church anathematizes.[72]

In maintaining this position, the Nicene Creed does not say anything radically new, as this position is also attested, for instance, in the writings of Theognostus of Alexandria (ca. 210–ca. 270 CE), one of Origen's pupils. Similarly to what we find in the Nicene Creed, Theognostus believes that the Son is born or has emanated from God and denies that he came forth from nothing:

The substance of the Son is not a substance devised extraneously (οὐκ ἔξωθέν τίς ἐστιν ἐφευρεθεῖσα ἡ τοῦ υἱοῦ οὐσία), nor is it one introduced *from things that are not* (οὐδὲ ἐκ μὴ ὄντων ἐπεισήχθη); but it was born *from the substance of the Father* (ἀλλὰ ἐκ τῆς τοῦ πατρὸς οὐσίας ἔφυ), as the reflection (τὸ ἀπαύγασμα) of light or as the steam of water. For the reflection is not the sun itself, and the steam is not the water itself, nor yet again is it anything alien; neither is he himself the Father, nor is he alien, but he is an effluence/emanation (ἀπόρροια) of the substance of the Father (ἀλλὰ ἀπόρροια τῆς τοῦ πατρὸς οὐσίας), this substance of the Father suffering the while no partition (οὐ μερισμὸν ὑπομεινάσης τῆς τοῦ πατρὸς οὐσίας). For as the sun remains the same and suffers no diminution from the rays that are poured out by it, so neither did the substance of the Father undergo any change in having the Son as an image of itself (οὕτως οὐδὲ ἡ οὐσία τοῦ πατρὸς ἀλλοίωσιν ὑπέμεινεν εἰκόνα ἑαυτῆς ἔχουσα τὸν υἱόν) (Theognostus of Alexandria, *Seven Books of Hypotyposes or Outlines*, fr. book 2, *apud* Athanasius, *Defence of the Nicene Definition* [*De decretis Nicaenae synodi*] 25,2).

The Nicene Creed works with the same antithesis between generation from God and from nothing, and it seems to tacitly assume that indeed *creation*, by definition, is *creation from nothing*: it attacks the Arian view that the Son is created, but does not challenge the view that creation as such is conceived as creation from nothing. This tacit, implicit authorization of the view that creation happened "from nothing" explains why the Pauline-Stoic sense of creation "from God" was totally eclipsed and eventually lost. It is in some way ironic that the Nicene Creed, which criticized the extreme Arian position of creational and christological nihilism, shares and authorizes a semi-nihilistic position of creational nihilism. Not only do its creedal statements entail the denial of the Son's generation from nothing, but it also fixes and authorizes the view of the

[72] Denzinger [43]2012, nos. 125–26, with minor changes in translation.

creation of the cosmos from nothing, thereby settling the cosmological debate. Thus the notion of creation from nothing, which had grown into the most prominent theorem – preferred over the deficient Platonic concept of creation from pre-existing, disorderly matter, which was deemed to infringe upon God's omnipotence – was authorized, almost in passing, as the definitive view. As we shall see below, the Stoic position of creation from God was not really reconsidered on its own merits, as all attention was drawn first to the undesirability of the Platonic position, and subsequently to the challenges posed by the extremely nihilistic Arian position. Both the Stoic and the Platonic views were surpassed in the contest between the extreme nihilistic and the semi-nihilistic position. Thus an ontological rift between creator and creation, which had been absent in the Platonic and Stoic views, was made visible. Although views within the Pauline School had oscillated between Stoicizing and Platonizing positions, in all cases the cosmos – whether in its beginning, its end, or its present stability – was seen as closely related to God. Stoicizing Paulinism entails a worldview that is basically panentheistic, because creation emerged from God and is expected to return into and subsequently fully identify with God (cf. 1 Cor 15:28). Platonizing Paulinism assumes an uninterrupted "chain of being," according to which the visible world is "grounded" in an invisible reality (cf. Arthur Lovejoy), an image that embodies a transcendent paradigm. In different but comparable ways, both types of Paulinism assume an ontological continuity between creator and creation. All of this was threatened in the nihilistic/semi-nihilistic controversy.

On the other hand, although the Nicene Creed is part of this nihilistic development, from a cosmological perspective the creed is not as radical as Arianism in its creational nihilism. To be sure, the view that creation is to be understood as creation from nothing was by no means confined to Arianism, but was a broad early Christian consensus that had established itself as the most efficient response to the Platonic infringement upon the omnipotence of God; the assumption of pre-existent, disorderly matter – which in (Christian) Platonism was assumed to be coeval with God – was now challenged by the concept of creation from nothing, which could do justice to God's omnipotence. However, if the cosmos was created *from nothing*, then the only ontic relation between creation and its creator was dependent on the Logos. If this Logos was also created from nothing, as the Arians argued, then the entire creation, including the Logos, would collapse into the nihilistic abyss, and the only relation between creator and creation would be determined by the creator's omnipotence and will; creation would be entirely exterior to God, brought into existence from nothing. By asserting that the divine Son was not created from nothing, but was generated from God himself, the Nicene Creed effectively mitigates the extremity of the creation from nothing theorem, because this creation is brought about "through" him who is from God.

Although the creed affirms that the one God, the Father, the Almighty is "*the creator* of all things, those visible and those invisible" (πάντων ὁρατῶν τε καὶ ἀοράτων ποιητής), it also asserts that he performs this role not by himself alone, but "through," "by the agency of," or "by (the instrumental) means of" (LSJ διά A.III.a–b) the one who is from his substance:

And [we believe] in one Lord Jesus Christ, the Son of God, the Only–Begotten, generated from the Father, that is, from the substance of the Father, God from God, light from light, true God from true God, begotten, not made, one in substance with the Father, *through whom all things came into being, those in heaven and those on earth* (δι' οὗ τὰ πάντα ἐγένετο, τά τε ἐν τῷ οὐρανῷ καὶ τὰ ἐν τῇ γῇ) (Denzinger [43]2012, no. 125, with minor changes in translation).

In this way, the Nicene creed prevented the total collapse of creation into the nihilistic abyss. Had it not avoided this, Paul's "natural theology" – according to which creation, because it emerged "from God," intrinsically possesses God's qualities of "everlasting, eternal power and divine nature/divinity" (ἥ τε ἀΐδιος αὐτοῦ δύναμις καὶ θειότης, Rom 1:20) – would have been disabled. But as the one "through" whom God created the cosmos is the very same one who was "the Only–Begotten, generated *from* the Father (γεννηθέντα ἐκ τοῦ πατρός), that is *from* the substance of the Father (τουτέστιν ἐκ τῆς οὐσίας τοῦ πατρός), God *from* God (θεὸν ἐκ θεοῦ), [...] one in substance with the Father (ὁμοούσιον τῷ πατρί)," this threatening, extreme ontological gap was narrowed. Through his closeness with creation, in his capacity as God's creational instrument, the Son-who-is-consubstantial-with-the-divine-Father is at least able, via this contact, to impart some of God's own ontological vestiges to creation, almost as a kind of divine DNA transmitted whilst "touching," moulding, or permeating creation. This yields a closer relation with creation than when creation is merely called forth from nothing by the omnipotent God, solely as an act of will.

This mitigating position was not invented in the Nicene Creed, but was already evident prior to the Council of Nicaea, and was moreover confirmed after Nicaea. In the period before the Nicene Creed, for instance, in the last quarter of the second century CE, Theophilus of Antioch had already adopted the notion of creation from nothing as part of his critique of the Platonic view of the coevality of matter with God. Nevertheless, Theophilus believes that the Logos, who is involved in this creation, is the Stoic "interior, immanent Logos" (λόγος ἐνδιάθετος) of God and is begotten from God:

God made all things from things that are not (ἐξ οὐκ ὄντων τὰ πάντα ἐποίησεν); for nothing was coeval with God (literally, "nothing flourishes at the same time as God": οὐ γάρ τι τῷ θεῷ συνήκμασεν) [...]. God, then, having his own Logos internal within his own bowels (Ἔχων οὖν ὁ θεὸς τὸν ἑαυτοῦ λόγον ἐνδιάθετον ἐν τοῖς ἰδίοις σπλάγχνοις), begat him, vomiting him forth along with his own wisdom before all things (ἐγέννησεν αὐτὸν μετὰ τῆς ἑαυτοῦ σοφίας ἐξερευξάμενος πρὸ τῶν ὅλων). He had this Logos as a helper in the things that were created by him, and by him he made all things (τοῦτον τὸν λόγον ἔσχεν ὑπουργὸν τῶν ὑπ' αὐτοῦ γεγενημένων, καὶ δι' αὐτοῦ τὰ πάντα πεποίηκεν). He is called "governing principle," because he rules, and is Lord of all things fashioned by him (οὗτος λέγεται ἀρχή, ὅτι ἄρχει καὶ κυριεύει πάντων τῶν δι' αὐτοῦ δεδημιουργημένων) (Theophilus of Antioch, *To Autolycus* 2,10).

Because God "vomits forth" the Logos (imagery that, as we have seen, is derived from Ps 44[45]:2 LXX) and the Logos is so closely involved with creation, the ontological gap between creator and creation is minimized, although it nevertheless exists, due to the notion of creation from nothing. This gap becomes even more minimal when one considers that, despite the notion of creation from nothing in this passage, there is also a hint that the Stoic Logos – which is interior to and immanent within God, and which resides in his mind (the λόγος ἐνδιάθετος) – becomes the exterior Logos (the λόγος προφορικός) which is uttered and expressed in creation, as in the prologue to the Gospel of John, which contains a similar transition from the interiority of the Logos within God to the Logos's subsequent creation of the cosmos (John 1:1–3). In this way, creation is seen as an expression from deep within God himself. There is a striking similarity here not only with John's prologue, but also with Paul's Stoic concept of the emergence of creation from God. It can hardly be a coincidence that the closer we come to a Stoic understanding of creation, the closer we seem to be to Paul's cosmology.

The same holds true for the views of Pseudo-Hippolytus in the early third century. In his *Refutation of All Heresies*, he develops the same view – that the Logos, as God's interior Logos, generated and emanated from him, also became intimately involved in creation, as he (albeit in a more Platonic sense) "possessed in himself [...] the forms conceived in the Father's mind," after which the cosmos was created:

This singular and universal God first conceived of and fathered a Logos (Οὗτος οὖν <ὁ> μόνος καὶ κατὰ πάντων θεὸς Λόγον πρῶτον ἐννοηθεὶς ἀπογεννᾷ), a Logos not like a voice, but the immanent reasoning power of the cosmos (ἀλλ' ἐνδιάθετον τοῦ παντὸς λογισμόν). Now he gave birth to him exclusively *from existing things* (τοῦτον μόνον ἐξ ὄντων ἐγέννα) [i.e., from God himself, from his substance; cf. below in 33,8]. The Father himself is Being, and from Being came the offspring (τὸ γὰρ ὂν αὐτὸς ὁ πατὴρ ἦν, ἐξ οὗ τὸ γεννηθέν). [33,2] The Logos was the cause of beings that are generated (<κ>αὶ αἴτιον τοῖς γινομένοις Λόγος ἦν). He carried in himself the will of the generating God and was not unversed in his Father's design (οὐκ ἄπειρός τῆς τοῦ πατρὸς ἐννοίας). At the very moment that the Logos emanated *from his Father* (ἅμα γὰρ τῷ ἐκ τοῦ γεννήσαντος προελθεῖν), he became his firstborn (cf. Col 1:15b). He possessed in himself a voice, the forms conceived in the Father's mind (φωνὴν εἶχεν ἐν ἑαυτῷ, τὰς ἐν τῷ πατρικῷ <νῷ> ἐννοηθείσας ἰδέας). From these forms, at the Father's command, the cosmos was generated, and the Logos completed the good pleasure of God in each single detail (ὅθεν κελεύοντος πατρὸς γίνεσθαι κόσμον, τὸ κατὰ ἓν Λόγος ἀπετέλει τὸ ἀρέσκον θεῷ). [... 33,8] The Logos alone is generated *from God himself* (τούτου ὁ Λόγος μόνος ἐξ αὐτοῦ). Thus he is God, existing as a divine substance (διὸ καὶ θεός, οὐσία ὑπάρχων θεοῦ). But the world is made *from nothing* (ὁ δὲ κόσμος ἐξ οὐδενός), and so it is not God (Pseudo-Hippolytus, *Refutation of All Heresies* 10,33,1–2, 8; text and transl. Litwa 2016, with minor changes).

Although the cosmos is believed to have been created from nothing, the nihilism of this view is tempered by the conviction that the cosmos is generated by the Logos, who was begotten from the divine Father as the immanent Logos of the cosmos.

Furthermore, in the year prior to the Nicene Council, Alexander of Alexandria, in a letter to Alexander of Byzantium, emphasizes the vast (ontological) difference between the self-existent divine Father and the creatures which have been created from nothing, whilst this distance is bridged by the Son, who is the divinely begotten mediating nature through which the Father creates the cosmos from nothing. Complaining about the Arians, he writes:

These inventors of idle tales assert that we, who reject their impious and unscriptural blasphemy concerning the creation of Christ from things that are not (ἐξ οὐκ ὄντων), teach that there are two unbegotten beings (ἀγέννητα δύο). For these ill-instructed men contend that one of these alternatives must hold; either He must be believed to have come from things that are not (ἢ ἐξ οὐκ ὄντων αὐτὸν εἶναι φρονεῖν), or there are assuredly two unbegotten beings (ἢ πάντως ἀγέννητα λέγειν δύο). The unexercised do not realize how vast must be the distance between the unbegotten Father, and the creatures, whether rational or irrational, which were created by him from things that are not (ἀγνοοῦντες [...] ὡς μακρὸν ἂν εἴη μεταξὺ πατρὸς ἀγεννήτου καὶ τῶν κτισθέντων ὑπ' αὐτοῦ ἐξ οὐκ ὄντων, λογικῶν τε καὶ ἀλόγων); and that the mediating only-begotten nature, through which the Father of the Logos of God created the cosmos from things that are not (μεσιτεύουσα φύσις μονογενής, δι' ἧς τὰ ὅλα ἐξ οὐκ ὄντων ἐποίησεν ὁ πατὴρ τοῦ θεοῦ λόγου), has been begotten from him, the self-existent Father (ἐξ αὐτοῦ τοῦ ὄντος πατρὸς γεγέννηται) (Theodoret, *Church History* 1,4,44–45 [1,3 NPNF, ed. Parmentier and Scheidweiler, p. 20,4–12] = Opitz, *Urkunden*, Urk. no. 14 / Dok. no. 17: Alexander of Alexandria to Alexander of Byzantium [324 CE]; transl. NPNF, series 2, vol. III).

This passage by Alexander, who deposed Arius in Alexandria, aptly illustrates my point. The ontological gap between the self-existent creator, on the one hand, and creation (which has been created from nothing), on the other, is so vast that it can only be bridged and mediated by the Son, who has been begotten from the Father, but who indeed possesses the nature that can mediate this ontological gap.

This semi-nihilistic position, with its assertion of creation from nothing, mitigated by the Son's generation from and consubstantiality with the divine Father, is also reaffirmed subsequently to the Nicene Creed. In an oration on the occasion of the 30th anniversary of the reign of Emperor Constantine, Eusebius reflects on some of the central elements of the Christian faith. As one aspect of this, he also elaborates on the close involvement of the divine Logos, begotten from God, with the cosmos; he describes creation almost as an act that prefigures the Logos's incarnation as the condescending movement of an intermediary who comes from the unbegotten God, is himself begotten from God, and thus constitutes the link with creation (which is created from nothing and, ontologically speaking, is immeasurably far removed from the unbegotten God):

[11,11] How much more, then, is our admiration due, not to the visible mechanism of the cosmos, material as it is, and formed of the self-same elements; but to that invisible Logos who has moulded and arranged it all (τὸν ἀφανῆ καὶ ἀόρατον λόγον τὸν δὴ τοῦ παντὸς εἰδοποιόν τε καὶ κοσμήτορα), who is the only-begotten Son of God (ὄντα τοῦ θεοῦ μονογενῆ), and whom the Maker of all things, who far transcends all being, *has begotten from himself*, and appointed Lord and Governor of this cosmos (ὃν ὁ τῶν ὅλων ποιητὴς ὁ πάσης ἐπέκεινα καὶ ἀνωτάτω οὐσίας αὐτὸς ἐξ αὐτοῦ γεννήσας ἡγεμόνα καὶ κυβερνήτην τοῦδε τοῦ παντὸς κατεστήσατο)? [11,12] For since it was impossible that perishable bodies, or the rational spirits which he had created, should approach the Supreme God, by reason of their immeasurable distance from his perfections, for he is unbegotten, above and beyond all creation (ὁ μὲν γὰρ ἦν ἀγέννητος, ἀνωτάτω τε καὶ ἐπέκεινα τῶν ὅλων), ineffable, inaccessible, unapproachable, dwelling, as the divine words assure us, in the light which none can enter; but they were created *from things that are not*, and are *infinitely far removed from his unbegotten nature* (ἡ δ' ἐξ οὐκ ὄντων προβεβλημένη πορρωτάτω τε διεστῶσα καὶ μακρὰν τῆς ἀγεννήτου φύσεως ἀπεσχοινισμένη); well has the all-gracious and Almighty God interposed as it were an intermediate Power between himself and them, even the Divine omnipotence of his only-begotten Logos (εἰκότως ὁ πανάγαθος καὶ θεὸς τῶν ὅλων μέσην τινὰ προεμβάλλει τὴν τοῦ μονογενοῦς αὐτοῦ λόγου θείαν καὶ πανάλκη δύναμιν). And this Power, which is in perfect nearness and intimacy of union, with the Father which abides in him, and shares his secret counsels, has yet condescended (συγκατιοῦσαν), in fullness of grace, and as it were conformed itself (συσχηματιζομένην) to those who are so far removed from the supreme majesty of God. How else, consistently with his own holiness could he who is far above and beyond all things unite himself to corruptible and corporeal matter (ἄλλως γὰρ οὔτ' εὐαγὲς οὔθ' ὅσιον τὸν τῶν ὅλων ἐπέκεινα καὶ ἀνωτάτω ὕλῃ φθαρτῇ καὶ σώματι συμπλέκειν)? Accordingly the divine Logos (διὸ δὴ λόγος θεῖος), thus connecting himself with this cosmos (ἀναμὶξ τόδε τὸ πᾶν ὑπελθών), and receiving into his hands the reins of the cosmos (καὶ τὰς ἡνίας τοῦ παντὸς ἐνδησάμενος), turns and directs it (ἄγει καὶ φέρει) through a incorporeal and divine power, skilfully as a charioteer according to his own will and pleasure (Eusebius of Caesarea, *Oration in Praise of the Emperor Constantine, Pronounced on the Thirtieth Anniversary of His Reign* [*De laudibus Constantini*] 11,11–12).

As in the other instances, the Logos, begotten from God himself, is intimately involved with the moulding and arrangement of the cosmos, which was created from nothing. This is also, finally, what we find in Augustine, according to whom, in his *Confessions*, the creation of the cosmos takes place not simply from nothing, but in the divine Wisdom which is born from God's own substance: "in that Beginning which is from you (Prov 8:22), in your Wisdom, which was born from your substance, you made from nothing – something. For you made heaven and earth" (Augustine, *Confessions* 12,7; transl. LCL).

All of these examples show that, in contrast to the radical nihilism that characterizes the Arian position, these authors preserved a sense of the ontological closeness of creator and creation in the Christ-Logos, which counterbalances and mitigates the nihilism of creation from nothing.

7. The Sparse Direct Critique of the Stoic-Pauline Concept of Creation from God

So where does this leave us vis-à-vis Paul's Stoic concept of creation as an emergence from God himself? Why and how did it disappear from the radar over the course of the second and third centuries CE? If I am correct, the Pauline-Stoic concept of creation from God himself gradually disappeared in two stages, and its disappearance went almost unnoticed because attention was fixed on other issues. It was an incidental, collateral loss rather than an intended target.

Firstly, it was marginalized because the *ex nihilo* theorem was shaped mainly as a response to what was seen as the infringement of the Platonic creation from disorderly, pre-existent matter upon the omnipotence of God. Secondly, it was then eclipsed by the Council of Nicaea's authorization of the *ex nihilo* theorem – a point on which it agreed with the Arians. The Nicene Creed implicitly authorized this position: when thinking of creation, we indeed assume creation from nothing. Hence, there was hardly any direct attack on the Pauline-Stoic concept of creation from God. As we have briefly seen above, such a criticism of the Stoic position was indeed expressed by Hermogenes around the last quarter of the second century CE, when he established his Platonic concept of creation from pre-existing, disorderly matter over against the Stoic and Nihilistic alternatives. According to Hermogenes, in a characteristically Platonic anti-Stoic argument, "He [God] could not have made all things [...] from himself; because whatever things the Lord made from himself would have been parts of himself; but he is not dissoluble into parts, because, being the Lord, he is indivisible, and unchangeable, and always the same" (Hermogenes *apud* Tertullian, *Against Hermogenes* 2). But when Tertullian, in his turn, criticizes Hermogenes's Platonic concept of creation, he free-rides on Hermogenes's critique of the Stoic notion of creation. He does not need to elaborate on it (Tertullian, *Against Hermogenes* 15), but takes its effectiveness for granted. In this way, the Stoic view slides into the background, and the Platonic view takes centre stage and is seen as the Nihilists' main antagonist.

One of the rare passages in which we still find an instance of the resonance and criticism of the Stoic view is in Augustine's *Confessions*. In the continuation of the passage we have just quoted above, Augustine asserts that God has not created the cosmos from himself:

> [I]n that Beginning which is from you (Prov 8:22), in your Wisdom, which was born *from your substance*, you made *from nothing* – something. For you made heaven and earth, *but not from your own self*. For then what you made would be equal to your only-begotten Son and through him equal to yourself as well: it would not be right at all that anything should be your equal which was *not from your own self*. Apart from you there was nothing existing from which you could make these things, O Trinity in unity and unity in Trinity. Therefore you made heaven and earth *from nothing*, something great and something small (Augustine, *Confessions* 12,7; transl. LCL).

Augustine's critique turns itself against the implication that a creation *from* God indeed implies the divinity of creation. But that was exactly Paul's point when he asserted that the cosmos intrinsically possesses not only the divine quality of eternal power, but also God's divine nature itself: "his invisible characteristics (τὰ [...] ἀόρατα αὐτοῦ), perceived by the mind ever since the creation of the cosmos through the works (ἀπὸ κτίσεως κόσμου τοῖς ποιήμασιν νοούμενα), are beheld (καθορᾶται), both his eternal power and his divinity (ἥ τε ἀΐδιος αὐτοῦ δύναμις καὶ θειότης)" (Rom 1:20). Paul's Stoic substantialism, according to which the cosmos has arisen "from God," seems to be confirmed by the fact that he sees creation as visualizing (and hence sharing in the divine nature of) the invisible God. Yet this share in God's divine nature would not necessarily mean that the cosmos is equally as divine as God. In Paul's understanding, the Son, through whom the cosmos was created (1 Cor 8:6), was somehow closer to God than the cosmos, which (subsequently) evolved from God. This is perhaps clearer in John's Gospel, as a result of its use of the terminology of the Logos, which is not only identical with and dynamically distinguishable from God (John 1:1–2), but is also the medium through which the entirety of the cosmos was created (1:3) and through which human beings, if they receive this Logos, can be regenerated from (!) God (1:12–13) and become deified (10:35). Conceptually, a kind of differentiation between generation from God in the first and the second degree would address Augustine's criticism. This is also how Hegel, in his view of the trinitarian self-development of God, sees the generation of the Son within the immanent Trinity, the creation of the cosmos, and the incarnation of the Son as part of the economic Trinity: as successive phases in the gradual unfolding of this theological and cosmological process.[73] All of these christological and cosmological moments are instances of divine self-differentiation and the positing of otherness, followed by return to the self. In a sense, the successive stages of the Absolute Spirit as self-identity, self-differentiation (through both alienation within the immanent divine and into the non-divine), and return to the self are quite consistent with a Pauline-Stoic concept of creation from, through, and back into God.

Apart from Hermogenes and Augustine, there do not seem to be many other examples in which this Pauline-Stoic understanding of creation from God is criticized. Another relevant passage may be found in Athanasius's *On the Councils*, which we have discussed in part above, and in which Athanasius, almost in passing, endeavours to discredit the Stoic meaning of the preposition "from" in Paul's statement that all things are "from" God (1 Cor 8:6). He argues for the metaphorical rather than the literal meaning of the preposition:

> [A]ll the creatures, though they be said to have come into being *from God*, yet are not *from God* as the Son is (τὰ μὲν γὰρ κτίσματα πάντα, κἂν ἐκ τοῦ θεοῦ λέγηται γεγενῆσθαι,

---

[73] Cf., for instance, Schlitt [2]2012; Hodgson 2005, 127–40; and O'Regan 1994, esp. 171–87.

ἀλλ' οὐχ ὡς ὁ υἱός εἰσιν ἐκ τοῦ θεοῦ); for they are not offspring in their nature, but works (οὐ γὰρ γεννήματα, ἀλλὰ ποιήματά εἰσι τὴν φύσιν). [...] And though the Apostle has said, "One God, from whom all things" (1 Cor 8:6), yet he says not this, as reckoning the Son with other things (εἰ δὲ ὁ ἀπόστολος εἴρηκεν· «εἷς θεός, ἐξ οὗ τὰ πάντα," ἀλλ' οὐ τὸν υἱὸν συναριθμῶν τοῖς πᾶσι τοῦτό φησιν); but, whereas some of the Greeks consider that the creation was held together by chance, and from the combination of atoms; and spontaneously from elements of similar structure, and has no cause; and others consider that it came from a cause, but not through the Logos; and each heretic has imagined things at his will, and tells his fables about the creation; on this account the Apostle was obliged to introduce "*from God*" (τούτου χάριν ὁ ἀπόστολος ἀναγκαίως συνείρηκε τὸ ἐκ τοῦ θεοῦ), that he might thereby certify the Maker, and show that the cosmos was framed *at his will* (ἵνα καὶ τὸν ποιητὴν γνωρίσῃ καὶ τὴν ἐκ τοῦ βουλήματος αὐτοῦ τῶν πάντων δημιουργίαν ἀποδείξῃ). And accordingly he straightway proceeds: "And one Lord Jesus Christ, through whom all things" (1 Cor 8:6), by way of excepting the Son from that "all" (for what is called God's work, is all done through the Son; and it is not possible that the things framed should have one origin with their Framer), and by way of teaching that *the phrase "from God," which occurs in the passage, has a different sense in the case of the works, from what it bears when used of the Son* (καὶ ἵνα τὸ 'ἐκ τοῦ θεοῦ' λεγόμενον ὧδε ἄλλως ἐπὶ τῶν ποιημάτων αὐτὸ σημαίνεσθαι διδάξῃ, ἢ ὡς ἐπὶ υἱοῦ λεγόμενον νοεῖται); for he is offspring, and they are works (ὁ μὲν γὰρ γέννημα, τὰ δὲ ποιήματά ἐστι): and therefore he, the Son, is the proper offspring of *his substance* (διὸ καὶ ὁ μὲν υἱὸς ἴδιον τῆς οὐσίας γέννημα), but they are the handywork of *his will* (τὰ δὲ τοῦ βουλήματος δημιουργήματα).

36. The Council [of Nicaea], then, comprehending this, and aware of the different senses of the same word, *that none should suppose, that the Son was said to be "from God" like the creation* (ὑπὲρ τοῦ μή τινας ὑπονοεῖν κατὰ τὴν κτίσιν οὕτω λέγεσθαι καὶ τὸν υἱὸν 'ἐκ τοῦ θεοῦ'), wrote with greater explicitness, that the Son was "from the substance" (ἐκ τῆς οὐσίας). For this betokens the true genuineness of the Son towards the Father; whereas, *by the simple phrase "from God," only the creator's will in framing is signified* (ἐκ μὲν γὰρ τούτου τὸ γνήσιον ἀληθῶς υἱοῦ πρὸς τὸν πατέρα γνωρίζεται, ἐκ δὲ τοῦ λέγεσθαι ἁπλῶς 'ἐκ τοῦ θεοῦ' τὸ βούλημα τῆς δημιουργίας τοῦ κτίζοντος σημαίνεται) (Athanasius, *On the Councils of Ariminum and Seleucia* [*De synodis Arimini in Italia et Seleuciae in Isauria*] 35,4–36,2).

Thus, according to Athanasius, Paul's assertion that all things are "from" God makes use of only the metaphorical meaning of the preposition in his critique of the Epicurean view that the cosmos came into being by chance, without the involvement of the gods. This is a beautiful passage that demonstrates how early Christian exegetes had to argue once they had forgotten about Paul's Stoic use of prepositions. The generation of the Son from the Father is *from his substance*, but the creation of the cosmos from God is *by his will*.

The only other critique of creation from God is a different type of critique, addressed against a particular Gnostic understanding of the provenance of matter "from" a lower goddess, the figure of Sophia-Achamoth. According to Irenaeus in his *Against Heresies* (composed in 180–189 CE), particular Gnostic groups who did not believe in creation from nothing believed that matter derived from "the passions" of Achamoth, "whom they call the Enthymesis [LSJ ἐνθύμησις III. *anxiety, worry*] and impulse of the Aeon that went astray"; "they tell us that all moist substance proceeded from the tears of Achamoth, all lucid substance from her smile, all solid substance from her sadness, all mobile substance from her terror," believing that she "produced from her passions aforesaid the vast material substance of creation," asserting "that matter was produced from the Enthymesis of an Aeon going astray, and that the Aeon [referred to] was far separated from her Enthymesis, and that, again, her passion and feeling, apart from herself, became matter" (Irenaeus, *Against Heresies* 2,10,3–4).

This report can be supplemented with the report Tertullian gives on the Valentinians in his *Against the Valentinians* (written in ca. 203 CE). According to Tertullian, this Sophia-Achamoth meets Jesus-Soter, "through whom all things were created" (1 Cor 8:6), who releases her from her passions and vices by transforming them into matter: "such vices as had become inveterate and confirmed by practice he throws together; and when he had consolidated them in one mass, he fixes them in a separate body, so as to compose the corporeal condition of matter" (Tertullian, *Against the Valentinians* 16). Despite some resemblance to the Stoic notion of creation from God, this Gnostic understanding is clearly based on a negative understanding of matter that is alien to the Pauline-Stoic understanding of creation, issuing as it does from the vicious passions of a lower goddess. So Irenaeus's and Tertullian's critiques are here aimed at a particularly Gnostic view, and if anything, Tertullian regards this view as similar to Hermogenes's Platonic concept of creation from pre-existent matter. As he adds to his report, "This will prove to be matter, which has set us in battle array against Hermogenes, and all others who presume to teach that God made all things from matter, not from nothing" (Tertullian, *Against the Valentinians* 16). Direct critiques of the Stoic theorem of creation from God are thus rather rare, and this leads us to our concluding reflections.

VI. Concluding Reflections: The Disappearance of a Pauline-Stoic Proto- and Eschatological Ontology

In my contribution to this volume on views on the origin and end of the cosmos in Platonism and Christian thought, I have argued that Paul's cosmology, as well as both his protology and eschatology, are strongly Stoic. Paul frequently expressed his view that the cosmos was created "from God, through, and into God," which is fully in line with the Stoic view that the cosmos is "from God" and will return "into God," and also entirely consistent with Paul's other cosmological views, such as the process in which the "scheme of the cosmos" is enveloped, its final identification with God, and the eschatological understanding of corporeality as a "pneumatic body" (σῶμα πνευματικόν). Consequently, Paul's cosmology is not linear, but cyclical, in the sense that the eschatological end is a return to the origins of creation in God. Thus there is also a strong ontological continuity between creator and creation, as all things have arisen from God. Of course, one should not worship the creation instead of the creator (Rom 1:25), but that is precisely *because* creation's origins lie in the creator. Only when this was forgotten, when human beings "worshipped and became devoted to the creation *alongside of* [with the implication of superiority above; LSJ παρά C.I.7], *beyond* (LSJ παρά C.III.1), and *over and above* (LSJ παρά C.III.2) the creator" (ἐσεβάσθησαν καὶ ἐλάτρευσαν τῇ κτίσει παρὰ τὸν κτίσαντα, Rom 1:25), did life become distorted (Rom 1:26–32). As such, however, there is no ontological gap between creator and creation, and it would be interesting to explore where and how the common assumption of a strong antithesis between creator and creation in Judaism and Christianity has arisen.

Expressions of such an ontological closeness are not limited to Stoicism, but also occur in the Jewish Scriptures. In Proverbs 8, Woman Wisdom, God's collaborator in creation (7:22–31), is said to have been "begotten" by God (8:25). As we have seen, the synonymy of "begotten" with "created" (8:22) and "established" (8:27) in this passage left it to the Arians and the anti-Arians to decide which meaning was decisive. (Did "begotten" mean "created," or did "created" mean "begotten"?) In any case, a close ontological relation between the co-creatrix and the creator is feasible here. In Psalm 90, the Psalmist lauds God himself for having given birth to creation: "Before the mountains were born, and (before) you travailed with earth and world – from everlasting to everlasting you are God!" (Ps 90:2).[74] As Martin Tate states in his Word Biblical Commentary on this Psalm, here "[c]reation is conceptualised in the cosmogonic mode of being given birth [...] the verb 'travailed with' in 2b refers to God; it is God who has given birth to the earth and the world, along with the mountains (v 2a)" – a very specific conceptualization that is easily overlooked – "especially when creation is defined in terms of the narrow scope of creation out of nothing."[75] Paul's protological views are not very different from the expressions found in Psalm 90 and Proverbs 8, but his protology, as well as his eschatology, has been cast in Stoic terminology and embedded in the Stoic worldview.

This does not make Paul a Stoic, however. As we have seen, Paul ultimately transposes his Stoicism into a Platonizing mode, because after the return of the cosmos into God, the cosmos is subsumed in an eternal intimacy with God in heaven. Nor does Paul's Stoicism remain unaltered within the Pauline School, as the author of the Pseudo-Pauline Letter to the Colossians clearly adopted a more Platonizing view of the cosmos, emphasizing its present coherence and

[74] Transl. Tate 1990, 431. This meaning is partially overridden in the Septuagint, which reads: "Before mountains were brought forth (πρὸ τοῦ ὄρη γενηθῆναι) *and the earth and the world were formed* (καὶ πλασθῆναι τὴν γῆν καὶ τὴν οἰκουμένην), and from everlasting to everlasting you are" (Ps 89[90]:2 LXX).

[75] Tate 1990, 440.

stability over above the cosmic process. Subsequently, however, the fundamentally Stoic outline of Paul's eschatology was restored and further developed in the Pseudo-Pauline Letter to the Ephesians, the author of which characterized Christ's ongoing dealings with the cosmos as a "recapitulation." As we have seen, this oscillation of Pauline views between Stoicism and Platonism is nothing unusual in the contemporary ancient philosophical schools, as individual Stoic and Platonic philosophers decided how to place their own emphases in their various cosmologies; some Stoics became Platonists in this respect and abandoned Stoic eschatology, whereas some Platonists read their Plato through a Stoicizing lens and believed that the cosmos emerged "from" God, who "holds the beginning, the end, and the centre of all things that exist."

I have also tried to answer the question of why this Pauline-Stoic understanding of the cosmos, its origins, and its ends has almost passed into oblivion. It was never directly contested, but rather marginalized and then eclipsed, as all attention was devoted to countering the views of the alternative school, the Platonic School. The Platonic concept of the creation of the cosmos from pre-existing, disorderly matter – which, according to some Christians, such as Hermogenes, was seen as a good theodicean explanation for the existence of evil – was seen by a growing number of Christians as an undue limitation of God's omnipotence. These Christians reached for the notion of creation from nothing, which was already current in both Hellenistic Judaism and early Christianity, to clarify the resurrection as a renewed creation from nothing. The creation from nothing theorem articulated the full omnipotence of God, who also created matter from nothing. The effectiveness of this notion in answering the Platonic challenge explains why interest in the Pauline-Stoic notion of creation from God dwindled. To some extent, this is ironic – or at least unnecessary – insofar as Stoicism could also have provided a rationale for the resurrection, because "resurrection" was equivalent to the Stoic "reconstitution" (ἀποκατάστασις). Moreover, unlike Platonism, Stoicism had no problems with maintaining God's omnipotence, since matter was not conceived as independent from God, but as emerging from him in creation. Yet somehow the notion of creation from nothing, already so popular as a rationale for resurrection, was the more attractive theorem with which to combat Platonism. This direct confrontation between the "Nihilistic" and Platonic theories of creation seems to explain why there were hardly any direct arguments against the Stoic concept of creation from God himself. It was mainly the Platonic view that triggered the further development and application of the theorem of creation from nothing. It is the Platonic position that drew the Nihilistic fire, whereas direct assaults on the Stoic position are almost completely absent from the historical record.

As we have seen, however, the adoption of the notion of creation from nothing gave rise to an even more extreme nihilism: that of the Arians, who argued that not only had creation been created from nothing, but that Christ also came into being from nothing, through an act of creation. Even though the Nicene response to this Arian nihilism managed to avoid the total collapse of creation into the nihilistic abyss – as it insisted that the divine Son, through whom the cosmos was created, was begotten from God –, its semi-nihilistic position never restored the full ontological, intrinsic relation that characterized the Pauline-Stoic view on the relation between creator and creation.

When seen through the prism of the present volume, focused as it is on the relation between Platonism and Christian thought in protology and eschatology, Platonism and Paulinism interacted in the following ways. Firstly, Platonism coloured Paul's adoption of Stoicism. It played a role in the transposition of Paul's Stoicism into a different, Platonic key, at least with regard to his eschatology. After the cosmos returns into God, creation is forever embraced in an eternal intimacy with God: human beings enter into their eternal dwelling in the heavens (2 Cor 5:1), having been dragged from their mortal bodies (Rom 7:24), and creation shares in their freedom in being released from its bondage to decay (Rom 8:21) and fully identified with God (1 Cor 15:28); corporeality becomes the sort of pneumatic body (σῶμα πνευματικόν, 1 Cor 15:44) that characterizes the Stoic god after the conflagration of the cosmos, when all things have been subsumed into God's *hēgemonikon*. Paul agrees with the Stoics in their non-linear, cyclical view of the cosmos's return into God, but due to this Platonic transposition, there is no periodic renewal of the cosmos after its full identification with God. Yet the resulting position is not Platonic either, as there is now no longer a cosmos, which would be unthinkable in Platonism, given its view that, although frail, the cosmos is eternal due to God's goodness. Moreover, in Platonism, souls eventually return back to earth from heaven in the periodic transmigration of souls. The philosophical souls that reach the stars (Alcinous, *Didaskalikos* 16,2 = GBS 10B) and leave their lower souls and bodies behind (Plutarch, *On the Sign of Socrates* 591d–f = GBS 9R) seem to descend again in due time. Precisely because souls (and the cosmos) are immortal, this cycle of descent and ascent continues. As Alcinous says, "From the argument that souls are immortal it follows that they enter bodies, becoming engendered within the formative structures of the embryo, and that they exchange one body for another – both human and non-human – many times" (Alcinous, *Didaskalikos* 25,6 = GBS 9Kk; transl. GBS). The souls are sent down into the eternal cosmos to enrich it (see Taurus, fr. 34t, ed. Gioè = GBS 9A), as the souls exist for the cosmos, not the cosmos for the souls.[76] If the philosophical souls end up among the stars, this seems to be only a temporary endpoint. Only in very exceptional cases is a soul really united with its principles after re-ascending (Numenius, fr. 42, ed. des Places = GBS 10J); such rare souls seem to escape the cosmos and the cycle of reincarnation for good. In Paulinism, however, heaven is the eternal destiny

[76] For this emphasis, see Boys-Stones 2018, ch. 9.2.1 and ch. 9.6.

of all those redeemed. Thus Paul's views on protology and eschatology, although they are in close conversation with Stoic-Platonic thought, are ultimately rather distinctive.

Secondly, Platonism influenced the discussion between members of the Pauline School. It provided an alternative model within the school, as the author of Colossians demonstrates through the affinity of his cosmological thought with Platonic cosmology. As we have seen above, this provoked a Stoicizing response from the author of Ephesians in return.

Thirdly and finally, from the perspective of the reception history of Paul's cosmology, Platonism also caused Paul's Stoicism to be forgotten, as the Platonic concept of creation from matter triggered the development of the theorem of creation from nothing, which became the standard Christian view. Read through the lens of the theorem of creation from nothing, Paul's views became confused; they lost their Stoic meaning and consistency, and an ontological gap opened between God and creation. In this sense, the Pauline-Stoic creation "from God" suffered a collateral loss due to the joint attack of the Arians and the anti-Arians, with their creation from nothing, against the Platonist theorem of creation from matter. Paul's Stoicism was never the intended target, but it became a victim in this debate between the Platonists and the Nihilists. Despite their mutual differences and varying degrees of nihilism (whether solely cosmological or cosmological and christological), both the Arians and the anti-Arians continued on the track of the anti-Platonic critique of the late-second and early third centuries CE. Hence the Pauline-Stoic notion of an ontic creation "from God" was eclipsed by the anti-Platonic, Nihilistic position that emphasized God's voluntaristic omnipotence, which could create from nothing.

In a final return to the initial sketch of the continued relevance of ancient philosophical cosmologies well into the twentieth century, as presented in the introduction to this contribution, it is intriguing to see, in the light of the findings of my research here, which options are still on the table. Since the 1950s/1960s, both the (Platonic) view of disorderly matter that always existed before it was used in creation and the (Aristotelian-Peripatetic) view of an eternal, non-generated cosmos that was and forever remains in a steady state have been ruled out. However, both the Stoic and the Nihilistic positions – which assume a beginning, either from an original singularity or from nothing – remain topics of discussion. Indeed, some forms of modern cosmology discuss a true creation from nothing, while others are less appropriately referred to as cosmologies "from nothing," as the nucleus from which the cosmos came into being was invisible (insofar as space and time were still absent), yet it was not nothing, but rather an infinitely dense nucleus. As the cosmologists John Barrow and Frank Tipler put it:

It is, of course, somewhat inappropriate to call the origin of a bubble universe in a fluctuation of the vacuum "creation *ex nihilo*," for the quantum mechanical vacuum is not truly "nothing"; rather, the vacuum state has a rich structure which resides in a previously existing substratum of space-time [...]. Clearly, a true "creation *ex nihilo*" would be the spontaneous generation of everything – space-time, the quantum mechanical vacuum, matter – at some time in the past. Such a true creation *ex nihilo* has been discussed by cosmologists in both classical and quantum gravity.[77]

It is this invisible kernel or nucleus, which "is not truly 'nothing'," that reminds me of the Stoic divine *hēgemonikon*, from which the cosmos emerges and into which it is to return. In this sense, whereas several ancient cosmological models have been proven wrong, the Pauline-Stoic and "Nihilist" models seem to retain their philosophical relevance.

Bibliography

Adams, E. (2007), *The Stars Will Fall From Heaven: Cosmic Catastrophe in the New Testament and Its World* (Library of New Testament Studies 347), London: T&T Clark.

Barrow, J.D. and Tipler, F.J. (1986), *The Anthropic Cosmological Principle*, Oxford – New York: Oxford University Press.

Boys-Stones, G. (2018), *Platonist Philosophy 80 BC to AD 250: An Introduction and Collection of Sources in Translation* (Cambridge Source Books in Post-Hellenistic Philosophy), Cambridge: Cambridge University Press.

– (2019), 'Difference, Opposition, and the Roots of Intolerance in Ancient Philosophical Polemic', in: *Intolerance, Polemics, and Debate in Antiquity: Politico-Cultural, Philosophical, and Religious Forms of Critical Conversation*, ed. G. van Kooten and J. van Ruiten (Themes in Biblical Narrative 25), Leiden – Boston, MA: Brill, 259–81.

Cook, J.G. (2000), *The Interpretation of the New Testament in Greco-Roman Paganism* (Studies and Texts in Antiquity and Christianity 3), Tübingen: Mohr Siebeck.

Cotton, H.M., Hoyland, R.G., Price, J.J., and Wasserstein, D.J., eds. (2009), *From Hellenism to Islam: Cultural and Linguistic Change in the Roman Near East*, Cambridge: Cambridge University Press.

Denzinger, H. ([43]2012), *Compendium of Creeds, Definitions, and Declarations on Matters of Faith and Morals*, ed. P. Hünermann, R. Fastiggi, and A. Englund Nash, San Francisco, CA: Ignatius Press.

Dillon, J. (1989), 'The Theory of Three Classes of Men in Plotinus and in Philo', in: *Of Scholars, Savants, and Their Texts*, ed. R. Link-Salinger, New York: Lang, 69–76 (reprint in idem, *The Golden Chain: Studies in the Development of Platonism and Christianity*, Aldershot: Variorum, 1991, 69–76).

– (2001), 'Plutarch and the Separable Intellect', in: *Estudios sobre Plutarco: Misticismo y religiones mistéricas en la obra de Plutarco*, ed. A. Pérez Jiménez and F. Casadesús Bordoy, Madrid: Ediciones Clásicas, 35–44.

Dörrie, H. and Baltes, M. (1996), *Die philosophische Lehre des Platonismus* (Der Platonismus in der Antike 4), Stuttgart – Bad Cannstatt: Frommann-Holzboog.

[77] Barrow and Tipler 1986, 440–44, at 441.

Donner, F.M. (2012), *Muhammad and the Believers at the Origins of Islam*, Cambridge, MA: Harvard University Press.

Eco, U. (1992a), 'Interpretation and History', in: *Interpretation and Overinterpretation*, ed. S. Collini (Tanner Lecturers in Human Values), Cambridge: Cambridge University Press, 23–43.

– (1992b), 'Overinterpreting Texts', in: *Interpretation and Overinterpretation*, ed. S. Collini (Tanner Lecturers in Human Values), Cambridge: Cambridge University Press, 45–66.

Fowden, G. (2014), *Before and after Muhammad: The First Millennium*, Princeton, NJ: Princeton University Press.

Grabar, O. (2006), *The Dome of the Rock*, Cambridge, MA: Harvard University Press, 2006.

Hawting, G.R. (1999), *The Idea of Idolatry and the Emergence of Islam: From Polemic to History*, Cambridge: Cambridge University Press.

Hodgson, P.C. (2005), *Hegel and Christian Theology: A Reading of the Lectures on the Philosophy of Religion*, Oxford: Oxford University Press.

Hoyland, R. (2012), 'Early Islam as a Late Antique Religion', in: *The Oxford Handbook of Late Antiquity*, ed. S. Johnson, Oxford: Oxford University Press, 1053–77.

Islam, J.N. (1983), *The Ultimate Fate of the Universe*, Cambridge: Cambridge University Press, 1983.

Kotter, P. B. (1981), *Die Schriften des Johannes von Damaskos*, besorgt von – (Patristische Texte und Studien 22), Berlin: De Gruyter.

Krämer, H. (2014), 'ΕΠΕΚΕΙΝΑ ΤΗΣ ΟΥΣΙΑΣ: Zu Platon, *Politeia* 509b', in: idem, *Gesammelte Aufsätze zu Platon*, ed. D. Mirbach, Berlin – Boston, MA: De Gruyter, 122–48.

Kropp, M. (2011), 'Tripartite, but Anti-Trinitarian Formulas in the Qur'anic Corpus, Possibly Pre-Qur'anic', in: *New Perspectives on the Qur'an: The Qur'an in Its Historical Context*, ed. G.S. Reynolds, New York: Routledge, vol. II, 247–64.

Litwa, M.D. (2016), *Refutation of All Heresies: Translated with an Introduction and Notes* (Writings from the Greco-Roman World 40), Atlanta, GA: SBL Press.

Long, A. A (2006a), 'The Stoics on World-Conflagration and Everlasting Recurrence', in idem, *From Epicurus to Epictetus: Studies in Hellenistic and Roman Philosophy*, Oxford: Oxford University Press, 256–82.

– (2006b), 'Astrology: Arguments Pro and Contra', in: idem, *From Epicurus to Epictetus: Studies in Hellenistic and Roman Philosophy*, Oxford: Oxford University Press, 128–52.

Long, A.A. and Sedley, D.N. (1987), *The Hellenistic Philosophers*, 2 vols., Cambridge: Cambridge University Press.

May, G. (1994), *Creatio ex Nihilo: The Doctrine of 'Creation out of Nothing' in Early Christian Thought*, trans. A.S. Worrall, Edinburgh: T&T Clark.

Mayer, W. and Neil, B., eds. (2013), *Religious Conflict from Early Christianity to the Rise of Islam* (Arbeiten zur Kirchengeschichte 121), Berlin – Boston, MA: De Gruyter.

Neil, B. (2013), 'The Earliest Greek Understandings of Islam: John of Damascus and Theophanes the Confessor', in: *Religious Conflict from Early Christianity to the Rise of Islam*, ed. W. Mayer and B. Neil, Berlin – Boston, MA: De Gruyter, 215–28.

Neuwirth, A. (2010), *Der Koran als Text der Spätantike: Ein europäischer Zugang*, Berlin: Verlag der Weltreligionen, 2010.

Opsomer, J. (2006), 'Éléments stoïciens dans le *De E apud Delphos* de Plutarque', in: *Les platonismes des premiers siècles de notre Ère: Plutarque, L'E de Delphes*, ed. J. Boulogne, M. Broze, and L. Couloubaritsis, Brussels: Ousia, 147–70.
– (2014), 'Plutarch and the Stoics', in: *A Companion to Plutarch*, ed. M. Beck, Oxford: Blackwell, 88–103.
O'Regan, C. (1994), *The Heterodox Hegel*, Albany, NY: SUNY Press.
Ramelli, I. L. E. (2013), *The Christian Doctrine of "Apokatastasis": A Critical Assessment from the New Testament to Eriugena* (Vigiliae Christianae. Supplements 120), Leiden – Boston, MA: Brill.
Reynolds, G.S. (2004), *A Muslim Theologian in a Sectarian Milieu: 'Abd al-Jabbār and the* Critique of Christian Origins (Islamic History and Civilization 56), Leiden – Boston, MA: Brill, 2004.
–, ed. (2008), *The Qur'an in Its Historical Context*, New York – London: Routledge.
Reynolds, G.S. and Samir, S.K. (2010), *'Abd al-Jabbār: Critique of Christian Origins – A Parallel English-Arabic Text*, edited, translated, and annotated by –, Provo, UT: Brigham Young University Press.
Runia, D.T. (2001), *On the Creation of the Cosmos according to Moses: Introduction, Translation, and Commentary* (Philo of Alexandria Commentary Series 1), Atlanta, GA: Society of Biblical Literature.
Sahas, D.J. (1972), *John of Damascus on Islam: The 'Heresy of the Ishmaelites'*, Leiden: Brill.
Schlitt, D.M. ([2]2012), *Hegel's Trinitarian Claim: A Critical Reflection*, Albany, NY: SUNY Press.
Schofield, M. (1991), *The Stoic Idea of the City*, Cambridge: Cambridge University Press; repr. 1999.
Sharples, R.W. and van der Eijk, P.J. (2008), *Nemesius: On the Nature of Man*, translated with an introduction and notes by – (Translated Texts for Historians 49), Liverpool: Liverpool University Press.
Smith, Q. (1992), 'A Big Bang Cosmological Argument for God's Nonexistence', *Faith and Philosophy* 9: 217–37.
Stead, C. (1998), 'The Word "From Nothing"', *Journal of Theological Studies* 49: 671–84.
Sterling, G.E. (1992), '*Creatio temporalis, aeterna, vel continua*? An Analysis of the Thought of Philo of Alexandria', *The Studia Philonica Annual* 4: 15–41.
– (1997), 'Prepositional Metaphysics in Jewish Wisdom Speculation and Early Christological Hymns', *The Studia Philonica Annual* 9: 219–38.
Tate, M.E. (1990), *Psalms 51–100* (Word Biblical Commentary 20), Dallas, TX: Word.
van Kooten, G.H. (2003), *Cosmic Christology in Paul and the Pauline School: Colossians and Ephesians in the Context of Greco-Roman Cosmology* (Wissenschaftliche Untersuchungen zum Neuen Testament II/171), Tübingen: Mohr Siebeck.
– (2008), *Paul's Anthropology in Context: The Image of God, Assimilation to God, and Tripartite Man in Ancient Judaism, Ancient Philosophy and Early Christianity* (Wissenschaftliche Untersuchungen zum Neuen Testament 232), Tübingen: Mohr Siebeck.
– (2014), 'The Divine Father of the Universe from the Presocratics to Celsus: The Greco-Roman Background to the "Father of All" in Paul's Letter to the Ephesians', in: *The Divine Father: Religious and Philosophical Concepts of Divine Parenthood in Antiquity*, ed. F. Albrecht and R. Feldmeier (Themes in Biblical Narrative 18), Leiden – Boston, MA: Brill, 293–323.

– (2017), 'Paul's Stoic Onto-Theology and Ethics of Good, Evil and "Indifferents": A Response to Anti-Metaphysical and Nihilistic Readings of Paul in Modern Philosophy', in: *Saint Paul and Philosophy: The Consonance of Ancient and Modern Thought*, ed. G.-J. van der Heiden, G.H. van Kooten, and A. Cimino, Berlin: De Gruyter, 133–64.

van Kooten, G.H. with Wischmeyer, O. and Wright, N.T. (2015), 'Quaestiones disputatae: How Greek Was Paul's Eschatology?', *New Testament Studies* 61: 239–53.

Young, F.M. (1991), '"Creatio ex Nihilo": A Context for the Emergence of the Christian Doctrine of Creation', *Scottish Journal of Theology* 44: 139–52.

List of Contributors

Andrea Falcon is affiliated with Concordia University (Montreal, Canada) and the University of Milan, Italy (La Statale).

Jörg Frey is Professor of New Testament with special focus on Early Judaism and Hermeneutics at the Theological Faculty of the University of Zurich, Switzerland and Research Associate of the University of the Free State Bloemfontein, South Africa.

Marc-Antoine Gavray is Professor of ancient philosophy at the University of Liège.

Benjamin Gleede is Heisenberg fellow at Tübingen University.

Alain Lernould is Research Fellow at the National Center of Scientific Research, member of the UMR 8163, "Savoirs, Textes, Langage" (CNRS-Université de Lille).

Marije Martijn is Professor of history of philosophy at VU Amsterdam.

Geert Roskam is Professor of ancient Greek literature at KU Leuven.

Einar Thomassen was Professor of the Study of Religion at the University of Bergen until his retirement in 2021.

George van Kooten is Lady Margaret's Professor of Divinity at the University of Cambridge and Fellow of Clare Hall.

Gerd Van Riel is Professor of Ancient Philosophy and currently Dean of the Faculty of Philosophy at KU Leuven.

Joseph Verheyden is Professor of New Testament at KU Leuven and Director of the Louvain Centre for Eastern and Oriental Christianity.

Index of Ancient Authors and Texts

Aeschylus
Agamemnon
1223–26 48

Aetius
Placita
1,7,21 18
1,7,33 184
2,4,2 20

Alcinous
Didaskalikos
16,2 232
25,6 232

Alexander of Alexandria 212–15 224

Alexander of Aphrodisias
Commentary on Aristotle's On the Heavens 7
Commentary on Aristotle's Prior Analytics
180,33–36 188
181,25–31 188

Alexander of Byzantium 224

Ammonius 69

Antiochus IV Epiphanes 202

Antipater of Tarsus 200

The Apostolic Constitutions
5,1 203

Aphrahat 154
Homily
22,24 154

Aratus
Phaenomena
5 190

Aristocles 184

Aristotle 2–3 7–22 51–52 56 69–70 74 77–78 81–82 85–86 91 94–95 170 206
Categories
12,14a26–b23 93
On Dreams
3,16b6–25 91
On Generation and Corruption 16–17
II 17
II 2–3 17
II 9–10 17
On the Heavens 9 11 13
1,1,268a1–3 11
1,2 9
1,2,269a8–9 51
1,3 9
1,3,270b20–23 18
1,10–12 8 10
1,11,280b1–20 86
2,8,290a20 36
Metaphysics
12 170
991a21–991b3 198

Meteorology 158
2,1,354a27–32 158
Movement of Animals 12–13
3 12
4 12
Nichomachean Ethics
5,8 1135b16–19 55
On Philosophy (frag. Ross) 8–11 13 15–16
16 13
18 12
19a 10 16
19b 10
19c 10
Physics
1,8,91b13–14 72
3,6,206a21–23.29–33 85
8 8–11 13 17 78 170
8,1,251b14–9 95
8,9,266a23–266b6 84
Rhetoric
2,13,1374b6 55
On the Soul
2,5,417a21–b2 81
2,5,417b8–419 82

Pseudo-Aristotle 201
On the Cosmos 217
392a5–9 18
397b9–18 200
397b14–15 174
On Melissus
1,975a4–17 170

Arius Didymus of Alexandria 5 14 188 190 211–15 219 224

Ascension of Isaiah 145

Athanasius of Alexandria 167 215–16
Defence of the Nicene Definition
26,6 198
35,7 214
35,12 214
25,2 220
On the Councils of Ariminum and Seleucia
15,1 214
16,2–5 213
16,5 215
17,4 213
17,5 215
17,6 215
35–36 216
35,4–36,2 228
36,4–5 214

Athanasius of Anazarbos 213

Athenagoras 169

Atticus 200–01
Frag. 5,8–10 201

Augustine 227
Confessions 225–26
12,7 225 227

Averroes 45

Epistle of Barnabas
6:13 133

2 Baruch 145

Basil 160–61
Nine Homilies on the Hexaemeron 161

Basilides 206–08

Bible
Genesis 92 161
1 102 155 168–69 204
1:1 101–02 162 169
1:2 102 169
1:3 102 134
1:5 204
1:6–7 156 160
1:8 204
1:10 204

- 2:7 162–63
- 2:23 175
- 21:19 150

Exodus
- 3:14 112

Leviticus
- 14:5 150
- 14:6 150
- 14:50 150
- 14:51 150

Numbers
- 5:17 150
- 16:32–33 154
- 19:17 150

2 Maccabees 203 206
- 7:28–29 202–03

Psalms
- 23 lxx 195
- 23[24]:8 lxx 195
- 23[24]:10 lxx 195
- 44[45]:2 lxx 214 223
- 89[90]:2 lxx 230
- 90 230
- 90:2 230
- 103:2–3 155
- 103:3 lxx 160
- 109[110]:3 lxx 198 214–15
- 148:4–5 161
- 148:4 lxx 160

Proverbs
- 7:22–31 230
- 8 230
- 8:22–25 211–12
- 8:22 226 230
- 8:25 198 230
- 8:27 230

Isaiah
- 40:13 lxx 173
- 43:10–11 lxx 112
- 45:12 lxx 112
- 51:6 154
- 65:17 lxx 186
- 65:18 134
- 66:22 lxx 186

Joel
- 4:2 154

Zechariah
- 14:8 150

Matthew 112 114
- 1:1 102
- 10:40 104
- 24:23ff. 160
- 25:34 156

Mark 111–112
- 9:9 112
- 14:61–62 112
- 14:62 113

Luke 112 189
- 3:38 102 190
- 10:16 104
- 15:12 190
- 15:30 190

John
- 1–17 103
- 1:1–18 99
- 1:1–5 100–01
- 1:1–3 104 223
- 1:1–2 99 101–03 227
- 1:3 102 227
- 1:12–13 227
- 1:14 4 108 110
- 1:15 103
- 1:18 112
- 1:19–34 112
- 1:30 103
- 2:4 108
- 2:11 109
- 2:22 109
- 3:3 150
- 3:13 105
- 3:14 108
- 3:16–17 114
- 3:16 102 104 106 114
- 3:17–18 134
- 3:17 104 106
- 3:18 113–14
- 3:22–26 112
- 3:32 105
- 3:35 106 114–15
- 4:7–15 150
- 4:19 112
- 4:23 113

4:24	183
4:26	112
5:19–20	105
5:22–23	113
5:24	114
5:25	113
5:26–27	113
5:26	105
5:30	105
5:37	105
6:26	112
6:33	105
6:38	105
6:39	113–14
6:40	113
6:41–42	105
6:44	105 113–14
6:46	105
6:50	105
6:62	103 105
7:28	105
7:37–39	150
8:16	105
8:18	105
8:58	103
10:28	106 114
10:30	112
10:35	227
11:1–45	113
11:25–26	113
11:26	114
11:43–44	113
12:16	109
12:31	134
12:32	114
12:44–45	105
13:3	105
13:20	104
13:31–32	110
14:1	105
14:2	153
14:7	113
14:9	113
14:25–26	109
14:26	110
15:18	102
16:13–15	110
16:13	109
16:16–19	113
16:28	215
16:33	109
17	102–03 108
17:1	110
17:2	105
17:5	99 103 105 110
17:9	105 114
17:24	99 102–03 106 115
19:28–30	108
20:17	160
20:28	112
20:31	112
21:22–23	113
Acts	189
1:11	160
3:19–21	189
17:18	190
17:28	190
17:31	190
17:32	190
Romans	5
1:20	172–73 222 227
1:25	230
1:26–32	230
1:28	173
2:14	172
4:17	203–04
7:23–25	173
7:24	232
8:3–4	104
8:21–23	114
8:21	232
11:34	173
11:36	172–93 204 215
12:2	173
14:5–6	173
1 Corinthians	5
1:27–30	204
1:29–30	204
2:1–3:3	182
2:16	173
7:29–31	177–78

7:31 176–78 180 192
8:6 172–93 204–05 227–29
11:2–16 175
11:8 175
11:11–12 175
11:12 192 204–05 216
15 164 184
15:24–28 179
15:28 159 179–81 184 192 221 232
15:35–49 153
15:39 181
15:42 159
15:44 181–92 232
15:50–55 114
15:51–53 190–92

2 Corinthians
4:16–5:10 185 191–92
4:16 185
4:17–18 185
4:18 185
5:1–3 185
5:1 185 192 232
5:3 185
5:4 185 191
5:5 185
5:8 185
5:16 160
5:17 186 205
5:18 134

Galatians
4:4–5 104
6:15 186 205

Ephesians 5 171 193–95 200 231 233
1 99
1:3 194
1:8–10 194
1:8–9 194
1:10 194–95 197
1:22–23 194–95
3:10 194
3:14–15 193 195 197 204
4:6 193 195
4:10 194–95
4:15 194 197
6:10–16 194
6:12 194

Philippians
2:6 1[illegible]0
3:21 184

Colossians 5 171 192 194–98 200 231 233
1:15–17 19[illegible]–99
1:15–16 19[illegible]
1:15 19[illegible] 223
1:16 196–97
1:17 198
1:18 195
1:19–20 197
2:9–15 197
2:9–10 198
2:9 199
2:19 199
3:1–2 199

1 Thessalonians
4:15–17 190
4:17 114 191
5:23 181

Hebrews
1:2 212
4 130
6:19–20 157
10:20 157

James 114

2 Peter 99 114 190
3:3–7 186
3:5–13 99
3:7 186
3:10–13 186
3:10 186
3:12 186
3:13 186

1 John 113
2:18–22 114
2:28 113
3:2 113

4:9–10 115
4:9 104
4:10 104

Revelation
7:15–17 150
21:6 150
22:1–2 150
22:17 150

Boethus of Sidon 14–15 200–01

Calcidius
Commentay on Plato's Timaeus
140–41 25

Cleanthes
Hymn to Zeus 190

2 Clement
1:7–8 203 205

Clement of Alexandria 135
Excerpts from Theodotus
22,4 124 126
23,2,32–33 125
29 127
36 126
42,1 124
78 136
The Instructor
1,6,26,2 136
1,6,27,3 136
1,28,3 135

Pseudo-Clement 204

Codex Bruce
Untitled 13 150
Untitled 242,24–253,2 142

Constantine 212 219 224

Corpus Hermeticum
On Regeneration
13,1–2 127

Cosmas Indicopleustes 5
Topography
1,1 156
2,6–23 156
2,31–36 158
2,35–36 157
2,37–82 158
3,51–53 157
3,85 157
4,4–6 156
5,33–47 157
5,33 157
5,34 158
5,254 156
6,28 156
6,29 156
7,11–17 157
7,83–86 156
7,90–91 157
9,8–11 157

Critolaus of Phaselis 3 7 14–18 20

Cyprian 203
Exhortation to Martyrdom, Addressed to Fortunatus
11 203

Damascius
On Time, Space, and Number 93

Dead Sea Scrolls
4Q471C, 6 & 11 145

Democritus 8 170

Diodore of Tarsus 155 159 161–62
On Fate (Cod. 223 220b5–19) 155

Diogenes of Babylon 14–15 200

Diogenes Laertius 176
Lives of Eminent Philosophers
7,134 173 210
7,135–36 210
7,137 175 178 210

7,142 210
7,147 174 193

Edictum contra Origenem 161

1 Enoch
22:8–10 145

3 Enoch
3–16 145

Epicurus 170

Epiphanius 18
Panarion
31,5,4 127

Eusebius of Caesarea 206 213 224
Commentaries on the Psalms
1285,55–56 187
Letter to Alexander of Alexandria
2–3 213
Life of Constantine
2,69,1 212
Oration in Praise of the Emperor Constantine
11,11–12 225
Preparation for the Gospel 188
11,17,10 206
11,21,5–7 206
15,5,2, 7–9 201
15,14,2 184
15,19,1–2 189
Proof of the Gospel
5,1,25 206

Eusebius of Nicomedia 211–12 214

Gregory of Nyssa 5 159–61 163–64 195
Against Eunomius
3,4,20 160
Antirrheticus 160
On the Ascension of Christ
9,326,26–327,4 195
On the Dead 159
Great Catechism
16 137
16,59–62 137
Homilies on Ecclesiastes
8 187
On the Interval of Three Days 160
On the Soul and the Resurrection
129,4–5 186
129,8–23 187
148,1–2 157
156,30–32 137

Hellanicus of Tripolis 214

Heraclitus
Frag. DK B60 134

The Shepherd of Hermas
1:6 206
26:1 206

Hermias
Commentary on Plato's Phraedrus 23

Hermogenes 208–11 226–27 229 231

Hesiod
Theogony 170
453–62 63

Pseudo-Hippolytus 211
Refutation of All Heresies 122–24 210
6,18 141
6,31,2–6,32,1 123
6,31,7 124
6,34,7 124
6,42 141
7,21,1 207
7,21,4 206–07
7,22,2 207
7,22,3 207
7,22,4 207
7,22,7 207
7,25,1 207

7,26,2 207
7,27,4–5 207
7,27,10–11 207
10,6,2–10,8,1 211
10,6,4 211
10,7,7 211
10,9,1–10,29,3 211
10,28,1 211
10,33,1–2 223–24
10,33,4 211
10,33,8 211 223

Homer

Iliad
15,362 179

Iamblichus 46 206

On the Mysteries
1,5 206

Irenaeus 123–24 229

Against Heresies 228
1,1,1 127
1,2,1 127
1,2,4 124
1,2,5–6 123
1,3,1.5 124
1,3,3 121
1,4,1 124
1,6,1 124
1,7,2 121 124
1,11 125
1,11,1 127
1,14 127
2,10,3–4 229

John Chrysostom 154–55 159

Homilies on Romans
31,3 154

On the Incomprehensible Nature of God
2,473–89 154

John of Damascus 218–19

On Heresies 218
100,10–13 and 17–22 218

John Philoponus 3–4 69–97 158

Against Aristotle 69
Prologue 70
1–5 70 84
6–7 70
6 91
8 70 76
fr. 63 W 86
fr. 77 W 94
fr. 79 W 94
fr. 108–13 W 78
fr. 114 W 73
fr. 115 W 71
fr. 115–16 W 86
fr. 116 W 74 76 89
fr. 121–22 W 90
fr. 121 W 87 90
fr. 122 W 90
fr. 123 W 95
fr. 129 W 89 92
fr. 131 W 72 76
fr. 132 W 76
fr. 134 W 77

Against Proclus 69 81 83
3,2,46,3–47,17 81
3,4,48,14–49,8 82
3,42,1–43,24 81
3,42,2–4 81
3,45,6–19 81
3,63,2–16 82
4,3,63,4–16 89
4,7,13–70,1 81
4,7,73,20–74,1 82
4,8,75,4–21 84
4,9,76,22–77,5 88
4,9,77,5–78,6 82
4,9,78,6–79,15 88
4,10,79,16–81,28 88
4,11,83,15–84,7 82
4,12,85,1–88,11 82
4,13 88
4,14–16 88
4,68,23–69,4 82
5,2–4 90
5,3,108,5–13 90
5,3,110,21–28 87
5,3,113,28–114,14 91
5,4 95

6,4–6 77
6,8,144,16–149,26 86
6,9,153,9–16 87
6,11,155,5–158,23 86
6,13–29
7,74,7–19 82
8,4 87
9,1 87
9,9,340,25–1,23 72
9,11,350,9–351,1 74
9,17,378,25–379,25 74
9,17,380,10–17 73
11,10,448,3–14 74
11,10,449,13–450,25 74
11,10,455,15–25 74
11,12,458,19–26 74

On the Creation of the World 158
1,8–22 162
1,16 162

Justin Martyr 135 169 206

1 Apologia
61,12 135

Dialogue with Trypho
4,1 206

Pseudo-Justin Martyr

Questions and Answers to the Orthodox Faithful
472c,5–7 187

Lactantius

Divine Institutes
7,23 188

Letter of the Synod of Antioch 216

Leucippus 8

Ma'aseh Merkabah 9 145

Macarius of Jerusalem 214

Macarius Magnes 203 208

Apocriticus 180
4,1 181
4,2–3 155
30 203

Marcellinus

Chronicles 65

Marcion 210

Marcus Aurelius

Meditations
4,29,1 177
5,34,1 177
11,1,2 178

Methodius 203

Discourse on the Resurrection
1,14 203

Minucius Felix 203

The Octavius
34 203

Nag Hammadi Codices

NHC I,3 *The Gospel of Truth* 4 119–22 130–31
16,34–17,1 119
17,4–9 119
17,10–20 120
17,23–25 121
18,11–24 120
18,36–19,7 131
24,28–25,3 121
26,21–27 121
27,11–28,16 121
27,26–34 122
27,34–28,4 121
28,24–32 121
29,26–32 121

NHC I,5 *The Tripartite Tractate* 122 126 130–31
57,3–8 127
62,6–26 131
64,28–65,3 124
65,3–12 124
65,4–67,34 126
65,7 126
65,9 126
65,20 126
65,27 126
66,6–8 124

66,19–20 126
66,31–32 126
66,32 126
67,33–34 126
118,14–138,27 127
123,19 130
123,27–124,4 130
124,25–31 122
126,9–24 130
126,9–17 122
127,25–36 127
128,19–129,34 127
128,30–32 127
133,6–8 130

NHC II,1 *The Apocryphon of John* 136–37 150
4,19–5,11 128
4,19–28 143
5,2–4 128
5,5 150
5,18–20 128
5,30–32 128
6,10–18 139
6,23 128
8,28–9,24 144
31,22–25 138
31,23–24 128

NHC II,2 *Gospel of Thomas* 134
3 135
18 133–35
24 135
49 135
50 135
51 135
113 135

NHC II,3 *Gospel of Philip*
67,27–30 121

NHC III,2 *Gospel of the Egyptians* (also IV,2) 136 139 147 150
43,1 150
62,25–63,23 138–39
64,9–68,1 138
66,22–67,10 139

NHC IV,2 *Gospel of the Egyptians* (also III,2)
74,9–75,11 138–39
74,29 139
75,3 139

NHC VII,5 *Three Steles of Seth* 133–34 136
127 128
127,20–21 128 133

NHC VIII,1 *Zostrianos* 5 133–52
6,7–7,22 144
6,17–18 144
7,1b–22a 144
7,4–6 144
7,13 144
7,18–19 144
15,1–18 146
22,4–12 146
23,17–24,1 147
24,28–25,22 146
53,15–24 144–45
61,14 144 147
81,6–20 143
117,1–4 141

NHC X *Marsanes* 136 142

NHC XI,3 *Allogenes* 5 133–52
45,21–37 149
45,22–30 143
48,15–17 143
48,34–38 149
49,5–26 143
59,14 148
60,14–61,22 148
66,30–38 142

NHC XIII,1 *Trimorphic Protennoia* 136 147 150
38,11–16 150
45,6–8 138
45,12–20 138
48,7–33 138
49,22–50,12 138
49,28–35 138

Nemesius 190
On the Nature of Man 187
section 38, 111,14–112,3 188
section 38, 112,3–6 189

Numenius
Frag. 42 232

Ocellus of Lucania 3 7 16–20

On the Nature of the Universe 15
- 13,5–17 = § 9 — 15
- 13,24–14,5 = § 11 — 16
- 20,1–7 = § 37 — 17
- 20,7–11 = § 37 — 18
- 21,15–18 = § 43 — 17

Origen 139–40 156 160–63 182 206 220

Against Celsus
- 4,14 — 183
- 5,20–23 — 189
- 6,64 — 206

Commentary on the Gospel of John
- 13,21,125–28 — 183
- 13,21,128 — 184

On First Principles
- 1,4,3 — 162

On Prayer
- 23,2 — 160

Orphic Argonautica
- line 16 — 141

Panaetius of Rhodes 3 7 14–15 20 200–01

Papyri Graecae Magicae
- 4 — 142
- 4,943–44 — 141
- 4,1716–1870 — 142

Parmenides 87

Phanes

Orphic Hymns
- 52,5–6 — 141

Philo of Alexandria 10 157 169 182

On the Cherubim
- 124–27 — 174
- 229 — 174
- 233 — 174
- 235–36 — 174

On the Creation
- 26–28 — 169

On the Eternity of the World
- 10–11 — 12
- 20–24 — 10 16
- 28–34 — 10
- 39–44 — 10
- 45–51 — 14
- 55–64 — 14
- 70 — 15
- 76–77 — 14 200
- 117–49 — 14

On the Life of Moses
- 2,103 — 158

On the Special Laws
- 1,81 — 174
- 4,187 — 204

Philogonius of Antioch 214

Pseudo-Philolaus

On the Soul 18

Photius 155

Plato 2–3 5 14–15 20 86–87 91 95 138 163 170 176 183–90 198 201 206 211 231

Cratylus
- 403b — 185
- 410b6–7 — 18

Gorgias
- 523a–27e — 45
- 523e — 159 185

Laws
- 715e–16a — 201
- 903b–05d — 45
- 904 — 51

Phaedo
- 107c–15a — 45

Phaedrus 3 30–32 42–43 63
- 246a–49d — 45

246e–47a	43
246e4	43
247a1–2	32
249d	199
252c4	28 30
Politics	30
Republic	3 45–46 65
2	62
4	48
9,588b–589d	185
491de	53
509b	206
592b	197
616bc	47
617d	54
617d5	49
617e3	50
617e5	53–54
617e6	53
618b3	50
619b7–d1	47
619b9	53
619c1	50
Sophist	
248d	82
Spuria	
366a	185
Statesman	57
272b–274e	201
272e5–6	57
Symposium	30
210–11	146
Theaetetus	
166d	205
Timaeus	20 23–44 47 51 59 62 65 70 74 85–86 91 168–69 201
28a–30a	176
28a–c	196
28c–29b	197
29a–b	197
30a	196 202 204
30c2–5	141
31b–34b	24
31b–32c	199
34b–37c	24
35b–36b	25
36b6	28
36e3	33
37c–39e	24
38b6–c3	86
38c5	36
39e–40e	24
39e	143
39e3–40a2	141
40d6–41a6	24
40d6–41a2	43
41a–b	20 169 211
41a4	38
41a7–d3	24 85
41c6–8	28
41d–42d	42
41d4–42d5	3 23
41d4–e1	25
41d5–6	28
41d5	41
41d6–7	29–30 41
41d8–42d2	25
41d8–e4	24 42
41d8–e1	37
41d8	25
41e1–2	33
41e1	25 30–31 41
41e2–3	51
41e5	35
42a	30
42bd	45
42b5	41
42c	59–60
42d2–5	26
42d4	35
42e	58–60
90e–92c	45
92c	197–98
202e9	30
248a2	28
271d6–8	30
Plotinus	5 139–40 142 182 206
Enneads	
1,7,1	206
1,8,6	206
2,9[33],6,14–21	141

3,8,[30],9,29–39 149
4,3[27],20–24 162
4,3[27],9–12 163
4,8[6],7,12–16 156–57
5,1,8 206
5,4,2 206
5,6,6 206
5,8,10,40–44 149
6,3[44],8 153
6,7,15,31–32 149
6,7[38],17,6–43 142
6,7,40 206
6,8,16 206
6,8,19 206
6,9,11 206

Plutarch 180 182 208

Against the Stoics on Common Conceptions
1067a 186

The E at Delphi
388e–f 180
393e–f 180 182
393f 199
393f–394a 180 199

Platonic Questions
3,1001e 198

On the Sign of Socrates
591d–92c 182
591d–f 232

On Stoic Self-Contradiction
1053b 183

Porphyry 47 50 54–56 61 65 86 180 206

Against the Christians
Frag. 69 (Harnack) 61

Commentary on the Parmenides
Frag. 12,22–29 (Hadot) 206

On Abstinence
2,8 65

On Free Will
271F (Smith) 56

On What Is Up to Us
79–81 54
268F (Smith) 50

To Gaurus
1,26 81
12,20 81
12,23 81
13,62 81
14,35–36 81

Proclus 3 [illegible]5–67 69–70 81–82 86 92

Commentary on Plato's Alcibiades
17 55
137,13–19 62

Commentary on Plato's Cratylus 29
105 63
107,11–13 63
149 64

Commentary on Plato's Phaedrus 29

Commentary on Plato's Republic 23 29
1,4,29 46
1,6,1–4 46
1,11,5–14,14 47
1,104,28 53
1,121,23–27 46
2,3,9 30
2,75,8–10 63
2,92–93 46
2,92,20–95,24 46
2,93–95 49
2,93,11–13 47
2,94,26–95,7 49
2,95,21–24 49
2,96,10–15 47
2,99,12–101,12 46 53
2,100,24–101,10 46
2,105,24–106,14 45
2,130,1–2 58
2,256,27 49
2,257–64 52
2,257,24–266,26 50
2,261,3–264,30 57
2,263,17–18 49
2,264,4–16 49
2,264,5–16 49
2,264,15–16 50
2,282,13–16 55
2,283,1 55
2,290,25–292,22 54

2,291,5–11 48
2,291,12 53
2,291,16–17 50
2,292–98 54
2,292,5–10 55
2,292,12–16 55
2,292,12–13 54
2,292,17–21 55
2,292,21–22 55
2,292,23–25 54
2,292,23 46
2,292,26–294,3 56
2,292,27 56
2,293,1–294,3 57
2,293,1 57
2,293,4–6 57
2,293,7–21 58
2,293,19–22 58
2,293,26–29 57
2,294,5–10 61
2,294,18–20 62
2,294,20–21 61
2,294,25–26 62
2,294,26–27 62
2,295,3–6 62
2,295,3 62
2,295,10–12 62
2,295,17–18 62
2,295,21–24 62
2,296,1–15 63
2,296,16–18 63
2,296,18–21 63
2,296,22–27 63
2,297,5–7 64
2,297,10–15 64
2,297,15–17 57
2,297,21 58
2,297,26–28 65
2,298,3–5 65
2,331,10–332,3 29

Commentary on Plato's Timaeus
1,5,3–5 32
1,12,26–27 27
1,34,21–23 63
1,79,6–9 63
1,111,14–19 29
1,142,20–21 33
1,144,12–15 33
1,167,30–32 63
1,267,12–268,6 85
1,277,32–286,19 45
1,289,6–1 201
1,366,20–368,11 45
1,429,6–7 63
2,70,27 33
2,140,11–142,14 27
2,148,31–149,16 27
2,148,321–150,5 27
2,230,7–9 29
3,131,18–20 35
3,162,1–166,29 63
3,165,5 30
3,193,18–194,15 43
3,230,15 39
3,235,11–21 62
3,235,25–29 33
3,235,28–30 32
3,236,31–238,26 34
3,238,5 32
3,242,9–310,2 23
3,242,9–260,4 26–30
3,244,22–24 28
3,245,14–19 28
3,245,19–246,28 28
3,247,26–250,28 31
3,257,5–9 28
3,257,10–11 27
3,257,18–20 27
3,258,10 30
3,258,20 30
3,259,11–27 28
3,259,15 30
3,260,17–18 28
3,260,18 30
3,260,25–26 31
3,261,12–263,22 35
3,261,12–19 37
3,261,20–262,6 38
3,262,1 30
3,262,6–263,5 38
3,262,7 30
3,262,30 30
3,263,22–265,12 30–31
3,264,4 32
3,264,19–265,1 29
3,265,6–12 38

3,265,8 30
3,265,9 38
3,265,15–268,21 32
3,266,1–5 33
3,266,5–7 32
3,267,1–3 33
3,267,5–10 32
3,268,10–20 33
3,273,25–274,13 57
3,274–75 51
3,274,23–24 51
3,274,25 51
3,274,26–28 51
3,275,1–5 51
3,275,12–13 52
3,275,14–15 52
3,275,15–280,32 52
3,275,26–30 32
3,276,8–9 40
3,276,22–30 34
3,276,22 39
3,276,23 32
3,277,3–5 52
3,277,7–31 52
3,277,22–23 52
3,278,25–32 52
3,279,11–30 63
3,279,20–22 52
3,279,21–24 52
3,279,21 52
3,280,22 39
3,290,18–23 41
3,290,30–291,6 30
3,291,7–17 31
3,295,20 62
3,298,2–299,9 34
3,298,27–28 32
3,304,3–11 39
3,304,30–305,4 35
3,305,11–307,12 35
3,305,26–28 39
3,306,13–307,12 37
3,306,29–307,5 40
3,307,3 41
3,307,26–309,20 35
3,307,26 35
3,307,32–308,7 36
3,308,5–6 36
3,308,7–9 3[illegible]
3,308,9 4[illegible]
3,308,10–24 4[illegible]
3,308,14–18 3[illegible]
3,308,17 3[illegible]
3,308,24–309,2 3[illegible]
3,308,26 3[illegible]
3,309,2–10 3[illegible] 41
3,318,27–31 5[illegible]
3,318,30 6[illegible]
3,319,29–320,2 6[illegible]
3,352,26 5[illegible]

Elements of Theology
7 84
26 84
28 84
29 84
77 84
181–83 29
184–211 23
184 29–30
185 29
202–03 29–30
204 63
211 53

Platonic Theology
4,4,18,1–2 43
4,5,19,17–21 43
5–6 23
5,5,24 63
5,28,20–25 64
6,15 32
6,15,74,27–75,1 32
6,18–22 43
6,18,85,3–5 32
6,21,96,10–29 43

On Providence
10–11 57
11–12 51
11 63
56–60 52
61 52

Protagoras

Testimonia
part 2, doctrine D9 205
part 2, doctrine D38 205

Ptolemaeus Euergetes 158

Qur'an
3:59 219
112:3 219

Rufinus
Apologia ad Anastasium
4 153

Seneca
Letters
9,16 178

Severus 200–01
Frag. 6t 201

Sextus Empiricus 18
Against the Logicians
7,60–61 205
10,316 18
Against the Professors
9,75–76 210

Simplicius 3–4 69–97
Commentary on Aristotle's Categories 70
7,23–32 70
Commentary on Aristotle's On the Heavens 69 72
25,22–6,7 70
119,7–120,12 86
137,19–28 71
138,3–6 87
139,23–27 94
140,9–12 91
271,19 69
288,28–289,15 13
462,20 69
Commentary on Aristotle's Physics 93
3,6 85
8 70 72
8,10 83
59,23 69
183,18 69
192,14 69
492,12–495,17 85
773,8–800,25 93
774,35–37 93
886,12–16 188
1117,6–12 75
1122,3–11 86
1129,28–1131,7 78
1131,9–19 79
1131,29–1132,3 79
1133,16–1134,29 78
1134,29–33 78
1134,33–1135,15 78
1135,15–21 79
1135,28–32 78
1136,3–10 79
1137,27–1138,11 80
1138,12–16 80
1138,16–29 80
1138,29–1139,2 80
1139,2–10 80
1140,4–8 78
1140,10–12 86
1140,11–17 73
1141,11–24 71
1142,4–14 74
1142,21–28 89
1142,28–1143,2 75
1143,20–22 73
1144,10–12 72 75
1144,16–21 75
1144,30–31 75
1145,7–13 74
1145,7–11 71
1145,22–24 75
1145,25–7 76
1150,34–1151,6 72
1152,2–10 92
1152,2–5 72
1152,5–10 73
1155,20–6,3 95
1157,6–9 87
1157,27–1158,29 90
1158,29–1159,7 90
1158,30–9,7 95
1159,8–27 87
1159,11–14 93
1160,20–40 93
1160,40–41,9 93
1161,29–1162,2 93

1163,3–24 94
1163,25–1164,6 94
1164,7–30 95
1165,3–10 91
1173,11–13 89
1173,20–31 92
1174,6–33 92
1175,5–10 92
1177,22–26 76
1177,22–24 72
1177,38–1178,5 76
1179,31–36 85
1182,28–39 91
1198,18–20 92
1326,38–1336,34 83
1326,38–1327,5 83
1327,19–20 83
1328,5–7 85
1328,23–30 85
1329,7–10 95
1329,19–33 84
1329,33–1331,7 84
1330,37–1331,7 81
1331,7–1335,16 84
1331,7–25 85
1334,34–39 85
1334,40–1335,16 92
1335,17–1336,34 84
1363,8–9 69

As-Sijistānī
Muntakhab Siwān al Hikmah
237 94

Socrates 188–90

Suda
Δ 114 162

Syrianus 23

Taurus 86
Frag. 34t 232

Tertullian 164 167 203 208–09 211 226 229
Against Hermogenes 209
1 210
2 208–09 226
8 209
10 208
15 209 226
33 210
34 203
Against Marcion 210
1,15 210
5,19 203 210
Against the Valentinians 229
16 229
Apology
48 203
On the Resurrection of the Flesh
11 203 210
52–62 164

Theodore of Mopsuestia 155–56 159 161–63
Commentary on Romans
11:15 163
Frag. 21 158

Theodoret
Church History
1,4,44–45 224
1,5,3 214
1,5,5 212

Theodosius 155

Theodotus 136

Theognostus of Alexandria
Seven Books of Hypotyposes or Outlines
Frag. book 2 220

Theophilus of Antioch 211 222
To Autolycus
2,4 209
2,10 209 223

Theophrastes 14

Valentinus 125

Victorinus
Ad Candidum
14,11–14 142

Xenarchus of Seleucia 3 7 19–20

Xenophon
Anabasis
4,4,15–16 205

Zacharias of Gaza 82

Zeno of Tarsus 14

Index of Modern Authors

Abramowski, L. 155
Adams, E. 186
Adamson, P. 50
Agamben, G. 56
Alexander, P. 145 187
Amand, D. 162
Annas, J. 45 48 50 54
Apelt, L. C. 170
Arendt, H. 56
Armstrong, A. H. 149
Arruzza, C. 47
Attridge, H. W. 119
Aubry, G. 81

Backman, J. 56
Bakhouche, B. 25
Baltes, M. 28 176
Baltzly, D. 46 61
Barrow, J. D. 233–34
Barry, C. 136
Baudry, J. 201
Baur, F. C. 107
Bechtle, G. 140
Becker, J. 103
Blank, J. 113
Bockmuehl, M. 119
Bodewitz, H. W. 137
Bodnár, I. 75
Bornkamm, G. 119
Boys-Stones, G. 168–69 192 201 232
Brennecke, H. C. 212
Brisson, L. 24–26 29
Bruns, P. 163
Bühner, J.-A. 104–05
Bultmann, R. 4 100 104 107–08 113
Bury, R. G. 18

Chase, M. 75
Chazelle, C. 155
Conway-Jones, A. 157 159
Cook, J. G. 181
Cornford, F. M. 23–26 28 30 41
Cotton, H. M. 213
Couvreur, P. 23
Crafer, T. W. 181
Croke, B. 65
Culpepper, R. A. 101

Dahl, N. A. 119 129–30
Davies, J. G. 160
Davies, S. 134
de Boer, Y. 45
de Haas, F. A. J. 74
Delcomminette, S. 45
Denzinger, H. 217 220 222
des Places, É. 201 232
Destrée, P. 45 49
D'Hoine, P. 42 63
Diehl, E. 23 59–60
Diels, H. 14 18 83 184
Dillon, J. 46 49–50 53 57 182
Dodd, C. H. 129
Dodds, E. R. 23 29 32
Dörrie, H. 176
Donner, F. M. 218
Dorandi, T. 81
Dottin, G. 141

Eco, U. 191
Eliade, M. 137
Eliot, T. S. 133
Endo, M. 101
Eshel, E. 145
Évrard, É. 69–70

Falcon, A. 2–3 7 9 11 18–19
Festugière, A.-J. 23 30 33–35 40 46 55–57 64–65
Finamore, J. F. 24 30 32 52 63
Fortier, S. 75
Fowden, G. 218
Frey, J. 4 99–103 106–09 111–13
Furley, D. 10

Gavray, M.-A. 3 69 82 91
Gebhardt, E. 195
Gioè, A. 201 232
Gleede, B. 5 153 159–60 164
Götte, M. 99
Golitsis, P. 69–70
Grabar, O. 219
Greenbaum, D. G. 50 56
Guinot, J. 154
Gunkel, H. 133
Guthrie, K. S. 15–18

Habermann, J. 101
Hadot, I. 69
Hadot, P. 206
Hahm, D. 10 14 18
Hahn, F. 104
Haleem, A. 219
Halliwell, F. S. 45 48 50
Hamerton-Kelly, G. 101
Harder, R. 15–16
Harnack, A. von 61 167
Hawting, G. R. 218
Heine, R. 183
Hengel, M. 104 111
Henrichs, A. 47 61
Hodgson, P. C. 227
Hoegen-Rohls, C. 109
Hoffmann, P. 70 84
Hook, B. S. 48 62
Hoyland, R. 218
Hoyle, F. 167–68 170
Hubble, E. 167

Ilievski, V. 53
Inglebert, H. 155
Islam, J. N. 170

Jaeger, W. 9–10
Janowitz, N. 145
Jonas, H. 139

Käsemann, E. 4 107–08
Kavvadas, N. 163
Ketteler, F.-H. 162
Kiel, N. 153
Kiessling, A. 158
Klauck, H.-J. 101
Köckert, C. 161
Kotter, P. B. 217–18
Krämer, H. 206
Kroll, W. 23 46 64
Kropp, M. 219
Krüger, R. 155
Kunath, F. 99–101 103
Kutash, E. 24 30 32 52 63

Lang, T. J. 119
Lasson, A. 167
Lerner, R. 45
Lernould, A. 3 23 27
Linguiti, A. 51 57
Litwa, M. D. 207 210 224
Loader, W. R. G. 104
Long, A. A. 168 188–89 194
Louth, A. 218
Lovejoy, A. 221
Lucarini, C. M. 23

MacDermot, V. 142
MacRae, G. W. 119
Martijn, M. 3 42 45 63
May, G. 206
Mayer, W. 218
Mazur, Z. 141 144
McPherran, M. L. 50 53
Meeks, W. A. 104
Meijering, E. P. 167
Merz, A. 111
Miranda, J. P. 104
Moreschini, C. 23
Morgan, K. 45
Mueller-Jourdan, P. 74

Neil, B. 218
Neuwirth, A. 218

O'Meara, D. J. 29
Opitz, H.-G. 212–16 224
Opsomer, J. 24 52 59 180
O'Regan, C. 227

Painchaud, L. 124 126–27 130
Parmentier, L. 212 214 224
Pearse, R. 181
Popkes, E. E. 106
Price, J. J. 218

Ramelli, I. L. E. 161 187
Rashed, M. 86
Reeve, C. D E. 47
Rengstorf, K.-H. 105
Reynolds, G. S. 218
Riggs, T. 52
Roskam, G. 1
Ross, W. D. 10 12–13 16
Runia, D. T. 12 169
Russi, C 51
Ryle, M. 168

Sachau, E. 162
Saffrey, H. D. 23
Sahas, D. J. 218
Samir, S. K. 219
Sandbach, F. H. 16
Santas, G. 45
Schäfer, P. 145
Scheidweiler, F. 212 214 224
Schimanowski, G. 104
Schiwietz, S. 154
Schlitt, D. M. 227
Schmidt, A. 158
Schmidt, C. 142
Schnackenburg, R. 104
Schnelle, U. 100
Schofield, M. 194
Scholten, C. 158
Schulthess, F. 216
Schultz, J. 61
Schwartz, E. 216
Schwemer, A. M. 111
Sedley, D. N. 168 188
Sedley, D. 14
Setzer, C. 153
Share, M. 75
Sharples, R. W. 10 14–16 18 188–89
Sheppard, A. 46 55
Smith, A. 50 56
Smith, Q. 163
Sorabji, R. 69 82
Soulier, P. 85
Staab, K. 163
Stead, C. 211
Steel, C. 53
Sterling, G. E. 169 172 174
Stroumsa, G. G. 137

Tarrant, H. 36–37 40 52
Tate, M. 230
Taylor, A. E. 25–26 28 30 36 38
Theiler, W. 15–16
Theissen, G. 111
Theobald, M. 111
Thomassen, E. 4 119 121–27 130 135 142
Thompson, G. L. 212
Tipler, F. J. 233–34
Tóth, J. 161
Trouillard, J. 23
Turner, J. D. 4–5 128 133 136

Ueberschaer, N. 113
Uthemann, K. 155
Uzunova, M. 45 63

Van den Berg, R. M. 62
van der Eijk, P. J. 188–89
van Gennep, A. 136
van Kooten, G. H. 5 167 177 179 181 191 194 197–99
Van Riel, G. 1 57
Verheyden, J. 1
Verrycken, K. 69
Versnel, H. S. 47–48

Walzer, R. 16
Wasserstein, D. J. 218

Weder, H. 100
Wehrli, F. 15
Weizsäcker, C. 167
Westerink, L. G. 23
Wilberding, J. 50–51 54 56 61
Wildberg, C. 69–70 76 83–84
Wilde, C. 218
Winkelmann, F. 212
Wischmeyer, O. 191
Wolska, W. 155–57
Wright, N. T. 191

Young, F. M. 217

Zeyl, D. J. 20

Studien und Texte zu Antike und Christentum

The series *Studien und Texte zu Antike und Christentum/Studies and Texts in Antiquity and Christianity* is dedicated to researching the whole spectrum of antique Christianity in its diverse manifestations and contexts from its beginnings until around the seventh century. Included are studies on classical histories of dogmas, ideas and theology as well as examinations of social history, the formation of relevant institutions, and the piety and mindset of antique Christianity. Special emphasis is given to research exploring how ancient Christianity interacted and contended with contemporary Judaism and its Greco-Roman environment. For that reason, theological volumes find their place alongside studies from the neighbouring classical disciplines of ancient history, classical and ancient eastern philology, archaeology and ancient philosophy. A variety of formats, such as monographs, text editions, conference volumes and collections of essays by individual authors, are published within the STAC series.

ISSN: 1436-3003
Suggested citation: STAC

All published volumes at *www.mohrsiebeck.com/stac*

Mohr Siebeck
www.mohrsiebeck.com